Mark A. Sammut Sassi

FLYING
at the
FALL of DUSK

COMMENTARIES ON PHILOSOPHY, HISTORY, CINEMA, LITERATURE *and* JOSEPH MUSCAT

"OCCRP 2019 Person of the Year in Organized Crime and Corruption"

Edited by
André P. Debattista

ISBN: 978-1-912142-36-1

Front cover image by Medialink.
Author image by H. Sammut Sassi.
Photos throughout the book by different people.
Book design by A. Carbide.

First edition 2021.

marksammutsassi@gmail.com

About the Author: Dr Mark A. Sammut Sassi LL.D., M.Jur., M.A., LL.M. (Lond), GradDipMgt (LSE), PGCHist St (Oxon), FSALS (Lond), (1973), has co-/written a number of books in English and Maltese, on law, history, and politics, published in Malta, the UK, and Italy. He studied law and translation at the University of Malta, legal history and legal theory at the University of London, historical sociology and management at the London School of Economics, and historical studies at Oxford University. He is a Fellow of the Society for Advanced Legal Studies (London), as well as a member of the Malta Historical Society, the Royal Historical Society (London), and the European Society for Comparative Legal History. For a while he taught history of law at the University of Malta. He was given the warrant of Notary Public by the President of Malta in 1997.

Other books by the same author include *Essays in Maltese Legal History and Comparative Law*.

FLYING
at the
FALL of DUSK

COMMENTARIES ON PHILOSOPHY, HISTORY,

CINEMA, LITERATURE *and*

JOSEPH MUSCAT

INTERNATIONAL EDITION

the crazy idea that things happen in reality so that a book can be written about them
"In his *Philosophy of History*, [Hegel] offers a wonderful characterization of Thucydides's history of the Peloponnesian War: 'In the Peloponnesian War, the struggle was essentially between Athens and Sparta. Thucydides has left us the history of the greater part of it, and his immortal work is the absolute gain which humanity has derived from that contest'. One should read this judgment in all its naïveté: in a way, from the standpoint of world history, the Peloponnesian War took place so that Thucydides could write a book on it. The term 'absolute' should be given here all its weight: from the relative standpoint of our finite human interests, the numerous real tragedies of the Peloponnesian War are, of course, infinitely more important than a book; but from the standpoint of the Absolute, it is the book that matters. One should not be afraid to say the same thing about some truly great work of art: the Elizabethan era occurred in order to produce Shakespeare; Shakespeare's work is the 'absolute gain which humanity has derived' from the vicissitudes of his era"
– Slavoj Žižek, *Less than Nothing: Hegel and the shadow of dialectical materialism*, pp. 471-72

"The Owl of Minerva spreads its wings only with the falling of dusk"
– G.W.F. Hegel, *Philosophy of Right*, Preface

A murdered journalist. Shady offshore deals. A tiny nation in the grip of large-scale criminal interests. These are the leading factors behind the selection of Maltese Prime Minister Joseph Muscat as the Organized Crime and Corruption Reporting Project (OCCRP) 2019 Person of the Year in Organized Crime and Corruption. Under Muscat's leadership, criminality and corruption have flourished — and in many cases gone unpunished — in the small Mediterranean archipelago of Malta, creating an environment that led to the 2017 murder of investigative journalist Daphne Caruana Galizia, investigators and government critics say.

The Maltese government's investigation into the killing of the journalist, who exposed corruption at the highest levels of Muscat's government, foundered for years. But that changed in November when authorities arrested the alleged mastermind, a Maltese businessman who is a close friend of Muscat's longtime associate and former top aide, Keith Schembri. Schembri was detained and questioned in connection with the killing. Throughout the process, Muscat was openly dismissive of the allegations and refused to remove those involved from their government posts.

"Muscat has shown a total disdain for the media, free speech, and has allowed corrupt figures to order killings with impunity," said Louise I. Shelley, the founder and director of the Terrorism, Transnational Crime and Corruption Center at the Schar School of Government and Policy at George Mason University. "OCCRP through this award honors the courageous investigators of the heinous murder and shows that the powerful can be brought to account."

Shelley is one of eight experts in the field of organized crime, corruption, and terrorism who sat on the judging panel that unanimously named Muscat the OCCRP Person of the Year. The annual award shines a light on the individual or institution that has done the most to advance organized criminal activity and corruption in a given year.

"Failed political leadership, as exercised by this man, represents the current crisis that is shaking the foundations — freedom of speech and rule of law — of the European Union," said Saska Cvetkovska, editor-in-chief of the Investigative Reporting Lab in Macedonia and a member of OCCRP's board of directors.

Since 2012, OCCRP has named a Person of the Year in Organized Crime and Corruption from nominees put forward by journalists and members of the public. OCCRP is a non-profit media organization providing an investigative reporting platform for a network of 45 non-profit investigative centers in 34 countries, scores of journalists, and several major regional news organizations across Europe, Africa, Asia, the Middle East, and Latin America.

From the OCCRP website

CONTENTS

ACKNOWLEDGEMENTS

I'LL START OFF BY THANKING TWO PEOPLE FIRST. Dr Simon Busuttil, the Secretary-General of the European People's Party, who left a profound impression on me when, as Malta's Leader of the Opposition, he cited Maltese poet Ružar Briffa during a political rally, but more importantly who encouraged me in 2016 to start writing political commentaries. And Malta's current Leader of the Opposition Dr Bernard Grech, the politician who, when I was dithering and told him about it, encouraged me to go ahead and publish this book.

Then, there are Malta's former Chief Justice Dr Vincent Degaetano, who repeatedly insisted that these essays deserved being collected in book form; and all the friends, present and past, at Standard Publications, and others such as Ann V., Frank Muscat, former European Court of Human Rights Judge Dr Giovanni Bonello, Joseph Cassar, Joseph A. Debono, Karen C., Dr Martin Testaferrata, and quite a few others, for their friendship and comments when they read these essays.

Almost needless to say, I would like to thank from the bottom of my heart the researcher and public intellectual André P. Debattista for editing these essays.

Last but certainly not least, I'd like to thank Providence. For the good times and the bad times, you know I've had my share.

THE MUSCAT TIMELINE

12 June 2004   MEP elections held in Malta; Joseph Muscat is elected with 36,958 votes

2007   Joseph Muscat is awarded a PhD from the University of Bristol; it is rumoured that Dr Mario Vella wrote parts of it

8 March 2008   Malta goes to the polls; the Nationalist Party wins the election with a relative majority of 49.3% of the votes. Labour Leader Dr Alfred Sant announces his resignation paving the way for a leadership election

8 June 2008   Aged 34, Dr Joseph Muscat is elected leader of the Malta Labour Party. In the second round of votes, Dr Joseph Muscat wins 574 votes against Dr George Abela's 291 votes

1 October 2008   Dr Joseph Muscat is sworn in as Leader of the Opposition

9 March 2013   Malta goes to the polls; the Labour Party wins the election with a large landslide garnering 54.83% of the votes. Dr Joseph Muscat is sworn in as Prime Minister

3 April 2016   Data leaked from Panamanian law firm and corporate service provider Mossack Fonseca implicates Minister Konrad Mizzi and the Prime Minister's Chief of Staff Keith Schembri. Daphne Caruana Galizia alleges that another company – Egrant – belongs to Michelle Muscat, the wife of Prime Minister Joseph Muscat

3 June 2017   Dr Joseph Muscat calls a snap election; the Labour Party is returned to office with a larger landslide and 55.04% of the vote

16 October 2017	Daphne Caruana Galizia is assassinated in a car bomb just as she was leaving her house in Bidnija, limits of Mosta
1 December 2019	Following widespread protests in response to alleged links between Government officials and the assassination of Daphne Caruana Galizia, Dr Joseph Muscat announces his intention to resign as Prime Minister and Leader of the Labour Party
27 December 2019	Dr Joseph Muscat is named '2019 man of the year in organised crime and corruption'
10 January 2020	Dr Joseph Muscat delivers his last speech as Prime Minister
13 January 2020	Dr Joseph Muscat resigns as Prime Minister and is replaced in the role by Dr Robert Abela

CRITICAL INTRODUCTION

Chronicling a 'Political Earthquake':
The Muscat era through the eyes of a conservative essayist

André P. DeBattista

ON THE 6ᵀᴴ JUNE 2008, MINUTES AFTER HIS ELECTION AS LABOUR LEADER, DR JOSEPH MUSCAT PROMISED HIS FOLLOWERS AN "EARTHQUAKE OF CHANGE." He reassured his followers that the Malta Labour Party is turning a new page in its history:

> we will show you a progressive party which will exceed your expectations in the environmental, economic and social sectors so that Malta can be the best in Europe... We should forget the past and concentrate on a future which unites us in building a new future.[1]

He vowed to create a "movement" which transcends party lines and draws the support of those individuals who did not usually support the Malta Labour Party. There were hints of this in his first speech:

> My vision is one where the Labour Party will be the basis of a movement of progressives and moderates, a movement for all those who identify themselves with the left and social democracy, with environmental rights and social justice, and a movement for those who from time to time base their thoughts on what they view as the best for themselves and their families."[2]

This was not the first of its kind in Maltese political history. Dom Mintoff galvanised his support around his *"Moviment tal-Ħaddiema"* (Workers Movement) while Dr Eddie Fenech Adami's movement in favour of Malta's EU membership led to one of the most defining constitutional milestones in post-colonial Malta.[3] It is a tactic used to mask brash partisanship and create

---

1   *Joseph Muscat: "An earthquake of change"*, Times of Malta, 6 June 2008
2   Charlot Zahra, *Joseph Muscat reaches out to lost Labourites*, MaltaToday, 8 June 2008
3   See also André P. DeBattista, *Dom Mintoff and Eddie Fenech Adami: Portraits of Persuasion and Charisma* in Mario T. Vassallo (2012) *Public Life*

a political 'broad church' involving those who may politically sit on the fence or who do not traditionally identify with a particular party due to historical baggage and family affiliation. In effect, Dr Muscat's new movement sought to whitewash and, in some cases, re-write history.

The Malta Labour Party got a new name, a new flag and a new logo. It was de-listed from Socialist International in December 2014 after failing to pay its fees in 2012. This re-branding was not accidental – it is central to the re-shaping of the party in the image and likeness of its new leader. It provided the necessary visual break with the past to depict the Muscat era as a *tabula rasa*.

This fresh start allowed the Labour Party to campaign on new platforms and to enter into new alliances and forge electoral inroads in cleavages never dreamed of before. The changes championed by Dr Muscat were revolutionary, in the sense that, as with all revolutions, they were aimed at shaping and creating "a new man" – a more liberal and individualistic man living in a *laissez-faire* society tinged with amoral familism.[4]

In the General Election held on the 9th March 2013, the Labour Party faced a Nationalist Party which had been in office since 1987, barring a brief period between October 1996 and September 1998. The party in government was torn apart by internal factions and fatigue. It was weighed down by accusations of corruption and scandal. In contrast, Dr Muscat promised a fresh start. The result paid off. The Labour Party was elected with 54.83% of the vote.

Four years later, the Muscat-led Labour Party improved its lead and garnered 55.04% of the votes despite being mired in corruption and scandal – the gravest of which prompted by the Panama Papers leaks.[5] Dr Muscat seemed unassailable – *Invictus*, as a particularly tacky piece of ink drawing claims.

This was a political earthquake like no other. However, Dr Muscat's choice of words on that balmy June evening was unfortunate. Unwittingly, he failed to realise that earthquakes leave considerable damage in their wake: the stronger the earthquake, the more long-lasting the damage.

---

in Malta: Essays on Governance, Politics and Public Affairs in the EU's Smallest Member State, Malta: Department of Public Policy

4 This concept is explored further in Edward C. Banfield (1958, 1967 ed.) *Moral Basis of a Backward Society*. London: Simon and Schuster. This concept has been explored in a Maltese concept in André P. DeBattista, *Amoral Familism*, Times of Malta, 13 May 2018

5 See also Mark A. Sammut (2016) *L-Aqwa Fl-Ewropa: Il-Panama Papers u l-Poter.*

A Fresh Menu

Dr Mark A. Sammut Sassi's essays published in *The Malta Independent on Sunday* between January 2018 and May 2020, chronicle the last months of the Muscat administration. His work is refreshingly honest. His style is erudite and, like every essayist worth his salt, he turns political writing into an art form. At times polemical, these essays serve to challenge the status quo.

Dr Sammut Sassi's political commentary blends in various elements. Each carefully crafted essay contains references to law, philosophy, history, poetry, film and literature. The author of these essays is a voracious reader who ruminates over what he reads and allows it to challenge his ideas and his writings. Thus, the reader is presented with more than just political writing. Each essay also serves as a commentary on the literary, cultural, architectural, and artistic scene.

Dr Sammut Sassi does not limit himself to commenting on the rampant sources of political injustice, the nonsensical statements, the triumph of Mammon and the general impunity on corruption cases. He realises that the political malaise runs deeper and its consequences are also social, as well as political. Thus, in various pieces, Dr Sammut Sassi raises the plight of the elderly and the dangers of loneliness. He defends the rights of the unborn, thus giving a voice to those who do not have one. In many ways, he shares the Burkean vision of society as being an association between the dead, the living and the unborn bound together in trusteeship.[6]

He challenges the contradictions of the liberal establishment. He calls out the inconsistencies of 'liberal fascism' – a phrase he borrows to good effect from the American author Jonah Goldberg.[7]

This collection questions the Whiggish interpretation of inevitable and constant progress – now staple elements of the political narratives.[8] In doing so, he provides a conservative analysis and a counter-narrative which questions whether all that glistens is gold.

There are three overarching observations which can be made about Dr Sammut Sassi's conservatism. Firstly, it is a conservatism which is profoundly shaped and rooted in its surroundings. Secondly, it is a conservatism which

---

6   Edmund Burke explores these themes in the book '*Reflections on the Revolution in France*' first published in 1790

7   Jonah Goldberg (2009) *Liberal Fascism: The Secret History of the American Left, From Mussolini to the Politics of Change.* New York: Random House

8   See also Herbert Butterfield (1931,1965 ed.) *The Whig Interpretation of History.* London: W. W. Norton & Company

rallies against the ugliness proliferating in our society, thus reminding readers that the conservative needs to have both an aesthetic sensibility and a social conscience. Thirdly, it is a conservatism which cannot accept individualistic liberalism. Instead, this form of conservatism is concerned with the human person.

The words "individual" and "person" are often used interchangeably. However, a distinction needs to be made between the two. Both extol the virtue of freedom, yet the former exalts the freedom to do as one pleases so long as others are not harmed. At the same time, the latter is a freedom which is not closed in on itself for it implies being open to other persons and growth within a community.

Dissecting a Movement

IF NEWS REPORTAGE IS THE FIRST "ROUGH DRAFT OF HISTORY," THEN AN OPINION COLUMN MUST BE THE "ROUGH DRAFT OF POLITICAL SCIENCE."[9] Dr Sammut Sassi's insights shed some light on the effects of this sudden shift in the political zeitgeist.

He believes the changes instituted were part of a comprehensive project to transform Malta into a liberal state – though Dr Sammut Sassi contends that this is a "travesty of liberalism" for it is "economically laissez-faire and socially libertine." He is concerned about that fact that this ideology developed "in conditions different to ours" and was "imported lock, stock, and barrel and imposed on an unsuspecting people."

Economic neoliberalism is a "new religion and the new homeland" bolstered by religious and patriotic trappings. Indeed, he argues that "the Market has become like a pre-Christian god who demands human sacrifice but, this time, in the name of endless economic growth." Our landscape – once dominated by Baroque parish churches, wayside chapels and niches – is now also being redefined in the name of this new religion. Mature trees are uprooted, roads are widened, and ghastly soulless buildings replace traditional buildings: "Neo-liberalism – the contemporary religion – manifests itself in high-rise glass towers and skyscrapers, usually flashing the name of the patron brand on their topmost parts."

Dr Sammut Sassi goes to great lengths to dissect the type of 'liberalism' that the new movement embraces. It is not classical liberalism, which would, at the very least, be tolerant of conservatism. Instead, in its liberal fascistic incarnation, it elevates politics to the level of religion and attempts "to make everybody believe in and practise the tenets of that religion." This is exemplified

---

9   This phrase is often attributed to *Washington Post* President and Publisher, Philip L. Graham (1915 – 1963)

through the measures adopted to silence or sideline those who do not accept the dogmas and creeds of the new intolerant religion.

The premise underpinning this collection of writings is that Dr Muscat's revolution "was not really and truly a Progressive one, but a revolution in laxity, in corruption." Since the economy was doing well, a blind eye was turned to this laxity and corruption. Good economic results were used to justify the culture of impunity. It bred a cynicism which knows the price of everything and the value of nothing. Proof of this lies in the random and wanton destruction of Malta's urban and natural environment. It reached its depths with the assassination of journalist Daphne Caruana Galizia (1964–2017) outside her family home in Bidnija. The investigation of her assassination revealed links to the highest corridors of power.

The events described above took place amid calls and promises of a "Second Republic." Dr Sammut Sassi reflects on this too:

> His insistence on a New Republic, a New Constitution, was meant to hit two birds with one stone: keep the people distracted by dangling this possibly much-expected carrot while, at the same time, imply that since the current Constitution is on its way out, it need not really be observed.

As an antidote, to this, Dr Sammut Sassi prescribes a "revolution" and a "change in mentality":

> Not the neo-liberal earthquake foggily promised and punctiliously delivered by Muscat's Movement. But a conservative, non-neo-liberal revolution. A return to certain perennial, immutable principles. That said, I am still waiting to see who will rise to the political occasion.

Envisaging a Conservative Alternative

IN THE PROCESS OF READING THIS COLLECTION OF ESSAYS, I HAVE FOUND MYSELF IN AGREEMENT WITH DR SAMMUT SASSI ON THE NEED TO FORMULATE A CONSERVATIVE ALTERNATIVE. What constitutes this conservative alternative? The claim by the new movement to have unleashed progressive liberal forces was intentionally done to ensure that anything conservative can be defined as being "anti-progressive" and, therefore, a regressive measure opposed to freedom.

The leading conservative thinker of the 20th century, Sir Roger Scruton (1944–2020), offers an excellent starting point – an invitation – into this great tradition which is neither regressive, nor anti-progressive, nor opposed to freedom.[10] Rather than being an international cause, conservatism is nurtured in a specific time and place and "all disputes over law, liberty and justice are addressed to a historic and existing community."

This specific community helps to nurture attachment and identity. In this regard, conservatism differs drastically from liberalism. The latter believe that identities shift and morph and "all boundaries are in essence, negotiable." Sir Roger argues that: "for liberals, it is not the specifics of our local history and acquired obligations that should govern our political behaviour, but the universal ideals of the Enlightenment."

At the heart of every conservative alternative – rather than revolution – is the idea that communities require a form of loyalty which is more durable than politics. This pre-political loyalty "causes neighbours who voted in opposing ways to treat each other as fellow citizens, for whom the government Is not 'mine' or 'yours' but 'ours', whether or not we approve of it." Nonetheless, for such a system to work, there needs to be a reliable system of accountability – and such a system is only possible if the electorate can transcend individual political preferences and place trust in those institutions and persons tasked with governing in the name of a collective "we." Loyalty and trust are essential to the conservative worldview:

> Trust enables people to cooperate in ensuring that the legislative process is reversible when it makes a mistake; it enables them to accept decisions that run counter to their individual desires and which express views of the nation and its future that they do not share. It is to the maintenance of that kind of trust that conservative politics has always been directed.[11]

This is not to say that individual freedom is not given its importance in the corpus of conservative thought. Most conservatives will agree that every person is endowed with the gift of liberty, which allows for free choices in the pursuit of meaning and happiness. However, most conservatives also believe that every human person exercises such freedom within a society which values liberty "as shared culture, based in tacit conventions." In other words, "true liberty arises only from a culture of obedience, in which law and community are shared assets maintained for the common good."

Contrary to what the neo-liberal consensus tries to argue, this form of conservatism is not nostalgia, bigotry and prejudice, and it is not the opposite

---

10   Roger Scruton (2017) *Conservatism: An Invitation to the Great Tradition.* New York: All Points Books
11   Ibid. pp. 4 – 5

of "progressive." Instead, conservatism is an invitation to re-discover the meaning of the human person and the context within which he lives and thrives. Sir Roger is, as ever, eloquent on the matter:

> We human beings live naturally in communities, bound together by mutual trust. We have a need for a shared home, a place of safety where our claim to occupancy is undisputed and where we can call on others to assist us in times of threat. We need peace with our neighbours and the procedures for securing it. And we need the love and protection afforded by family life... We rational beings need customs and institutions that are founded in something other than reason, if we are to use our reason to good effect.[12]

Pursuing the Permanent Things

TRUST, COMMUNITY SPIRIT, INSTITUTIONS AND LIBERTY – THESE ARE FOUR PILLARS WHICH HAVE BEEN REDEFINED BY THIS MOVEMENT. Trust has been replaced by suspicion. This was partially fuelled by the fact that the "*Malta Tagħna Lkoll*"[13] slogan cynically uses the notion of community to justify blatant partisanship and the manifest lack of meritocracy. This casts doubt on the independence of institutions and redefines the concept of liberty. Some now define "Liberty" as being a by-word for libertinism, profligacy and impunity.

The leader of this movement, Dr Joseph Muscat, can rely on his personal charisma and communicative skills. Dr Sammut Sassi examines these in excellent detail in this book. These skills served to reinforce an aura of invincibility and infallibility among his supporters. Thus, loyalty and identification in the movement and its leader have been strengthened at the expense of commitment to the community and concern for the common good. However, charismatic leadership has its defects and limitations. In encouraging this "Midas cult," we may run the risk of forgetting the main moral of that story:

> Midas, king of Lydia, swelled at first with pride when he found he could transform everything he touched to gold; but when he beheld his food grow rigid, and his drink harden into golden ice,

---

12   Ibid. pp. 10 – 14
13   Malta Tagħna Lkoll – "Malta for All" – the slogan used during the 2013 and 2017 elections by the Labour Party. The slogan was meant to represent inclusivity and meritocracy.

then he understood that this gift was a bane and in his loathing for gold, cursed his prayer.[14]

The antidote is a return to the 'Permanent Things' as defined by T.S. Eliot (1888-1965): "those enduring truths and ways of life and standards of order."[15] Naturally, there will be resistance. As Russell Kirk (1918-1994) rightly observed, the "permanent things" will have enemies and such enemies "do not believe that there are permanent standards of behaviour or indeed an unchanging human nature." Thus they try to "create political systems that will make everyone happy without much effort."[16]

We get glimpses of these permanent things in traditional institutions, faith, history and literature. These, in turn, inform our understanding. It is, perhaps, a literary reference which best sums up the main pitfall of the neo-liberal state. As Isabella, in William Shakespeare's "Measure for Measure" observes, "O, it is excellent to have a giant's strength, but it is tyrannous to use it like a giant."

---

14   Claudian, *In Rufinem*, quoted in Carol Graham (2009) *Happiness around the World: The Paradox of Happy Peasants and Miserable Millionaires*. Oxford: Oxford University Press, p 1

15   Russell Kirk, *The Permanent Things of T.S. Eliot's Politics*, Lecture presented at The Heritage Foundation on 9 February 1989.

16   Russell Kirk (2016) *Enemies of the Permanent Things: Observations of Abnormality in Literature and Politics*. Tacoma: Cluny Media.

PREFACE

Muscat the Mythoman(e)

"Myths," tells us Mary Midgley in her 2004 book *The Myths We Live By*, "are not lies. Nor are they detached stories. They are imaginative patterns, networks of powerful symbols that suggest particular ways of interpreting the world. They shape its meaning."

This is what Joseph Muscat sold the Maltese people: a bagful of myths. I use the verb "sold" purposefully. There's no other way to make any sense of the Panama companies opened by Muscat's *maîtresse-en-titre* Konrad Mizzi and *éminence grise* Keith Schembri.

But we have to understand Muscat in the Maltese context, which is, if I may be allowed this provocation, a Medieval context. The Maltese are still trapped in a collective psychological time warp. They live in the 21st century, but their mentality is still of the 15th or 16th. The Maltese State is not a modern State, in the Weberian sense of an impersonal machinery ruled by laws made on behalf of the people. The Maltese State is a sort of personal belonging, and its owner is the Prime-Minister-Prince who exercises a sort of *dominium*, which could be defined as private power over public matters. The Maltese electorate temporarily invests the Prime-Minister-Prince with personal sovereignty instead of delegating administrative power to him to administer in the name of the real sovereign (the People). Loyalty is expressed toward the Prime-Minister-Prince rather than to the homeland, and loyalty to the former is rewarded but rarely, if ever, is loyalty to the latter. When somebody who is loyal to the Prime-Minister-Prince's contender is rewarded, it is portrayed as a sign of the ruling Prime-Minister-Prince's magnanimity. The Prime-Minister-Prince is perceived as a sort of absolutist ruler who need not really keep his word and be accountable toward the electorate, as any delegated administrator would; his only objective is, as Machiavelli describes his Prince, the attainment and maintenance of power, and this he does by convincing the electorate to judge him positively at the end of the legislature, and then again, not necessarily on what he does publicly but privately. Politics is experienced as continuous warfare, between the ruling Prime-Minister-Prince and his contender; the bond between the Prime-Minister-Prince and his followers is never ideological, it is perennially personal, almost as if it were a feudal bond, the bond between liege and vassal. Muscat's creation of a ministerial post for the implementation of the electoral manifesto was a tongue-in-cheek implicit admission of this setup. Helena Dalli's explicit declaration that Muscat's government had duped the electorate confirms this reading.[17]

Muscat has thus to be understood in this context of Prime-Minister-Prince. In this context he sold (at least) three myths, three ways of interpreting the world and shape its meaning.

Myth # 1: Muscat the Great

MUSCAT CONVINCED THE MALTESE PEOPLE THAT HE WAS THE SOLUTION TO MALTA'S WOES. He proposed and pushed the myth of the Great Man.

The myth of the Great Man is a nineteenth-century theory that explains history in terms of the impact of heroes. These "great men" are unique individuals born with natural attributes (intelligence, courage, divine inspiration, and so on) and through these attributes they impact history. The notion seems to have been primarily elaborated by the Scottish essayist Thomas Carlyle in his book *On Heroes, Hero-Worship, and the Heroic in History* (1841):

> Universal History, the history of what man has accomplished in this world, is at bottom the History of the Great Men who have worked here. They were the leaders of men, these great ones; the modellers, patterns, and in a wide sense creators, of whatsoever the general mass of men contrived to do or to attain; all things that we see standing accomplished in the world are properly the outer material result, the practical realization and embodiment, of Thoughts that dwelt in the Great Men sent into the world: the soul of the whole world's history, it may justly be considered, were the history of these.

The late nineteenth-century German philosopher Friedrich Nietzsche came up with a similar view in his concept of the *Übermensch*. In Nietzsche's view the hero should be revered, not for the good he has done for the people, but simply out of admiration for the marvellous. The hero's justification lies in his self-conception as a man chosen by destiny to be great. Life is a struggle, and the hero views himself as a conqueror, growing stronger through conflict. He is not ashamed of his strength and instead of the Christian virtues of meekness,

---

17   "When we were about to introduce civil unions in 2014, there was a poll which showed that 80% of the people were not in favour, even though the majority had voted for this. But you know electoral programmes, it's a package, and they didn't realise because we just put in equality as a major pillar for this government," were the exact words – Yannick Pace, "PN says Helena Dalli can't be taken seriously after 'admitting' to misleading voters", *Malta Today*, 19 March 2018.

humility, and compassion, he lives by the heroic virtues of courage, nobility, pride, and the right to rule.

I'll put it bluntly. This is all nonsense and nothing but excessive and obnoxious narcissism. It is nonsense because history is the product of enormous underlying forces on which no individual has any real control. An individual can take advantage of circumstances, but much depends on social, economic, ideological, and other forces. The individual is like a mariner navigating the great currents of society's development. He needs to be a skilful mariner, but if there's no current, the skill and the effort bring no result. And if the current is too big, it will drown the mariner. It ultimately boils down to prowess *and* fortune. Only the narcissist believes he can control the great forces around him and that not only is he endowed with super-human powers but he is also entitled to use them.

One of the staunchest believers in the Great Man myth and that Muscat was a Great Man is Labour politician Owen Bonnici. According to *The Malta Independent*, on Monday 2 December 2019 Dr Bonnici claimed that "leaders of Muscat's level 'are born once every 25 years'".[18] Not only does Dr Bonnici believe in this myth, but he's scientific in his approach: he's even knowledgeable about the phenomenon's periodic nature.

Myth # 2: Progressives and Moderates

TAKING IT FOR GRANTED THAT EVERYBODY WAS ON BOARD WITH HIS RADICAL PLANS TO CREATE A NEW ETHOS AND A SHIFT IN THE PHILOSOPHY OF THE LABOUR PARTY, MUSCAT MOVED NARCISSISTICALLY TO SHAPE THE PARTY IN HIS OWN IMAGE. *Imago Muscati* one could say. Muscat sold the myth that a marriage was possible between the two genders of liberals (the "progressives" and the "moderates"), that that marriage was made in heaven, and that it was the only *ménage* possible.

The glaring contradiction caught the eye of a number of people, including public intellectual Lino Spiteri (1938-2014). In possibly one of the best articles the former Labour Minister ever wrote for *The Times of Malta* in 2010,[19] Mr Spiteri opined:

> Under a new leader, changed style and all, the Labour Party is in the process of attempting to reinvent itself. [...]
> The biggest change came at the top. Alfred Sant, despite good

---

18   Neil Camilleri, "Justice Minister says he was 'shocked' by photo of Melvin Theuma and Keith Schembri", *The Malta Independent*, 2 December 2019.
19   Lino Spiteri, "Labour Party on the move", *The Times of Malta*, 1 February, 2010.

qualities, which not everybody recognises adequately, carried too much baggage, not least with his preference for a Malta outside the EU. Dr Muscat, though young in years, had spent half his lifetime in politics and mostly at Dr Sant's side by the time he made it to leader.

Nevertheless, his four successful years as an MEP turned him into a convinced European. He threw Labour's anti-EU baggage overboard as soon as he took over the helm. He says he wants to do more than that. He is striving to build a movement of "moderates and progressives". That contains inherent contradiction. On certain things you cannot be progressive and moderate at the same time. [...O]ne cannot be all things to all men.

Needless to say, Mr Spiteri was right in his assessment, and I agreed with and elaborated on his last point (the contradiction inherent in a movement of "progressives" and "moderates") in my 2016 book *L-Aqwa fl-Ewropa. Il-Panama Papers u l-Poter*. James Debono had also contributed to this analysis, arguing that this coalition of moderates and progressives was "bas[ed...] on vague, half-baked and contradictory messages"[20] – Mr Debono had seen through the dishonest nature of Muscat's discourse.

With his "progressives and moderates" oxymoron, Muscat was obviously paving the way for the introduction of his libertine (I prefer the proper word to the euphemistic "socially liberal") agenda. This is not an original idea of Muscat's. In his 2017 book *Decadence, Radicalism, and the Early Modern French Nobility: The Enlightened and Depraved*, Chad Denton writes,

> The libertine nobleman and his more elusive and rare companion the libertine noblewoman refuse to remain consigned to early modern France. Despite being unquestionably figures of antiquated systems of privilege and power, they were also in a very real sense pioneers of Western modernity, laying the groundwork for a society where many people can choose to openly reject the religious and social values one is born into and use one's knowledge of the world around them to justify that decision. Of course, even now in this postmodern era of radical choice in identity, some degree, or in some cases a great deal, of privilege is still required to truly and easily assert one's individuality.

Muscat sold the tried and tested idea that we can all be like the libertine nobility of the former system in France. Sex sells, and Muscat wanted to

---

20   James Debono, "Labour general conference: Programming the progressives", *Malta Today*, 24 January, 2010.

make a killing. Labour was getting excited at the prospects of "liberation". One instance that epitomises the teenage-like excitement that pervaded Labour was the broadcast on the Party's TV station of a news item on the wall paintings in a Pompeii brothel. The excitement contagion reached Parliament, particularly with the worldview constantly promoted by Parliamentary Secretary Rosianne Cutajar. In March 2020,[21] *The Times of Malta* covered Ms Cutajar's excitement with commerce in sex and reactions to the Labour politician's excitement:

> Prostitution risks becoming further unregulated if the buyers of sex are criminalised. Her announcement caused an immediate uproar among a coalition of over 40 NGOs who are advocating the so-called 'Nordic model' that proposes to decrease the demand for prostitution by holding the client liable for prosecution while decreasing the vulnerability of the sex worker through decriminalisation. However, [...] Ms Cutajar remained steadfast in her views. "In countries which are following the 'Nordic Model', we have seen prostitution being driven underground which is extremely dangerous," she said. She said that rather than copy other countries' models, it was necessary to find an approach that suited the Maltese context. While there were some women who were driven into sex work because of their vulnerability, others freely chose it as a profession. "We need to keep in mind both of these realities and find a legal pathway to protect both of them."

Literature on the psychological burdens of prostitution abounds. But I have found one article which summarises in its conclusion much of what we know about the subject:[22]

> Prostitution is the business of sexual exploitation. Well-documented risks of harm to the person used as product

---

21   Kristina Abela, "'When buying sex is a crime, prostitution is driven underground'", *The Times of Malta*, 7 March, 2020.
22   Melissa Farley, "Risky Consumption: Risks of Prostitution: When the Person Is the Product", *Journal of the Association for Consumer Research*, Volume 3, Number 1 (January 2018). Melissa Farley is the executive director of the non-profit organisation Prostitution Research & Education, San Francisco, California.

in the sex trade are ignored or denied. Pimps, traffickers, and sex buyers exploit the vulnerabilities of a dehumanized, devalued, and commodified class of women who have been set aside for men's sexual use. Anyone who is familiar with the daily life of those in prostitution understands that safety in prostitution is a pipe dream. Advocates of legal and decriminalized prostitution understand this but rarely admit it. Still, evidence exists. For example legalizing prostitution in Australia resulted in prostitution's being seen as a normal job. However the Australian governmental agency responsible for worker safety recommended hostage negotiation training for those entering prostitution. This reflected the government's awareness of prostitution's dangers, contradicting the notion of prostitution as a job like any other.

[...]

The activities of sex buyers and distributors/traffickers—the commoditizers—are predatory in the extreme. Those who profit from selling women in prostitution know of the risks just as surely as tobacco companies knew of the risks of smoking. As a nod to these risks, some have proposed harm or risk reduction based on the assumption that people will inevitably continue to engage in prostitution. Risk reduction interventions therefore aim to reduce *but not eliminate* risk of harm. At its extreme, a harm reduction approach becomes a laissez-faire ideology more concerned with protecting individual rights to certain behaviors, no matter how risky, than with protecting the health of these same individuals, their families, and the public. Harm reduction approaches to prostitution (such as male condom distribution) may have some benefits but fail to address the roots of the problem. A risk reduction-only approach is dismissive of the alternatives for risk elimination: not entering prostitution, or helping individuals to completely avoid these highly risky activities.

The complicity of governments sustains prostitution. When the sex trade expands, women are less likely to compete with men for jobs. When prostitution is incorporated into states' economies, governments are relieved of the necessity of finding employment for women. Blood taxes are collected by the state-as-pimp in legal and decriminalized prostitution. Banks, airlines, internet providers, hotels, travel agencies, and all media are integral to the exploitation and abuse of women in prostitution tourism, make huge profits, and are solidified as part of a country's economy.

The existence of prostitution anywhere is society's betrayal of women, especially those who are marginalized and vulnerable because of their sex, their ethnicity, their poverty, and their history of abuse and neglect. [...] Decriminalized prostitution as a public health response to HIV is not warranted, given the current empirical evidence. The social and ethical challenges to those who promote legalized (or decriminalized) prostitution are overwhelming. Until vulnerability is removed and equality is in place, women will continue to enter prostitution as a last-ditch survival maneuver. This perspective has been elaborated in the Palermo Protocol, an international legal agreement [...] that makes consent to prostitution irrelevant with respect to whether or not trafficking (pimping) has occurred. Another ethical issue is poverty and the financial inducement that compels people into prostitution [...] Until income and sex equality exist, poor women will be vulnerable to prostitution. And finally, since legalization of prostitution has been associated with increased trafficking, those most vulnerable are at increased risk for harm.

[...] A number of countries have passed legislation that recognizes prostitution as sexual exploitation: Sweden (1999), South Korea (2004), Iceland, (2008), Norway (2009), Canada (2014), Northern Ireland (2015), France (2016), and Republic of Ireland (2017). In these abolitionist approaches to prostitution, sex buyers are penalized (as are pimps and traffickers) and people in prostitution are decriminalized and are also provided with exit services and job training. Once prostitution is understood as a form of violence against women, this legal approach makes sense.

But first we have to move past the pimps' and profiteers' deceptive narratives that deny the risks of prostitution to the person who is sold as product. Ultimately, it is necessary to look at the structural origins of race, sex, and economic inequality. Public education is needed regarding the humanity of those who are bought as products, the risks and the violence of the experience of being bought for sex, and the predatory criminality of the sex buyer.

Then again, who am I to agree with the experts when there's a politician who knows better? Rosianne Cutajar is a radical believer in Muscatism. Like all radicals, she probably thinks she has been handed the keys to the Kingdom. Because indeed, this is a question of neither progressives nor moderates. This is a question of radicals.[23] In Italy, the positions ensconced in Muscatism were the positions that Marco Pannella (1930-2016) and Emma Bonino and their Radical Party[24] flagrantly campaigned for.

Muscat's chimera of a libertine society, built on the twin pillars of the on-the-counter mentality (morning-after pill, gender changes, and possibly abortion in the future) and the Liberal Fascist mentality (the criminalisation of psychological help to homosexuals, the removal of religious symbols from public places, and so on), included divorce.

As a matter of fact, prior to the introduction of divorce in 2011, annulment served the same purpose. The snag was the 1992 Church-State agreement that, in the reality faced by people, permitted abuse, resulting in unnecessary lengthy proceedings at times motivated by spite. This could have been solved via amendments to procedural law. Instead, divorce was introduced. The fundamental difference between annulment and divorce, on a psychological level, is that in annulment there is the understanding that love never existed while in divorce the understanding is that love existed at first but it fizzled out along the way. The second proposition is obviously fallacious, since real love cannot die. If the feeling died over time, then it was not love, it was something else. Real love is forever. Consider the love of a (normal) parent toward their child: it's life-long.

Putting such musings aside, let's look at the demand for divorce, and how Muscat's chimera and myth were divorced from reality. When the divorce referendum was held in 2011, the question the electorate was asked was: "Do you agree with the introduction of the choice of divorce in the case of a married couple who has been separated or has been living apart for at least four (4) years, and where there is no reasonable hope for reconciliation between the spouses, whilst at the same time ensuring that adequate maintenance is guaranteed and the welfare of the children is safeguarded?"

According to the Department of Information, 71.57%, cast their votes of which 0.93% were invalid. Of the approximately 70% of the adult

23   See Peter Serracino Inglott's Postface in Giuseppe Mifsud Bonnici and Mark A. Sammut, *Il-Liġi, il-Morali u r-Raġuni* (Malta, 2008).
24   Self-described as *"liberale, liberista e libertario"*.

population of Malta that cast its vote, only almost 53% agreed with the referendum question. That is **not** 53% of the population of Malta; that's 53% of the approximately 70% who cast their vote validly. In other words, out of the **entire population of Malta, only 38%** agreed with the proposition found in the question.

That almost 30% of the electorate did not express an opinion can only mean that either the question was not couched properly or the public debate was not carried out properly. All arguments in favour of extrapolation are *ab initio* fallacious – otherwise we would use a system based on extrapolation from a sample rather than having recourse to universal suffrage. A University Professor once suggested that strategy to save money, but his suggestion never gained traction. I will not enter into the merits of the argument as to whether all voters should be made to vote (as is the case in certain countries) or of the other argument on the legal meaning of the result when many people do not vote. I am here looking at society not at the political mechanism utilised in referenda.

In other words, the argument that that referendum represented the opinion of the population is clumsy at best. That it was all an illusion is confirmed by the aftermath. In 2018, information given by Minister Owen Bonnici showed that there had been 2,328 divorces since the remedy's introduction.

It is clear to me that it was more a question of ideological fuss than real necessity. Those more or less 300 divorces per year could have been easily dealt with under reformed and therefore more efficient annulment procedures. The result would have been the same, but the ideology would not have shifted toward the idea that marriage has an opt-out. In annulment, the marriage is deemed to have been non-existent because it was faulty from the beginning; in divorce, the marriage is deemed to have been valid and existent but things went awry over time. The ideological shift is significant, because by the next generation it will have ushered in the mentality that marriage is like a car: you buy it and if you don't like how it runs, you get rid of it and buy a new one. Or you take public transport.

It becomes obvious upon further reflection that the chimera of an alliance between progressives and moderates was just that: a chimera. In reality, Muscat was only an implement facilitating the shift necessitated and dictated by late capitalism, a shift from the family as the individual's first community to the individual who has no community except that created on the workplace. All said and done, it is not that different from the situation of the negro slaves on antebellum American plantations.

Myth # 3: The Economic Miracle

EVEN AFTER HIS RESIGNATION, MUSCAT CONTINUED PEDDLING THE MYTH THAT HE'S AN ECONOMIC GURU WITH HIS PREDICTIONS ON THE POST-CORONA VIRUS PANDEMIC MALTESE ECONOMY. But here we are interested in Muscat as Prime Minister and his incessant propaganda to convince the electorate that he single-handedly turned Malta's economic fortunes around and made Malta's fortune. His conceited insistence on the surplus bears witness to this. That this was but a charade, however, came definitively to the fore in 2020. In January of that year, *The Times of Malta* ran a telling headline: "Malta's financial surplus drops sharply in Q3 2019".[25] The article beneath it claimed that "[t]he government surplus reached €57.4 million in the third quarter of last year, half of what it was in the same period the year before." This was also the news reported by *The Malta Independent* on that same Monday: "Sharp drop in Malta's financial surplus in third quarter". But it had already been the trend earlier in 2019. Indeed, the web portal LovinMalta had reported that "Joseph Muscat's government ha[d] recorded a deficit of €16.5 million for the first quarter of 2019".

With his post-pandemic predictions, Muscat played his usual tune: it's everybody's fault but mine. The trick depends heavily on the public forgetting that the downturn in Malta's finances *predates* the 2020 pandemic. The surplus had disappeared already by the beginning of 2019. It was just a chimera, an illusion, like most of the other conjuring tricks magician Muscat offered the Maltese public.

In fact, what Muscat really managed to achieve was ideological. He managed to transform the Labour Party from a social-democrat political force protecting workers living and working in a market economy to a liberal political actor promoting the market society which Muscat himself laid the foundations for. A market society is a society that orbits round the market. Muscat successfully initiated the process of removing the human person from the centre of society, to be replaced by the market and its needs, expectations, and claims.

Take the environment as an example, though there are quite a few others. The well-being of the human person was pushed aside, its place

---

25   13 January, 2020.

to be taken by the well-being of the construction industry and the market it needs to thrive. (How long-lived that well-being is yet to be seen.) In an interview published by *The Times of Malta* in June 2020, Environment Minister Aaron Farrugia stated, "There should have been smarter development. Development should happen, but smartly and sustainably",[26] further proof – if any was actually needed – of Muscat's ideology of the market society.

Mary Midgley can help us understand better. I'll quote again from *The Myths We Live By*. She speaks about the shift that has been taking place for some time now:

> We are still using the familiar social-contract image of citizens as essentially separate and autonomous individuals. But we are less likely now to defend it on humanistic or religious grounds than by appealing to a neo-Darwinist vision of universal competition between separate entities in an atomised world, which are easily seem as machinery – distinct cogs or bytes put together within a larger mechanism. Social atomism strikes us as scientific.
> This same reductive and atomistic picture now leads many enquirers to propose biochemical solutions to today's social and psychological problems, offering each citizen more and better Prozac rather than asking what made them unhappy in the first place. Society appears as split into organisms and organisms into their constituent cogs. The only wider context easily seen as containing all these parts is evolution, understood (in a way that would have surprised Darwin) as a cosmic projection of nineteenth-century economics, a competitive arena pervading the development, not just of life but of our thought and of the whole physical universe.

These are the currents underlying the modern world. Muscat felt them and, inspired by his deep-seated, egosyntonic narcissism, naturally followed them, to acquire power (and more), for himself and his friends.

Muscat's success(ion)

FOR INDEED, MUSCAT WAS NEVER ALONE. Behind Muscat's mythical Great

---

26   Bertrand Borg, "Interview: 'There should have been smarter development' – Aaron Farrugia. Malta's environment and planning minister on hunting, the PA and recycling", *The Times of Malta*, 1 June 2020.

Man persona there was not a great woman; there lurked an *éminence grise*: factotum and "catalyst" Keith Schembri. Victor Calleja provided an insightful snapshot of Mr Schembri in a piece he wrote for *The Malta Independent on Sunday* in May 2020. You might agree or disagree with it, in part or in whole, but here it is:[27]

> Up to a few months ago, the prime minister of Malta was a certain Joseph Muscat. At least that was the official version for the history books. But the whole world knew that the real power behind Castille's throne, the de facto prime minister, was Keith Kasco Schembri.
>
> Schembri was the real king and Joseph Muscat was just a smiling, grimacing figurehead.
>
> Joseph Muscat was a good mouthpiece for Schembri. He allowed himself, enticed by all sorts of horrors and riches, to be totally led by his chief of staff. Schembri held the string that pulled Muscat who performed to perfection. Schembri was the ventriloquist, Muscat the happy-to-indulge puppet.
>
> Then the world around Muscat erupted. He lost his smile and swagger and, when the going got too hot, out he went. Keith Schembri needed just one more important chess move.
>
> To Labourites and people in general Muscat was a marvellous super-hero, the man who gave the Labour Party dynamism and invincibility.

Mark A. Sammut Sassi
1 May 2021

---

27   Victor Calleja, "Keith Schembri: come back, all is forgiven", *The Malta Independent on Sunday*, 31 May 2020.

AUTHOR'S NOTE

THE READER WILL NOTICE THAT AS TIME WENT BY, I STOPPED REFERRING TO JOSEPH MUSCAT AS "DR MUSCAT" AND STARTED REFERRING TO HIM SIMPLY AS "MUSCAT". This was not to follow the policy I deeply disagree with followed by certain newspapers that expects correspondents to refer to each other by their surname. My decision was based on the fact that at one point I decided that Muscat had lost the right to be referred to by his academic title, or even by any title. At the time of writing, I am not privy to any sure knowledge on Muscat's involvement in the assassination of Daphne Caruana Galizia. My instincts do tell me something, it goes without saying; but there is no smoking gun. That said, the circumstances are so murky, his covering up for his friends' Panama adventures so brazen-faced, that as far as I'm concerned he deserves to be referred to simply as "Muscat".

Which indirectly serves to criticise the policy taken up in the last few years by a number of Maltese newspapers to refer to people by their surnames. I once sent in a reply to something most probably silly penned by that toffee-nosed Martin Scicluna, and referred to him – obviously enough – as "Mr Scicluna". The newspaper asked me to remove the title and refer to him simply as "Scicluna". I refused because, even though I strongly disagreed with the tomfooleries which this silly old man was trying to pass off as deep thoughts, I still felt I was bound to address him as "Mr Scicluna". This was not a pub brawl; despite Mr Scicluna's conceit, pomposity and resemblance to Quentin Tarantino's Stephen Warren (the black slave in *Django Unchained* who calls the other slaves "nigger" and "boy"), the debate was still civilised and governed by a certain etiquette. I felt – and still feel – that calling with their surnames people who are still alive or, if dead, still remembered by the living, is not only bad manners but also disrespectful toward the dialogue. Certain enlightened newspaper editors think otherwise... and, long story short, my reply to Mr Scicluna was never published.

This phenomenon is the twin sibling of that other phenomenon – undoubtedly imported from Britain in the most abject form of servile neo-colonialism – of addressing on first-name basis somebody you hardly know, the idea being that you connect with the person and thus lubricate a sale. A facile metaphor would lend itself perfectly here, but I will resist the temptation. I think such a sale is in reality a hard sell, and I'm allergic to hard sells.

So we have the situation that people you barely know address you on a first-name basis while certain newspapers mention other people on a surname basis. The courtesy used in the Francophone countries, of using "Monsieur", is fast disappearing in the Anglophone world. Italy is somewhere in the middle. The educated still use "Lei", or even "Ella" ... the others use "tu".

It is my conviction that the cinema of the 1970s foresaw much of this (or, vice-versa, that the roots of all this is found in the counterculture of the late '60s/early '70s). For instance, the silly American movie of 1973 *Group Marriage* enumerated the progressive-liberal programme (divorce, abortion, homosexual "marriage", polyamory – only euthanasia was left out). In the classic restaurant scent from the Italian movie of 1971, *Trinity is Still My Name*, the literally unwashed Trinity (played by Terence Hill) and Bambino (Bud Spencer) look at the French waiter is forcing himself to smile at them while describing their food, ending with "*petits pois*" on literally a high note. Trinity asks him, "*Ma perché ridi tanto?*" – "What so funny, huh?" Trinity uses "tu" (the familiar form) when any Italian knows that "Lei" (the polite form) would have been in order.

If you think about it, it's all a matter of social interactions, of – but I risk a lot of flak for using this – "class struggle". And yet, the struggle goes on. And only a politically blind person does not see that, as Slavoj Žižek[28] points out during a discussion with Robert Pfaller, Peter Pilz, Judith Ransmayr held in Vienna on April 2019,[29] at the root of political correctness (or its variants) there's a "class dimension". On that occasion, the Slovene philosopher said,

> I think that the problem with the Left is that we live in the negative legacy of '68, which brought about this 'culturalisation', as it were, of Leftist politics. I notice how systemically social and political problems are 'culturalised'. Like, we have racism,

---

28   At the 2019 Holberg Debate, Žižek was challenged by free-market economist Tyler Cowen about his political views. Citing citing China as an example of the failure of Communism, Cowen argued that Žižek was, in fact, not really a communist, but a conservative! https://www.youtube.com/watch?v=2Sy8 xbhaX68&t=306s

29   Full video: https://www.youtube.com/watch?v=udqlXkBV6fQ

you do a totally fake kind of psychoanalysis and you say, 'It means that we are not open enough to the others, we project our traumas unto the others' and so on and so on. This brings me to one of the most stupid statements (– I almost become Goebbels here and say, 'Let's burn books where they claim this'): 'an enemy is somebody whom we were not ready to listen to, to hear his story'. So Hitler was our enemy because we didn't... ? No! We have to accept that there are real enemies out there. They might be Islamist Fundamentalists and so on and so on. The Left should stop this attitude of 'We are our own enemies whenever we project something unto our enemy', and so on and so on. So I think we should critically analyse this cultural turn of the Left. I think this is the origin of the catastrophe. The extent to which, although beneath the surface, political correctness in the United States has a class dimension. Although they would not admit it, but it's the enlightened, intellectual classes' way to dismiss ordinary people who still mistreat their wives, and so on and so on... you cannot understand resistance to political correctness without the class dimension, and that is what Donald Trump used in a masterful way.

Žižek obviously interweaves many thoughts, trying to say things without saying them, or saying one thing but giving the impression he's saying something else. That said, I think that what he means is quite clear.

I think the vast majority of the Maltese are conservative. The radical liberals are a minority – a vociferous minority no doubt, but a minority none the less.

What do we understand with "conservative" and "radical liberal"?

Probably the debate's essentials are captured in two expressions: (1) Chaos *versus* Order and (2) Individual *versus* Community. To my mind, Chaos occurs when Individuals are detached from their Community, and believe and act as though their desires take precedence on the needs of their Community. Chaos also exists when the Collective forces Individuals to sacrifice their aspirations for an ideological goal. This is where traditional ideology – that purportedly ended in 1989 – becomes relevant. In the Communist countries, say, individuals were forced to sacrifice their freedom for Marxist-Leninist ideology, or for whatever other ideology their country's dictator imposed on them in the name of Marx and Lenin.

Order, on the other hand, is achieved when there's harmony between the Individual and the Community, when a gentle equilibrium is found. The problem lies in society's ever-changing nature, which means that to find the equilibrium you have to adapt constantly.

So it's a paradoxical mindset: you've got constantly to adapt to changing circumstances in order to attain the rigid objective of finding the point of equilibrium between Individual and Community. To achieve that equilibrium you need steadfast principles, and a lot of compassion. If your principles aren't steadfast, and you follow the flow, then instead of finding the gentle point of equilibrium thereby restoring Order, you find yourself stoking the fire of Chaos.

That's how I understand conservatism; that's my conservatism. It probably differs from other types of conservatism.

What does it mean in practice? It means taking positions against the radical liberals and castigating the socialists for forgetting the "needful". (I use this dated word on purpose.) Against the liberals who, in the name of some ill-defined personal freedom, demand, for instance, the introduction of abortion. The elimination of an unborn human for the mother and/or father to continue with their lives, self-evidently violates the principle of Life. Being pro-life is neither religious nor ideological; it's the self-evident truth that all humans are created equal, to borrow the wording of the American Constitution. Humans are created when an ovum gets fertilised, and from that moment onwards they are equal. Being equal, they all have the freedom to live. Abortion means that the freedom of the unborn child to live is superseded by the supposed freedom of the mother and/or father (who together created that child) to move on with their lives.

The unborn child's potential for the Community cannot be sacrificed for anybody else to attainment their individual desires, including the parents. That would mean that the parents' potential is more important/valuable than the unborn child's. It would mean that all humans (born and unborn) are "equal", but the born are more equal than the unborn.

The logic of seeking the equilibrium between Individuals' desires and the needs of the Community applies throughout the spectrum of social issues.

Then, the socialists. These deserve to be castigated for abandoning the vulnerable. Why should pensioners, say, keep living under the stress of having to strive to make it to the end of the month? The conservative applies compassion, and understands the plight of pensioners and suchlike groups.

Slavoj Žižek argues that ideology is what we don't know that we know. Quoting Donald Rumsfeld, he argues that we know what we know; we know what we don't know; we don't know what we don't know. But – he adds – we also don't know what we know. What we don't know that we know is "ideology". It's what we're fed by media, movies, magazines, 'and so on and so on'. Ideology is conformism. It's delegating your thinking to somebody else.

But is that somebody else looking after your interest or their own?

Being conservative means tending your own garden. With compassion though. Because it's compassion that's crucial in determining in an orderly fashion the gentle point of equilibrium between the needs of Individuals and those of the Community.

Flying at the Fall of Dusk

The Elderly, Hipsters and Agriculture

WHEN I WAS A BOY, ITALIAN TV STATION RETE 4 USED TO BROADCAST A JAPANESE ANIMATED SERIES CALLED *STAR BLAZERS*. It featured the sunken WWII battleship *Yamato* – 'Yamato', Japan's traditional name, resounds with patriotic fervour in Japanese hearts – which is brought up from the bottom of the sea and refurbished as a spaceship. It then embarks on a quest for survival.

The metaphor of post-war Japan rising from the ashes was so striking – the original Japanese dialogue was even replete with sexual innuendo signifying the nation's potent regeneration (the Italians duly sanitised it) – that some have even considered the cartoon series nothing but Fascist in tone and outlook.

It represented the rebirth of a nation, the post-war quest for economic growth at all costs.

Like other vanquished peoples before them, the Japanese started to imitate their conqueror. In the post-war years, Japan imported the American nuclear family model to replace the extended family of Japanese tradition.

The economic experiment succeeded, and Japan flourished.

Not only did the economy bloom, but the country experienced a second baby boom accompanied by another, enormous boom in housing, a necessity dictated by the new wave of young 'soldiers' (and their families) who manned industry in the economic war that a demilitarised Japan declared against the world.

The enormous housing estates, called *danchi* and constructed on pristine farmland on the outskirts of big cities, attracted people who could satisfy strict requirements. For instance, only those who earned 5.5 times the rent could apply for an apartment.

These once-desirable flats today look like chicken coops, one on top of the other, in rows of soulless blocks extending as far as the eye can see. One *danchi* outside Tokyo is so large that two train stations had to be built to cater for the droves of workers who would commute six times a week to the burgeoning city. Now its population has dwindled, and it's mostly old people who live there.

Economic growth at all costs cost a lot in social, environmental and human terms.

A few weeks ago, *The New York Times* carried an article on what the Japanese call "lonely deaths". Old people die all by themselves, forgotten and lonely, having spent the last years of their lives enduring daily depersonalising loneliness.

Almost eerily, this scenario had been foreseen by Jonathan Swift (1667-1745) in his *Gulliver's Travels*. In one of his travels, Gulliver visits a country where people called 'struldbrugs' attain immortality at the age of 80. Then they find that their friends and immediate family have all passed away and they envy them; they have no contacts among the younger generations whom they envy for their youth. They become detached from society, and society strips them of virtually all their rights.

In his book *L'origine des systèmes familiaux* (2011), the French anthropologist Emmanuel Todd argues that the English nuclear family system could explain the rise of capitalism, 'because it permits the social flexibility necessary to uproot farmers and the individual mobility necessary to try out new technologies' (p. 18). So, perhaps, Swift's "prediction" was not so eerie after all.

Japan is not alone in having lonely elderly. In March 2017, *The Guardian* published an article claiming that a survey found that 'three-quarters of older people in the UK are lonely'.

In 2013, Italy's *Corriere della Sera* ran an article entitled 'The Elderly: more loneliness, more hardship', claiming that even in the South (where, according to one oft-cited study, there used to be "familism") 'social support is lacking'.

Late capitalism's Onanistic quest to maximise wealth for wealth's sake, its hard-headed insistence on reducing people to means of production whose social and family ties are severed, and its staunch belief that the economy should guide politics, have reduced people to atoms floating in the void of loneliness and depersonalisation.

Indeed, depersonalisation at the very beginning and at the very end of the human being's existence is a defining characteristic of late, neoliberal capitalism.

As usually happens, the hyenas and the jackals prey on the vulnerable. One week after *The New York Times* published the article I mentioned above, the same newspaper published a follow-up opinion piece. 'Japan's aging, dying, atomized present is one version of our future,' opined the writer, 'and a not-so-distant one, already visible in late-middle-age despair and elder exploitation.'

Exploitation: that's where the hyenas and jackals enter the scene. Just one extreme example: an article published in *The Guardian* in October 2011 entitled 'Japan's 77-year-old porn actor: unlikely face of an ageing population', claims that in recent years one-fifth of Japan's adult movie industry (worth almost a billion euros every year) consisted of movies featuring actors in their 60s and 70s, with names such as 'Forbidden Elderly Care'. Clearly, the demand in Japan to overcome old-age loneliness is very present, and is worth something like €200 million per year in adult movies alone.

For all those hipsters who wave the flag of anti-censorship, dope-smoking, libertarian values and all that 1968 stuff, they had better re-think their objectives, as their enthusiasm for what they cherish has led other countries along paths that the liberals could never have imagined (or at least, one hopes they could never have imagined).

And no, this is not bigotry, but simply reading the signs of the times.

To be a true hipster today, you have to be conservative.

The Really Right Question to Ask is: Who Really has Rights?

ONE THING THAT INTRIGUES ME IS THE NAME OF THE 1789 DEC-LARATION OF RIGHTS ISSUED BY THE FRENCH AT THE BEGINNING OF THEIR 10-YEAR-LONG GREAT REVOLUTION: *THE RIGHTS OF MAN AND OF THE CITIZEN*. Already in the 1790s, French women realised that 'rights' were probably literally meant for men and not for all humans, irrespective of sex. Their pleas to be included in the polity were largely ignored, as women's place was at home raising the children, the *enfants de la patrie*. Since then, thanks to the efforts of many (women and men), women have become full members of the polity, equal to men. In other words, no longer confined to the private sphere of the "private" family but welcomed into the greater family, or brotherhood, of the nation and, therefore, its political manifestation, the State.

Ideologically speaking, women had always been human but they became equal to men only after a relentless struggle. They finally became ... *citizens*. In politics, ideology is always more important than biology. I have italicised 'citizen' because of its implications in this context. I am not referring to 'passive' citizenship, but to 'active' citizenship – being an active member of the polity. Children, for instance, are 'passive' citizens, as they can exercise no political right even though they enjoy some protection at law.

Indeed, the idea of citizen and citizenship is problematic, because of the discord between ideology and biology. It would seem that not all biologically human beings are human on the ideological level. Again, consider children. They start their biological existence as small foetuses, growing into infants, children and finally adolescents, before achieving full citizenship. With each phase, the law grants them more protection and more active participation in the polity. What changes is not the biological existence of the individual (whose form 'evolves' over time), but the status given to the individual in accordance with a political construct.

The debate on whether to give 16-year-olds the vote, for instance, fits into this view. The debate will weigh biological considerations (psychological maturation, say) against political exigencies. At the end of the day, however, politics will no doubt have the upper hand.

In other words, it is politics (or political ideology) that decides when the biological human being becomes a political human being, and therefore a human being endowed with the right to exercise and enjoy rights.

In the past, not all human beings were members of the polity: consider slaves, who were treated like incomplete humans by one ideology and then emancipated by another ideology. Let us not forget, however, that when the black slaves of Haiti revolted and demanded emancipation in the 1790s, France agreed on condition that the Haitians pay it 90 million francs as compensation for loss of property (slaves) and income. The sum, settled only in 1947, was equivalent to more or less US$21 billion.

Political ideology may decide one day that androids have rights and can exercise them – a theme explored even in movies, such as *Bicentennial Man* starring Robin Williams.

Indeed, last October, Saudi Arabia granted citizenship to robot Sophia – the absolute victory of politics over biology. A machine was adopted into the human race and given one of humanity's most precious gifts: state citizenship.

A few weeks later, *The New York Post* reported that Sophia, the machine produced by Hanson Robotics and granted Saudi Arabian citizenship, now wanted a baby.

One victim of the victory of politics over biology is the unborn human being. Denied citizenship, the unborn human being is also denied full political and legal protection in the present dominant ideology. Biology has nothing to do with this ideological position.

All talk about "bunch of cells", "undifferentiated tissue", etc., is simply nonsense and inconsequential.

Just like with teenagers being given the right to vote, the legal situation of the unborn depends solely on politics: the same politics that, at different historical moments, decided that slaves were full citizens, later that women were full citizens and now, just a couple of months ago, granted Saudi Arabian citizenship to a (female?) robot manufactured in Hong Kong.

Muscat's Mistake and Other Stories

PEOPLE ASK AND SAY: "BUT WHAT DO WE REALLY CARE ABOUT CORRUPTION? It has little, if any, effect on our lives!"

Only recently, something happened which has had a small but highly significant impact on the lives of each and every one of us. Had Malta not been in the throes of debating corruption and dealing with the surreal situation we are facing on a daily basis, we might have noticed. Instead, we were all hustling making a fool of our country, with sensible people calling for the resignation or removal of Mizzi and Schembri while blindfolded folk were defending the indefensible.

And while we were engaged dissecting the ins and outs of secret offshore companies as if we were all experts, with the more intelligent clamouring "Proof! Proof! Proof!" and the more gullible arguing that you don't open a secret company to deposit the rent of a small house in outer London – the Council of Europe chipped away at the real enjoyment of one of our individual rights.

I might be wrong and I stand to be corrected, but I cannot remember a single drop of ink wasted on the effects of the protocol to the

European Convention for the Protection of Human Rights and Fundamental Freedoms Malta signed this week.

The Convention has been amended to shorten, by two months, the time limit given to the individual to file an application before the Court. Now, the time limit is no longer six but four months. The official purpose is to "help maintain the effectiveness of the European Court of Human Rights". But, as a lawyer friend told me, the reality is that the amendment will have a serious impact on individuals for whom four months are not enough to find a lawyer able and willing to take the case to Strasbourg.

The enjoyment of our fundamental human rights has been tampered with and we were too busy wasting our time to notice simply because Messrs K&K are still occupying important positions when their position has clearly not been tenable for a very long time.

Now that's how corruption affects your life. Apart other things, it distracts you from the serious matters.

* * *

IN THE MEANTIME, TO MY MIND, JOSEPH MUSCAT HAS MADE A SERIOUS MISTAKE WHEN DEALING WITH THE AMERICAN UNIVERSITY OF MALTA FIASCO. Replying to a journalist this week, he said that he thinks there are traces of success in the AUM. The mistake was not the drivel he dished out to the journalist. Muscat is not the first and will not be the last politician to talk nonsense just to save face. His mistake was to use his trademark smile while conveying untruths to a public who is in a position to compare his fanciful statements with the truth.

Muscat would have been wiser simply to admit that there are problems at the AUM. He might have chosen to qualify them as teething problems, but to lie through his teeth like that, when we all know the enormous flop the AUM has turned out to be, has essentially given his trick away.

I don't know about you, but I simply adore Spaghetti Westerns. One trope in these old movies is when the hero enters the saloon, sits down at the table where the big shots are playing poker and joins the game. He loses the first round on purpose, as it allows him to observe how the other plays give their bluffs away - nervous ticks, eye movements, or similar behaviour which can be easily associated with bluff.

Muscat has just given away how he bluffs.

Now whenever we see him replying the same way he replied to the AUM question, we will know that it is certainly not the winning hand he's keeping close to his chest.

* * *

MANY JOURNALISTS AND OTHERS TOO, MOSTLY BELONGING TO THE GENERATION AFTER MINE, ARE DOING A GOOD JOB AT EXPOSING THE CORRUPTION AND MALADMINISTRATION OF THIS GOVERNMENT. But – at least in my humble opinion – they are making two cardinal mistakes by using the English language.

One. They are alienating that part of the electorate which speaks Maltese and resents other Maltese speaking the English. Mostly it's because of the unwarranted social stratification subtext. Essentially, those who resent English spoken in the Maltese-English accent can't digest this silly idea that because you speak English you think you're something better. If these activists are wise (in the philosophical and the street sense), they'd better switch to Maltese and do their job in Maltese.

Two. They are promoting the Maltese Islands image instead of the Malta image. I don't think I need to clarify that I am all for "Malta", and not at all for the "Maltese Islands".

Despite Mizzi's and Schembri's best Panama efforts, we are not a Caribbean former colony. We are an Italic (not Italianate or Italian) former British colony, and our identity is Latin and Catholic. Even the Anglophones are Latin; and even the atheists are Catholic. Just spend some time in England and you will realise that we are not English and analyse deeply our culture to see that it's not Protestant, not even Anglo-Catholic.

I very much dislike this phenomenon so aptly described in Joseph Conrad's *The Nigger of the Narcissus* and by Martti Koskenniemi in his *The Gentle Civilizer of Nations: The Rise and Fall of International Law*. The latter is a brilliant book which speaks of how the former (mostly African) colonies bought the white man's worldview as the ticket to board the ship of civilisation.

We Maltese (or at least many of us) have been civilised for at least nine hundred years, and the ship often moored here. We don't need to buy any ticket.

Manipulation, Ideology, and Poetry

MUCH OF MANIPULATION CON-SISTS IN EMPHASISING THE FORM TO DRAW ATTENTION AWAY FROM THE CONTENT. If you happen to like the TV show *Fool Us*, starring top Las Vegas magicians Penn and Teller (you can watch the episodes on YouTube), you will notice that 'magic' is essentially a game of manipulation. One magician who guest-starred on the show explained the mechanics of the game in very explicit terms: he said that you have to gain your audience's trust in order to fool them.

I must admit that I have learnt a lot from watching Penn and Teller's *Fool Us*. Not about prestidigitation, in which I am not greatly interested, but about the creation of an illusion. It is a fantastic art and after you watch a dozen or so episodes of the series, you start seeing what magicians see – the sleight of hand, card forcing, pre-show work, apparently random on-stage movements, persuasive pseudo-scientific talk and all the other tricks that magicians, mentalists, and other fellow professionals who ply this ancient trade make use of to fool the audience.

Unfailingly well-groomed, elegant, polite, calm, self-possessed and endowed with grace and self-confidence, the typical conman is out to pull a fast one on you. His form is impeccable and you are fooled into freely giving him your trust. And then, hey presto! – he stings you with his confidence trick.

But since you're mesmerised by the elegance of the form, you don't realise what's boiling on the content front, and once the legerdemain is done, you think it's magic. In fact, it is but simple trickery and the conman has had you.

The other day I was watching a NET TV journalist – the not-un-easy-on-the-eye and spirited Lisa Spiteri – as she interviewed different members of the Labour administration, including Prime Minister Joseph Muscat, on the (so far attempted) rape of Żonqor Point.

My impression was that these people are being coached to be collected, composed, and cool while they dish out dollops of sound-bites to journalists. Again I confirmed my impression – outlined in my book on the Panama Papers – that Prime Minister Muscat governs the country as if he were a magician.

* * *

I DO NOT THINK I AM THE ONLY ONE TO HAVE THIS SOLID CONVIC-TION THAT WE ARE IMPORTING ENGLISH IDEOLOGICAL STANCES

SKIPPING ALL SORT OF CULTURAL QUARANTINE.

This post-colonial trend has been exacerbated under Muscat's government. This is quite ironic, as the other Labour believed in the *mitna ta' xejn, mitna għall-barrani* narrative ["we died needlessly, we died for the foreigner"] (again, you can listen to Paul Abela's beautiful song, sung by Renato, on Youtube). Muscat's Labour government, instead, adopted a new narrative based on shallow readings of ideological material churned out by Anglo-American leftish-liberals who have little in common with social democrats and socialists.

Prime Minister Muscat, when confronted with the clamorous U-turn on same-sex matters, admitted he read a couple of books and changed his mind. Just like he signed away an enormous swathe of pristine countryside in Żonqor Point in under five minutes of conversation with a Jordanian construction magnate, so he signed away the right of children to have a parent from each sex after reading a book or two.

I have no doubt that the books Muscat read contained Anglo-American gender ideology and that the Maltese who until yesterday had *mitna għall-barrani*, now cower before the neo-liberal Anglo-American ideologue.

I don't write these words out of airy-fairy nationalistic sentiments. I am inspired by other considerations, of a tangible, cultural nature, and on the democratic mandate. Luckily, on the subject of abortion, Muscat had to concede that his government does not have a mandate. (Needless to say, the hawk-eyed will have seen that the ultimate objective is the introduction, sometime in the future, of this abominable practice.) But on other, less controversial, matters the mandate argument is put aside and strident campaigning stokes support through top-down manipulation presented as if it were bottom-up demand – another example of the politician-magician who gains the audience's trust in order to fool them.

But mostly what is of concern to me is that an ideology which developed in conditions different to ours is imported lock, stock, and barrel and imposed on an unsuspecting people. Take one of the cornerstones of abortion ideology: the usurpation of Darwin's theory of evolution. When this theory was made public in the 19th century, it was criticised not only on religious but also on social grounds. Many people at that time saw it as a projection unto nature of the *laissez-faire* liberalism of the dog-eat-dog Victorian society, of the cut-throat competition that sanctioned the survival of the fittest in the domestic market and justified the imperialist colonisation of inferior races in the wider world.

Clearly Darwinian theory provides a convenient template for the abortion ideology. Just as a humanoid ape evolved into the modern human, so the foetus 'evolves' into the individual. Little does it matter what Darwin really thought. Ideas – called 'mentifacts' by evolutionary biologist Julian Huxley – take a life of their own and influence people and behaviours: they form cultures.

But cultures are endemic to populations. In the book of which he was a co-author, *Malta: Culture and Identity*, Henry Frendo explains that in Malta 'nation' and '*heimat*' overlap. The latter is a German word meaning 'home' but also the identity and culture in which one feels at home. When a foreign culture is imposed – surreptitiously, fraudulently or otherwise – the identity of a people is displaced by a foreign identity that evolved in a different socio-economic environment and history. Where this can lead is anybody's guess, but for sure a people that stops feeling at home in its own country can only expect social tensions.

A Normal Country?

IN 1995, ITALIAN POLITICIAN MASSIMO D'ALEMA PUBLISHED A BOOK CALLED *UN PAESE NORMALE: LA SINISTRA E IL FUTURO D'ITALIA* (A NORMAL COUNTRY: THE LEFT AND ITALY'S FUTURE). I didn't manage to read it all, because the layout was horrible and the text bored me to tears, but I have always cherished that title as a politico-moral compass. *A normal country.*

D'Alema synthesised the message of his book in three sentences: "My generation's duty is to take the Italian Left to government. Previous generations have done fundamental things: they acknowledged democracy and renewed the country. For us, now, the problem is government: we want to prove our mettle."

Twenty-three years later, and almost five after the Maltese "Left" has been elected to power again, I find myself asking whether Malta is a normal country.

By many accounts it is not.

I will focus only on three: Keith Schembri and Konrad Mizzi, the urban environment, and culture.

Schembri and Mizzi
SEEMS LIKE THE NAME OF A STAND-UP COMEDY DUO. Only it's not. These two are more like the Cat

(Mizzi) and the Fox (Schembri) from Collodi's *Pinocchio*.

Anyway. We have now learnt about the secret memorandum being signed months before the call for expressions of interest in the hospital privatisation project, and about involvements in recycling. In a normal country, the Cat and the Fox would have been made to resign. Not in Malta, though, where they are kept in their positions (secret companies and all) ... To serve as catalysts for other projects?

Urban environment
LIKE EVERYBODY ELSE, I AM FOLLOWING WITH A HEAVY HEART, NEWSPAPER REPORTS ON THE RELENTLESS ONSLAUGHT ON OUR ARCHITECTURAL HERITAGE.

The Gozitans are worried about unrestrained "development" in Victoria's historical core. Others are concerned about the transformation of a Sliema cloister into a hotel and the obliteration of a former cinema in Birkirkara. Others still, about the forest of high-rise buildings which will forever change the landscape. The list goes on and on.

Needless to say, I fully subscribe to the subtext in all these cases: Joseph Muscat's *laissez-faire* policies are destroying the country's heritage. But let us be frank and honest. Villa Birbal, Borg Olivier's villa and the de Fremaux Żejtun *palazzo* – to mention but three examples – were not demolished on Dr Muscat's watch.

The problem seems to me deeper than Joseph Muscat and his everything-goes policies where the only value is money. It's a matter of what it means to be a "normal country".

When campaigners protest against the remorseless demolition and destruction of our architectural heritage and, essentially, Malta's character, they fail to come up with a coherent philosophy of preservation. Or, at least, if such a philosophy exists, it does not form part of public discourse, it is simply absent from the public arena.

I believe that in a "normal country", the thinking part of the public (only a minority of which votes for Dr Muscat, by the way) should articulate a philosophy of urban conservation. And that philosophy should not only be made public, but it should form part of the culture of the people. Only when such a coherent philosophy starts occupying public discourse will there be a real context to the protests of campaigners. Otherwise, they are all destined to be perceived as the protests of fussy people, who have nothing better to do with their lives. Which is manifestly wrong and simply rubbish.

Of course, campaigners are right. They are insisting on the

preservation of the urban character of the country, which contributes to the nation's unique or almost-unique identity – a selling point for tourism but also a point of reference for our collective psychological well-being.

But this communitarian ideal clashes, and violently to boot, with the right (real or perceived) of individuals to capitalise on their property. The issues here are complex and require careful philosophical analysis. Yes, philosophical. (But our philosophers are more interested in liberal issues, such as abortion, MAP, euthanasia, gay adoption, thought policing, and other such rubbish imported from the Anglo-American globalist-capitalist world, than in saner, more practical and mundane problems which interest not the fringes but the entire local population.)

The problems exist on two levels and both are intimately related to Justice, with a capital "J".

One, community versus individual. Why should the right of the individual to capitalise on private property be curtailed by intangible community benefits accrued from conservation? Since the benefits to individuals are easily quantified, how to quantify community benefits?

Two, individual versus individual. If individuals have already had a chance to capitalise in the past, why shouldn't other individuals be given the same opportunity in the present and the future? This is a very serious question, and so far I have read or heard nobody dealing with it in a philosophical way.

(By "philosophy" I mean the drawing up of a theoretical framework which outlines the path of justice to be followed if we are to maintain social peace.)

Culture

In the meantime, instead of solving these problems, we are regaled with the most inane cultural production imaginable: a concert featuring the favourite music of Prime Minister Joseph Muscat. I cannot say "Bang your head against the wall" because heavy metal seems not to be on the menu.

Let's compare Prime Minister Joseph Muscat with his predecessors.

Under Mintoff, we got *Ġensna*. Fine, many might find it a distorted interpretation of history, almost a Whiggish rehash of history as an evolution leading to Mintoff's 31 March 1979.

But that's not my point. My point is that under Mintoff, the people were told a story about the nation, and the message that Mintoff is the Saviour of the Nation is oblique. Ray Mahoney actually did a fine job when he wrote the lyrics to that rock opera.

Under Eddie Fenech Adami – and surely thanks to Peter Serracino Inglott's input – Malta got some serious cultural stuff: the Malta Jazz Festival and the Malta International Choir Festival are but two examples.

Alfred Sant didn't have much time to do anything as Prime Minister. Military re-enactments "celebrated" the bicentenary of the French occupation, but otherwise not much else in those twenty-two months. Yet, under Dr Sant's leadership, the Labour Party produced the high-quality *Iljieli Mediterranji* on an annual basis, with people such as the late Joe Attard, Joe Borg, Tony Degiovanni, Narcy Calamatta, my late father, and many others, creating and promoting popular yet beautiful and artistically-valid representations.

To my mind, Lawrence Gonzi adopted a more austere attitude, preferring work to play.

But now we come to Joseph Muscat and we find that the pinnacle of his government's cultural programme is a concert to celebrate the Prime Minister's musical tastes!

So let us sum up all of this. Shady dealings go on, while the Prime Minister's Chief of Staff and favourite Minister open secret companies. The Prime Minister's *laissez-faire* policies usher in an era of remorseless urban devastation. And all this happens with the Prime Minister's favourite music as soundtrack. "Malta: A Normal Country" – what a horror movie!

Fringe Liberalism and the Environment

THERE IS A PERVERSE WIND BLOW-ING IN THE SAILS OF THIS GOV-ERNMENT'S SHIP AND INSTEAD OF WORRYING ABOUT IT, THE CAPTAIN ACTUALLY RUBS HIS HANDS WITH GLEE.

The document called Constitution of Malta might have shortcomings, but removing the Catholic Church from its constitutional position should certainly not be a priority. Whom is the Church bothering anyway?

There can be no sane answer, as the perverse wind of ideology keeps blowing and blowing, driving the ship forward towards a weird Liberal Utopia.

In a sane world, the priorities should be elsewhere. To my mind, the built-up environment is one priority which needs urgent attention.

Two interesting articles in the present constitutional document have a role to play.

One of these articles reads thus: "The State shall safeguard the landscape and the historical and artistic patrimony of the Nation" (article 9).

The other states, "The State shall encourage private economic enterprise" (article 18).

The way Malta's economy has evolved seems to indicate that a balance between the two cannot be struck – private economic enterprise has to thrive by laying waste the landscape and the historical patrimony of the nation.

But this is nothing short of folly. When the entire country will end up as one 400-km^2 mass of pure, unadulterated concrete, what are we going to do? Emigrate *en masse* to Pachino in Sicily or to the Barbary Coast?

Frankly, I must admit I do not have a solution to offer. As a matter of fact, I do not occupy any public office. Instead, the captain of this ship driven forward by the perverse wind of fringe liberalism – a liberalism that is economically *laissez-faire* and socially libertine – seems oblivious to the impending disaster and not ready to spend a moment deliberating the problem.

We *must* find a solution whereby private economic enterprise can be encouraged without having to sign the death sentence of the environment!

We simply *cannot* give up.

We *cannot* accept as Revealed Truth the *lassiez-faire* theology of the God of the Market. Are we going to remove the Clergy of the Christian God from the constitutional document to bring in the Clergy of the Fringe-Liberal God?

The problem is multi-faceted.

It is not only a question of wanting to resist the *laissez-faire* politics of this government. It is also a question of calibrating the situation to attain Justice.

The over-urbanisation of the country reflects a deep, psychological need related to Justice.

Stopping people from "developing" their land or the property they inherited smacks of injustice. Perhaps not in the strict legal sense, but in the moral and psychological sense, it smacks of expropriation.

We are all born with an innate psychological need to be treated equally. Society then tames this need by indoctrinating us that some are more equal than others are. And since this is inculcated into our heads from a very tender age, we accept it as a true reflection of the world and live according to its dictates.

This explains, for instance, why the fight for women's rights has necessarily turned into a fight and not an exercise in good-mannered persuasion. The same applies to the emancipation of other groups of people, whose predicament is marked either by an imposed inferior status or by exploitation, or both. Ultimately, it is the violence necessary to overcome the equally violent social power structures that engender and legitimise exploitation.

But this taming is only partial. It is applied with regard to positions of power and industrial production. With regard to other aspects of social life and the economy, the taming is weak.

The system we live in has its origins in the French Revolution of 1789. This important event didn't just happen; the legal, economic and social changes which erupted in its wake had been long brewing. The idea of freedom of enterprise is one of them and the new order ushered in by the Revolution wanted to do away with two fundamental restrictions: restrictions on the enjoyment and capitalisation of land and other property, and restrictions on market equality between economic actors.

In other words, a revolutionary idea which has now become mainstream responded to humanity's innate need for equality: all men were born equal and had the sacrosanct right to trade and make money freely and without discrimination, while land could not be entailed or otherwise kept off the market.

It is this idea which makes it difficult to protect the environment. If all men are equal, why should some be allowed to develop their properties and others not? If all men are equal, shouldn't all properties be eligible for development?

This big problem needs to be

solved for the two above-mentioned articles of the Constitution to work like a politico-legal hole and shaft in the engineering fit of the State.

Instead, we have a Prime Minister who thinks it might be a good idea to spend public money and waste public time to debate (and hold a referendum on) whether to remove Catholicism from the Constitution!

Public money and public time should be used to find ways to save the environment while allowing people to make money.

But since that's not fringe, it's not cool. Spending, how much? one million euros?, to ask voters whether they want to do away with Catholicism in the Constitution, on the other hand, is.

A Mockery of Democracy

If you study Joseph Muscat's political style you will find a truly interesting characteristic.

Shrouded in a sort of humility, Dr Muscat often repeats that he (and/or the extension of his persona, the government) is not perfect. This earns him not only a respite of credibility and some political mileage but also, more importantly, the possibility to buy time. In the game of democracy, each government has a constitutionally-limited lifespan, so buying time to postpone the payment of political penalties is absolutely of the essence. Every seasoned politician knows that if he or she can survive a crisis for more than a week or two, then the chances are that they need not do anything about it or quit the game so soon.

So Dr Muscat keeps playing, over and over again, this "we are not perfect" tune. Now he has taken it to the next level. Not only is he "not perfect", there is really no alternative to him.

This is quite a telling manoeuvre. It is no longer the case that Dr Muscat is not perfect, but we have to lump it because there is no alternative.

This extraordinary assessment was evident in the accusation levelled at the Nationalist Opposition that when in government they were simply "administrators", whereas he "leads".

The verbal trickery actually amounts to a mockery of democracy. In a democracy, the politicians in government *administer* – which is why we call it the *Administration* as in the "Labour Administration". Politicians in government administer the State on behalf of the People, who are the embodiment of the Nation's Sovereignty.

In a democracy, leadership is relegated to party politics, not state affairs. When the Leader leads the Nation and declares to embody Sovereignty, it's a democracy no more.

Dr Muscat speaks as if he went up Mount Sinai, spoke to a burning bush, and climbed down carrying two Stone Tablets he claims were given to him by the God of Liberalism to lead his people to the Promised Land of economically *laissez-faire* milk and socially libertine honey.

Coming from a politician who continuously preaches secularism – to the point that he thinks Catholicism should not feature in a new constitutional document – these pseudo-religious discourse and referencing mark the absolute zero of political incoherence. Dr Muscat brazen-facedly uses religious un-dertones to convey messages about himself as the one who has been touched by divinity, the anointed one, the Messiah.

I am, of course, not the first to make this observation. I must give credit to somebody else who first noticed this trait: that insightful commentator of Maltese politics and brilliant maverick, Joe Demicoli of *Banana Republic* fame.

Already in 2008, when Dr Muscat took over the leadership (not administration) of Labour, Mr Demicoli had published a song, called *Inhobbkom*, depicting Dr Muscat as the Messiah. Over the years, it got more than 230,000 views on YouTube, and given that it's in Maltese, that number is truly impressive. It might have had the (undesired?) effect of inoculating the adoring masses against the truth, or even of signalling that it was fine to accept the new leader as ... Messiah. Irony can at times pay Customs duty on behalf of the truth.

These considerations apart, it becomes patently clear to whoever seeks to be objective, that this elaborate PR exercise – "we are not perfect but there's really no alternative" and "let the nation unite behind the Anointed One, he who has the gift of the second sight, the Chosen One, the Leader" – is a far cry from democracy.

Does it really matter? If the hay is abundant and the sun keeps shining, should we really care?

According to experts in economics, the growth will not last long; soon the economy will start cooling down. It goes without saying that Dr Muscat is fully aware that nothing lasts forever. This might lend new insight as to why he is slowly "transitioning" toward his exit (and it's not only because of the Mizzi-Schembri shenanigans).

But once he leaves, we shall have to deal with a messy messianic legacy. I seriously wonder whether it will be healthy for the development and maintenance of democracy in Malta.

One of the basic tenets of democracy is that no member of society is divine. This stance has a long-standing pedigree.

For instance, King Charles I of England was convinced he could cure people with his touch. King James IV of Scotland, who later became James I of England, famously said that "even by God himself they [kings] are called gods".

The divinity of kingly rule was mainstream ideology in the past, but its head was (luckily and literally) chopped off a few times to drive the point home that kings are not divine. In a democracy all humans are born equal; nobody is divine in a democracy.

Democracy thrives on the accountability of politicians and the transparency with which they conduct their political business. The politician who believes he or she is not to be held to account and whose dealings fall short of transparency (because "we are not perfect" but "there is no real alternative" since "we lead" and "the others only administer"), damages democracy no end.

Do we stand to lose anything if this happens? Should we care?

Though the answer is obvious to the intelligent, it is much less so to the others.

Is 'Liberal' an Insult?

IS BYZANTINE AN "INSULT"? Probably the backward Normans who, engaged as mercenaries by the Arab rulers of Sicily a thousand years ago, met the Byzantines and were overwhelmed by their inexplicable sophistication, used "Byzantine" as an insult. The word "Byzantine" is today used to describe the Byzantine Empire (that fell in 1451) as well as to denote something excessively complicated.

The same applies to "liberal" – it can mean somebody who adheres to "liberalism" or the opposite of "bigot".

Were the Byzantines, "Byzantine"? Are opponents of liberalism, bigots?

Before developing my argument, I want to tease the reader with a question.

What keeps the liberal construction industry from developing that prime ODZ land with fantastic sea-views occupied by a few dilapidated buildings known as Ħaġar Qim and Mnajdra? Why doesn't the Malta Developers Associations talk to journalists and – more importantly – to our liberal Prime Minister Joseph Muscat, to argue the case for a phenomenal 69-storey tower built on that plot currently occupied by a heap of pinkish, mouldy stones known as the Ħal Tarxien Neolithic Temples?

Even entertaining the idea – let alone the act – of demolishing Neolithic structures and erecting modern, shining towers on their sites, is absolutely shocking.

The question is, Why?

And the answer is found in one word: "taboo".

It is (and hopefully will forever be) a taboo even to consider such hideous projects as demolishing prehistoric buildings.

And yet, the liberals have demolished other, non-physical age-old institutions, because the taboo that shielded them has been eroded and, unlike the temples, no protective tent was erected over them to shelter them from the elements of "liberalism".

In my book *L-Aqwa fl-Ewropa*, I devoted a longish chapter to analysing Joseph Muscat's politics. I quoted from one of my favourite thinkers, the French Alain Supiot who argues that "a politics of deregulation of personal status is actively promoted in the name of a struggle against the 'last taboos'" (*Homo Juridicus: On the Anthropological Function of the Law*, p. 37).

The liberal agenda is, indeed, one which seeks to remove the "last taboos".

To what "liberal" are we referring?

A short book by the Italian public intellectual Marcello Veneziani, written in the late 1990s, can serve as a good introduction to the subject. Titled *Comunitari o liberal. La prossima alternativa?* [*Communitarians or liberals. The next alternative?*], it suggests that in the post-1989 world the divide is no longer between capitalists and communists, but between liberals and communitarians.

Essentially, the liberals seek an atomised society in which the individual is directly linked to the State. By removing the "last taboos", the State deregulates personal status but asks for full subjection in return. Human rights, I would add, thus become indispensible in such a scenario, as they are the individual's only defence which claim to originate from an authority higher, and other, than the State.

The communitarians seek buffers between the State and the individual: intermediating associations of people which attenuate the relentless encroachment of the individual's freedom by the State. The primary among such associations is based on nature: the family.

No wonder that the family is one of the prime targets of the liberal approach to politics.

Some liberals claim they want to embrace new ideas, opinions and behaviour. Let's consider prostitution as one example of such "novelties".

Prime Minister Muscat claimed in 2017 that he had the people's mandate to launch a reform of the laws regulating prostitution. The irony behind this "progressive" so-called mandate is that the "liberal" idea of regulating prostitution is as medieval as they come!

In 1988, the French historian Jacques Rossiaud published a book on prostitution in the Middle Ages which has now become a classic. I found the Italian translation, *La prostituzione nel Medioevo*, in a second-hand bookshop in Florence and never bothered to buy the English translation. This, however, is from the blurb of the English translation, which you can find online: "public prostitution may in fact have been viewed by secular and religious authorities as a means of social control and of preserving marital stability – a means by which the virtue of wives and daughters was actually protected".

In the Middle Ages, prostitutes were charged with public duties. Among these was the duty to "take care" of foreigners, by offering an outlet for their aggressive traits as well as protecting women of good repute (Rossiaud, p. 59 of the Italian translation).

Malta is experiencing a high turnover of foreign workers, who spend only a couple of years in the country because of the "inflated property market" (as claimed by the president of the Malta Employers Association). I might be wrong, but this influx seems to cast light on the government's intention to regulate the prostitution industry.

In July 2017, the Prime Minister referred to it as "a black market industry which could be enslaving women". But by regulating it, Dr Muscat's government would only be transforming it into a legitimate industry, which does not necessarily solve the "enslavement" issue.

For the purposes of my argument, however, such regulation is nothing new at all! It would simply amount to a throwback to medieval times, when there was a "social climate that encouraged even respectable men to use [the] services [of prostitutes]" (again from Rossiaud).

So much for "new" ideas and behaviour! Unless, that is, we really are in the "new Middle Ages", as John Rapley pithily put it in his famous *Foreign Affairs* article of 2006. In that sense, it would be a case of a novelty and a throwback at the same time. And this can only be achieved by removing the "last taboos", and – to put it bluntly – forgetting those who are left behind by the "new" system.

So, is "liberal" an insult? No, I would not say so. It's an ideology. But, in my opinion, it's a rotten one.

Depressive Liberalism

ALL HUMANS NEED LOVE, AND TRUST. They need to trust each other in order to share the same living space.

The problem with love and trust, of course, is that they are scarce. Not having enough love and trust for everybody they meet, individuals need structures within which to express and receive both. Some of these structures are natural (e.g., the family), others are man-made (e.g., clubs, congregations... companies).

This is where social liberalism finds the enormous hurdle it cannot overcome.

I prefer to define 'social liberalism' as that political ideology that seeks to 'liberate' the individual from the constraints ensuing from belonging to a group, and this through the direct intervention of the State. One example is State-sponsored 'freedom' from the so-called 'patriarchal family'.

(Never mind that this narrative is clearly flawed, as there is no real patriarchy. All intelligent men listen to their wives. The dim ones don't, and end up courting trouble at home. Men and women who don't listen to their equally intelligent partner ultimately harm their children, and that is as dim-witted as can be.)

Liberalism needs the 'atomised' individual – an individual who belongs to no structure, apart from the multicultural State or, nowadays, the market.

The individual is 'freed' from family ties, but also religious and even national ties. He or she floats about, responding to the demands of an omnipotent, fluid market.

Not even company loyalty remains a top priority – the new culture seems to favour employees who continuously flit from one job to another, using one company job as a trampoline to spring to the next.

This atomisation leads to depression.

A few years ago, *The New York Times* published an article called 'Why Conservatives are happier than Liberals'. The article echoed research that has been going on for a number of years and consistently produces the same result: liberalism is related to depression.

In 2014, the *Journal of Applied Psychology* published a paper called 'The Subjective Well-Being Political Paradox: Happy Welfare States and Unhappy Liberals' (available online).

One of the conclusions was that "measured in terms of enacted values (i.e., what the government actually does), liberalism corresponds in higher subjective well-being, but when politics is measured in terms of espoused values (i.e., what individuals believe), greater conservatism coincided in higher subjective well-being".

This should serve as backdrop to the concerted, aggressive pro-abortion media campaign we are currently witnessing.

A commissioner from the Council of Europe and an unknown lady claiming to be from a strange association called 'Catholics for Choice', have recently set out to convince the Maltese public that abortion is a human right and that it's okay for Catholics to abort. (Former member of the Council's Parliamentary Assembly Michael Asciak has argued that the commissioner is probably breaking council rules.)

Former European Court of Human Rights Judge Giovanni Bonello has already clarified that abortion is not a human right; others have made clear the real Catholic position on abortion.

So there's no need to repeat what has already been said.

However, it is worth underlining that whereas abortion is one of the accepted tenets of modern-day liberalism, holding liberal values is related to depression.

Abortion defies both love and trust. It annihilates the maternal bond of love and the bond of trust there should be between father and mother, by removing the father from the equation.

A culture in which abortion is legal and therefore easily available, makes (decent) men paranoid. (The less decent ones follow another set of rules.)

But it makes women paranoid too.

A Romanian friend married to a Swede once told me how when she informed her husband about her first pregnancy and he didn't suggest an abortion, she was a tad surprised and only then concluded he was a decent man. The liberal ideology behind this short anecdote is shocking.

Bonds of love and trust add value to life, and help avoid depression. By normalising abortion (in the name of free choice, feminism, and other abstract ideological terms), a culture devoid of love and trust has been engendered in the West.

Considering abortion and the other negative aspects of liberalism, one can only invite pro-abortion preachers to go preach their deadly gospel elsewhere.

A Liberal State

JOSEPH MUSCAT'S PROJECT IS TO TRANSFORM MALTA INTO A LIBERAL STATE. My contention is that his project is a travesty of liberalism.

In a liberal State, justice works. Court cases are managed professionally, delays avoided, alternative resolution mechanisms encouraged and given massive publicity and visibility, international commercial practices (such as international arbitration) rendered more understandable to all involved…

In a liberal State, education imparts to all children the skills to take care of money and avoid being ripped off.

In a liberal State, traffic is managed properly, and fast. Daily gridlock is bad for business and for the psychological well-being of the population.

A liberal State enjoys excellent (not low-cost) air connections with other countries to facilitate trade, exchange of ideas, investments…

In a liberal State, the government pushes for the opening up of capital for export-oriented industry owned by local entrepreneurs. It dilutes bureaucracy for new inventions; incentivises new inventions, research and development, and other wealth-creating intellectual property; makes access to the stock market easier and attractive, by publicising it heavily.

In a liberal State, the environment is not ruthlessly and shamelessly raped, harassed and abused, but the freedom to enjoy it is safeguarded for future generations. People are allowed the freedom to live without the anxiety caused by savage over-development.

In a liberal State, the State does not get involved in shady deals but treats the national health service as the most sacred of sacred cows. It engages in healthy eating campaigns, discouraging junk food consumption.

A liberal State – *with a social conscience* – is all this and more. It is not a club whose two main objectives are the enrichment of its members (through corruption and shady deals) and the dismantlement of the country's social fabric (by pushing the agenda of fringe groups).

A liberal State is constitutionally geared to ensure the proper, well-oiled functioning of its institutions and minimise abuse of power, by politicians and other PEPs.

In a liberal State, business should not depend on the government of the day to launch projects and see them through. Business should depend on rules applied and upheld in an equal fashion for one and all. This was the essence of the liberal-bourgeois revolution which begun 200 years ago in parts of Western Europe, not the demolition of the social fabric. France flirted with such silly ideas for 10 years from 1789 to 1799, and then for a long time adhered to a conservative social policy. The socially conservative period – which dominated the West – allowed the business class to consolidate its wealth. Malta needs that; the current demolition of the social fabric is not conducive to the creation of wealth. It will make *almost* everybody poorer.

No compassion for the liberals

THE UNITED KINGDOM HAS EMBRACED A HEIGHTENED LEVEL OF SOCIAL LIBERALISM. The NHS website gladly announces that "one in three women will have an abortion in their lifetime" as if that were some national achievement to be proud of.

The UK has a humongous problem with loneliness. Prime Minister Theresa May even appointed a Minister for Loneliness.

Now, the London *Times* has published an article about the culture of neglect reigning at a Lothian hospital where old patients at the end of their lives were not given the care they needed, and were verbally and physically abused, to boot. On a regular basis. An official report cites "a poor culture that lacks compassion, respect for patients and respect for colleagues".

When you care only about yourself – not even about your (unborn) children – and about your liberty to do as you please, how can you practise compassion? When the dominant ideology fixates on the sole attainment of one's pleasure and (slippery and, at times, delusional) self-actualisation, how can there be compassion? For the liberals, there is no compassion. Is this what we want for Malta?

Buleben

SO NOW IT SEEMS THAT AFTER SENDING EVICTION LETTERS TO FARMERS AND CREATING A VERITABLE MEDIA FUSS, THE GOVERNMENT IS BACKING DOWN ON THE CRAZY IDEA OF BUILDING UP HUGE SWATHES OF PRISTINE LAND IN BULEBEN. What happened?

Is this really a government that listens?

I don't know. But this story reminded me of an anecdote a Belarussian friend once told me. When the government of Belarus takes a decision that turns out to be unpopular, the people take to the streets and protest. The protests are given a lot of prominence by the media (in this supposed dictatorship...). Following the ruckus, the President speaks to the people assuring them that it was a genuine mistake, that

the minister never really wanted to implement the measure, etc etc etc. The government backs down and the people are happy because the government listens.

And the dictatorship that listens goes on. A sort of democratic dictatorship. Possibly even socially liberal.

Sandro Chetcuti and dog-dinner making

AS USUAL, THAT PARAGON OF BRILLIANCE AND WISDOM SALVU BALZAN BUNGLES UP ANY ARGUMENT HE DECIDES TO TACKLE. The latest example of this *soi-disant* journalist's cogent and coherent thinking was the attack on Sandro Chetcuti in 2018.

Now let me be clear. I don't even know Mr Chetcuti, and I'm as disgusted as the next man with the appetite for destruction which characterises the "development" industry.

But is attacking Mr Chetcuti and his lobby the answer? What should developers do? Retire *en masse*? Go and spend the rest of their lives in a monastery to practise self-flagellation?

Salvu Balzan is as silly as a goose. These people have found the goose which lays the golden eggs and, despite the destruction, the government will let it lay till the goose's dead.

If Mr Balzan were honest in his journalism, he would attack the government not the developers' lobby.

The government has to find ways to open up new business opportunities for people like Sandro Chetcuti to channel their energy and entrepreneurship in ventures that don't ruin our natural and urban environment forever.

Mr Chetcuti has no such duty. His only duty is to obey the law. It's the government's duty and responsibility to create a legislative framework to usher in economic liberalism.

Instead, Government is wallowing in the mud of *laissez-faire* and doing next to nothing to promote real liberalism, by which I mean availability of venture capital, a courageous, visionary and lean bureaucracy, an efficient and egalitarian judicial system, etc. This is what makes a market economy work.

But, of course, Salvu Balzan opens fire on Mr Chetcuti to save Joseph Muscat from well-deserved criticism.

What an expert at making a dog's dinner of an argument he is!

Calm After the Storm

THE PRO-ABORTION LOBBY IS TRYING TO CREATE A MEDIA STORM TO TAKE THE PUBLIC BY STORM AND IF THEY SUCCEED IN THEIR INTENT, THERE WILL BE CALM.

'Calm after the storm' is one way of translating the title of Giacomo Leopardi's poem *La quiete dopo la tempesta*. The poem, or *canto*, is divided in two parts. In the first part, Leopardi celebrates the return to normal, everyday life after the storm. In the second part, he reveals his true thoughts: life is sorrowful and the only joys we have are short respites from pain.

Leopardi is not just the greatest Italian poet of his century and one of the world's greatest poets of all time, but probably also the most pessimist of them all. And although pessimism is a sin against life, his philosophical verses make you stop and reflect on the meaning of life, and how nature plays with us as if we were little dolls in a doll-house.

His extreme, depressive pessimism helps us to assess our own lives in their proper perspective.

When I read about the pretended right to terminate the life of a fellow human being in the foetal stage of life, I cannot help but remember Leopardi's poetry. This poet from the Marches in central Italy suffered from a severe deformation of the spine; he must have feverishly desired a medical way out of his predicament. Unable to find any, he sought refuge in poetry.

When I read about the handful of ladies who, being a bit of a handful, stood outside Parliament in Valletta to declaim their vision of life and death, I thought about Leopardi because those who are in favour of abortion justify their position by arguing that terminating the life of an unborn child can be a way out of suffering, of a harsh predicament. Unlike Leopardi, they do not seek refuge in merciful poetry, but in the cold steel of the abortionist's merciless tools.

The closing lines of Calm after the storm are graceful and replete with shades of meaning. Leopardi first addresses Nature (1), then he refers to humanity in general (2):

(1) You scatter sorrow with a free
hand, grief
Spontaneously appears, and the
happiness, that so often
Through a freak of nature and some
miracle
Grows out of trouble, is a great
reward.

(2) Humanity
Dear to the gods! Happy to find
Some breathing room
From sorrow: is blessed
When all sorrows are finally relieved
by death.
(Translation by John B. Valerio.)

The Festival of Life's Victory Over Death

IN 2018, IN PADUA, ITALY, A SCULPTOR AND A TEAM OF UNIVERSITY ACADEMICS UNVEILED A 3-D VERSION OF THE MAN WHOSE FIGURE WAS IMMORTALISED, LITERALLY, IN THE TURIN SHROUD. They re-created his bodily appearance: a man 1.8m tall, robust and extraordinarily handsome, with long hair and a beautiful beard.

They opined that the man who was wrapped in that ancient sheet was the same man whose death, and what happened in its wake, are commemorated in the Easter festival.

The festival is a celebration of the story of the death and resurrection of a man who aspired to the grandest of grand designs: the love of, and for, all humanity.

For Christians, it is the story of how God loved humanity to such an extent that he sent His only Son to die for the sins of humanity and redeem us all from the eternal damnation consequent to the original transgression against God's will.

For others, however, he was one of their own who sided with the rabbinical school of Hillel, which, in those days, was locked in controversy over the Law with the school of Shammai. The Shammites held fundamentalist views on Scripture and the Law; the Hillelites were more lenient and sought a balance between the love for God and the love for one's neighbour.

For others still, he did not really die on the cross, as God saved him at the last, most crucial moment by sending somebody else to take his place while raising him alive to heaven. They hold him as the penultimate prophet and eagerly expect his second coming, when he will fight a false Messiah.

For the atheist, or the agnostic, it is either the story of a fool who died for lofty ideals, or of a freedom fighter, a descendant of the House of David who was executed for the political crime of sedition, having dared to claim his rightful throne by freeing his people from Roman imperialism. How else to interpret the triumphant entry into Jerusalem riding the foal of a donkey and "INRI"? The atheist or agnostic observer might even see it as a mythological story, a rehash of the Persian/Roman Mithras or the Egyptian Horus.

For yet another group, he represents a metaphor, of psychological death and psychological resurrec-tion. After all, the belief in God is a requisite for the success of the twelve-step programme to recover from alcoholism or sex addiction, as traditionally administered by Alcoholics Anonymous and others involved in such kinds of therapy.

But it is not only a metaphor for overcoming death caused by "sin" and resurrecting to a new life. It is also an allegory for the sacrifices life asks of us, when our ego has to die for the love of those dear to us. One need not give one's life like the French gendarme Arnaud Beltrame did a few days ago to save a hostage.

That is heroism on a grand scale. There is heroism on a more mundane scale, when the ordinary does however become extraordinary. One can, and should, sacrifice – on the psychological level – one's ego for the love of others. To borrow Freud's intuition, there is either Love or Death. Love thus becomes equal to Life.

One need not have an addiction or be religious to understand that the Easter festival conveys a message of courage and hope, of Life/Love overcoming Death. It is probably the most positive of messages one can imagine.

Life and death
OUR TIMES ARE CHARACTERISED BY THE BELIEF IN RIGHTS (OFTEN AT THE EXPENSE OF OBLIGATIONS). Some scholars have tried to establish a timeline for the present rights-based culture, even going back to the High Middle Ages. Others – and I think *these* are right – argue that our contemporary

rights-based culture came into being with the French Revolution and the revolutionary idea of the Rights of Man. (Regrettably, it took quite a while for women to be included in "Man".)

But this flurry of rights has brought about a systemic dilution of values, and eventually disrespect for human life. Just look at one aspect of our culture: entertainment. Young people play videogames that encourage them to go back and "finish off" their virtual adversaries. They gain points for killing "enemies". Cinema portrays violence as if it were a normal reaction to life events, and recently Hollywood has even normalised the killing of "descendants".

This is part of a broader construct, of an ideology which has removed the sense of a higher moral authority. The aftermath has been that we have become desensitised to human life, possibly on a scale not experienced in living memory.

I do not adhere to that school of thought which idealises the past. I think *passatism* is wrong. There were no ancestors who "in their simplicity" lived a morally better life. Violence was always there, in various forms. But violence in the name of rights for all is a novelty, one that is not easy to unravel as we are imbibed in the ideology that a right must necessarily be right.

And yet, some "rights" are plainly wrong. Just like the privileges to which rights served as antidote, were wrong.

There is, to my mind, only one thing which is always right: Life. Everything else is, and has to be, subservient to it.

Giving one's life for another
THE SCEPTICS BELIEVE THAT THIS IS JUST MEDIEVAL PIOUS CLAPTRAP, LONG DEFEATED BY RATIONALISM AND SCIENCE. The selfish gene makes the world go round and survival of the fittest is the order of the day. I think that much of this modern scientific claptrap is simply the projection of the liberal worldview unto the natural world, essentially liberal anthropomorphism.

The greed underlying liberalism necessarily has to demonise religion. (That greed is the archenemy is conveyed in the story of the apostle who betrays his master for money.)

One way to demonise effectively is to claim that the message of religion makes no sense either rationally or scientifically. And yet, as the Slovene philosopher Slavoj Žižek has demonstrated in *Living in the End Times* (2010), p.92, one finds a paradox here:

> The 'reason' of which the Pope speaks is a pre-modern tele-

ological Reason, the view of the universe as a harmonious Whole in which everything serves a higher purpose. Which is why, paradoxically, the Pope's remarks obfuscate the key role of Christian theology in the birth of modern science: what paved the way for modern science was precisely the 'voluntarist' idea – elaborated by, among others, Duns Scotus and Descartes – that God is not bound by any eternal rational truths. While the view of scientific discourse as involving a pure description of facticity is illusory, the paradox resides in the coincidence of bare facticity and radical voluntarism: facticity can be sustained as meaningless, as something that 'just is as it is', only if it is secretly sustained by an arbitrary divine will. This is why Descartes is the founding figure of modern science, precisely when he makes even the most elementary mathematical facts like 2 + 2 = 4 dependent on arbitrary divine will: two plus two is four because God willed it so, with no hidden or obscure chain of reasons behind it. Even in mathematics, this unconditional voluntarism is discernible in its axiomatic character: one begins by arbitrarily positing a series of axioms, out of which everything else is then supposed to follow. The paradox is therefore that it was the Christian Dark Ages which created the conditions for the specific rationality of modern science as opposed to the science of the Ancients.

For the naysayers Žižek is an atheist Marxist and Lacanian philosopher.

My Personal Library

The Missing Jesus: Rabbinic Judaism and the New Testament (2002) is a collection of scholarly essays written by Jewish experts (including one who is Pope Benedict's favourite Jewish interlocutor).

The essays are all breath-taking, but I love one in particular ('The Gospels and Rabbinic Literature') in which the author, Herbert W. Basser, a Jewish theologian, makes two beautiful statements: 'It seems that the Evangelists had little idea about the details of Jewish laws, and only by careful analysis can we establish what lay behind their words' and 'Not only can the New Testament confirm the antiquity of legal principles of early Rabbis, it can also for medieval and modern ones'.

Professor Basser's observations taken together clearly signify that the Evangelists faithfully transcribed real legal discussions of 2,000 years ago without necessarily understanding the legal details

– a clear clue pointing at the historicity of the Gospels.

Bart D. Ehrman's books, such as *Lost Christianities* (2005) and *The Orthodox Corruption of Scripture* (2011), are brilliant books that indirectly prove that tradition is perhaps more important than what's written in the Book.

Professor Ehrman is a former born-again, fundamentalist Christian who then lost his faith.

Despite his being an avowed atheist, Ehrman is a staunch defender – basing himself on proper research and studies – of the historicity of Jesus' life and death.

So there's a thought for those who wonder whether Jesus was an invention, a literary creation, rather than a real, flesh-and-blood historical figure.

The Act of Killing

... IS ALWAYS AN ACT OF MORBID FASCINATION. It is a fleeting moment of God-like omnipotence, and a supposed shortcut to solving problems. After all, *mors omnia solvit.*

Or does it? Does death by murder really solve everything?

Ghosts haunt murderers. Humans seem to be genetically programmed to live with the psychological aftermath of killing only if the act is carried out as a group exercise, in the form of war, when the Enemy is completely dehumanised. When done individually, the wicked end up like the tossing sea, which cannot rest, whose waves cast up mire and mud. Ghosts are a metaphor not only of the murderer's guilty conscience but also of the falsity of the proposition that murder is the shortcut to solving problems.

When the Mafia calculated that by whacking Giovanni Falcone and Paolo Borsellino it would be solving its "harassment" problems, little did it realise that that double murder would actually turn out to be a watershed moment, galvanising civil society against the honoured society.

Whoever commissioned Daphne Caruana Galizia's gruesome murder will sooner or later discover that it was a misguided decision of colossal proportions. Even if they are not caught, even if they drown their conscience in whisky, vodka, or rum, the masterminds behind the assassination will eventually discover that they have unleashed forces they could have never foreseen.

Killing always unleashes forces that are beyond any one individual's, or coterie's, control.

Killing the unborn, the new nigger
MUSCAT'S GOVERNMENT IS ON THE WARPATH, AND LIFE IS ITS ENEMY. It is intent on passing a law making it legal to kill unborn human beings, on the premise that the unborn human being is an object, not a person. The historical precedents of this shameful position are well-known, the most repulsive of which was the treatment reserved for non-whites, particularly in the United States.

I recently read of a case in antebellum Louisiana, *Valerien Joseph v. Calmes and Buford* (1857): two white slave patrollers, Calmes and Buford, were on the lookout for runaway slaves when they encountered Joseph, a black free man. Despite his protestations, they beat him up and whipped him some 50 times to subdue him and take him away as a slave. Finally, and with the help of onlookers, Joseph managed to escape. He then sued the two white men, framing his lawsuit in a strange fashion. Instead of describing the violence inflicted upon him, he framed the case as a debt action, claiming that Calmes and Buford owed him money for their illegal assault on his property: his body. The jury found in his favour and the judge condemned the two men to pay him money for assaulting his property, his body.

This is indeed a strange case, but serves to illustrate the idea of the exclusion of certain categories of humans from the purview of the law. The 'nigger', Joseph, won his case because he based it on a law which viewed him as property, not on a law which considered him a person.

This is exactly what Muscat's government is proposing *vis-à-vis* embryos – that a certain category of human beings be treated as property, excluded from the purview of legislation which protects a person's rights, foremost among which the right to live. Property has no such right; property simply belongs to somebody, without any inherent right to live.

The legislation permitting embryo freezing (and death by thawing or by disposal) is a return to the obscurantist laws which allowed slavery and racial abuse in the 18th and 19th centuries.

The unborn is the new nigger. Then the nigger was the Afro-American; now the nigger is the unborn child.

In all such cases, humanity is denied to human beings. Some humans are not human enough, or simply not human.

My Personal Library

Umberto Eco's *Foucault's Pendulum* (1988) has been described as 'the thinking man's *Da Vinci Code*'. The novel is an ironic depiction of grotesque believers in conspiracy theories. It addresses the basic human need to make sense of disparate, unconnected events.

Unlike García Márquez, who looks for meaningful but acausal coincidences, Eco underlines the stupidity of trying to find causality between events that simply happen at the same time but are not connected.

However, Eco's dismissal of fake conspiracy theories doesn't mean that all conspiracy theories are fake, in the same way that the fact that some horses are brown doesn't mean that all horses are brown. Muscat's government seems to have embarked on a risky funambulism of sorts. It is trying to shove down the throat of its hardcore vote the conspiracy theory that journalists from all over the world are ganging up against Labour by proposing fake conspiracy theories on Daphne Caruana Galizia's murder. It's very much an Eco-like scenario. The government has its very own conspiracy theory to explain away what it claims to be a fake conspiracy theory!

Two Very Short Stories

The Secret Service Always Rings Once

FOR THE PRIME MINISTER, LEADING THE COUNTRY WAS NO WALK IN THE PARK. Not only did he have to deal with the embittered loser in the leadership race, but he also had to find ways to co-exist with a domineering predecessor, who so many years after "abdicating" still viewed the socialist party as his own private property.

But the Prime Minister was trying to implement a revolution, perhaps oblivious to the truism that revolutions have a long history of eating their progenitors. Moreover, attempting a revolution when you have two other centres of power in your fold might turn out to be nothing short of a reckless gamble. Much to the annoyance of those closest to him, the Prime Minister was probably inspired by an "easy come, easy go" philosophy.

As the saga unfolded, it became increasingly clear to one and all that the arm wrestle between the Prime Minister and his predecessor would eventually harm the Prime Minister.

The spectators included the political class in a neighbouring country, a dictatorship. The relations between the Prime Minister's party and the dictatorship had a chequered history, but the most important aspect for the purposes of our story was that the dictatorship viewed the Prime Minister's country as a satellite.

The Prime Minister received a message from the dictatorship's secret services. While his predecessor would be bathing in the usual cove, a diver would grab his leg and hold him beneath the surface of the water for some minutes. The ensuing death would appear as an accident, and the Prime Minister's problem would be quietly and efficiently solved. But the Prime Minister was a man of principle, and declined the offer. The rest is history.

The Notary and the Two Ladies

THERE WAS IN THE MID-2000S A NOTARY WHOSE FATHER WAS A VERY CLOSE ASSOCIATE OF THE THEN LEADER OF THE OPPOSITION.

One dark wintry evening, two women visited the notary in his office, purportedly to ask about the expenses associated with buying a house.

Had they been Yin and Yang, the bespectacled one would have been the Yang, the symbol of masculinity. That said, both women had a mannish hairstyle and their attire was unmistakably dandy.

The notary could not fail to notice that they were intimate with each other, as if they were a married couple. He had never met them before, and did not know them even though one of them was probably already a public figure militating for minority interests. He tried to answer all their questions to the best of his knowledge, but kept struggling with a nagging inner voice suggesting that they were not really interested in buying a house but had used it only as an excuse to meet him.

The meeting did not last longer than half-an-hour, after which they quietly stood up, thanked him, and left the office. The notary gently closed the door behind them and went back to his desk and to whatever business he had been engaged in before the two women had paid him their visit. He never met them again after that dark wintry evening.

It was only in the mid-2010s that the notary realised that his inner, nagging voice had been right. Those two women had visited him only because they thought they could get in touch with the then Leader of the Opposition through him. Clearly, they had succeeded in having his successor's ear, who brazenly uses them whenever he needs to distract the electorate from the shenanigans of the Fox (his closest aide and right-hand man) and the Cat (his favourite minister).

My Personal Library

Radclyffe Hall's *The Well of Loneliness* (1928) occupies a place of importance in my personal library not because it's a great work of literature (it isn't), but for its honest depiction of the inner world of lesbians. It's a sincere novel, and – though one might disagree with the ideas it promotes espoused by the German psychologist Richard von Krafft-Ebing but disregarded by the psychoanalysts – it certainly makes a persuasive case against isolation and derision. My only real objection to this novel is the foreword by Havelock Ellis, a progressive who experimented with psychedelic drugs, entered an open marriage with a lesbian, and was impotent until he turned 60 but claimed to be an expert on sexology. He was also a eugenicist and believed that abortion should be widely available in order to weed out certain bad elements in the human genetic pool and allow only the fit to perpetuate the human race (an orthodox eugenicist, he wrote *The Task of Social Hygiene* in 1912). His lover was Margaret Sanger, the founder of the organisation that would eventually become the abortion-providing behemoth Planned Parenthood.

Science:
Abuses and Blunders

IN THE CURRENT EMBRYO-FREEZING ATMOSPHERE SERVING AS PRELUDE TO THE POSSIBLE INTRODUCTION OF ABORTION, THE WORDS "SCIENCE" AND "SCIENTIFIC" ARE BEING BANDIED ABOUT AS IF THEY WERE SPELLS WHICH CAN MAGICALLY SHUT UP OPPONENTS. Pro-life exponents are expected to genuflect reverently before the high altar of science.

The idea that science is something definitive and foolproof is as unscientific as can be. Science – a branch of knowledge – is like the universe: ever-expanding.

I am tempted to repeat what was written quite some time ago, namely that most propositions are not false but nonsensical.

That any so-called "expert" should publicly say that the human being in his or her early stages is a bunch of cells, is not false but nonsensical. The "expert" merely fails to understand the logic of our language. Embryo, child, adult are simply words with no inherent relation to reality except that which we impose on them.

Indeed, the deepest problems are in fact not problems at all, but instances of lack of clear thinking mostly owing to inaccuracies of language.

But I shall resist, and shall instead present the argument that science has made an inordinate number of errors in the past.

I shall give examples, in the hope that I convince those who persist in presenting science as some infallible, static body of truths to stop being fundamentalist and to accept that science is open to error as any other branch of human thought: error of observation or calculation and error of language, which can be subjective and inaccurate despite our best efforts.

The worst error science ever made is beyond the shadow of a doubt the classification of humans into different races. Not only was it bad science, but it also allowed barbaric political acts, such as slavery, colonialism, and genocide.

In the early 20th century, anthropologists wrote about races as a biological explanation for differences in psychology and intelligence between groups of people. Races were also used to explain – biologically – why certain peoples were more successful than others. Why, even as late as 1997, in his highly popular *Guns, Germs, and Steel*, Jared Diamond had to use science to debunk the "science" behind race.

So which is right? The early 20th-century science of racial superiority and inferiority, or the late

20th-century science which believes that races are figments of the imagination, instruments of political domination whereby the powerful exploit the weak?

Even Einstein made two serious blunders. 'There is not the slightest indication that energy will ever be obtainable from the atom,' he said just before the atomic age was born.

Astrophysicist Mario Livio explains in his book *Brilliant Blunders* that in his equations describing how gravity works, Einstein included a term he called the cosmological constant, based on his belief that the universe was static. When, later, astronomers found that the universe is expanding, Einstein removed the constant from his equations.

However, in 1998 – long after Einstein had passed away – astronomers found that the only way to explain new data about the expanding universe was actually to retain the cosmological constant Einstein had erroneously removed.

Darwin's notion of heredity was totally mistaken, and his theory is marred by his incomplete knowledge.

It was only in the beginning of the 20th century that the concept of heredity devised by Mendel was understood – but that was decades after Darwin had published his theory of evolution.

Perhaps the worst offender was Lord Kelvin who ignored the advice of other scientists on how heat is transported, leading him to calculate incorrectly the ages of the Earth and the sun. The problem with Kelvin, writes Livio, was that he 'was used to being right far too many times'.

A worthy contender for the title of worst offender was Linus Pauling, who won the Nobel Prize twice, just by himself.

Pauling was convinced that the DNA molecule was a triple helix, whereas the correct model was the double helix proposed by Francis Crick and James Watson.

Science and fundamentalism are by their very nature incompatible.

Taking science as if it were a religion, presenting it as Gospel truth, is the *nec plus ultra* of anti-science.

Science, like evolution, is always works-in-progress.

The Clown and the Children

IN HIS POSTFACE TO THE BOOK IL-LIĠI, IL-MORALI U R-RAĠUNI, PETER SERRACINO INGLOTT SPOKE OF 'THAT SORT OF SCHIZOPHRENIA WHICH LEADS ONE TO ACT AT VARIANCE WITH ONE'S BELIEFS'. *Il-Liġi, il-Morali u r-Raġuni* is a long conversation, published in book form, between former Chief Justice Giuseppe Mifsud Bonnici and I; Professor Serracino Inglott was praising Professor Mifsud Bonnici by implication for living according to his beliefs.

PSI undoubtedly had a subtle mind, equipped with vast knowledge, and it is a pity that he has still not been studied enough. The only published work I am aware of which analyses Serracino Inglott's thoughts is Mario Vella's *Reflections in a Canvas Bag*, of 1989.

Serracino Inglott viewed himself as a clown, who I understand as the incarnation of the joke made in the spirit of the sadness engendered by curiosity. If you are curious, you set out to seek knowledge, and when you find that it is impossible to harness all there is to know, you become sad, and then joke about it. Or, if you cannot joke about it, you simply fall silent. Not because you would have said all there's to say, but because you realise that some things you simply cannot talk about. Mostly because language is not sophisticated enough to deal with everything.

Sometimes, the sadness can be due to the fact that you know that there is no real audience for your joke. A joke is like a neurotic question: it maddeningly needs an answer. The implied question is: 'Isn't the potentially sad situation described in the joke in reality funny?' If the audience agrees, then it answers by laughing, and a cathartic moment follows. If no answer is forthcoming, then the joke, which was meant to elicit hilarity, ends up being a vehicle for sadness. Sometimes, the joke is not a vehicle but is itself sad, because there is no audience for it, and it remains an unanswered question.

I think that when PSI appeared before the Parliamentary Committee, he could have chosen to remain silent on embryo freezing. Instead, he chose to talk and I suspect he was playing an intellectual joke, which has to be partly understood in the context of his relationship at the time with the party then in government.

Christianity and Catholic dogma
THE JOKE COULD ALSO BE UNDERSTOOD IN THE LIGHT OF THE FACT THAT IN THE MIDDLE AGES, FOR ALMOST 500 YEARS, CATHOLIC DOGMA WAS THAT THE EMBRYO JOINED HUMANITY ONLY WHEN ITS

LIMBS HAD FORMED. BEFORE THAT MOMENT, IT WAS CONSIDERED FIRST LIKE A VEGETABLE THEN LIKE AN ANIMAL. (Reminds you of the famous "embryo is not a human being" insight.) In the Middle Ages, there were those who believed this moment happened on the fortieth day, others on the eightieth. Ironically, it would seem that it was Martin Luther who believed that humanity was there from the moment of conception. In a classic example of "double irony", Luther is a hero for certain elements within the Labour Party: Lutheranism is associated with Modernity which, in turn, is associated with anti-Catholicism.

For a long time, the Protestant idea that humanity is there from the very beginning was considered heresy. It was only in the 17th century that a papal physician called Paulus Zacchias declared that the embryology supporting that particular idea was sound science. For all those who speak about dogma, intolerance, and what not, there you have it. Modern Catholicism accepted a Lutheran idea which had at first been considered heretical. Modern Catholicism abandoned the very same medieval idea being advocated by Muscat's government.

But things are even more complicated. The argument about the moment when a human being joins humanity had been going on since Antiquity. The Stoics believed in humanity at birth; Aristotle, on reaching a certain stage of embryonic development. Therefore, the argument is absolutely not new. What has changed is that in the mid-20th century, technological advancement made it possible to terminate pregnancies without major risk to the mother's health. But the philosophical argument has been raging for more than two thousand years, and the medieval position was identical to the position taken by Muscat's Liberal-Progressive Government.

The Role of Science

THE NOTION THAT MODERN SCIENCE DEFEATS CHRISTIANITY IS PREPOSTEROUS. The argument harks back to pre-Christian, pre-Modern, pre-Scientific Age times! It is essentially a pre-Christian, pre-Modern philosophical argument, and cold-hearted to boot. It completely bypasses compassion, the hallmark of Christianity. Just recall the story of the Good Samaritan, the principle that the Law is made for Man not Man for the Law, Jesus' approach towards the adulteress and other "sinners", and so on – and you will find that, like other utopian philosophies, Christianity hinges on the quintessential value of Compassion. (I am purposely avoiding controversy by treating Christianity simply as an ethical system.)

Science clearly is not an ethical system. As Max Weber argued in *Science as a Vocation*, science can teach neither values nor why one should hold to such values. Science is mostly descriptive; what we make of that description belongs to philosophy. Two friends look at the skies on a cloudless night; one sees distant suns or lonely planets, the other sees next year's horoscope; when they spot shooting stars, one sees meteoroids while the other sees the opportunity to express a wish.

Embryo freezing and bortion

THE IVF PROCEDURE FULFILS THE WISH OF PEOPLE TO BEGET CHILDREN, AND THIS IS THE MOST WONDERFUL THING IN THE WORLD. It should not, however, engender ethical problems, such as the freezing of embryos and their destiny.

One consequence of freezing embryos is that it paves the way for the introduction of, at least, early-term abortion. Many pro-abortion arguments I have heard or read seem to me child-like. 'My body, my choice' and other similar battle cries seem like children who want to play football but then won't bear the responsibility if they break a windowpane. They are the arguments of people who want to extend childhood as much as possible, who are afraid of growing up.

My Personal Library

Philippa Pearce's *Tom Midnight Garden* (1958) is a book for children about a boy, Tom, who wants to grow up as late as possible. It's also about the old lady whom he befriends as a girl when they meet in the 'midnight garden', a magical extension of the old lady's dreams about her childhood. As the story unfolds, the girl grows into a young lady who falls in love with a young man and they get married, whereas Tom remains a boy. Later, in a truly moving scene, Tom meets the old lady in the real world and they resume their friendship. Perhaps Tom will grow up, after all.

Like good children's novels, *Tom's Midnight Garden* can be understood on different levels. There is the story for children, of magic and friendship, and the fear of growing up. Who has never been asked by a child, "What do grown-ups do?" or "What's it like to be a grown-up?" Then there's the story of the adult reading the book with the child, and it can have two meanings: post-war Britain looking at her Victorian past (but this is not pertinent here), and, well... grown-ups who want to remain children all their lives, and avoid their responsibilities.

Muscat's Social Contract

ALL POLITICIANS ENTER INTO A CONTRACT WITH THE PEOPLE. Some terms and conditions are specific to a particular politician, others are common to them all.

I am not referring just to promises, as each politician makes promises. To borrow Machiavelli's words, the politician then has to decide whether the promise given was a necessity of the past and the word broken a necessity of the present. I am referring to the terms and conditions of the social contract which apply to all politicians. I think I would be right to argue that these "contractual" terms and obligations form part of the constitutional set up of a State, even when they are not written.

Now it must be said that, whereas all societies have a vague notion of this social contract, not all societies share the same notion.

Some societies, particularly those influenced by the Protestant ethos, are quite strict with their politicians. Others are more lenient and others still simply accept non-observance as a fact of life, even considering any mention of the contract as naïveté.

Our own Joseph Muscat is aware of his contractual obligations toward the Maltese people.

However, he repeatedly tries to wriggle out of them by citing a number of exceptions or mitigating circumstances.

For the first months of his administration, Muscat begged the People for forgiveness because the Administration was still green. As time passed, and this excuse expired and lost its efficacy, he resorted to at least three other different approaches.

Muscat argued by implication that since the Nationalists had also done certain things, then there was really no contractual obligation. I disagree with those who read this defence of his as meaning that, since the Nationalists also did certain things, then he should not be held accountable. I think what Muscat meant was this: his critics were inventing higher standards which obviously did not exist, since not even they themselves had abided by them in the past.

The second approach was to accept the existence of certain contractual obligations, whilst requesting that evidence be put forward in support of their contravention.

The third approach was to accept the existence of the contractual obligations and to accept that they had been contravened, but the breach could be justified by arguing that the persons involved were too precious to be sacked, despite the blatant breach of social contract.

Frankly, I find none of these excuses acceptable. Being green is neither here nor there, as such an argument denies the role of the Civil Service. Claiming that contractual obligations do not exist is a non-starter because, in politics, rules evolve. The insistence on evidence makes little if any sense at all in politics – politics is based also on perception. Lastly, retaining for whatever reason individuals who have clearly schemed to fatten their pockets, is the wilful injection of a deadly virus into the social organism.

But Muscat can still get away with it, because he keeps appearing as the doctor curing two ailments: the aspirations of certain minorities and the economy. As Italian philosopher Benedetto Croce said, politicians are often like doctors or surgeons. You don't care whether your doctors or surgeons are personally honest; you only care that they cure you.

The Nationalists need to persuade the electorate that while Muscat could be a good doctor for some of Malta's ailments, he is also the cause for new ailments which he cannot cure, but they can.

Who is a human being?
THE IVF DEBATE HAS RAISED AN IMPORTANT QUESTION AND IT IS NOT WHETHER THE EMBRYO IS A HUMAN BEING. The important question is whether we who have been born are human beings.

One of the most insightful answers to this important question was given by the Neapolitan philosopher Giambattista Vico: we are human beings because we bury our dead.

I argue that if showing respect to the lifeless bodies of those we have loved is what makes us human beings, then we are human beings also because we show respect to those we have yet to love.

Whether the embryo is viable, potential, actual or any other of these words, is of no real import. One part of the crux of the matter is that the embryo is somebody's progeny. Even if still in the form of eight undifferentiated cells, it is still somebody's child.

Another part of the same crux is that not all desires imply an obligation of fulfilment. We are human beings because we neither kill our offspring nor do we commodify them. We are human beings because we respect all those who belong to humanity because, to borrow an ancient phrase made famous by Thomas Hobbes, we are not wolves to one another.

My Personal Library

Leonardo Sciascia's *The Day of the Owl* (1960) (*Il Giorno della Civetta* in Italian) is a novel about contractors in Sicily paying kickbacks and protection money to the Mafia and the murder of one small construction contractor who refused to follow suit. An upright policeman from mainland Italy tries to solve the murder but his efforts are foiled by the whacking of a key witness. A film of the same name inspired by the novel and directed by Damiano Damiani, was released in 1968.

At the time the novel was written, there was resistance in Italy towards accepting that the Mafia really existed. Sciascia's publication proved instrumental in overturning the situation.

The novel contains the famous subdivision of humanity by the local Mafia boss into five categories:

> I have a certain experience of the world; and what we call humanity
> – all hot air, that word – I divide into five categories: men, half-men,
> pigmies, arse-crawlers – if you'll excuse the expression – and quackers.
> Men are very few indeed; half-men few, and I'd be content if humanity
> finished with them... But no, it sinks even lower, to the pigmies who're like
> children trying to be grown-ups, monkeys going through the motions of
> their elders... Then down even lower we go to the arse-crawlers who're
> legion... And, finally, to the quackers; they ought to just exist, like ducks
> in a pond: their lives have no point or meaning.

The Republic Problem

WHAT IS THE STATE? The answer can be borrowed from a verse of the Creed: 'all that is, seen and unseen'.

The State itself is never seen; what we see are its symbols and the exercise of its powers. The State is very much like God. You can see symbols reminding you of God and you can see the exercise of God's power, but you can never see God Himself. That is how the State works: you can see its flags, its coats-of-arms, its currency, and you can see the implementation and enforcement of its laws, but you can never see the State. You do not really *know* that the State exists; you *believe* that it exists because you see its symbols and its effects.

There is a huge difference between the Government and the State. The Government is only one channel the State uses to exercise its powers. Another channel would be the Courts of Law, say. The State is larger than the Government.

In the system we have inherited from our former colonial masters – the constitutional monarchy – the Monarch does not have absolute powers to do whatever s/he likes, but at the same time s/he is the ultimate symbol of the State. The Monarch is the living symbol of the State. The British monarch is shrouded in a god-like aura, a sort of semi-divinity. Even if the monarch were not the supreme governor of the Church of England, British monarchy would still be based on theological grounds, and the Monarch considered as God's representative on Earth.

Whether one is a believer or, paradoxically, atheist or agnostic, one still wittingly or unwittingly accepts the dominant ideology that the British monarch is a divine being, or, at least, somebody who reigns by divine right. It would seem that the notion of divinity can exist even in the absence of a belief in God.

This almost-divine quality infuses the Monarch with extraordinary moral authority while providing the nation with a unifying figure transcending the divisiveness and pettiness of party politics and politickeering.

I use these theologically sounding terms for a specific reason. The British monarch is constitutionally bound to silence and neutrality. But that does not prevent the unconscious psychological phenomenon whereby the person of the monarch is invested with a sort of "holiness".

The Monarch is the head of a national hierarchy, and the word "hierarchy" ultimately comes from the Ancient Greek words *hieros* (meaning "holy") and *arkho* (meaning "rule").

This "holiness" or semi-divinity creates a sense of "shame" or "taboo" in the Monarch's subjects, and to my mind has a positive effect in imposing on the subjects a sense of probity, be it fleeting or lasting.

This is where we face our Republic Problem

DESPITE THE MORAL CHARACTERISTICS OF THE INDIVIDUALS OCCUPYING THE OFFICE OF PRESIDENT OF MALTA, THE OFFICE ITSELF LACKS THE SAME ALMOST-DIVINE QUALITY OF THE BRITISH CROWN. Not because Malta is tiny and her history as an independent nation young, but because the President of a Republic is not above politics, and remains willy-nilly part and parcel of politics.

The Office of President – irrespective of the personal qualities of the office-holder – lacks the institutional wherewithal to allow the office-holder to instil a sense of "shame" that would lead to an inner search for principles and action which prefer right to wrong.

I am not advocating a return to the pre-1974 arrangement. Retaining the British monarch as Head of State of Malta is out of the question. In 2017, Australian historian Jenny Hocking revealed that in 1975 the Queen intervened to topple the then-Prime Minister of Australia, Gough Whitlam.

Instead, I am addressing the need, expressed time and again in online comments for instance, for a guarantor of the Constitution. This would go beyond the role of the Constitutional Court, as I think people want a political guarantor, who, unlike the institutionally shackled Court, would act quickly and discreetly.

Democracy is dependent on constitutional "life support equipment", otherwise it dies. Democracy is not the natural state of affairs; tyranny is. Indeed, democracy is an effort – to obtain respect for the rights of the individual and for minorities, and to contain arbitrariness and abuse by those who govern. Tyranny is easy as the powerful impose their plans, ideology, or whims.

Antonella Cesarini's *Una rivoluzione in forma di legge. Malta 1974: storia di una anomala revisione costituzionale* [A revolution in the form of a law. Malta 1974: the history of an anomalous constitutional revision] (1997), is an interesting monograph which attempts to describe and analyse the "anomalous" constitutional amendments of 1974.

Oddly enough, I cannot seem to find any review of the book published at the time of its publication. It is a pity, as it would have been instructive to read in retrospect what Maltese reviewers would have made of it 20 years ago, also because the Italians have a knack for making explicit all that the English keep implicit.

All in all, it is a book worth reading and cherishing in one's library as it lends more insight to the on-and-off debate on constitutional development.

I think it should be read together with Ugo Mifsud Bonnici's succinct but illuminating *Kif Sirna Repubblika* (1999).

The Ideology Blitz

WHAT EXACTLY WERE THEY HAPPY ABOUT? Why the celebrations? Why should a medical procedure lead to... celebrations? 'We are free!' some of them chanted. Free from what?

These were some of the questions that darted through my mind on reading the news that the majority of the Irish voted to remove the constitutional ban on the medical procedure known as "abortion". There are many things to say, and everybody and their dog have their opinion. I guess everybody has their opinion on lobotomy too, another liberating medical procedure, but certainly no sane government would allow a referendum on it! Why on abortion then?

Because it is not a question of healthcare. If healthcare were a matter of democratic decision – by non-experts no less – then we would have reached the nadir (or pinnacle) of imbecility. Healthcare is a matter for the experts (and even they sometimes bungle it up – take the insulin shock therapy as an example).

Abortion is a political issue, not a healthcare issue. It is not about the freedom to choose healthcare. You do not choose healthcare – healthcare is a necessity. If you need surgery, you need it; you don't choose to turn up at the operation theatre and expect to undergo surgery if you're healthy.

So "healthcare" – a necessity – is used in the most Orwellian of fashions to denote a choice. The blitz of confused ideas is extraordinary! But a blitz it is, an ideology blitz. And because ideology is full of contradictions, it is up to certain members of society to ask the pertinent questions to untangle those contradictions.

The political class, the mainstream media, and other opinion swayers bombarded the Irish with pro-abortion ideology. It could be called "Marketing", or even "Public Enlightenment and Propaganda". But that's no way to have a democracy. The democratic system – probably originally intended to permit intelligent discussion to find the most rational and sensible solution to problems – has been turned into a marketing exercise, in which the tools employed to induce people to buy products (even unwanted ones) are used to persuade people to buy ideas.

If it were not so, why the celebrations? Why celebrate that parents can kill their own offspring? Why shed tears of joy? "Oh gosh, what a relief! Now we can have unprotected sex and face no music afterward!" Shouldn't abortion be a sad, grave decision taken after serious deliberation?

The truth is that the joy was for the marketing victory. It must have been the same joy experienced across tobacco company boardrooms when the industry penetrated the female smoking market almost 100 years ago. The 'Torches of Freedom' marketing campaign persuaded women to take up smoking cigarettes as the next step in emancipation and the acquisition of equality with men. The only party really to benefit from that "liberation" was the tobacco industry. Women just ruined their lungs while never outgrowing their supposed penis envy.

The techniques involved in marketing – harvested from psychology and transplanted on the unsuspecting market – have two aims: to create demand where there's none and to keep increasing it thereafter. This is the marketing of ideology. While ideologies abound, only one dominates. And there's no antitrust setup to contain abuses of the dominant position.

The current dominant ideology...
... DOES NOT SUPPORT REFERENDA ON A THREE-DAY WORKING WEEK, NOW THAT TECHNOLOGY WOULD ALLOW IT. Instead, it supports referenda on sexual freedom. The reason why sex and sexual relations should be more important than labour and labour relations is probably that the population should be kept occupied fighting futile personal battles on the private and family fronts.

If it were about population growth, the same ideology would not promote surrogate motherhood, *in-vitro* fertilisation, gay marriage, and the other sexual "liberation" objectives that increase the population. Therefore, it's about something else, not "population growth" (which, like "healthcare", is used in an Orwellian fashion). The current dominant ideology promotes the free market and ever-increasing consumption for ever-increasing profit making.

It's not a novel idea to say that everything revolves round the distribution of available resources among members of the community. And – again to put it in a way which is not novel – history has been a repetition of the same pattern: one part of the community exploits the other(s) to keep to itself the limited resources available.

The dominant ideology seems to be telling us that as a species, our evolution over the millennia had the ultimate goal of reaching the free market economy stage. We evolved in such a way that some of us are exploiters, and the others are the exploited. If it weren't so, we would be using democracy to change society, and instead of voting on, and in favour of, killing our own offspring (to be "liberated" ... from what exactly?), we would use democracy to improve our working

conditions, to work less and earn more (efficient resource sharing), and so on. Instead, the dominant ideology suggests that living like a perpetual adolescent (according to adolescent spending behavioural patterns) is the ideal.

Abortion fits this lifestyle like a glove: have fun but no children, as "no children" equals more money to spend on non-child-related but fun products and services.

Ideology holds us in bondage and we simply cannot imagine ourselves not in bondage. We passively accept that there is no alternative to ideological bondage. So in reality, we live in apparent freedom, subjected to the order imposed on us in the name of Freedom – the freedom to kill our offspring but not the freedom to improve, in tangible ways, our working and living conditions.

There's an unusual film – John Carpenter's *They Live* of 1988 – which explains ideology's hold on us. The protagonists wear special sunglasses that, according to philosopher Slavoj Žižek, 'function like a critique of ideology. They allow you to see the real message beneath all the propaganda, glitz, and posters and so on. ... When you put the sunglasses on you see the dictatorship in democracy, the invisible order which sustains your apparent freedom.'

More or less, that's it.

The best pro-abortion book I've read is called *A Defense of Abortion*, written by David Boonin and published in 2002 by Cambridge University Press. Professor Boonin starts the book by telling us that there were photos of his son Eli on the desk right beside him while he was writing this book. The main argument of his book is that it's fine to end the life of one's own offspring still in the womb because they lack organised cortical brain activity. (I don't remember him mentioning the possibility that in the future we might detect such activity; he seems to imply that there's no chance of technological improvement.)

So the best defence of abortion is to promote the ideology that movement in that part of the brain called "cortex" is what makes us human and endows us with rights, including the right to live. Unlike others, Professor Boonin does admit that the foetus and the future postnatal being are the same substantial being, but he proposes that the foetus lacks certain value-making properties, which thus deny it the right to live. It seems to me that this proposition is a sort of synecdochic fallacy: it elevates a represented part (organised cortical activity) to accurate reflection of the whole it is taken to stand for (the one and same substantial being). It's as if my skin colour (one of my parts) reflected my entire being, my whole; as if my rights were dependent on my skin colour or my cortical brain activity (one of my parts, be it a characteristic or a bodily activity).

But the point I want to make is that it is all ideology. Boonin's interpretation is but one of many competing beliefs. It neither flows nor follows from "facts". It is simply an interpretation of them. Ideology – or the arbitrary interpretation of "facts" – is constantly hammered into our heads, dominating our worldview, holding us in bondage to apparent freedom. The questions to ask are always two: who will benefit? And, who pays the price?

To my mind, as things have turned out (by which I mean that there was no original conspiracy; things simply happened, and events unfolded), the benefits of all these supposed freedoms accrue only to those who milk the system. They keep the exploited embroiled in their illusion of freedom and wellbeing or in the tragic situations created by the supposed freedom of others. (Depression does not come from no-where.)

Had abortion been legalised abroad to benefit the poor, then why were social services not incremented instead? The money was there when the banks were bailed out of the mess of their own making. Millions for the banks and nothing for the poor? And then abortion as the solution for poor families, while spending millions to fund abortion-providing facilities? It's clear that it has nothing to do with poverty and the poor.

As to who pays the price, I think it is obvious that children always have to pay the price. Perhaps this is the ultimate message of Christianity (now deemed one of the archenemies of late free market ideology).

Perhaps today Christianity is the most pro-child ideology available on the market of ideas. But being outside the ideology, it is underrated and considered *passé*, and to make matters worse, its marketing department seems to have lost its spirit and given up the ghost.

So it Shall be Written. So it Shan't be Done

WHILE GIOVANNI BONELLO IS GOING HOARSE PREACHING THE GOSPEL OF REASON WEEK IN, WEEK OUT, A FORTNIGHT AGO KEVIN AQUILINA MADE A POWERFUL INDICTMENT PUBLISHED BY *THE MALTA INDEPENDENT*. Both seem to me to have been met with a tomb-like silence.

Professor Aquilina is not some new kid on the block. He is Dean of the Faculty of Laws at the University of Malta which, in a normal country, should mean a lot. The phrase from his article of a fortnight ago which struck me was this: 'as the law is applied today (not as it is written down)'. This simple phrase, if its implications are allowed to soak in, is nothing short of earth-shattering. 'As the law is applied today... not as it is written down'! One is left almost speechless. What does it even mean: that the law is not applied as it is written down? Then what is applied? Somebody else's idea of what the law should be? And who is that somebody? Who empowers that somebody to apply their own law rather than the law of the State?

I'll be very frank about this. I was shocked but not surprised. And I was shocked not by the statement itself, as bewildering as it may be, but by the utter silence with which it was met. Not a reaction from the Chamber of Advocates, from the Law Courts, from the omniscient Minister of Justice, from the Minister for Home Affairs. Nothing but complete silence. Ear-shattering silence and this is what shocked me.

I was not surprised because I had been made immune to this phenomenon when I was still a young man, and somebody stopped me in Republic Street, Valletta, not far from Wembley Store, to tell me that I was an eccentric to believe that the law should be applied as it is written down! Then I was taken aback. This gentleman was sort of telling me to get off my high horse and accept the facts of life: the law is not applied as it is written down! On that occasion he used the Merchant Shipping Act as an example.

Some 16 or 17 years have since passed and I still believe that the law should be applied as it is written down. Am I an eccentric? Possibly. Do I care? Not at all! Why should I be an eccentric to believe that the law should be applied as it is written down? Now, the legal theorist among readers will smile at that (rhetorical) question, because the legal theorist knows that there are many issues to raise, such as the different approaches to interpretation and the relationship between one individual provision and the legislation of which that provision forms part and the entire corpus of laws and human rights, and so on. The legal theorist knows that the intention of the legislator has to be sought in the wordings of legal provisions. The legal theorist knows that some laws are like living trees, they grow and their growth reflects their environment – in the sense that a tree which grows in a wind-swept field will have a shape different from a tree of the same species which grows in a sheltered wood.

Whereas I do not dispute the legitimate reaction of the legal theorist, I would gracefully tell him or her that that is not my point. I have argued elsewhere, for instance, that we Maltese should not quote legal arguments made by Italian scholars on provisions of their Civil Code of 1942 which have no equivalent in our Civil Code (loosely based on their Code of 1865). But my point here is not legal; it is political and cultural and is that one cannot have a system in which the law says one thing, and the State behaves in a different way.

Kevin Aquilina wisely and rightly called his article of a fortnight ago 'Legal uncertainty and disproportionality'. I will now commit a mortal sin and quote from Wikipedia: 'Legal certainty is a principle in national and international law which holds that the law must provide those subject to it with the ability to

My Personal Library

Constitutional Law in Malta (Wolters Kluwer, 2018) is not only Kevin Aquilina's latest book but also one of my latest acquisitions. It arrived the same day I received two other publications: a pamphlet of 1838 called *Quelques Notes sur les Avantages du Jury en matière criminelle* and *Histoire du droit pénal et de la justice criminelle*, by Jean-Marie Carbasse. But it was Professor Aquilina's book that got my immediate attention.

The Author with Prof Kevin Aquilina, Msida, Malta 2012.

It is a succinct work, collating the different legal instruments making up Malta's *droit constitutionnel*. I am using French because the English word 'law' fails to deliver because it can mean both *droit* (*id-dritt*) and *loi* (*il-liġi*). Kevin Aquilina covers all the *lois*, *il-liġijiet*, found in the *droit*, *id-dritt*.

He starts by giving a historical outline of the Constitution of Malta and a general introduction to the Maltese State set-up. He then goes on to discuss the sources of Maltese law (international law, European law, domestic sources). He logically proceeds to discuss the form of government, and then moves on to describe the State and its subdivisions. He concludes by analysing citizenship and fundamental rights, and other issues such as religion, economic activity, the armed forces... in brief, it's a veritable tour de force which anybody interested in Malta should read or at least consult every now and then.

When you consider Professor Aquilina's skill at treating such a complex subject not only with dexterity but also by disarmingly, unassumingly and artfully employing apparent simplicity, you can easily understand why the indictment he made in his article of a fortnight ago acquires such tremendous weight.

regulate their conduct. Legal certainty is internationally recognised as a central requirement for the rule of law.' If we live in an environment in which the law says one thing, and the State does another, we do not have the Rule of Law. We have a jungle. And to survive in a jungle you need either to be big and strong or else to enjoy the protection of somebody big and strong. This defeats the ideal of equality in the eyes of the law.

Should we care about ideals? Yes, because ideals are the antidote to the state of nature. Without ideals of order and equality we go adrift, carried by the conflicting currents of existence and ending up sinking in the whirlpool of chaos.

The Dick Whittingtons of Our Times

A FEW DAYS AGO HENRY FRENDO, HISTORY PROFESSOR AT THE UNIVERSITY OF MALTA, WROTE A LETTER TO ANOTHER NEWSPAPER COMPLAINING ABOUT PUNDITRY AND THE FREQUENT PEDDLING OF FACTOIDS. I wrote an online comment to his letter.

Professor Frendo was reacting to an article which had argued that, in 1919, the Maltese masses were manipulated by Fascist-leaning Maltese politicians who wanted Malta to join the Kingdom of Italy. He wondered whether writing history books is really worth the hassle. My online comment was that the Fascists had published their manifesto on the eve of the Maltese riot, and therefore the two were linked. Even Balbo, Diotallevi and Casaubon would confirm this. I should have added that we have always called it *Sette Giugno*, a dead giveaway that they were Fascists. Needless to say, my *ironic* comment was loosely based on Umberto Eco's analysis of the fantastic links one can "see" between disparate facts. The three chaps I referred to are the three protagonists of Eco's *Foucault's Pendulum*, a novel built on anachronisms and bizarre associations between unrelated facts.

(The article which rightly irritated Prof Frendo seemed unaware of the fact that Italian Irredentism – that is, claiming 'Italian' territories for the Kingdom of Italy – predated Fascism, among other salient facts.)

My point, however, is that pundits peddling factoids distort our understanding of our past, present and future.

The migrants saga
WE ARE RELENTLESSLY BOMBARDED WITH FACTS AND FACTOIDS IN THE MIGRANTS SAGA, MAKING IT DIFFICULT TO DISTINGUISH THE FORMER FROM THE LATTER. We are told about the black African invasion. It is certainly true that there are many blacks in Europe. It is also true that it can be difficult for them to integrate. And it is also true that they are more visible than white immigrants – mostly because their skin is black.

Is this an invasion? Numerically speaking, I think the facts show that it is not an invasion. The numbers are relatively small (And I think they should remain small). Culturally speaking, I think the facts show that it is an invasion. Who is to blame? To my mind, the promoters of multiculturalism and similar airy-fairy utopias. I wonder how much the West has to learn from black African culture with regard to State-building and organisation,

I am sorry to say. I visited Senegal last year, and the only thing I can say is that it's the ideal place for an anthropologist or some other scholar interested in pre-State societies and how they were devastated by Western colonialism. Otherwise, there is nothing to learn. I was shocked by the chaos I saw; it's beyond description.

There was a hit in 1947 called *Civilization*, which stayed in the charts for a number of weeks. It narrated the story of a black African laughing at the "educated savages" who want to "civilise" him – he tells them he prefers the Congo to civilisation. And I can understand him. The intelligent black African prefers being somebody in Africa than a slave in Europe. Ultimately, Europe is no El Dorado. And despite the lip service, Europe will never really accept the black Africans. Needless to say, there are those who run away from war and other conflicts. For these I have the greatest sympathy; for the economic migrants, much less.

But let's go back to factoids and facts. Europe is being swamped with black Africans (not true). European civilisation and African culture can co-exist (also not true). The facts are that Europe has developed the State; the Africans have not. This basic difference accounts for the inadequacy of multiculturalism. Unlike the racist notions hopefully of yesteryear, the French theory of nationalism is that, irrespective of your skin colour, if you accept French civilisation you become French. It is absolutely not multicultural, and I think they are right. When in Rome, do as the Romans do.

Roma locuta, sed causa non est finita

THE GOVERNMENT OF MATTEO SALVINI AND LUIGI DI MAIO HAS DECIDED TO FLARE UP ANTI-IMMIGRANT SENTIMENTS, BULLYING MALTA IN THE PROCESS. Both stances are unacceptable. Racism is rubbish and bullying is despicable. But, again, we have to ask a number of questions. For instance, what is Malta doing to avoid the root causes of this situation? As far as I can tell – but I stand to be corrected – absolutely nothing.

Has Malta put any pressure on France to stop meddling once and for all with internal politics in Africa? Has Malta put any pressure on her European partners to help Africans develop their domestic economies? Taking in refugees is a cure for the symptoms. Instead, the root causes have to be cured.

Like Matteo Salvini and Giorgia Meloni, I believe in no more European neo-imperialist meddling in African politics; no more neo-liberal exploitation of African economies for European gain. We need an Africa for Africans. We need African nationalism, African State-building, African acclimatisation of other elements of Western civilisation. And this because the Africans have understood that the Western ideas about the State form are the only viable shell within which to develop into modernity.

What has Malta done in this respect? Does the newly-opened mission in Ghana, for instance, help towards the attainment of this goal? Closing Malta's ports is a stop-gap, myopic solution. We need a radical solution. We need to stop Africans dreaming that they are some latter-day Dick Whittington who left his native Lancashire to seek his fortune in London, having heard that the streets there were paved with gold, only to find himself cold and hungry... and was saved when taken in by a wealthy merchant... Well, you know the story.

Europe's streets are not paved with gold. Italy and Greece are facing real crises. Malta has registered a €78 million deficit in the first five months of this year. Where are the gold-paved streets? (I am obviously ignoring the Fourth Floor Federation.)

Apart from alleged secret agreements with Matteo Renzi, Malta has done nothing to help resolve the root causes of mass migration. Instead, Malta is embracing neo-liberal policies stemming from Malthusian prejudices which account for Europe's demographic decline and which nutty liberals want to counterbalance by importing boat-loads of illegal immigrants.

Has skin colour got anything to do with my ire? Absolutely not. What irks me is that the supposed right of a woman to kill her child in her womb ends up – via a series of labyrinthine links – fuelling the boats carrying illegal immigrants.

If Europe were not experiencing demographic decline, there would be no justification for NGOs to sail close to the Libyan shore to load illegal immigrants and ship them to Europe.

Human rights
THE HUMAN-RIGHTS ASPECTS OF THIS VERITABLE MODERN-DAY SLAVE TRADE, WHICH KEEPS REMINDING ME OF THE SLAVE TRADE CONDUCTED FROM SENEGAL AND OTHER WEST AFRICAN OUTPOSTS 200 YEARS AGO, ARE COMPLICATEDLY INTRICATE. The immigration crisis has been unfolding not only in the Mediterranean region but also on the North American continent. Does the solution lie in a fairer distribution of wealth among nations? What is Malta doing toward this end?

My Personal Library

Martti Koskenniemi's *The Gentle Civilizer of Nations: The Rise and Fall of International Law 1870-1960* (2001) is a unique analysis of imperialism and colonialism from an international law perspective. But it's not strictly a history of international law; it is a history of the ideas that shaped international law. It speaks of civilisation, of sovereignty, of universalism and particularism, of "Europeanness" and "Otherness".

One of the central themes is the 'myth of civilisation: a logic of exclusion-inclusion':

> exclusion in terms of a cultural argument about the otherness of the non-European that made it impossible to extend European rights to the native, inclusion in terms of the native's similarity with the European, the native's otherness having been erased by a universal humanitarianism under which international lawyers sought to replace native institutions by European sovereignty (p. 130).

This is self-evidently relevant to today's human rights discourse. Are the Others – the migrants – who are manifestly breaking the law to seek their fortune, still eligible for their human right to life? Is the cultural threat they pose enough to deny them their human right to life? And then, to kick it up a notch, are the illegal migrant and the embryo so different from us that they do not deserve to enjoy their human rights?

I have to mention Jared Diamond's Pulitzer-Prize-winning *Guns, Germs and Steel: The Fates of Human Societies* (1999) at this juncture. He claims that the Europeans have managed to dominate other peoples not because the Europeans are genetically superior but because they had guns, they had immunity to the germs they got from domesticated animals and which they carried on them wherever they went, and they had the steel to build railways to transport armies and goods quickly and efficiently.

Diamond's book is fantastic: it gave me goose-bumps when I first read it 19 years ago. But the documentary based on it was even more poignant. Professor Diamond argues that the imposition of the European lifestyle erased African millennial traditions.

For instance, the Africans used to live in small villages on hilltops, away from water sources. The Europeans made them move and settle in new cities built in riparian areas, so that they could load cargo on steamships navigating the rivers. By so doing, the Europeans wiped out the strategy the Africans had used since time immemorial to avoid malaria. During a visit to a hospital in Black Africa where children are dying after having been bitten by the deadly malaria-bearing mosquito, tears roll down Diamond's cheeks while he describes the human disaster provoked by the White Colonial Master.

I too cried.

And just like John Paul II, when he visited the Senegalese island of Gorée from where slaves were shipped to America for two centuries, prayed for forgiveness for the way the blacks were treated, so too I pray.

The United States left the United Nations Human Rights Council a few days ago because of what it has called a "cesspool of bias". Is this a signal that the world is turning its back on human rights? I doubt it. Traditionally, the US was inward-looking. It is not the first time the US has withdrawn from an international engagement because of human rights. In April 2005, it withdrew from the Optional Protocol of the Vienna Convention on Consular Relations because the Protocol placed the US under the jurisdiction of the International Court of Justice and the US had just lost three cases in a row which dealt with consular law but had a strong human rights dimension. What was remarkable was not that the US withdrew, but that it signed up to the international court jurisdiction in the first place. So the recent withdrawal from the UN Human Rights Council seems to fit in this inward-looking pattern of the US.

But is Europe inward-looking too? Despite the claims (of important polemicists such as Tariq Ali, author of *The Obama Syndrome: Surrender at Home, War Abroad,* among others) that the US follows an imperialist policy, I think present-day American imperialism is different from the European imperialism of former times. I cannot say that Europe looks inward.

And yet, despite her obvious historical debt toward Africa, Europe seems uncertain as to how much she wants to adhere to human rights which are not related to sexual freedom. In the sense that when sexual freedom is at stake, human rights generosity abounds; but when it's human rights for black Africans, Europe becomes stingy.

In this case, by human rights I do not mean the right of the economic migrant to play Dick Whittington.

I mean the right of every African to pursue happiness and achieve his or her full potential in a prosperous Africa.

Questions of Identity

IN HIS BOOK ON FRANCE IN THE MALTESE COLLECTIVE MEMORY, CHARLES XUEREB MAKES AN INTERESTING OBSERVATION: WITH DOM MINTOFF'S DEATH, MALTA'S QUEST FOR IDENTITY, WHICH HAD PREOCCUPIED AT LEAST ONE OR TWO GENERATIONS, DIED A NATURAL DEATH. Dr Xuereb might be right. Indeed, the post-war generations had been overly preoccupied with our national identity, a question rendered both actual and urgent by the quest for political independence. Were/are we truly Europeans; were/are we Latinised Arabs? Were/are we ambivalent Europeans?

Indeed, for decades, a good chunk of public debate was devoted to the Maltese language, the communication medium which defines us as a nation. The Araboid language that many of us speak, preoccupied us until, more or less, Dom Mintoff's death. Since more or less that time, the frequency of articles and letters in the papers on the Maltese language seems to have abated.

The difficulty with Charles Xuereb's observation is that Mr Mintoff's death took place one year before Joseph Muscat's election to power. Muscat's liberal-progressive government distanced itself from national identity problems and em-braced individual identity politics. Until 2012/13, public discourse was preoccupied with our national identity; post-2013, it was taken over by gender-related issues. Muscat's battle cry – The Best in Europe – implied two consequences: (1) we are European, (2) now we have to be the best Europeans. (At bit like being more Catholic than the Pope?)

Needless to say, for Muscat "being European" means "being liberal", as if Europe were bereft of conservatives and traditionalists. So Muscatian Malta became the number-one pro-LGT country in the world. (I have seen nothing done for the Bs so far, and I doubt anything will be done for the Bs any time soon, because for the Bs to attain equality with the Ls and the Gs, and be able to formalise their relationships, bigamy would have to be removed from the Criminal Code.)

For those who try to read more than is written, my stance is that I have many, many problems with same-sex adoption. Otherwise, I adhere to the traditional "live and let live" mentality of the Maltese and other Catholic nations. (But more about this later.)

A couple of years ago, more or less, I went to dinner with Fr Mark Montebello, a lawyer and university professor who first invited himself and then outdid himself trying to dominate the conversation. Between bursts of questions fired submachine-gun-like by the professor at Fr Mark, I managed to waddle and proffer two observations as if they were precious vases, and they caught the rebel priest's attention. Despite my protestations, one of them he dismissed as rhetoric; the other, however, intrigued him. Fr Mark was all ears when I opined that we Maltese are an unfortunate lot, as we tend to end up with counter-movements without having previously experienced the phenomena which should give rise to the counter-movement in the first place! The philosopher in the man of the frock was hooked. He wanted to know more.

In spite of the professor's valiant attempts at limelight monopolisation, and to catch Fr Mark out on some family tree business, I managed to convey some of my thoughts to the brilliant but unorthodox Dominican. I argued that we had experienced a fierce counter-reformation without having ever faced any serious Protestant threat. Our pedantically ideological church architecture, trumpeting a counter-reformation which was as redundant as it was unnecessary in the local context, has marked our national character with a "baroqueness" that keeps exuding pedantic exaggerations in many aspects of public life. Similarly, this government's exaggeratedly pro-gay rhetoric and stances were completely out-of-place in a country that was essentially tolerant of "deviant" behaviour.

I could sense Fr Mark's impatience but, as the true intellectual that he is, he allowed himself to be swayed to listen to more.

When our Criminal Code was being prepared, the British administration wanted to punish "deviant" behaviour; the Maltese resisted with all the means at their disposal. (I use the term 'deviant' in a historical sense, devoid of value-judgments.)

To my mind, if we left out for a moment the vote-catching strategy, Muscat's government's rhetoric would make sense in a Protestant country because it is the Protestants who have had tumultuous relationships with the non-heterosexual segment of their populations. The Puritan ethos drove the British to want to forcibly cure homosexuals, for instance. The Catholic-Latin attitude was more relaxed. During the discussions on our Criminal Code, in the first half of the 19th century, the Maltese were against the punishment of "deviant" sexual behaviour. Andrew Jameson, the Scottish lawyer engaged by the colonial administration to oversee the new

Code, even explicitly complained about the lax moral character of Southern Europeans!

So, in the local context, this government's pro-LGT vote-catching overdrive was as historically useless and meaningless as the Church's counter-reformation: both were a charge on a non-existing enemy. The one extolled the power of the Catholic Church in a country which had shown no desire to embrace Protestantism. The other pushed a legislative agenda for a minority using the language of a justice agenda in a country which had never persecuted that minority, but had actually showed ample tolerance.

I wanted to elaborate this line of thought, and Fr Mark seemed game... but we were derailed by the relentless professor's insistence on his fascination with family trees, and we were too polite. I don't know if my assessment was right. I was quite annoyed I could not have Fr Mark's knee-jerk reaction to my intellectual provocations. But if my assessment is correct, we have solved the national identity debate by embracing a radical rainbow agenda.

Public discussions on our language as the definer of our national identity have been eclipsed by the counter-reformation-like LGT crusade. That's a pity, as our national identity keeps being an issue, and

our language keeps being the lynchpin of it (even for those who, paradoxically, don't use it but still define themselves as Maltese).

Maltese is what defines us because it is the repository of our history, probably the Latinisation of a Siculo-Arab community. We have forgotten it, but our ancestors inverted the meaning of Arab words, like *daġħwa* (دَغْوَ) and *issalli* (or, to be more precise, *salla* (لَ صِ ى)). The first word means 'proselytism' in Arabic, and the second, 'to pray'; we have inverted them to mean 'blasphemy' and 'to use foul or vulgar language' respectively. The historical significance of this inversion is tremendous, not only with regard to the obvious question as to whether it was done consciously or unconsciously, but also to the more important question: if it was done consciously, why was it done? Why was the meaning inverted of words intelligible only to Maltese-speakers and not to Romance-speaking Christians hailing from other parts of Christendom? Was there widespread knowledge of Muslim religious jargon across Christendom, inducing the Maltese to want to impress their foreign, Christian masters with their newly-found faith? Would this explain opting for inversion rather than erasure?

I do not have the answers. But the questions are there, and perhaps somebody more knowledgeable than I could shed light on the mechanics and dynamics of the semantic inversion of *dagħa* and *salla*.

Whatever they are, the inversion is part of our collective heritage and therefore psyche. It resides in our collective unconscious, possibly having seeped to our cultural genome which, despite Mr Mintoff's death and Muscat's ascension to power, we still have to unravel and decipher. Those Maltese who have adopted English as their mother tongue (as if we did not have a history) have also adopted the history contained in the 'genetic material' of that language.

The influx of tens of thousands of foreign workers will further erode our history. We will lose our national identity but, thanks to the government, we will acquire a rainbow of sexual identities.

"Being Maltese" will become emasculated, and if you are a man and want to become a woman, it's as easy as pie.

My Personal Library

I was thinking of spending a few words on Anthony Luttrell's *The Making of Christian Malta* (2002), but instead I'll bring to your attention Achille Mizzi's *Ġenesi* (2017).

The reason is... personal. My late father used to tell me repeatedly that Mr Mizzi uses our little language to discuss topics of a universal nature. He was convinced that Achille Mizzi's poetry is of a world level, even if written in a lesser-used language.

Mr Mizzi's *Ġenesi* is beautiful. Profound also, and at times brimming with intertextuality, but always intellectually stimulating and emotionally satisfying. But it is its beauty that I want to highlight. Listen to this (p. 106):

> *Qasira wisq l-eternità*
> *biex għalik nixxennaq*
> *u nħobbok...*

There is a temptation, with Mr Mizzi's poetry, to agree with Mr Mizzi's own self-evaluation (p. 132):

Mhux poeta jien
li nitkellem mal-kotra

Well, that might be a plus. But in reality, I don't think it's really the case. Mr Mizzi might not address the crowd from a pulpit or write poetry to advocate, but readers will appreciate *the burning tears flowing down his cheeks during the night as he awaits his poetry to dawn like a late narcissus.*

If that image is not beautiful, then I wouldn't know what is!

Beauty is sometimes appreciated by the uncouth, but always by the refined. In other words, you can't be refined and not have Mr Mizzi's books in your library.

I particularly like this stanza (p. 173):

Baħnan
f'għerfu l-bniedem
bħal triq li ma tinfidx
... minn imkien
ma twasslek imkien.

That series of negatives confirms that Mr Mizzi has been, and still keeps going, places.

Peace, Security and Social Progress Among all Nations

"There is no immigrant crisis," said philosopher Slavoj Žižek to the journalist during an interview on UK's Channel 4 a couple of years ago. His point was that, beyond the heart-rending images used by the media to prick our consciences, we should seek the causes behind the flow of economic migrants and bona fide refugees.

I would say that Western economic neo-imperialism (the scramble for oil, French meddling in Western and Central African monetary systems and currency management) make it impossible for poorer countries to become rich, even though they are literally sitting on unimaginably vast natural resources, or they can't get rich because of those resources.

I keep asking myself whose interests France seeks by keeping a representative on the governing bodies of the African Financial Community franc and the Central African Financial Cooperation franc. These two African currencies are not inter-convertible but each is fully convertible to the euro. In other words, the system is built to hinder inter-African trade, unless through the euro as a vehicle currency. This means that inter-African trade, which could create wealth for these peoples, is deliberately hindered by a system concocted and supported by France!

Is Malta putting any pressure on France to alleviate this situation? According to Article 1(3) of our Constitution, "Malta is a neutral state actively pursuing peace, security and social progress among all nations". How has Malta been pursuing these goals?

Western political neo-imperialism, then, accounts for the creation of failed States (Libya, Syria, Iraq, God-knows-who in sub-Saharan Africa) and the twin phenomena of the bona fide refugee exodus (Syria, Iraq) and of the inability to contain the sub-Saharan El-Dorado seekers (Libya).

Fortune, Prowess and our Fate

THE ENTIRE MIGRANT ISSUE MAKES ME WONDER ABOUT FORTUNE AND FATE. We live by the myth that we have free will. We believe that we go to school, or to university even, get good grades, and then we are free to choose what to become and if we want it hard enough, our will triumphs and our dreams come true. The truth is that some of us fail because the human being is flawed. Others fail because the system is flawed. Those of us who succeed and are insightful, humble, and sincere will admit that it has very little to do with us and a lot to do with Fortune. In certain ways, we are all predestined.

Machiavelli argued (rightly, I think) that our Fate is shaped by Fortune and Prowess. However, I do not think that it is a 50:50 situation. Prowess is much, much less consequential than Fortune.

If you are born beautiful or handsome, many doors will simply open before you, and that's Fortune. If you are born ugly, you will experience something different, and that too is Fortune. (Unless you are an actor with a sense of irony and can cash in on your ugliness – do you remember Marty Feldman or Jack Elam?) If you are born into a rich family, you have a headstart in life; if your family is poor, you start with a massive handicap. No matter how good or bad you are, your beauty and your family's riches will have an immense impact on your life. And your talents – which are, again, a product of genetics and the environment you grew up in – are also something you receive and not something you yourself create out of nothing. You might practise for 10,000 hours, but if you are tone deaf, you will never become a concert pianist. There's no way you can train your ear; it is just a matter of Fortune. If, however, your ear detects the right pitch and your family is supportive, then you can achieve something in the music business.

Lucky to be born in (Western) Europe now?

WE ARE PROBABLY FORTUNATE TO HAVE BEEN BORN IN (WESTERN) EUROPE, AND NOW; THE AFRICANS ARE PROBABLY UNFORTUNATE TO HAVE BEEN BORN IN AFRICA. That does not mean, however, that Africans should be condemned to live their lives in poverty because of Western (European) neo-imperialism.

We as Europeans should have as one of our sincere objectives the development of African countries. Unless, that is, the élite need them underdeveloped because, should they develop, Africans would simply overwhelm Europe.

If this is indeed the case, then the élite cynically need to maintain the *status quo*, to have human tragedies both in the Mediterranean Sea (in terms of lives lost) and in Europe (in terms of culture and social harmony lost).

What has Malta been doing in this respect? Apart from quarrelling with Italy, that is.

The more important question is: who stands to gain from the *status quo*?

The middle and working classes, or the rich élite?

Media dishonesty
HOW DO THE MEDIA BEHAVE IN THIS SCENARIO? Do they allow us to really understand what is going on? Or are the issues fudged by repeating emotional, do-gooder narratives with a view to distracting us from the root causes of the irregular immigration we witness on a regular basis? The media has a huge responsibility for the expectations being formed and the attitudes taking root. But are the media always honest? Or are they (knowingly or unknowingly) blindly following the agenda of the rich élite who need migration flows to destabilise the European working classes and to serve as cooling mechanism when Africa overheats under the pressures of exploitation?

Not all media houses adhere to the same levels of honesty. Let me give you an example from my own personal experience. Only recently, I won a libel case in which Media-Today's integrity came out heavily scathed. I was taken to court for allegedly asking a question on the MaltaToday website. It would seem that Mark Vella – brother of MediaToday's editor Matthew – won a literature prize in a competition where one of the judges was Immanuel Mifsud. It also seems that Mr Vella had, many years previously, published a book by Mr Mifsud. The situation begged the obvious, legitimate question. However, I was taken to court for allegedly asking something similar. But it seems that

MediaToday substituted whatever I had written with something they themselves cooked up, only then to take me to court for what they themselves inserted on their website under my name.

In court, MediaToday were not able to prove that what they were alleging that I wrote was actually written by me. In other words, it seems that they implanted the text and attributed it to me. Now consider this. They cooked up a statement and posted it under my name on something as small and insignificant as a question on whether Mark Vella won an almost-forgotten literary competition thanks to his past ties with one of the judges, Immanuel Mifsud. Just imagine what they could do when the stakes are higher.

This is just a miniscule example of media dishonesty, which I can attest to because I went through it personally. This kind of unethical behaviour pollutes public discourse, from small and insignificant events (like Mr Vella winning a competition, in the case of MediaToday) to big and significant issues, such as an honest and transparent public debate on migration.

Why I am fascinated by Slavoj Žižek
MY FASCINATION WITH SLAVOJ ŽIŽEK STEMS FROM THE FACT THAT HE HAILS FROM A SMALL COUNTRY AND HIS ACCENT IS THICK.

So much for certain local big heads who want to throw their weight around in our small pond but then lack the wherewithal to jump on a metaphorical dinghy, cross the metaphorical sea and risk their life to prove their mettle in Intellectual Europe.

My Personal Library

Amor Fati (2018) by Andrew Sciberras is an unusual little book of poetry. Unusual not only because the author invites donations to Puttinu Cares (a highly commendable initiative), but also because it's a collection of poems dedicated to the memory of philosopher Friedrich Nietzsche (1844-1900). Dr Sciberras is a quiet man, who likes to keep a low profile, but his poetry is something to write home about. Read what is effectively a 40-word rendering of the notions of Dominant Ideology and *pensée unique* in verse (p. 53):

Aħna l-bnedmin
sirna atomizzati 'ppulverizzati
fl-istess frammentazzjoni tas-sistema
'mmanipulata
bħal priġunieri sterilizzati
'mmansati biċ-ċimi tal-irmiġġ
fil-qigħan tal-għar imdiehex
b'nar iħeġġeġ warajna
naraw biss id-dellijiet vagi
tal-iskulturi tal-allat tat-terrakotta
fuq il-ħajt immoffat ta' quddiemna
nemmnu li dik hi l-unika realtà
eżistenti.

I don't know where he gets this skill to synthesise from, but it certainly is impressive. Or consider this little gem (p. 82):

Ħuti
meta tkunu kollha ċħadtuni
mid-deżert immens tal-iskorpjuni
b'bejtiet mostrużi
bħal kavallier erudit riekeb fuq żiemel
istintiv

nerġa' niġi lura b'għajnejja mħaffrin
gandotti mċajprin
u nfittex lil dawk
moħbijin fl-għerien tal-għoljiet
imdallmin
u did-darba nħobbkom b'differenza
f'dan il-vjaġġ tal-eżistenza.

That image of the erudite knight riding the instinctual horse reminds me of Don Quixote or of the Ego riding the Id (and being taken wherever the Id wants to take it...). You would say, okay it is a lucky choice of words. But then, as you re-open Dr Sciberras' book, the first thing you find is a quotation from Freud on Nietzsche. Dr Sciberras is indeed quiet and does keep a low profile, but, man, does he know how to play this particular game of cards!

Amor fati is Latin for "love of Fate"; the idea that you accept what Fate throws at you as part of your existence in this world. In other words, to say "yes" to whatever happens to you, to reality per se. To put it in the poet's words, '*U bħal reliġjuż li jemmen bid-dommi tal-fidi / xi darba nixtieq inkun biss / li għalkollox ngħid iva*' (p. 77).

If you watch the movie *Adrift* you might find a good example of *amor fati*. I don't like spoilers, so I'll just say that the protagonist loses two important people in her life, and yet fully accepts her fate, not passively, but by getting back in the saddle after the fall.

Best (Amateurs) in Europe

LIKE THOUSANDS OF OTHERS, I
WATCHED MICHELLE MUSCAT BE-
ING INTERVIEWED BY SALVU BAL-
ZAN ON THE STATE TV CHANNEL,
AND I FOUND IT HILARIOUS. Not
Mrs Muscat's performance, but the
show itself.

I have known Michelle Muscat
since 1992 or '93, when she was still
dating Sandro Mangion (the blond,
easy-going guy who would later become president of a gay rights association). My first impressions of
her, which have not changed over
the years, were that she was articulate, effervescent, self-centred, and
strong-willed. After watching the
Balzan interview, I felt that Mrs
Muscat's defining characteristics
are still those of all those years ago.
Indeed, nothing has changed.

Mr Balzan admitted that he had
been chasing both Mrs Muscat and
her spouse for more than a year to
get them to agree to be interviewed.
I can understand their reluctance.
Mr Balzan is probably Europe's best
amateurish journalist. His lack of
preparation, his lack of perspicac-
ity, his lack of tact, guarantee that
his show unfailingly turns out to
be, time and again, a missed opportunity. Had he been endowed
with a little knowhow, he might
have given us some insight into the
interviewee's ego and shadow, what

hides behind her persona... Indeed,
the interviewer has to be something
between a journalist, a novelist and
an analytical psychologist. Unfortunately, for us, Mr Balzan seems unable to answer to any of these call-
ings, or the mix required to make
a good interviewer. Any insight we
got was thanks to Mrs Muscat's own
exertions, not Mr Balzan's. So I can
understand why the Muscats have
been avoiding an interview with
the man for so long.

Instead, Mr Balzan managed to
muddle up an interview which was
at once simple to execute and full
of potential. "Simple to execute"
– indeed, Mr Balzan could have
killed it; instead he simply executed
the interview, in that other sense
of the word. I really do not understand why the Muscats have chosen
such an anatine ally. Just consider
this mumbo jumbo which succeeded in bypassing Mr Balzan's
filter (we have to assume he has
one): '*fil-qosor għax jien magħruf li
ma nagħmilx mistoqsijiet fil-qosor
imma xtaqt nistaqsik fil-qosor*' [be
brief because I am known not to
ask brief questions but I wanted to
ask you briefly]!

Or this other one: '*ma rridx
inpoġġi kliem f'ħalqek jew inpoġġi
kliem f'ħalq tiegħi*' (*sic*!) [I do not
want to put words in your mouth
or to put words in mouth of mine]!
Here I have to admit that I asked a

number of people to decipher what the guru journalist's lips were trying to pronounce, and there is a school of thought which argues that they heard, '*ma rridx inpoġġi kliem f'ħalqek jew inpoġġi kliem bħal tiegħi*' [I don't want to put words in your mouth or to put words like mine] – you can check for yourselves on YouTube, it's exactly at the beginning of the 53rd minute.

This Maltese luminary of European journalism was interviewing the wife of the Prime Minister of the land (variously known as the "First Lady") and he could bring himself neither to prepare a decent script nor to pronounce his questions in an intelligent or at least intelligible way. There were moments when the "First Lady" herself seemed unable to hold back her smile, even though she was narrating a harrowing experience for her, her nuclear family, her extended family, her intimate friends, her less-intimate friends, her foreign friends, the 'ex-President Emeritus' (a mix-up undoubtedly due to the nervousness caused by being in Mr Balzan's presence), her entourage, her supporters, her acquaintances, her followers... But I understand her. How can you hide your smile when your interlocutor's IQ is higher than Einstein's?

Or else consider this: Mr Balzan was comparing something to a '*ġlieda bejn il-klieb, b'kull rispett*

lejn il-klieb' [a dogfight, with all due respect to dogs]! Can you blame Mrs Muscat for forgetting her life-changing experience and spotting the hilarity in the anatine, duck-like performance unfolding before her own eyes?

Mrs Muscat is articulate but Mr Balzan needs to use, '*x'jgħidulu?*' [what's it called?]. Imagine somebody on BBC or Bruno Vespa on Rai Uno using the English or Italian equivalent of *x'jgħidulu?* when interviewing people of the rank of Mrs Muscat!

And then, Mr Balzan kept referring to Mrs Muscat in the masculine! '*Kont ċert?*' [Were you sure? – in the second person singular masculine] and '*konxju*' [aware, again in the second person singular masculine] pepper his questions! *Ċert? Konxju?* When addressing a lady? I know this is the heyday of gender identity *laissez-faire* – but there's a limit to everything! This was a prime time, state-television show, and the interviewer didn't even know the difference between masculine and feminine!

The greatness of Salvu Balzan lies in his ability to elevate mediocre amateurism to an art. (Umberto Eco saw something similar in Mike Bongiorno.)

I can (again) understand why Mrs Muscat told Mr Balzan '*il-gazzetti naqrahom meta jkolli aptit*' [I read the newspapers only when

I feel like it]. It would have been an insult had that phrase been addressed to any other newspaper editor (in his free time, when he's not busy sweating to prepare *Xtra sajf*, Mr Balzan is involved in the editorial process of at least two *soidisant* newspapers). But since it was addressed at Mr Balzan, I can understand Mrs Muscat – she was telling it as it is. (Or should I have said 'saying it as it is' in this case?) Was she telling Mr Balzan that she reads his newspapers only when she feels like it, because they are a bit like his programme...?

When Milan Kundera, the naturalised-French Czech author wrote his theory of the novel, he argued that the author stipulates a contract with his reader at the very beginning of the novel. The reader gets to know, more or less, what the novel will deliver, and after reading it will be able to judge whether the author has kept his word or not. Let's apply Kundera's theory to Mr Balzan's real-life sit-com. The opening signature tune is a macho riff played on the electric guitar at a menacingly low tempo. It manages to evoke images of a tough guy advancing in the light of a lamppost toward the dark alley where mobsters are hiding, with the clear intention of beating the living daylights out of them. This is what we expect from Salvu Balzan. That he'll give the politi-

cians and other puffed-up, big-ego big shots some hard talk and decidedly a hard time. Then you watch the show, and you see him crawl and prostrate himself before the powerful First Lady. At least the closing signature tune is more sincere. It's a vintage 8-mm film of a village festa accompanied by the Greenfields singing about the sales of their records (in the thousands).

Mrs Muscat shared some insight beyond her immediate life. She said this, and I think her analysis is correct: 'I am more passionate about social democratic values and I understand certain aspects and issues that are felt by the grassroots more than my husband can. Joseph is more centrist and knows how to work with all sides and strike a balance.' By "centrist" she meant neoliberal.

Tomás Eloy Martínez (1932-2010) wrote many novels but my favourite is *The Peron Novel* (1988). When *The New York Times* reviewed the English translation, it observed that Juan 'Peron's power, as Eloy Martínez teaches us, depended not on his character but on his essential emptiness. Peron's will for power gained control by being seemingly obedient to whomever he was speaking with. The rich, the poor, the generals, the anti-imperialist nationalists, the fascists, all could see themselves in the general. "The reason I've been a leading figure in history time and time again," he says, "is precisely because I have contradicted myself'".

Eloy Martínez's other well-known novel, *Santa Evita* (1995), is not as good as *The Peron Novel* and I think Michelle Muscat is right to say that the comparison with Eva Peron is trite. I think it has now been reduced to a *cliché* and I will not say anything about it, though the book does form part of my personal library. Readers might wish to read, or re-read, it. Though, as I said, it's not as good as the other one, it's not that bad either.

Trimming the Sails of the Materialist Boat

WHEN YOU THINK ABOUT IT, WE ARE A DIFFERENT TYPE OF NATION. Not only do we live on an island – and there seems to be the "island mentality" (isolated communities that perceive themselves as exceptional or superior to the rest of the world: *l-aqwa fl-Ewropa* and all that). But we also have a strident materialist outlook. I speak about the majority, obviously.

There is not much that can be done about the first. An island is an island is an island, and even if you reclaim land up to Sicily, it will still remain an island. The sole consolation is that we are not the only ones. There are many others who perceive themselves as exceptional and superior to the rest of the world... a sort of elite club made up of island-mentality societies.

The second characteristic – the materialist streak – is not geophysical, it is not carved in stone. It is an ideology, and as such can be overcome, if the political will is there. We tend to give more importance to material possessions than to other aspects of life, to judge others by their belongings, to gauge one's success in life by the quantity of things one manages to amass. We have invested material things with spiritual value. Needless to say, we are not the only materialist country in the world; but we do differ in that we do not value the non-materialist aspects of life. (Again, I speak about the majority.)

In other words, the Maltese seem to be a materialist-only nation. Other nations value material possessions and "spiritual" achievements. I do not mean religion or faith, but Man's spirit, those activities which cultivate the mind and the inner world. Poetry, architecture, sculpture, the visual arts, music, dance, theatre... and any other mode of expression which enables us to express what goes on inside us but often times fails to find proper verbal expression... these are Man's inner world. Those among us who are able to bring them forth do the rest of us a great favour by enabling us, individually or collectively, to resolve our inner tensions and other unfinished business.

Each community has its own bards and artists, poets and actors, writers and architects, sculptors and authors... A developed, mature community treasures them, endows them with public recognition, and engenders a mentality which looks to them for an explanation. This does not happen in other, possibly evolved, countries. Italy, for instance, takes her artists seriously. Leonardo Sciascia – whose novels changed the country's attitude to-wards the Mafia – was elected to Parliament. The poet Eugenio Montale was made Senator *ad vitam*. Even our own half-Italian Arnold Cassola – a Professor of Literature – was elected by the Italians. (I'm not saying he should be elected by the Maltese in the Maltese context! I'm just making a point about recognition, not about political ideas.) But Italy is a country which seems to have institutionally rejected majoritarianism. Possibly because Mussolini's regime used to wag its wolf's tail at the idea that it enjoyed wide consensus among the population. We have turned majoritarianism into a national disease. Among its numerous symptoms are low cultural standards (desolate inner world) and, even worse, abysmal environmental standards (desolate outer world).

There is an intangible link between our spiritual world and our environment. Wreck the environment, and you kill the spirit. Keep the spirit crude, and you sign the environment's death warrant. Let's call a spade a spade. The Maltese celebrate the destruction of the environment – be it natural or urban – mostly because their spirit is unrefined.

The only way to refine the spirit is through the spreading of positive ideology. There are two entities that can do something about this: the

Church and the State. The Church tries to inculcate some sort of environment awareness, but the Church advances under the State's pitiless fire. The State, at least under this administration, seems to have become enslaved to business interests for whom the environment is not a priority but a veritable obstacle. For the present administration, material wealth is the only objective worth pursuing. The outer world (the environment) and the inner world (culture) are but encumbrances.

Let me quote one example to illustrate my point. A few days before Ferrari CEO Sergio Marchionne passed away, Louis G. Camilleri was appointed to his place. Of Maltese ancestry, Mr Camilleri was born and raised in Egypt, though he had a stellar career in multinational companies. Prime Minister Muscat publicly congratulated Mr Camilleri on his appointment. (It remains to be seen whether Muscat's gesture will translate into Ferrari investment in Malta.)

A few days later, I found out that another Maltese Egyptian might have deserved Muscat's attention, though he received none. I discovered that last year the highly respected academic Pierre Cachia passed away. Professor Cachia had also been born and raised in Egypt, and had also had a stellar career becoming 'a key architect of Arabic

My Personal Library

John Gray made a name for himself with his book *Liberalism* (1986), a book which brims with quotable nuggets. Such as this: 'With the decline of the classical liberal system of thought, liberalism assumed its modern form, in which rationalistic intellectual hubris is fused with a sentimental religion of humanity'.

Professor Gray has written many other books, criticising capitalism and deregulation, our myths of progress, our self-conceit which brings along the destruction of the world...

But one thing about him leaves me with a sense of unease. George Soros actually praised his *False Dawn: The Delusions of Global Capitalism* (1998).

studies who made modern Arabic literature a serious academic subject in both the UK and the US'.

Did anybody mention him in Malta? As far as I can ascertain (but I always stand to be corrected), nobody spent a word on this important academic, even though – like Mr Camilleri – his ancestry was Maltese.My conclusion is that according to current dominant attitudes, Mr Camilleri deserves Maltese praise because he succeeded in material achievement; Professor Cachia, on the other hand, was completely ignored because he succeeded in spiritual achievement.

That's the sorry, shameful state of the country.

There is no political will to push forward a non-materialist ideology. The political will is the path of least resistance: trimming the political sails so that their angle to the wind of profit achieves the most power possible... to push the ship forward toward more and more... profit.

Of Human Bondage (To Stupidity)

IT IS NOT THAT I AM FEELING UNGENEROUS TODAY, IT'S BECAUSE I'M FEELING TIRED. I'm tired of much of humanity's stupidity. Yet this tiredness is in itself stupid, because, as the German poet Schiller wrote in his *The Maid of Orleans*, 'against stupidity, the gods themselves battle in vain'. But since this is the silly season, I hope I will be forgiven if I indulge in venting my pent-up frustration on human stupidity.

Although even somebody like Einstein put in his tuppence worth ('Only two things are infinite, the universe and human stupidity, and I'm not sure about the former'), it is my firm opinion that the number-one world-class expert on stupidity is Carlo Cipolla (1922-2000), an Italian professor of history of economics who wrote the classic treatise on the subject called *The Basic Laws of Human Stupidity*. You can download it, in PDF and for free, from the internet.

I think Cipolla's definition of a stupid person is particularly useful: 'A stupid person,' he writes, 'is a person who causes losses to another person or to a group of persons while himself deriving no gain and even possibly incurring losses.' Keeping this definition in mind, one can look around and identify the people who belong to this category. One wouldn't do this out of meanness of spirit, but out of a need for self-preservation and to try and enlighten others.

The first basic law states that 'always and inevitably everyone underestimates the number of stupid individuals in circulation'. That does not mean that the stupid belong to only one sector of society. Education or social class have nothing to do with stupidity. Indeed, the second basic law tells us that 'the probability that a certain person be stupid is independent of any other characteristic of that person'. You can find the same percentage of stupid people in all human groupings, from a conference of blue-collar workers to a gang of Nobel laureates. Stupidity 'is not affected by time, space, race, class or any other socio-cultural or historical variable,' writes Cipolla.

The problem is that those among us who are not stupid find themselves at a huge disadvantage when having to deal with stupid people.

Another basic law states: 'Non-stupid people always underestimate the damaging power of stupid individuals. In particular non-stupid people constantly forget that at all times and places and under any circumstances to deal and/or associate with stupid people always turns out to be a costly mistake.' Admittedly,

this seems to imply that, as a matter of fact, all of us are slaves to stupidity. But since this is the silly season, let's continue with the suspension of our disbelief.

The attack made by the stupid person is so stupid and irrational that the non-stupid person is 'generally caught by surprise by the attack', and 'even when one becomes aware of the attack, one cannot organize a rational defence, because the attack itself lacks any rational structure'.

Make no mistake. The fifth and last basic law of human stupidity warns us that 'a stupid person is the most dangerous type of person'. Why is this? Cipolla explains:

A stupid person is more dangerous than a bandit. The result of the action of a perfect bandit is purely and simply a transfer of wealth and/or welfare. After the action of a perfect bandit, the bandit has a plus on his account which plus is exactly equivalent to the minus he has caused to another person. Society as a whole is neither better nor worse off. If all members of a society were perfect bandits, that society would remain stagnant but there would be no major disaster. The whole business would amount to massive transfers of wealth and welfare in favour of those who would take action. If all members of society would take action in regular turns, not only society as a whole but also individuals would find themselves in a perfectly steady state of no change. When stupid people are at work, the story is very different. Stupid people cause losses to other people with no counterpart of gains on their own account. Thus society as a whole is impoverished.

Human groupings can be subdivided into four categories: the helpless, the intelligent, the bandits, and the stupid. Have a look at the figure here. It explains the consequences of the actions of different types of people, whether they accrue benefits for themselves and/or others, or whether they wreak damage to themselves and/or others. The ideal behaviour, needless to say, is that of the intelligent person whose actions are of benefit to themselves and to others. But ideals are ideals, and the real world is full of bandits, helpless people, and the most dreaded category of all: the stupid...

Now let us consider some examples of stupidity. The most offensive one that comes to mind right now is the stupidity which led to the collapse of the Morandi Bridge in Genoa, Italy. It seems that this was a foretold disaster. A number of intelligent people – engineers and businessmen among others – had been insisting for years that it was obvious the bridge would not last and that Genoa needed to build a bypass to divert the heavy traffic. Twenty-five million vehicles crossed over that bridge every year, including mastodontic trucks pulling containers coming from France: the collapse was bound to happen because of the particular characteristics of the bridge. But stupid politicians pandering to the stupidity of certain voters repeatedly blocked the bypass plan... and now at least 41 people have paid for that stupidity with their lives. (All of a sudden, it stops being the silly season, doesn't it?)

Let's consider more stupidity connected with roads and driving. There seems to be a movement in Malta in favour of legalising the recreational use of drugs. This is, to my mind, the *nec plus ultra* of stupidity. According to cannabis-support.com.au, driving under the influence of cannabis increases the chances of having a car crash by ... 300 per cent! Only the stupid ones can delude themselves that people would not drive under the influence (of cannabis). We already have to deal with those who drink and drive; why be stupid and add more headaches.

The current urge to widen or build more roads, to uproot mature trees, to destroy the natural and urban environment is another candidate for the Stupidity Academy Award. Only stupid people do not understand that ruining the environment means killing the goose that lays the golden eggs. I'm referring not only to tourism, but also to the healthy psychological, and therefore economic, benefits of a beautiful environment.

The barbaric destruction of traditional buildings to have them replaced by soulless brutalist or other raw "modernist" architecture is not only insane but also extraordinarily stupid. The nonchalance with which our urban architectural heritage is treated (keep in mind that, at the moment, the Barriera outside Valletta and Fort Ricasoli are literally collapsing into the sea) is so stupid, you feel that there are no words to express your dismay, distress, and disbelief.

Cipolla's treatise is an eye-opener. 'In a society which performs poorly,' he writes,

> the stupid members of the society are allowed by the other members to become more active and take more actions.
>
> Whether one considers classical, or medieval, or modern or contemporary times one is impressed by the fact that any country moving uphill has its unavoidable fraction of stupid people. However, the country moving uphill also has an unusually high fraction of intelligent people who manage to keep the fraction of stupid

people at bay and at the same time produce enough gains for themselves and the other members of the community to make progress a certainty. In a country which is moving downhill, the fraction of stupid people is still constant; however in the remaining population one notices among those in power an alarming proliferation of the bandits with overtones of stupidity and among those not in power an equally alarming growth in the number of helpless individuals. Such change in the composition of the non-stupid population inevitably strengthens the destructive power of the stupid fraction and makes decline a certainty. And the country goes to Hell.

Temple-by-the-Pool

THE NEWS THAT SOMEBODY EVEN DREAMT OF SUBMITTING AN APPLICATION TO BUILD A SWIMMING POOL A FEW METRES AWAY FROM THE ĠGANTIJA TEMPLES CALLS FOR SOME ANALYSING. I know neither who the applicant is nor the architect, and frankly it does not matter, as I want to raise a point of principle. Also because, from what can be gleaned from the press, the persons involved are not politically exposed.

As expected by the rational part of society, the Planning Authority rejected the application. So, kudos for that. Then again, it was no big deal. Only if the board were composed of certified lunatics would the PA have acceded to that application. One does understand the cynicism surrounding the PA, particularly the cynicism generated by the persistence of suspicions that friends of friends oil the wheels over there. However, there are circumstances when it is self-evident that those wheels can be oiled by no friend of friend, no matter how refined the lubricant. The Neolithic temples probably are the ultimate "development" taboo, the one zone nobody – no Minister, no Chief of Staff, no saint – can perform the miracle and get the go-ahead for its "development" or that of its neighbouring area. (Or, to put it differently, we have not yet reached that stage of collective insanity.)

What makes me shake my head in disbelief is that what I am saying should be obvious to one and all. It is so obvious that one is left speechless when an architect – somebody who has a University degree and should be endowed with a modicum of culture and common sense – submits such an application in the first place. Let us forgive the owner, who might be a victim of his own benighted miscalculations. But an architect should know better. Certain applications should not even been drawn up, letalone submitted. The client should have been politely shown the door.

And this is the point I want to zero in on. Let us make a comparison with other professions. Notaries have a duty, laid down in the law regulating their profession, not to draw up deeds which go against public policy. Notaries take this limitation to the freedom of the will of the parties very seriously and prefer to err on the side of caution. (The notary's prudent nature induces people to think that notaries know less law than advocates.) I stand to be corrected but it would seem that architects have no such duty. All ODZ applications (i.e., applications to deviate from known public policy) seem to be fine. Their profession seems somehow to remind one of advocates working in the criminal field, who take no decision but have to convince the Court to act on behalf of the public good (either by punishing somebody found guilty as charged and restore social harmony, or acquit an innocent person and avoid a graver injustice).

The architect has to argue that the environment (be it historical, urban, or rural) is the offender and that it is on trial for denying the applicant the full enjoyment of his rights as lawful owner of the property. In the case of the Ġgantija Temples, the argument would have had to be that the 6,000-year-old structure denies its neighbours their right to jigger away to their heart's content on their own patch of land. The architect has to base his case on the written law, very much like the criminal lawyer. The good criminal lawyer knows that where the law wants, the law says and that there is no offence if the law does not say so. Therefore, the prosecutor endeavours to convince the court that the facts before it match the facts envisaged by the law, and that the accused should therefore be found guilty as charged. The architect seems to follow a parallel strategy: convince the Authority that the proposed development satisfies the written law and that the environment should be punished for interfering with the full enjoyment by the applicant of his property. I find this quite disturbing. If a zone is declared outside development, how can it be even thinkable to apply for development? The logic seems to be akin to this: you cannot kill, but murder is sometimes justifiable or excusable, and therefore everybody deserves a fair trial.

Similarly, you cannot develop in an outside-development zone, but development is sometimes justifiable or excusable, and therefore everybody deserves the right to submit an application. Even if it means applying to build a swimming pool a few metres away from a world-heritage prehistoric site! To my mind, it is this ultra-liberal attitude that has to develop... from its current barbarity to some degree of civilisation.

The logic in planning should not be that of the advocates (convince the Court that your thesis is right), but that of the notaries (certain deeds are precluded in advance because they run counter to public policy). There are no two ways about it: it is not that a notary can publish the deed hoping to convince the court not to annul it. The notary cannot publish such deed, tout court. Similarly, architects should not be allowed to submit applications to develop in outside-development zones. *Tout court.*

All of this reminds me of an incredible sign I once read above a door in one of Milan's airports: *Pericolo: l'ingresso é assolutamente vietato* – 'Danger: access is absolutely forbidden'. What does that "absolutely" mean? Access is either forbidden or it is not; if there really is danger behind that door, access cannot be negotiable! The same with ODZs. Development is forbidden. *Tout court.* No qualification. Otherwise, what would the O in ODZ stand for? Optional? Obtainable? On-demand?

The rationale underlying the law has to change. It has to abide by the principle that no private ownership is absolute, but all ownership exists in the context of a community and necessarily has to respect the higher dictates of that community's common good. Nobody can abuse his or her right. The problem is philosophical. Originally, liberalism implied the freedom to exploit your capital to the maximum, with little or no shackles. In time, it expanded the idea of unencumbered exploitation from the ownership of things to the ownership of the body, with abortion, pornography, drug taking, formalisation of sexual freedom, and so on, being given free rein. It is an internally coherent ideology, but manifestly leads to self-destruction in the long term. It is true that 'in the long run, we're all dead', but

My Personal Library

A judge who sits on a foreign court recently messaged me about an ancient, legally romantic procedure invoked on one of the Channel Islands. It's called the *Clameur de Haro* and it's a cry for justice, asking the Prince to intervene because somebody's possession of their land is being disturbed or interfered with. It is an ancient injunction, harking back to the early customary law of Normandy, even to the times of William the Conqueror. The Law of Normandy still obtains in Jersey and Guernsey. The judge mused, 'Ah, if only something similar were available in Malta to avoid a certain type of real estate development!'

The Haro injunction is described in detail in *Le Grand Coutumier de Normandie: The laws and customs by which the Duchy of Normandy is ruled* (a 2009 publication of the Jersey and Guernsey Law Review somebody thought fit to gift me...).

It does not depend on a law enacted by the modern (liberal) State but on an ancient law which is still valid. One wonders whether the application of the ancient law of Normandy was limited only to the Duchy of Normandy, or whether it extended to the Norman Kingdom of Sicily (which included Malta). And in the latter case, could it be claimed that it would still apply to Malta today since it has never been explicitly repealed?

Ah, the foibles of the bibliophile...

it is death through suicide. The "it's my property/it's my body" ideology extends to our attitude toward the environment. If the exploitation of capital and body is unshackled, so should the exploitation of the environment be unshackled.

For the law to change, this mentality has to change. A revolution is needed. Not the neo-liberal earthquake foggily promised and punctiliously delivered by Muscat's Movement. But a conservative, non-neo-liberal revolution. A return to certain perennial, immutable principles. That said, I am still waiting to see who will rise to the political occasion.

Best Week in Europe?

Wake-up call

No, I mean literally. Not the "wake up and smell the coffee" meme but, literally, waking up Environment Minister José Herrera to tell him that Maghtab is burning! The fire broke out at 5 am on Friday morning but, according to the Minister himself, he was only informed at 7.30 am. The Minister fiddled with his toast and coffee while Maghtab burned!

So how does it work? Do Environment Ministry officials have instructions not to disturb His Majesty before 7:30 am? What's the intra-ministerial communication protocol for national emergencies? Is there no procedure to determine what is and what is not a national emergency? Whatever the answers are, the situation is pathetically amateurish.

Earlier in the week, the media quoted a scientific report that implies that the smoke belched out by cruise liners hugely reduces intelligence levels. Just imagine the smoke churned out by burning Maghtab! Anyway, this is probably a wake-up call for the Minister to come up with stiffer regulations to reduce air pollution caused by cruise liners. If His Majesty the Minister is reading this after 7:30

am, could he do something about it, please?

The Guardian quoted Xi Chen at Yale School of Public Health in the US, a member of the research team which produced the scientific report, as saying: 'Governments really need to take concrete measures to reduce air pollution. That may benefit human capital, which is one of the most important driving forces of economic growth.'

So, yes, we – 'human capital' – are one of the most important driving forces of economic growth!

We are not human beings but human capital!

Thank you so much, neo-liberalism.

AUM

THE AMERICAN UNIVERSITY OF MALTA WAS MEANT TO BE A HIT; INSTEAD IT KEEPS REPEATEDLY HITTING THE WALL. This week the media has reported that even this year the AUM failed to attract enough students to make it a viable tertiary education institution.

I must admit that when the idea of a second fully-fledged university was floated some five years ago, I was filled with overwhelming enthusiasm.

It's good for a flourishing intellectual environment to have more than one source of academic research.

But when I realised that not only did the project not pan out, but also that it was wrong from its inception, my enthusiasm was dampened and I for one was sorely disappointed.

If the idea really is to rid the country of academic monopolies, then the whole AUM sham should be shut down and replaced either by a new university (a public-private partnership) or by a radical change in the constitution of the University of Malta, transforming it from a monolithic structure into a federation of colleges allowing for competition in the realm of ideas and knowledge.

An added benefit would be that Malta would then be able to compete in the international tertiary-education market and attract serious numbers of foreign students, contributing not only to the economy but also to the intellectual climate in the country.

Now that's some good neo-liberal ideology instead of the dark version we have to contend with.

Neo-liberal uncharitableness

THE NEW DIRECTOR OF THAT ADMIRABLE INSTITUTION, CARITAS, WAS INTERVIEWED THIS WEEK AND SHED NEW LIGHT ON THE ABOMINABLE DARKNESS SPREAD BY THIS GOVERNMENT'S NEO-LIBERAL POLITICS. These are Anthony Gatt's words:

Caritas acknowledges the economic development and prosperity of part of the population, however the gap between the rich and the poor is growing. There are growing bands of society that are at risk of poverty, including those depending on pensions or non-contributory benefits, those with mental health issues, those completing a drug rehabilitation programme, young separated people who cannot make ends meet and elderly people who are not homeowners.

You would think we have a Thatcherite government. Instead we have a government calling itself a Progressive Movement. If this is progress, then let's regress to whatever there was before.

Let's not kid ourselves. Poverty is not something that punishes only the poor; it punishes society in its entirety. More poverty engenders more crime and disorder. Christian democracy is good because of the left-wing aspect of Christianity – giving is indeed receiving. But these post-Social-Democrats we now have in government think that taking is, well, taking.

Towers in Mrieħel
MRIEĦEL IS ONE PLURAL OF MERĦLA, MEANING HERD – THE OTHER PLURAL IS MERĦLIET. In our

collective memory, the herd evokes images of the undulant fever, the *deni rqiq* eradicated thanks to the research and discovery made by Temi Zammit.

I would say the country has been taken over by the herd instinct and by *deni oħxon* – the herd is being shepherded to allow the wolves in its midst to devour, gobble up and guzzle down, with no end in sight, in a frenzy of high-fever irresponsibility and short-termism. I would really like to know what will happen once the present phase of the economic cycle is over. What shall we do with all these "developments"?

I recently heard an interesting idea expressed by the Italian philosopher Diego Fusaro. We are experiencing something new and interesting. The cost of "development" is treated in a communist fashion: the public foots the bill. But the profits are treated in a capitalist fashion: they all go into private pockets.

The Neo-liberal Religion

My Personal Library

When I was at secondary school, we were given Ġużé Ellul Mercer's *Leli ta' Ħaż-Żgħir* (1938) to study. Mr Ellul Mercer was a Labour politician, who probably really believed it was right to help the workers improve their lot and the poor get out of their plight. The PN became electable again when it embraced these Christian values to the full.

Essentially, *Leli ta' Ħaż-Żgħir* is a tale of how ignorance is the forbear of exploitation. It seems to me that the 1980s experiment to inculcate this important moral in the heads of students failed abysmally. Had it been a success, the Muscat Administration would not be having such a field day.

In our times, *Ħaż-Żgħir* [Little "Town"] thinks it's becoming *Ħal Kbir* [Big "Town"] when, in reality, it's on its way to becoming *Ħal Mewt* [Death "Town"].

Too sudden, too much is deadly.

THE NEO-LIBERAL RELIGION – THE RELIGION OF THE MARKET – IS THE IDEOLOGY TO WHICH THE WEST HAS WHOLEHEARTEDLY AND UNRESERVEDLY CONVERTED. This religion's high priest in Malta is well known.

When travelling across Europe and you come across a Catholic church, there's a high probability that you will find the extravaganzas – so beloved to us Maltese, a Baroque nation – of the Counter-Reformation, when the Catholic ideology, then dominant, aimed to ensure that everyone understood the glory of the Church and that without the Church there is no salvation. That same determination to save humanity has been taken up by the new religion that has swept the West, ousting Christianity: neo-liberalism, the Religion of the Market.

It propagates the belief that without the Market, there can be no salvation, that economic growth is more important than individuals and that we all have our role in the Market's Salvific Plan. Peoples have to make sacrifices (austerity) to redeem themselves from sin (recession, crisis) and enter Heaven on Earth (ever-increasing economic growth).

But whereas in Christianity, it is easier for a camel to go through the eye of a needle than for a rich man to enter the Kingdom of God, in neo-liberalism it is easier for said animal to perform said feat than for wealth to be distributed fairly. In neo-liberalism, the fat grow fatter, the lean leaner, and the middle classes defend the system while the poor eye them with envy and resentment.

Religious Architecture

CATHOLICISM SPREAD ITS INFLUENCE THROUGH THE ERECTION OF CHURCHES. Similarly, neo-liberalism – the contemporary religion – manifests itself in high-rise glass towers and skyscrapers, usually flashing the name of the patron brand on their topmost parts. Wherever you go in the West, you will find these cathedrals dedicated to Holy Capital – from the major cities (Paris, London, Frankfurt, the American cities, Singapore) to the minor ones (Vilnius, Prague, Luxembourg).

Malta Cattolicissima is also converting to this new religion. To my mind, just like Muslim Malta became *Malta Cattolicissima*, so *Malta Cattolicissima* is fast becoming *Malta neo-liberalissima*.

Possibly this is because we are a frontier territory, and the periphery always faces the overwhelming temptation to prove that it belongs as much as the centre. The towers have to go up not necessarily to satisfy the demand for housing (this can rationally be met by making good use of the oversupply of vacant properties) but to satisfy the demand for psychological reassurances that we are not ambivalent but are prime specimens of the Contemporary Man, the neo-liberal.

At this stage, the question is obvious. If we have the third-largest unsupported dome in the world (Mosta), the sixth-tallest church dome in the world (Xewkija), and we are the best in Europe and these are best of times, shall we build one of the tallest skyscrapers in the world to show that, while in the past we were more Catholic than the Pope, now we are more neo-liberal than Whoever-It-Is?

Religious Behaviour

AT ITS CORE, THE QUESTION OF "SHOULD" AND "CAN" IS ESSENTIALLY RELIGIOUS. The religious code of conduct is replete with "shoulds", even if they are expressed as "shalls". (According to certain nitwits, it's impossible to make this distinction – *shall* versus *should* – in Maltese!)

But philosophy also explores this territory. Neo-liberal pundits – such as the pseudo-professor (in the sense of know-it-all) Martin Scicluna and the real professor Kenneth Wain – love (mis)quoting Immanuel Kant, one of the foremost philosophers of the Enlightenment. Kant argued that you *can* because you *must*. This imperative is important for liberalism, because it somehow justifies the autonomy of the individual by transforming an obligation (must) into an instance of freedom to act (can).

Slavoj Žižek, the contemporary philosopher and insightful follower of psychoanalyst Jacques Lacan, teaches that in our times the imperative has been turned on its head: from 'you can because you must' to 'you must because you can'. This is the danger (and pitfall) of neo-liberal religious behaviour: because you can do something, then you must do it. The possibility of choosing whether to do or not to do something unleashes an anxiety so big that it can be resolved only by doing that something. Not doing it will simply fuel the anxiety. It's a bit like antibiotics: you should not take them indiscriminately, but since you can, then you must take them, even if you know that you are contributing to the emergence of resistant superbugs.

All said and done, while Christianity is a religion of restraint, Neo-liberalism is a religion of satisfaction of demand.

This explains why abortion, for instance, has become a common method of contraception in much of Europe and even in Muslim countries where neo-liberalism has spread and abortion is allowed.

No nation-state, only market
WHEREAS IN A THEOCRACY, STATE AND RELIGIOUS INSTITUTIONS CONFLATE, IN THE NEO-LIBERAL SYSTEM THE NATION-STATE DISSOLVES INTO THE ACID OF THE MARKET, EMITTING A MIASMA OF DESPAIR. If you think about it, this receding of politics to allow power to be managed by economics was only bound to happen. When kings and other potentates used to decide to default on their loans, their creditors had to be mindful of the fact that their royal and noble debtors had armies and judicial mechanisms to carry out executions. The liberal constitutional system created legal ways and means to oblige the state to repay its debts toward private subjects of the law. Since power is money's faithful servant, it was only natural that power should leave the Chamber of Politics and move to the Chamber of Economics. The dissolution of the nation-state implies its replacement by supranational structures holding supranational markets. Is this a good or a bad thing?

For the so-called "populists", it is a bad thing. They clamour for national identity, traditional values, religious cohesion, work for local workers. For the neo-liberals, it is a good thing as they seek economic growth more than anything else, arguing that economic growth translates into personal growth and increased

My Personal Library

The books of Slavoj Žižek and Diego Fusaro are good guides for the times we are living in. Žižek is a Slovene philosopher referred to as the 'Elvis of philosophy' and Fusaro is an Italian philosopher who appears regularly on Italian TV talk shows. These two authors claim to be Marxists, but theirs is a strange Marxism.

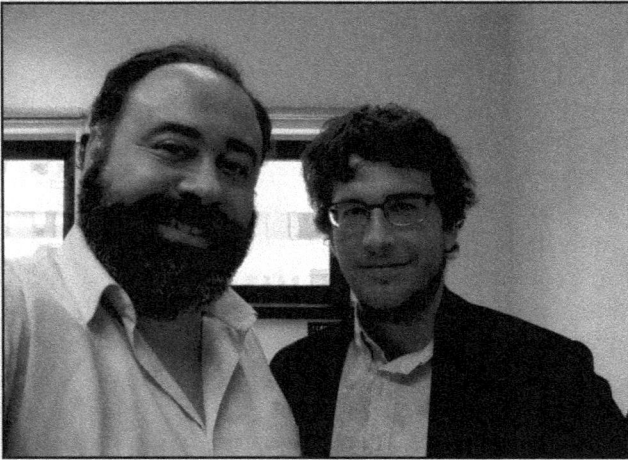

Only recently, Fusaro participated in a book published in German, in Germany, called *Marx von Rechts* [*Marx from the Right*], a way of reading Marx and waving goodbye to Marxism without falling for neo-liberalism.

One of Žižek's books is called *Living in the End Times* (2010), a title meant to gibe at a number of positions – but perhaps when you have rightists discovering, exploring and explaining Marx, we are really in the 'end times' and on the eve of something new and interesting.

In the photo: the Author with Diego Fusaro, Milan 2016.

autonomy for the individual. Clearly, the question is: which individual? Is economic growth egalitarian, or is it limited to the elite?

Mercatus nunc religio et patria
MY LATINIST FRIEND WHOSE NAME I SHALL NOT MENTION, WAS ADAMANT I SHOULD NOT USE THE SUBHEADING THAT I, IN MY IGNORANCE, HAD ORIGINALLY THOUGHT UP: *MERCATUS NOVA RELIGIO ET NOVA PATRIA EST*. Instead, he convinced me to use *Mercatus nunc religio et patria*, and I paid heed to his advice.

Indeed the Market, with its "religious" and "patriotic" trappings, has become the new religion and the new homeland. Modes of behaviour are exhorted in order to lubricate the wheels of the Market, and sacrifices are expected for its sake. To ease anxious consciences, the Neo-liberal Religion – for example – insists on waste separation (when many problems could be avoided just by using materials other than plastic) and publicises multi-million donations to charity by billionaire Big Business.

The Market has become like a pre-Christian god who demands human sacrifice but, this time, in the name of endless economic growth. The question is: just like Christianity in its heyday could not be stopped, is the Market Religion today also unstoppable?

Government, Society, and Public Thinkers

THERE IS AN IMPORTANT INTERFACE BETWEEN GOVERNMENT AND SOCIETY: PUBLIC THINKERS. We sometimes refer to them as "journalists" but, in reality, the interface consists of "opinion-makers". Historically, they were known as "pamphleteers"' and today as bloggers or columnists and to some, the public thinkers, people are useful to help the public analyse the changes underway.

Ordinary changes underway
THAT THE COUNTRY IS UNDERGOING PROFOUND CHANGES IS UNDENIABLE. Some of these are good: even though it still looks shabby and is so hopelessly disorganised, the country is getting a facelift and this is welcome. After all, as somebody recently put it (and I must say I liked it a lot), it's useless having 5-star hotels in a 1-star country.

General maintenance of public spaces is a duty of the government which derives from the basic principles of governance, and even from a certain reading of constitutional provisions. An Administration would be guilty of dereliction of duty if it did not devote part of the country's resources to the upkeep of public buildings, spaces, etc. So no particular applause for simply doing one's duty. Needless to say, having the vision and the energy to carry out one's duty is something that voters might wish to reward. But my point is that a Party that promises the electorate that it will carry out its duty – for instance by carrying out proper maintenance of the country – is actually a Party that's taking the electorate for a ride. General maintenance is nothing but an ordinary duty of the government of a functioning state, so it's no big deal to promise it and keep one's word. It's like parents who take care of their child. It's what's expected of them. If they don't take such care, they are condemned, but there are no special commendations for parents who do their ordinary duty as parents. Even though I must say that once – in a flea market – I discovered an old certificate dating from the 1920s, I think, given by the French Republic to a family for having had a particular number of children and for raising them. Nowadays I think we would consider the award of such a certificate as an unwelcome manifestation of Fascist or *étatist* ideology.

(I am obviously leaving out the aspect of the extraordinary in the ordinary, by which I mean the enormous sacrifices parents make for their children, which their children then appreciate, or at least should appreciate, as they grow older.)

Extraordinary Changes Underway
BUT THEN THERE ARE THE EX-TRAORDINARY CHANGES WHICH ARE TAKING THE COUNTRY BY SUBTLE STORM: SUBTLE BECAUSE THEY ARE CHANGES CARRIED OUT BY POLITICIANS IN BUSINESS SUITS WEARING BLUE TIES. Blue ties have nothing to do with the colours associated with the parties. I'm thinking more of one episode from that vintage British sitcom, *Yes, Prime Minister*, in which Sir Humphrey, the Machiavellian Permanent Secretary, advises Jim Hacker, the clueless Prime Minister, that if his message to the nation is sheepish but he wants it to appear strong, he should wear a red tie, whereas if his message is revolutionary but he does not want to upset people, he should wear a blue one.

The country is undergoing revolutionary upheavals, at a fast pace, but politicians are not wearing red ties. They are wearing blue ties, and manipulating minds. These current changes remind one of that decade in France, between 1789 and 1799, when the French revolutionised their entire society, breaking family ties in the name of free enterprise and individual freedom. Ultimately, they had to rein in their unbridled enthusiasm and restore some sort of social order. The pendulum always oscillates back, in its endless quest to find the position of equilibrium.

The French Revolution was a time of hopes and dreams, but also of chaos and destruction. The dream was that the people would leave the darkness behind them and embrace the light. The truth was that the highly imperfect former system, which had matured over the centuries, was swept away in one go, and instead of applying slow, ordered reforms, revolutionary ideas were experimented with and imposed on a population that was, by and large, mostly unprepared for them, and chaos ensued.

During the last election campaign, the Labour Party used as one of its slogans *Il-Ħolma Maltija* [The Maltese Dream] the name of one of my father's novels. It is a fictional autobiography of our greatest patriot, Mikiel Anton Vassalli, who was much influenced by the same intellectual currents which, in part, brought about the French Revolution. I am sure that the same revolutionary spirit animates this government, but it is subdued, because it is aware that if the Revolution is spelled out, people would open their eyes and there would be unrest. So, essentially, it's Revolution by Stealth. I think the spirit of this ongoing revolution was laid bare last March when that video went viral showing Minister Helena Dalli chuckling while she told an international delegation about the successful introduction of gender-related innovations in our legal system. On that occasion the Honourable Minister could not hold back her amusement at the incredulity of the Maltese people, who had been misled by Labour's election programme that had promised "equality" without specifying the details.

The values of Maltese society are being changed in an almost underhanded fashion. The less intelligent take longer to realise this; the more intelligent realise early on but they are also aware that they are a minority and it might not be gainful to say things explicitly. Then there are the public thinkers, who might even support the changes and therefore turn a blind eye to the indecent way things are being done. Ideally, in a democracy such changes take place following the direct expression of consent by the people. The only time this has happened in recent times was the introduction of divorce. And even there, I would argue that if we are to be honest with ourselves, the figures did not show a majority of all eligible voters. That said, the formality was at least followed and the people were asked for their opinion.

If the people – and not the politicians – are sovereign, then extraordinary (or revolutionary) changes should only take place with popular consent. And public thinkers have a duty to point this out: for two reasons. The first is because the form by which a people is governed is important. Form is as important as content. By this I mean that a good decision is good not only because of what it should bring about, but also because of the way it is made. This is why we have democracy – that is, decisions taken by the people because, let's be frank, dictatorships also do good things, but they do them the wrong way.

If our public thinkers stop making the distinction between the democratic and the dictatorial way of taking decisions, we risk losing democracy.

The second reason is because whether revolutionary, or extraordinary, changes need to be publicly discussed, given that their implication and conclusions are far-reaching.

Changes in "morality" not only affect the sector they directly regulate but they have a spill-over effect. Compartmentalisation does not exist; everything is interlinked.

"Morality" is like an ecosystem: one small change impacts on everything else.

The duty of public thinkers is, first and foremost, towards the public. Their personal convictions have to take second place.

Their first priority should be to think on behalf of the public, which is absorbed in its everyday chores and worries.

Otherwise, those who pretend to be public thinkers end up being just private thinkers who express their thoughts publicly.

A friend has given me an incredibly good book entitled *The Great Partnership: God, Science and the Search for Meaning* (2011), written by Rabbi Lord Jonathan Sacks, who at the time was the Chief Rabbi of the Commonwealth.

This collection of essays puts forward arguments which, even if you are not Jewish, you end up agreeing with – not just due to their persuasive style but mostly on account of the force and clarity on which their reasoning is based.

I'd like to quote a brief excerpt: 'A free political order is possible only when the fundamental political act is a mutual promise between the governor and the governed. But no human being can be trusted to keep his or her word when he or she has access to power – a power not available to opponents. Sooner or later... there is an inescapable risk of tyranny' (p. 133).

The Best-in-Europe Dream

JOSEPH MUSCAT'S AMBITION TO MAKE MALTA THE "BEST IN EUROPE" SEEMS TO HAVE BEEN THWARTED BY REALITY. Let us consider a few examples.

According to the most recent Worldwide Governance Indicators issued by the World Bank, Malta has experienced a veritable free fall in freedom of expression and accountability – the worst showing in 10 years. There has been a downward trend since 2014. The implications are clear. In the meantime, air pollution in Malta is the fourth worst in the European Union. According to EU officials, pollution accounts for 80 per cent of premature deaths as it causes lung disease and cancer and possibly Alzheimer's disease.

So not only are we not even remotely the best in Europe, but we are heading towards the opposite end of the spectrum. And we might end up kicked out of civilisation. Let me explain by giving an example that illustrates the uncivilised mentality regulating the Best Country in Europe. Enemalta announced last Thursday that it would suspend the supply in certain parts of Ħaż-Żebbuġ from 8 am to 2:30 pm. Seems civilised enough, except that they cut it at 7:30 am... oblivious to the hassle and problems they created to unsuspecting citizens. Are the Maltese bound to live with it? No, particularly when they were promised that their country would become the Best in Europe.

The Best in Europe is turning out to mean also an influx of foreign workers who swell the demand for housing and everyday necessities while exerting inordinate pressure on the infrastructure and resources as well as the social fabric and native culture of the country.

The Best in Europe is turning out to mean a dystopian cosmopolitan city-state, saddled with the ugliness of the megalopolis – haphazard urbanisation, overdevelopment, social decline – but lacking the beauty of the European metropolis, which essentially boils down to the pleasures of the mind. Malta is not becoming another Paris, London or Rome, where you find high-level theatre, shops selling unusual but interesting stuff, inspired architecture and well-kept public parks, but a jaded copy of some urban agglomeration in China or South America.

The Best in Europe is not even becoming another Venice, because Venice is a place from which the inhabitants can from time to time escape to find refuge and solace in their holdings in the hinterland away from the humid and densely occupied lagoon city.

The Best in Europe is quickly degenerating into a hotchpotch of overdevelopment and shoddy urban planning and barely-integrated migrants who have no roots here and possibly do not intend to ever settle here. Is this racist talk? No. Race has nothing to do it. This is demographics and sustainability. The physical and social environment is being threatened by a human deluge, by the wave of immigrants – irrespective of whether their skin colour is black, white, or whatever. The facts are that there simply is no space. And the country's culture is not urban, but "semi-urban" if not even provincial. Muscat thinks that a 55 per cent majority gives him the same right as an 80 per cent majority to transform the soul of the country beyond recognition. This is simply not the case. There is no physical space for his project, and there is no mental space either. He can try to change the latter, but it's difficult to increase the former, even if he were to push forward his land reclamation agenda. He might wish to buy Pantelleria – as an intellectual recently proposed – but, like Grand Master Pinto before him (who wanted to annex Corsica), he might find this to be but a chimera.

The influx of foreigners is worrying all those who have a good head on their shoulders. Not only those who can see that the overex-

My Personal Library

Last Wednesday, a dear friend of mine, a Frenchman, passed away. He was a doctor of medicine, a man of culture, an old-school gentleman, a connoisseur of cigars and wines and a lover of golf and Scottish kilts and clans, a devoted husband and a proud father, a traditionalist with whom I have had many wonderful conversations.

Dr Thierry Schaedgen, a Lorrainer, was preoccupied with European civilisation and its decay, the barbarisation of sexual mores (like, for instance, the use of abortion as a contraceptive method), the rise of the Extreme Right and the risks it poses to democracy and freedom...

He urged me to buy books by one of his favourite authors, the French Jew Éric Zemmour, which I did – and though I promised him I would read them and we would discuss them, I kept postponing, mostly because I'm a very slow reader in French and I'm always short on time.

One of Zemmour's novels, *Petit Frère*, deals with the breakdown of a neighbouhood in Paris' 19th *arrondissement* when a young Jewish DJ is murdered by an Arab childhood friend. The book's blurb reads thus: 'What the narrator discovers goes beyond a racist murder or a crime of passion: it's the decomposition of a neighbourhood subjected to increasingly more violent tensions, the ethnic conflicts which gnaw at French society, the lies of politicians, and the impostures of the intellectual elite'.

Dear Thierry, how I would have liked to discuss this novel with you! It's still on the shelf, waiting for its turn to be read. I will now read it in your honour.

But, if you will allow me one last instance of sincerity, the book I really would have liked to read was your Memoirs about which you spoke so many times but which I am sure you never found the time to write.

Those Memoirs would have been the repository of your spirit, the spirit of a good man, a gentle soul, a generous doctor, a genuine friend who left too young, too soon.

Adieu, mon ami !

ploitation of the environment will, sooner or later, sound the death knell of the territory. But also those who see clear threats to the culture of the people inhabiting the territory.

In his speech during the opening ceremony of the academic year, the Magnificent Rector of the University of Malta expressed the thoughts of many Maltese who have not been blinded by the gleam of the Best in Europe hype. He clearly stated that all foreigners who come to work in Malta should learn Maltese. The Professor is right. I for one am fed up of having to switch to English when I'm ordering food in a restaurant. When I'm in Malta, since I'm Maltese I want to feel at home. We all want to feel at home in Malta. Not only at restaurants – but everywhere. This is why the Magnificent Rector is right. He's talking about a deep psychological need: to feel at home when you're in your homeland. The foreigner has to adapt; we don't have to adapt to foreigners. Is this xenophobia? Of course not! Foreigners are more than welcome. But their numbers have to reflect the accommodation capacity of the territory and they have to adapt to our culture, not the other way round.

On top of that, let's stop deluding ourselves that we are really a functioning bilingual country. We are the Best Deluded Country in Europe. Just consider that there are British universities which do not take it for granted that Maltese students have the linguistic wherewithal to study in Britain.

I recently had a look at the website of a mid-ranking English university and its English language requirements: 'If you want to study for a degree from a UK university, and English is not your first language, you will need to take an English language test to prove that your English is of a sufficiently high standard.' So far, so good. But read on: 'You don't need to prove your knowledge of English if you're a national of, or if you have completed a qualification equivalent to a UK degree in, any of these countries: Antigua and Barbuda; Australia; the Bahamas; Barbados; Belize; Canada; Dominica; Grenada; Guyana; Ireland; Jamaica; New Zealand; St Kitts and Nevis; St Lucia; St Vincent and the Grenadines; Trinidad and Tobago; UK; USA.'

Jamaicans – whose *patois* is made up of phrases like *Inna di morrows* and *Weh yuh ah seh* – don't need to prove their standard of English but the Maltese do. Am I blaming the UK system? No. Because the British are right. The Maltese can speak no language properly – we've become a nation of Salvatores from Umberto Eco's *The Name of the Rose*. Maltese is degenerating; Malta's English is, not to put too fine a point on it, idiosyncratic; Malta's Italian is *vucumprà*-like (no idea of the polite form and its nuances, for instance). French and German are positively exotic if not even esoteric... and so on.

The implications of what the Magnificent Rector said are clear, at least to me. Instead of making things worse by tolerating foreign workers who speak English as they mishear or mislearnt it, let's get the foreigners to learn Maltese and let's try to save the language. Saving the language means saving the culture (the two are intimately intertwined). By saving language and culture, we can manage to keep Malta the home of the Maltese and avoid finding ourselves strangers in our own (strange) land.

But there's more to it. The Rector's idea would also bring about an indirect beneficial consequence: learning Maltese would be a sort of screening process – if a foreign worker is intelligent enough to learn Maltese, then the country would be benefitting from the influx of intellectually high-net-worth individuals.

Secular Morality: Promises and People

THERE IS ALWAYS THE TEMPTATION TO CONDENSE SPECIALISED KNOWLEDGE AND IMPART IT TO A NON-SPECIALISED AUDIENCE. The temptation is fuelled by the idea that spreading knowledge – even in a "coarse" fashion – helps to leave the tyranny of dark ignorance, and move toward the light. This temptation is particularly attractive to the French.

When travelling in France you will note, at airports and train stations, that kiosks sell philosophy and history magazines. You buy them with high hopes, but, more often than not, it's a letdown. The best word to describe what these magazines offer is premastication, or "kiss feeding", like when a mother physically breaks food down to feed her child who is incapable of chewing it by itself. Much of this premasticated stuff is Enlightenment propaganda. By which I do not necessarily mean that I disagree with the principles of the Enlightenment, but that there are important differences between the mantras of propaganda and historical "truths". For instance, there was no stable "religious" morality in the Middle Ages. The public thinking of the Middle Ages was mostly done by the Church, but it was not "stable"

– it was constantly evolving. The Christian theory of marriage, say, did become the dominant ideology but it took some three centuries to coagulate. The same applies to the theories on the beginning of life worthy of protection, and on prostitution, (one particular monastic order even argued the social necessity of the oldest profession).

To say "religious" seems to imply a dichotomy between "Church" ("God") and "State" ("Caesar") but this was hardly the case. In the 20th century, the Italian thinker Santi Romano persuasively argued that the Middle Ages were a stateless epoch, that is, a time when the State was so weak, it was virtually nonexistent. The grand state apparatus of the Caesars collapsed and disintegrated in Western Europe following the fall of Rome.

This is difficult for us moderns to understand, as we are fishes living in the aquarium of the State, and cannot imagine life outside that aquarium in a wide state-less sea. But that is how it was. The law has an intimate, bidirectional relationship with morality: it both shapes, and is shaped by, morality. And the State, which monopolises the creation of law, takes account of the winds of morality change.

But the Middle Ages were another planet. In the Middle Ages, the law was not made by the State.

There was no State to make the law!

The law was made by different, competing centres of power, all legitimate but all existing in utter chaos, reflecting the "natural" chaotic state of society. The law was simultaneously made by the Church, by notaries, by judges, by communes, and also, but limitedly, very limitedly, by kings and other potentates. It was also made by scholars who commented on the centuries-old *codex* of the (Eastern) Roman Emperor Justinian, and the rest of the old Roman law, only re-discovered in the 11th century after it had lain forgotten for hundreds of years.

The Middle Ages were a mishmash of competing laws, of local customs, of a complex and variegated tapestry of overlapping and stratified jurisdictions and legal systems. There was no stability, even though there was an evolving worldview.

This is the "historical truth", not the mantra forged by 18th-century propaganda in the furnace of the French Revolution.

De-Christianisation

THE "CIVILISATION" USHERED IN BY THE REVOLUTION NECESSARILY NEEDED TO DE-CHRISTIANISE EUROPE. The new socio-economic formation needed a worldview fundamentally different from the medieval one which had been moulded and buttressed by Christianity. It needed one, over-arching legal system to harmonise the different markets. But because law and morality are intimately intertwined, it also needed a new, secular morality based on one axiom: nothing is permanent, every obligation can be resolved, every contract rescinded, and this in accordance with the dictates of economic efficiency.

The moral idea found in Matthew 5:34-37, that all promises are binding, and which through Canon Law had shaped medieval law, was not useful to the new system. A new principle was introduced: there could be no "perpetual obligations". The new mentality pervaded all spheres of life, from employment relations to interpersonal relations: nothing is permanent, everything is fluid. From the consensualism of the Middle Ages, Europe passed to the contractualism of the Enlightenment.

What possibly started out as a good antidote to the excesses of the medieval system, ended up evolving (or degenerating, depending on one's viewpoint) into the (neo-)liberal system we have today, in which nothing is sacred anymore (except profit).

I do not quote Church documents or reactionary authors. I find solace in the leftist French legal thinker Alain Supiot who, in his *Homo Juridicus*, published by Verso in 2007, devotes an entire chapter to 'The Binding Force of the Word: *Pacta Sunt Servanda*'. Of the many points Supiot makes, I will choose only one. He argues that even though the modern contract arises in the wake of the Enlightenment, it could not have come into being without the medieval belief in God. Promises depend on trust and trust needs an all-seeing, all-powerful guarantor to thrive: God. (Remember the US dollar 'In God We Trust'?)

What happened was that with secularisation, the State (Caesar) took the place of God. It is the State which now guarantees that promises are kept. Supiot quotes Max Weber who, upon returning from a trip to the United States, reported a statement he had heard from a businessman: 'What someone believes is wholly indifferent to me, but if I know that a client does not go to church, then for me he is not worth 50 cents; why would he pay me if he does not believe in anything?'

The salient characteristics of secular morality
ONE CHARACTERISTIC OF SECULAR MORALITY IS THAT THE STATE (CAESAR) THINKS OF ITSELF AS GOD. On my Facebook page, I keep a ceiling fresco I saw in a church

in Little Italy, Montreal, Canada. It is an incredible scene, painted by Guido Nincheri, with Mussolini on one side and the Pope on the other, both beneath the angels and saints, and ultimately God. The official interpretation is that the painting commemorates the recognition of the Vatican State in 1929. To my mind, instead, it hints at the Fascist aspiration to elevate the State to divinity status, and to supplant Christianity with the Fascist religion. The official interpretation is one of co-operation; my own interpretation is one of competition.

To me, that painting represents a veritable preoccupation, because a Fascist State is the last thing I want to live in. A State that arrogates to itself the administration of my freedom of action and imposes on me what I can and cannot think is, to me, a suffocating prison cell where I can only keep a notebook with my thoughts jotted down. I do think, like Jonah Goldberg, that Liberalism in its current state has become Fascist. Goldberg's book *Liberal Fascism* (2008) sheds much light on the path followed by the progressive-liberals from Mussolini to identity politics.

In the medieval (or Christian) system, people internalised the belief that God watched them, and this imposed on them a moral duty to keep their word. In the post-Enlightenment (or secular, de-Christianised) system, people know that the State – despite CCTV cameras and the highly-intrusive mobile phone with its Google panopticon-like applications and what have you - does not really watch you all the time, because it simply cannot. Surely not like God, who also knew your intentions apart from your deeds.

On top of that, the secular system tells you that your word is plastic. So not only is there no real guarantor, but in reality there is no pressing need for one as, all said and done, giving one's word is a wishy-washy business. In the medieval/Christian system, you had worth in God's eyes, what you did was significant to Him, and you would be rewarded or punished in the afterlife for your deeds in this life. In the secular system, Darwin (whose face appears on British paper currency) has been made to tell you that you are just another animal in the evolution of species. Highly speculative astrophysicists insist that you live on a little blueish-white speck in a vast universe, that is neither unique nor special. Therefore, you are not worth anything to any Higher Being.

For secular morality, the only "God" there can be is Human Reason, which is self-evidently not higher than Humanity itself: Man (in his tower-like State) replaces God.

But Man is at the same time, and

paradoxically, reduced to a clump of cells, a human resource, a taxpayer, a slave to economic forces.So you can do whatever you like – you can kill your own unborn child, you can deprive your children of a mother or a father because your private peccadillo becomes your public persona, you can commit suicide when you're old, lonely and no longer useful to the consumer society, and so on – because ultimately you are insignificant. You are a little piece of shit, and you know it.

The narcissistic freedom to do as you please and to consume as much as you can becomes the wall which isolates you from the others, and ultimately from yourself.

Your only companion becomes an echo, which can only finish a sentence not started.

My Personal Library

Some books end up on your shelf not because you treasure them but because you had to buy them to read what their author had to say. Many of these books you'd want to burn after you read them were it not for the belief that only an ignorant Nazi pig burns books. (In reality, not only the Nazis were book-burning maniacs. Martin Luther, Louis XIV, and even Alexander the Great burnt books.) I would have very much wanted to impose this destiny on one particular book, but I restrained myself, not only because of my staunch belief that books shouldn't be burnt, but because of a short passage that saved it... a bit like when Abraham negotiated with God not to destroy Sodom if he managed to find x number of righteous men in the city. In the case of Sodom, these were nowhere to be found. In the case of Salvu Balzan's dull-as-dishwater, sophomoric autobiography of sorts, one episode saves it from the flames.

Mr Balzan closes his tedious little opus...cule by relating how he was once invited to a party and then-Prime Minister Eddie Fenech Adami introduced him to somebody thus: 'This is Saviour Balzan, one of my fiercest critics'. Mr Balzan was positively impressed by Dr Fenech Adami's attitude, and rightly so.

It is the only instance in which one can share Mr Balzan's reaction. The rest of the book is forgettable. Joyfully shreddable, to be more precise.

The Minister and the Friar

WHAT A BREATH OF FRESH AIR FR. IVAN ATTARD OF THE DOMINICANS! And what a totalitarian oppressive view from a top Minister of the State!

I am obviously referring to Fr. Attard's videoblog on contraceptives and the irate reaction of the Minister for European Affairs and Equality Helena Dalli to it.

Let's clarify some points.

1. It is Fr. Attard's duty to preach the teachings of the Church he belongs to. If he were to be silent, he would be a fraud, a parasite living on the donations received by the Church and other monies earned by his Order.

2. It is Fr. Attard's constitutional right to express his beliefs, without fear of reprimands from the State. Fr. Attard enjoys fundamental human rights under the Constitution, under the European Convention of Human Rights, and under a series of other international treaties.

3. When a representative of the State reprimands somebody for expressing views and beliefs which do not break any law, there is the possibility of chilling that person's inclination to enjoy their right to freedom of expression in a full, wide, and democratic fashion.

4. Yes, the views expressed by Fr. Attard are not contrary to the law. They are his views (and, incidentally, the views of quite many people). So Fr. Attard has the sacrosanct right not only to hold them, but also to express them freely.

5. Helena Dalli, the Minister in question, too has the right to hold views and beliefs and to express them freely, but she has to exercise that right with caution and circumspection, because she is not a common citizen: she is a Minister and when she speaks, it is the State that is speaking through her. Minister Dalli is not the Minister for Transport, say, or Agriculture. She is the Minister for European Affairs and Equality, and her comments therefore can be understood as the expression of formal government and therefore State policy.

6. The Minister speaks as if there were one truth - hers. This is a totalitarian approach. In a democratic environment (which is our European heritage), there is not a single approach. All lawful approaches are equally protected by the law and by the moral system on which the law is based.

7. It seems that the neo-liberals are day after day showing us their true colours: totalitarian liberals: you are either liberal like them or they (metaphorically) burn you at the stake.

What did Fr. Attard preach? Actually, if you listen to his videoblog you will find a very coherent critique of the neo-liberal system. It shows that he is extremely well-read, level-headed and can clearly read the signs of the times.

Fr. Attard made two points, essentially. One, contraceptives remove the need for self-restraint. He made an interesting contrast between self-restraint as self-discipline and self-restraint as self-oppression. Frankly, I see nothing wrong with this reasoning. Fr. Attard used the analogy with food ... and I smiled, because if only I could exercise the self-restraint Fr. Attard spoke about, I would not be overweight! So, as a life philosophy, Fr. Attard is proposing a praiseworthy model. Exercise self-restraint as self-discipline. Control your appetites and you will live a better, happier life, because you will free yourself from the oppression of your desires. What is there to censure in this? The learned Dominican was here criticising the libertarian aspect of neo-liberalism, which is the idea that you can (even should!) satisfy all your appetites (mostly sexual) because it is your right to do so. (In one of my recent articles, I quoted the contemporary philosopher Slavoj Žižek's observation that the current dominant ideology tells you that since you can, you should.)

Two, that contraceptives exist in a market economy. Here Fr. Attard was presenting a critique of late capitalism, namely the exaggerated form it has taken under the aegis of the neo-liberal worldview. Again I cannot find any grounds on which to disagree with the learned friar. Whereas the free market is probably a good thing, not all things should be freely traded. There are things that should not be in the market, because of their effects on human behaviour. Or else, their trade should be controlled.

Alcohol is a good example. There is the free market in alcohol (prohibitionism was not a great success in the US a century or so ago), but certainly it makes sense to preach self-control when consuming alcohol. Indeed, the State campaigns against drinking and driving. So why should the State campaign for the responsible consumption of alcohol, but – according to the Minister – a Dominican priest should not campaign for the responsible use of contraceptives (or no use at all, just like no drinking at all)? Both alcohol and contraceptives form part of the exaggerated capitalist mentality – the consumerist mentality – at the root of neo-liberalism.

Consume, consume, consume: that's the Commandment of the neo-liberal Religion. There are exceptions, obviously, and while the State campaigns for self-restraint with regard to alcohol consumption, a Minister of the same State criticises a priest for campaigning for self-restraint in matters sexual. Messy thinking, I would say, as both refer to instinctual appetites.

Readers' Comments
Some readers argued online that since the priest is celibate he should not preach on sexuality; they made two logical mistakes. First: as Leo Tolstoy famously pointed out, 'All happy families resemble one another, but each unhappy family is unhappy in its own way'. Your experience in your family or relationship(s) does not make you an expert. If you think otherwise, you are making the mistake of thinking that from one example you can extrapolate a universal principle.

Second: A psychologist need not have experienced the ailments their clients complain of to be able to help them. A lawyer need not be a businessman to represent a shop owner in court. And so on and so forth. Likewise, a priest need not have experienced the sexual act or marriage to be able to preach a philosophy of life. Umberto Eco's observation is the best explanation for these online commentators: in the past certain people used to speak their minds in bars and cafés where their friends would shut them up.

Now they take to the social media. With no sense of self-restraint.

Birth Rate
There is also another way of looking at the subject raised by Fr. Attard. Malta's birth is the fourth-lowest in the EU (1.37 births per woman in 2016, as reported in 2018 by Eurostat). What is the significance of this statistical datum in the current situation?

We have to consider three elements, to my mind. One, that Joseph Muscat is behaving – to borrow a phrase recently used by Romano Prodi – as if winning an election means that you get the country as your dowry. In other words, Prime Minister Muscat is behaving as if an electoral victory means he can radically change the country: he wants to import tens of thousands of foreigners for short- to medium-term economic growth. Long-term, this inflow will radically change the social fabric of the country, while overstretching its shaky infrastructure.

Two, in the long run, it would be wiser to adopt pro-family measures encouraging the Maltese to have more children (and move the birth rate up from the fourth-lowest) in order to have enough taxpayers to sustain the pensions system and the broader social welfare infrastructure in the future.

My Personal Library

Paolo Villaggio's *Fantozzi, rag. Ugo: La Tragica e Definitiva Trilogia* (2013) is the literary progenitor of the hit movies which have entered the collective imagination of the Italians, and I dare say, the Maltese. If the movies are funny, the books are even more hilarious. Every paragraph contains an exaggeration, a hyperbole, that is at once funny and a source of insight into the predicament of the average (Italian?) man. (I say "man" on purpose: *'maschilisimo rozzo e impotente'* [uncouth and impotent machismo] is one of the characteristics of Fantozzi that Stefano Bartezzaghi refers to in his Introduction to the book).

As they say, it's better to watch the movie before reading the book. That way you avoid the let-down, because the book is almost always better than the movie. The way Villaggio moulds the language to create a true but absurd and therefore impossible rendition of reality is breath-taking. It is this paradox between form (impossible, absurd, implausible) and content (true-to-life) that inducts Fantozzi to the Hall of Literature. Fantozzi is like Mythology: implausible stories meant to explain the true meaning of life.

In an interview Villaggio gave to a Swiss TV channel way back in 1975, he spoke of one of the biggest mistakes of contemporary Western ideology. He argued that the common man has been promised that if he buys and consumes, he will attain happiness. 'Is this consumerist society ... happy?' Villaggio asked. 'No, it's the devil, it's the opposite. This kind of happiness is highly unhappy.'

Reminds you of Fr. Attard's words.

Three, if we look at it in strictly non-religious terms, Catholic teaching (which is what Fr. Attard was preaching) is a pro-family ideology, and can therefore be useful in a population project meant to perpetuate the welfare state without shifting society in fundamental and ill-thought-out ways.

The European Court of Human Rights and the Two Ministers
A RECENT CASE DECIDED BY THE EUROPEAN COURT OF HUMAN RIGHTS SHOULD MAKE INTERESTING READING FOR OUR TWO ULTRA-NEO-LIBERAL MINISTERS: HELENA DALLI AND OWEN BONNICI. In *E.S. v. Austria*, the Court decided that where attacks 'go beyond the limits of a critical denial of other people's religious beliefs and are likely to incite religious intolerance [...] a State may legitimately consider them to be incompatible with respect for the freedom of thought, conscience and religion and take proportionate restrictive measures' (para. 43 of the judgment).

I feel that a State should always consider that any offence directed at any of the sane religions (Christianity, Islam, Judaism, etc) is not covered by freedom of expression, because it hurts unnecessarily and adds nothing to a democratic environment. Ultimately, democracy is like Valletta: a "city" built by gentle-men for gentlemen. Taunting people for their religious beliefs is neither gentlemanly nor productive.

Our Two National Heroes and the Kappillan of Gozo

IN THIS WORLD, THERE ARE TWO KINDS OF PEOPLE: THOSE WITH WORKING BRAINS AND THOSE WHO LICK. For those whose brains work, it is clear that the recent news means only one thing: our two National Heroes have to resign. There is no two ways about it. Of course, for those who lick (and therefore whose brains are either switched off or still wrapped in their original packaging), there's no wrongdoing and the difference between the attempted, frustrated, and consummated crime does not exist. But those who lick might have other priorities, and good governance is not one of them.

People with working brains are certainly considering two other matters.

1. We have come to know about the Panama secret companies only because somebody decided to leak the records of one legal firm. But we know that there are many legal firms giving the same type of service all over the world. So how can we be sure that our two National Heroes did not open other secret structures elsewhere?

2. If the power station deal was indeed influenced by the setup that surfaced recently, how can we be sure that other manoeuvres of the same kind did not take place? For instance, the Mrieħel towers: can we be sure there is no mysterious company somewhere paying some other secret company somewhere else?

I think all upright citizens have but one choice: to echo the call made by one pressure group to investigate all deals involving our two National Heroes, and to applaud the other pressure group which took the epoch-making initiative of going to the Police to actually file a report asking for a criminal investigation. This is democracy in action.

Please take my writing as a standing ovation to the courage and determination of these people.

The Language Question (again?)
IN 1934, THESE ISLANDS SAW THE ELEVATION OF THEIR NATIVE TONGUE TO LEGALLY RECOGNISED LANGUAGE. In 1964, that same language became the national language of the nascent nation-state. In 2004, it was added to the extended family of Euoprean Union official languages. And yet, we seem unable to grow out of the language question. It keeps cropping up time and again.

Recently, somebody filed a parliamentary petition to ask that the law be changed to allow all citizens equal access to court services. The wording of the petition is not exactly limpid, so the objective of the petitioner and the less than three hundred people who signed the petition so far is not all that clear. The petition mentions 'non-English speakers' and 'non-Maltese speakers' and their need to use either of the two official languages (Maltese and English) in Court. I wonder how this petition can help non-English, non-Maltese speakers, since the petition refers to equal access in Maltese and English but no other language. Despite the ambiguity of the petition, it seems to me that this petitioner has, possibly unwittingly, touched on an issue which will certainly acquire more importance in the years to come: namely the hotchpotch that will become the linguistic situation in Malta. Almost the entire population can more or less make itself understood in English. I say 'more or less' because this week, for instance, a British newspaper poked fun at Muscat when it reported that '[h]e went on to claim a closer union between the EU and Arab states could allow them to head in a direction "where others fear to tread".'

The poke was linguistic – the implication being that the Muscat does not know how to use the phrase in inverted commas, taken from a poem by Alexander Pope: 'For fools rush in where angels fear to tread'. Muscat had unwittingly admitted that the EU was made up of fools – music to the ears of the editor and readers of that newspaper, but certainly not what Muscat intended.

If even the country's Prime Minister faces these difficulties, we should not delude ourselves about many of the others. So, at the end of the day there are at least two points to ponder.

One. Not Being Left Out
THE MALTESE LANGUAGE REMAINS THE KEY THAT OPENS THE DOOR TO THE NATIVE COMMUNITY. All the talk about cosmopolitan Malta and all that are completely irrelevant. "Cosmopolitan" means being familiar with and at ease in many different countries and cultures. Very few individuals can aspire to be both familiar with and at ease in many different countries and cultures. Usually such individuals travel a lot and are not particularly attached to any one country. At times, children of diplomats grow into cosmopolitan adults, having spent their childhood in the different countries where their diplomat parent was posted. Otherwise, people who spend their entire lives in the same place, meeting the same people, and facing the same situations and conditions, do not become cosmopolitan overnight, even

if their beloved Prime Minister wants them to. Being cosmopolitan does not depend on willingness and will; it depends on life experience. I wonder how many Maltese know what it means to spend half the year under an incredibly shy sun and in temperatures of -25° Celsius, like the Nordics do.

And thus, we go back to the original statement: the Maltese language remains the key that opens the door to the native Maltese community.

If "cosmopolitan" is being used as a by-word for "turn a blind eye" to "weird" behaviour, then we are playing with fire, possibly fostering the culture of de-humanising foreigners... excessive neo-liberalism can lead to xenophobia. Too much political correctness ultimately begets hatred. But I will elaborate on this a bit further down, and again in future articles.

Two. The English as she is spoke
NON-EU NATIONALS, BUT EVEN EU NATIONALS, WHO ARE FLOW-ING INTO MALTA, HAVE DIFFERENT LEVELS OF ENGLISH. There are the native speakers, who most probably often feel frustrated that the nuances of the language go over the heads of the majority of the population. Then there are those whose English is inferior to that of the average Maltese, and these will have

to face difficult situations making them feel short-changed and filling them with resentment.

To me, it seems that the incoming migrant is not someone who necessarily wants to establish himself or herself here. This migrant therefore would not look for a local spouse, missing on the added benefit of having a shield from, and a sincere interface with, the local culture. Instead, migrants would be temporary residents, giving rise to a social phenomenon of indifference toward their plight or, even worse, a culture of abuse, viewing temporary residents simply as cows to be milked.

When all is said and done, in the long run abuse hurts both victim and abuser. If the foreigner is dehumanised, we risk a repetition of Mitteleuropa in the early 20th-century.

The Wealth of a Nation
WHEN THE POLICIES OF THE STATE ARE INSPIRED BY SHORT-TERMISM, TALK OF CULTURE ENDS UP OC-CUPYING A PLACE OF SECONDARY IMPORTANCE IN THE SCALE OF VAL-UES, THE UPPERMOST VALUE BEING SHORT-TERM GAIN AND THE MAX-IMISATION OF IMMEDIATE PROFITS. When people are reduced to chattel or to a replaceable resource, then the situation raises many ethical, social, and economic issues.

The Rector of the University of Malta recently argued that migrants should learn Maltese. This is an important idea for those who want to establish themselves permanently. Only a fool cannot reckon the wisdom of the Rector's words. But the temporary resident, who comes over to make some money while the boom lasts, might find that the prospect of learning Maltese not that attractive. And this is the sore point that needs immediate and careful attention. Language is the lubricant that oils social interactions. You don't live in a country; you live in a language. Wave after wave of migrants who aren't interested in local culture, and are in turn dehumanised, will ultimately erode the social fabric of the country, which is the real wealth of any nation.

The Kappillan of Gozo
COMMENTS ON THE SOCIAL MEDIA AND ELSEWHERE HAVE RIDICULED THE ŻEBBUĠ (GOZO) COMMUNITY FOR THE TRIUMPHANT ENTRY THEY RESERVED FOR THEIR NEW PARISH PRIEST. Let's analyse this rationally.

This must be a Gozitan tradition. I cannot remember and am not aware of any similar tradition on the island of Malta. Is it bad? No. Is it commendable? Indifferent. Should it be stopped? Of course not! Let the people enjoy themselves if it gives them joy to welcome their spiritual leader in that fashion! If it's harmless, why judge them? (I suspect that this is a fundamental liberal notion, elaborated by that liberal-socialist philosopher called John Stuart Mill: if an act is harmless, it need not be sanctioned and prohibited.)

The Labour Leader asked the Maltese to be "cosmopolitan", to be at ease with different cultures. Some people cannot even be at ease with the different regional cultures of our own country – how on earth can Muscat expect them to be at ease with cultures from other countries? As I said about Ultra-Neo-liberal Minister Dalli: 'messy thinking'. It seems the neo-liberals are remarkably good at it.

A Question of Meaning

IN POLITICS, THERE IS THOUGHT AND THERE IS ACTION. The latter is more important than the former when it comes to achieving results, but the meaning of the action depends on the thought.

Our little country is relatively young. Its institutions have still not grown out of their infancy or, at best, their adolescence. They have still not achieved full emancipation from the colonial past. State-building is still a work-in-progress. At the same time, Maltese society, which is much older than the country's modern status, has its needs - and they are pressing needs. Not just in respect of the vulnerable who need decent social accommodation, but everybody else - from people who need less air pollution because they are increasingly suffering from lung disease, to students afflicted with respiratory problems on account of mouldy classrooms, to the overall sensation gripping the country that there is no chance of saving the environment for future generations.

Action is required on both fronts: state-building is an important priority but social needs are equally important.

State-building
JOSEPH MUSCAT'S INSISTENCE ON WANTING TO PROTECT THE MIZZI-

SCHEMBRI DUO AT ALL COSTS IS A HUMONGOUS SPOKE IN THE WHEEL OF THE STATE-BUILDING PROCESS. How can the Maltese state function properly when its executive branch's topmost representative fails to take the action expected of him? When state officials see that clear misbehaviour is condoned, they will either feel demoralised or, worse, empowered to do likewise. When the population sees all of this, its respect for the authority of the State will plummet.

Benedetto Croce

IN THE INTER-WAR PERIOD, THE ITALIAN PHILOSOPHER BENEDETTO CROCE WROTE THAT PEOPLE TREAT POLITICIANS LIKE DOCTORS. When somebody needs a doctor to cure them, they don't care whether the doctor is honest or dishonest, moral or immoral. All they care about is that the doctor can cure them.

The same applies to politicians. People hardly care whether a politician is honest or not; what they do care about is that the politician can deliver and create wealth, stability and well-being.

Croce was writing at the time when Italy started experimenting with the Fascist regime. Whether you like Mussolini or not, the historical truth is that for a number of years, the regime enjoyed a high level of popular support. The Italians call that period *gli anni del consenso* (the years of popular approval). The regime created many structures and entities that are either still in place today or else served as the basis for further development down the years. These had social objectives and proved popular with the Italians. Most importantly, the regime tried to impose order on a population and country that had grown disorderly.

So Mussolini's morality was hardly important. What was important was that he was making something great out of Italy (or at least, so the propaganda said).

The question thus begs itself: Are Croce's words still valid today?

The morality of politicians

I WOULD SAY THAT CROCE'S WORDS ARE ONLY PARTIALLY VALID. Yes, social needs are important. But so too are matters of state-building.

Creating wealth is good. Distributing it fairly is better.

Having institutions that work is good. Not abusing government power is better.

The country needs a healthy version of this two-pronged vision: state-building on the one hand, social conscience on the other.

Despite all the talk about the rule of law and 'our institutions are working fine' and so on, it seems to me that Joseph Muscat's administration is failing miserably on both counts.

It seems to me that the more the Labour Government protests that there is the rule of law and all that, the less things are functioning as they should. Labour doth protest too much, methinks.

Wealth is being created but very badly distributed, to the extent that poverty is raising its ugly head.

State institutions are treated like ballast that hinders the rise of certain people's private air balloons.

Occupying a State position brings with it the obligation to obey an unwritten code of State morality.

The Mizzi-Schembri-17-Black imbroglio is of such far-reaching significance that it could wreak untold havoc on the State, its institutions and the country, to the extent that we end up with only pieces scattered here and there in the shadow of increasingly higher high-rise buildings.

Machiavellian politics
THE MIZZI-SCHEMBRI IMBROGLIO IS HISTORY IN THE MAKING. Somebody recently wrote an opinion piece criticising Joseph Muscat for being Machiavellian. I disagree with the author of that piece, because he seems to think that Machiavelli proposed an amoral prince as an abstract model for real princes to follow. Machiavelli might be understood as having meant that the end justifies the means, but the end itself was highly moral – at least for Machiavelli and those of his persuasion. The unification of Italy was such a high moral goal that some amoral behaviour could be tolerated.

Not so in the Mizzi-Schembri imbroglio, as the only goal is the lining of certain pockets through secret companies and secret bank accounts in shady jurisdictions: an absolutely immoral (not amoral) objective. The meaning very much depends on the context.

My Personal Library

Hayden White's *The Content of the Form* (1987) is an excellent, though high-brow, treatise on the problems of meaning in different historical epochs. White's ideas will be useful to future historians when they write about Joseph Muscat's political legacy.

Muscat's political legacy will have a meaning which, if we apply White's ideas, will reside in 'the content of the form', in the way that future historians will want their present to be the fulfilment of a past from which they will wish to have descended. I'm sure it will be a different past from the one Joseph Muscat is leaving them.

The Use and Abuse of Language

LISTENING TO KONRAD MIZZI AL-WAYS CAUSES CONSIDERABLE STRESS TO MY DIGESTIVE SYSTEM. I cannot stomach all the code-switching, the inability to start an answer in one language and finish it in that very same language, the penchant for peppering anything he says in Maltese with redundant English words. And yet I think that this Comedy Knights-like way of communicating can sway opinions. It's high time for us to analyse the scam.

Konrad Mizzi, the code-switcher
BECAUSE A LINGUISTIC SCAM IT IS. In larger countries, linguists study the language patterns used by politicians to draw conclusions on the sincerity or otherwise of their discourse. For instance, linguists have noted that Donald Trump seems to have dumbed down his language since taking to politics. It seems that he now uses a rudimentary kind of speech – repetitions and bad, incoherent sentence structure and all – as a means of getting closer to the core of his electorate. This does not mean that President Trump is stupid or uncouth; it simply means that he has chosen to bond with his electorate through that kind of language. It is actually an astute marketing ploy.

Dom Mintoff's speeches have also been analysed but, as far as I know, only for the imagery and metaphors used and not for the language itself. However, it is known that it was a certain kind of language meant to appeal to a certain kind of electorate. One need only listen to the cassettes issued by the Labour Party in the 1980s (the *Sensiela Kassett Soċjalisti*) or to recordings found on YouTube, to analyse the linguistic techniques skilfully used by Mr Mintoff to explain complex political situations and ideas to an electorate unprepared for such complexity but that could cast a vote.

Is Konrad Mizzi using a similar ploy? Why can't Dr Mizzi stick to one language? Why does he need to switch from Maltese to English, to use redundant (pseudo-) technical terms in English? Is it because he studied abroad? So many other politicians have studied abroad, and yet they do not resort to such tactics. To my mind, Dr Mizzi is resorting to a reverse strategy when compared to President Trump and Mr Mintoff. He "dumbs up" his language, and he does it for two reasons: to confound the smart and impress the sub-literate.

The smart
BY CONSTANTLY SWITCHING FROM ONE LANGUAGE TO ANOTHER, DR

Mizzi attempts to stupefy the smart members of the public, particularly when he is trying to cajole us into accepting his discourse through logical distortions and verbal contortions.

Just analyse the contortions in his short Facebook video clip and the short exchange he had with the press, when – despite the crystal-clear conclusions of the NAO report on the power station deal – he still insisted, with headstrong pigheadedness, that that very same report absolved him of all wrongdoing.

The sub-literate

The sub-literate (and not only) Konrad Mizzi impresses with the pretence that he's an expert, a whizz-kid. The message he indirectly tries to convey is that if he can use technical terms – or what could sound as technical terms – in English, then surely he must know what he is talking about.

In both instances, it clearly boils down to pulling wool over people's eyes.

The underlying messages are twofold: 'I'm one of you (and I made it)' and 'I'm an expert'.

This is the public image Dr Mizzi created of himself through skilful misuse of language and double-tongued linguistic devices.

The switchers

Every time you switch on the lights, remember that Konrad Mizzi code-switches to beguile and befuddle you. He does this by trying to make you forget that electricity originating from the interconnector would have been cheaper.

The ecstasy of gold

The truth is that code-switching and the implied messages it tries to convey do nothing to conceal the absolute, unadulterated greed which fuelled the efforts to create secret structures in secretive jurisdictions known for money laundering. Let us not forget that these secret structures were created only a few days after the elections of 2013. No amount of linguistic detergent can remove that stain.

This part of the NAO report is enough to morally convince anybody that the secret structures had not been set up for nothing:

> the NAO maintains serious reservations regarding the risk that Government was exposed to when the guarantees were in effect. The Office is of the opinion that such a situation could have been avoided through appropriate planning, with referral to the European Commission

undertaken at the earliest, possibly prior to the issuance of the Expression of Interest and Capability and the Request for Proposals. It is in view of the serious repercussions that could have materialised had the guarantees been called that the NAO advocates that any measure that could have mitigated the issuance of the Government Guarantees and the duration within which they were in effect, should have been considered.

The language of bureaucracy

BUREAUCRACY SPEAKS BUREAU-CRATESE. What is the NAO report saying here? It is saying that the fact that the State took on itself the bank guarantee burden at that stage of the process meant that not all bidders were treated in the same way.

In other words, other bidders would have behaved differently, had it been known from the beginning that the State would intervene to make a bank loan possible! Only those who have either switched off their brains or are sub-literate can keep stubbornly repeating that there is no wrongdoing here!

It's the economy...

SOMEBODY ADVISED ME TO STOP WRITING ABOUT THIS TOPIC BE-CAUSE, ALL SAID AND DONE, PEOPLE KNOW WHAT DR MIZZI DID, BUT COULD NOT CARE LESS. The economy is doing fine and that is what matters at the end of the day. I must say that that is a very powerful argument. But it is also short-sighted. Degradation – whether moral or physical – is a long-term story. It's like having a medical condition and not caring about it because things are going well for the moment... when it becomes chronic, it might well be too late. Degradation, like high blood pressure, is a silent killer.

But let us not flatter ourselves that the inability to see the common good and its long-term trajectory is a monopoly of the Maltese. It's a human, and tragic, trait. And has been like this since time immemorial.

I think it's one of the lessons the Old Testament tries to teach. But the Jewish tradition also teaches that prophets are usually not appreciated at home.

Such is the folly of humanity, such is its tragedy.

My Personal Library

Sometimes I find myself wondering how certain words I've never used in my life come to my mind while I'm writing. Words like "double-tongued" and "milksop", which I didn't even know I knew, emerge out of the deep recesses of my mind and present themselves, almost with a smile on their face, as if to announce their suitability to whatever I am writing. Since I don't know I know them, I need the dictionary to verify their suitability, to make sure that they can really deliver what they promise. It almost always turns out to be the case, and I'm always humbled by the mysterious linguistic games played by the unconscious mind. It has now dawned on me that there was a time, some 25 years ago or more, when I used to read (the very liberal) *The Economist* from cover to cover, religiously, week in, week out. Until I realised that it was taking up all of my time and had reluctantly to give it up. However, I do not regret all those hours spent soaking up every word in it, despite the magazine's liberal agenda. Indeed, I met the English language on its pages.

One benefit I certainly do not regret is that I kept abreast with the latest publications of a certain calibre. One such book was *Age of Propaganda: The Everyday Use and Abuse of Persuasion*, by A. Pratkanis and E. Aronson (1991). A few snippets from the Table of Contents will give you an idea of what a goldmine the book is: The Psychology of Factoids, The Credible Communicator, The Manufacture of Credibility, Self-Sell, Why Do They Keep Repeating the Same Ads?, If You Have Nothing to Say – Distract Them, How To Become a Cult Leader...

The book is replete with examples. One of them is the 1968 US presidential election and Richard Nixon's campaign in particular. When you watch Konrad Mizzi, or even his boss, on TV or elsewhere, keep these words in mind (written about Nixon's campaign) (p.101):

> television is a powerful means of seducing voters to vote for images of candidates rather than the candidates themselves. Or, as one Nixon staffer put it: 'This is the beginning of a whole new concept... This is the way they'll be elected forevermore. The next guys up will have to be performers'.

Sex, Money, and Let's Not Rock the Boat

POLITICS IS A HARD, STRESSFUL OC-CUPATION AND MANY POLITICIANS ASK THEMSELVES WHY THEY ARE IN IT. Some say they want to change society and do something for the common good, the definition of "common good" obviously being as elastic as it is idiosyncratic.

Stress for a politician can be created by past actions, by problems at home, by the other side's dirty tricks, strong divergences of opinions with one's own side, and possibly the politician's own reaction to all this. Too much stress can be lethal, so caution is advised, as nothing is more precious than one's health.

Then, of course, there are those who are having the time of their life. Just consider Konrad Mizzi – despite everything, he still wants to contest the next elections.

Stop nodding at the Panama shenanigans
THERE IS SOMETHING EXTREMELY WRONG WITH MUSCAT'S GOVERN-MENT. It is more than rotten, but I cannot find *le mot juste* yet. We are not alone to have this feeling. At least two Ministers – Evarist Bartolo and Edward Scicluna – seem to be somewhat embarrassed by the shenanigans going on at the top lev-els of the country's administration. With Muscat's Chief of Staff and what could be Muscat's equivalent of Madame de Pompadour messing around with secret companies in secretive jurisdictions, big business, energy and all that, it is a mystery how only Ministers Bartolo and Scicluna seem embarrassed.

Worse still, Muscat's fluffiest Minister not only seems not to be embarrassed... he actually seems to be enjoying the ride. Now I know for a fact that Owen Bonnici can be finicky if he wants to. At the same time, he can also forget the woods completely and just look at the trees, or vice versa, he can ignore the trees while embracing the view of the woods. He is quite intellectually "versatile".

But in the Panama Shenanigans Saga, Minister Bonnici is being *too* intellectually versatile.

Not only did he not keep his distance from the two honorary Panamanians, but he also engaged – as a person of trust no less – the mastermind behind the entire imbroglio! Brain Tonna, of the infamous Nexia BT outfit, has been engaged, at €5,000 a month, as a person of trust by Minister Bonnici. Unbelievable. The fiasco (for a fiasco it is) was even a Reuter's news item. Appalling. One has to ask to what extent the web is tangled. And one has to ask whether

We the People are also comfortably numb, unable to realise the untold damage being done to the country's reputation.

But for the moment, perhaps Minister Bonnici should stop nodding at the shenanigans and start behaving with something sort of close to dignity, inspired by the likes of Ministers Bartolo and Scicluna.

As for these two Ministers, upright citizens expect more of them if they are to retain the thinking public's respect. They should voice their concern loudly not whisper their disapproval *sotto voce.*

Otherwise, unless they really start putting Malta first, we might begin to suspect that theirs could be nothing more than mere pretence and ostentation.

Liberal Fascism

MY FRIEND RANIER FSADNI RECENTLY MENTIONED THE COLLOQUIAL USE OF THE ADJECTIVE "FASCIST" BY 'SOME OF THE MUSCAT GOVERNMENT'S CRITICS'. I have often referred to Muscat's government as neo-liberal. I have actually devoted an entire chapter of my book *L-Aqwa fl-Ewropa* to analyse its beo-liberal character. I have often said that I think the current strain of Liberalism is Fascist. So, here goes my friendly comeback.

I think there are at least three ways of using the term "Fascist".

There's the first way, which is historical. I certainly do not mean that (to use an American expression) Prime Minister Muscat is following in the footsteps of Prime Minister Mussolini.

There's the second way, which is, as Mr Fsadni pointed out, colloquial. "Fascist" can be used as a term of abuse, a byword for "authoritarian", or even "conservative".

Let's borrow an example from popular culture: a scene from Carlo Verdone's 1980 comedy, *Un Sacco Bello* [*Fun is Beautiful*]. Mario voices his worry that his son is not thinking about having his own family, and, what's worse, he has found a girlfriend, Fiorenza, who is certainly not family material. Fiorenza retorts that she has already spat in her own father's face and warns Mario, "Be careful, *fascio* [Fascist], it would take me nothing!' To which Mario angrily replies, 'You're calling me *fascio*? Me? Listen here, little tart, I'm not a Communist like this [he raises his left fist] - I am a Communist like this!! [he raises both fists]'.[30]

That's the term of abuse, in its colloquial manifestation.

But then there is the third meaning, which is the meaning I have in mind and refers to the inherent

---

30   You can watch the scene here: https://www.youtube.com/watch?v=bH5HUexDmwM.

contradiction of intolerant liberalism. Just a few examples to illustrate my point, all of which you can describe as "Fascist", even if they take place in democracies.

Incredible as it may sound, a few days ago German kindergartens were given a brochure instructing assistants on how to identify girls coming from far-right families: they usually wear dresses and braids. The kindergarten assistants were told how to deal with the children's parents in order to avoid further diffusion of far-right ideas. One criticism to this approach was that it resembled too much the modus operandi of the Stasi, the secret police of the former East Germany (a Communist State) which used to spy on people. What the criticism meant was that the approach was "authoritarian".

But let us look at examples from "fiction". Equating the tendency toward law and order to "Fascism" is a theme which appeared in movies and novels up to some time ago.

Consider the beautiful 1970 movie *Investigation of a Citizen Above Suspicion*, a political satire on the authoritarian practices of the police force in a democratic State (Italy), including the morally distasteful practice of keeping records on all the homosexuals living in a city. Then consider Manuel Vázquez Montalbán's *noir* novels,

which he started writing in the 1970s about the Spanish detective Pepe Carvalho, a former CIA agent and former Communist, whose girlfriend is a prostitute in Barcelona. In one of these novels, we find the Dutch Police keeping files on everybody... in The Netherlands, of all places, the avant-garde personal freedom haven *par excellence*. Then consider Alan Parker's 1982 movie, *Pink Floyd: The Wall*, and the in-your-face use it makes of fascistoid imagery to criticise the education system and the pop music industry, both happening in Britain, the mother of liberal democracies.

Some nine years ago, I was thinking to myself that the Liberals had stopped being liberals, because you either had to agree with them or they would "excommunicate" you. What kind of liberal does not tolerate conservatives? I deduced that it had to be a Fascist Liberal. I went through this reasoning on a flight to London, and – in a classic example of synchronicity – when I landed in Luton, I found a book in the airport bookshop called... *Liberal Fascism*, by Jonah Goldberg.

It had been a *New York Times* bestseller the year before, clearly demonstrating that many people were feeling uneasy with what liberalism had morphed into. I bought a copy and decided to adopt many of Mr Goldberg's views on Fascism.

Law as a tool of cultural hegemony
UNLIKE THE ORIGINAL INCARNA-
TION, THE NEW FASCISM, THE LIB-
ERAL VARIANT, IS SOFT. It does not
gas or otherwise dispose of you in
a concentration camp. Nonetheless,
it is as intolerant as its predecessor.
Because it believes, yet again, that
the State is omnipotent and that it
should, softly this time not harshly, regulate as many aspects as possible of the life and thinking of its
citizens. Fascism is the elevation of
politics to the level of religion and
the attempt to make everybody
believe in and practise the tenets
of that religion. Just consider the
French law banning and punishing
attempts to dissuade women from
having abortions. How can this be
a liberal law? Abortion is a liberal
"achievement". But – and this is the
big contradiction – to conserve the
"achievement", the Liberals have
to adopt Fascist tactics and punish conservatives who dare openly
to disagree with the liberal stance
and act upon that disagreement. In
other words, *everybody* has to be
liberal. Or else they are punished
by the Liberals and the laws they
enact. Take the case of Malta's gender identity law. It punishes (both
a fine and imprisonment are con-
templated) not only 'conversion
practices' if applied to 'vulnerable
persons', but also the advertisement
of such practices. The definition
of 'vulnerable persons' is so wide
that it could include anybody. Everybody has to be liberal, because
the State has so decided. I think
that when everybody is obliged
not to rock the boat and to adhere
to the dominant ideology (or else
face criminal punishment), we can
safely talk of Fascism. In this case,
Liberal Fascism.

My Personal Library

Jonah Goldberg's *Liberal Fascism: The Secret History of the American Left, From Mussolini to the Politics of Change* (2007, 2009) should be on everybody's reading list.

It explains the premises on which much of the social aspect of the neo-liberal agenda is built, and which are usually left unsaid. In these times of "populism", when there are serious attempts to rock the boat because of the latest phase in the Sexual Revolution, immigration, and money matters, this book acquires even more relevance.

It might actually provide the key to interpret the reaction of the people to the excesses of the neo-liberal agenda.

A Christmas Present

TELEVISION MALTA RECENTLY BROADCAST A PROGRAMME ABOUT A ŻEBBUĠI WHO ALL THE ŻEBBUĠIN LOVE: LELI ZAMMIT, A 60-YEAR-OLD WHO HAS DOWN'S SYNDROME AND IS REALLY THE MOST LOVED PERSON IN ĦAŻ-ŻEBBUĠ. For many years, Mr Zammit used to visit my office on his way home. He would knock on the door and enter, say hello, hug me and shake the hands of all my clients, sometimes even hugging them. It was not the first time that this little ritual made arguing clients stop to find an amicable way forward. Mr Zammit's presence would work miracles. I think it brought people to their senses, opening their eyes to the meaning of life.

Society has developed away from organised religion. Then again, society has not – and can not – develop away from the need for meaning. To find meaning in life is a deep human need: a meaningless life is so heavy that it can – and has – crushed people. Christmas is one of those symbolic moments of meaning. The ideology behind Christmas is the ideology of a new beginning, a new direction in life. (The "Testament" as in Old and New Testament, can also mean the giving of direction.)

Why should this be important in this day and age, when ignorance and superstition have (supposedly) been consigned to the dustbin of history? The short answer is that these things are always important. The long answer is that, when you think about it – and as funny or disrespectful as it may sound – many people live like caged hamsters. They run about their little cage, dash up and down the different plastic levels, sprint in the wheel – and it all adds up to a lot of activity and very little sense of achievement. Mostly, I would say, this is because of the economic model we inhabit, in which the processes of industrial production have been divided into small, almost meaningless, tasks which rob the work of any kind of dignity and direction.

In an agricultural setting, the farmer participates in the production of produce from beginning to end – from sowing to reaping – and has long resting periods in-between that he can use for recreation. In the industrialised world, on the other hand, the "salaried slave"– the factory or office worker, that is – participates in small, specialised tasks which to him appear disconnected from the rest and allow him little satisfaction and only brief spells of recreation.

Short of a full-blown revolution – which I am not advocating – there is really little scope for inner personal advancement. (Much of the current buy-to-rent frenzy is a symptom of this search for meaning. Once the chimera is understood for what it really is, the depression will be felt far and wide.) Of course, one can join the rat race, but there is no guarantee of success in terms of inner personal achievement and advancement. The spiritual path, on the other hand, offers a guarantee of achievement, because the journey is interior. Like all journeys, it offers a destination, and working one's way towards that destination can be a source of profound satisfaction.

Then again, reaching the destination, as Robert Browning tells us in his poem *Childe Roland to the Dark Tower Came* (1855), might not necessarily bring much joy. It's the journey itself which brings satisfaction.

Cut from the past

THE MAIN IDEOLOGICAL POINT BEHIND CHRISTMAS IS A CLEAN CUT FROM THE PAST. Christmas has, however, been hijacked by capitalism and its promise of instant happiness upon receiving presents. This consumerist ideology has been embodied in the figure of an overweight old man wearing a white beard and driving a reindeer-pulled sleigh while drinking a carbonated soft drink with past connections to cocaine! Somewhere I read that this figure could actually have come from Arctic folklore: people would spend the desolate wintry months holed up at home eating hallucinogenic mushrooms thrown down their chimneys by shamans dressed up as Amanita mushrooms (red clothes with white dots)!

That said, we could view the giving of presents as the celebration of the process of cutting off one's future from one's past. In other words, the future need not be a continuation of the past; it can be a "new" future, a new way of doing things with a more refined sense of ethics and duty. The spiritual journey, unlike the drab journey in the material world, can bring satisfaction because of a sense of achievement. The psychologist Carl Jung described Christ as the 'archetypal Man', the ideal to which we should aspire to emulate. In *Psychology and Religion*, Jung says: 'The drama of the archetypal life of Christ describes in symbolic images the events of the conscious life of a man who has been transformed by his higher destiny.' Transformation is fundamental to a meaningful life, a life that seeks a higher destiny.

More directly relevant to Christmas, in his *Collected Works* we find Jung saying that 'the individual ego is the stable in which the Christ-child is born'.

Overcoming one's selfishness and being of service to others

THE ECONOMIC MODEL IN WHICH WE LIVE – WITH ITS HIGH-RISE BUSINESS-TOWER CATHEDRALS AND ITS SHOPPING-CENTRE PARISHES – DOES NOT PROMOTE THE CHRISTIAN IDEAL. Instead, it insistently puts forward the religion of making more and more money, even at the expense of human dignity, ties and feelings. There are many reactions to this spiritual sterility. Some people hold the radical view that one should not bring children into this corrupted and wretched world. Crazy as it may sound, there are countries that even allow the legal action of wrongful birth. Others react by resorting to the age-old axiom that if you can't beat them, join them. They thus conclude that they should give free rein to their greedy desires. After all, since desire can never really be satisfied, these people will always be busy, like happy hamsters running on their ridged wheel, a bit like Sisyphus who was forced to roll an enormous boulder up a hill, only for it to roll down when it nears the top, and having to repeat this action forever. Until one day, that is, when *bumm bumm il-bieb!* ... Death knocks on your door. After a life spent meaninglessly, running (hamster-like) after material gain, your time is suddenly up.

Christmas, with its break-with-the-past ideology, is a yearly wake-up call to start afresh and take off on a journey through the inner world of one's spirit, the destination of which is a Better You.

Christmas commodification

THE ONE INTERVIEW WITH JOSEPH MUSCAT AND HIS FAMILY OF A COUPLE OF WEEKS AGO APPEARED VERY CLEARLY TO HAVE BEEN A PROPAGANDA EXERCISE. But it was the brazen-faced exploitation of the two daughters which I found ethically objectionable. The two daughters are not dauphines, they are not heiresses to a throne. They are not child prodigies either. They are two sweet children like many others, endowed with nice personalities and the innocence of childhood, but children to whom is being imparted a warped vision of the world and their place in it, and this is ethically objectionable. I wonder what the private thoughts of the Commissioner for Children are about this glaring example of child commodification. The image Muscat tried to portray of himself reminds me of Napoleon's propaganda strategy to portray himself as the heir to Charlemagne and Hannibal, and the redeemer of the French. We might now expect a series of David-like photos depicting Joseph Muscat riding on Cyrus Engerer's back, intent on crossing the Conservative Bigotry Alps to free the peoples who live beyond the mountains, with his finger raised toward the sky in the gesture typical of he who believes, acts and wins. Muscat's first ride, however, was not on Mr Engerer's back but on that of Joseph Cuschieri. Every Christmas I think of Mr Cuschieri, the sacrifice he was made to make, and the reward he was given. In 2008, Mr Cuschieri was made to give up his seat in the House to make way for Muscat's co-option. There is a lot that could be said about the pressure exerted on Mr Cuschieri and the great disappointment through which he later had to go, which apparently even manifested itself psychosomatically (shingles, mostly). It is an important indicator of Muscat's cheeky personality that he rewarded Mr Cuschieri by appointing him to an official role in Greece. I can imagine Mr Cuschieri's daily woes having to deal with everything in the Greek alphabet. Literally everything, but everything everything, is Greek to him now. Christmas is the time to be nice and kind to one's neighbour. Perhaps with Mr Cuschieri, Muscat had to be nice and kind all year round. You gauge the moral intrinsic value of a man by the way he treats his friends and his enemies. It seems difficult to classify Mr Cuschieri: he seems to be neither Muscat's friend nor his foe. He too rather seems to have been commodified.

My Personal Library

Frances Hodgson Burnett's *Little Lord Fauntleroy* (1885) is a children's novel (and a much-beloved 1980 Christmas movie starring Alec Guinness, Connie Booth and Ricky Scroder) which forcefully but delicately drives home the message that it's never too late to experience the Christmas changeover. (Spoiler alert.) An old English Earl's son marries a commoner, an American to boot, whom the Earl never accepts on account of her social class. When the Earl's son dies, the widow and her son move to England. Ultimately, the grandson's love and innocence win over the grandfather, and the old man's heart melts, accepting his daughter-in-law and even taking an interest in his hitherto-ignored tenants' lives and economic predicament. Even though he is old, and old habits die hard, the Earl breaks with the past and embraces a new future.

Women's Year?

As the end of the year approaches, some friends have asked me why I keep writing, in this idealist-like fashion, and whether one of my New Year's Resolutions will be to stop. When all is said and done, they argued, all that people care about is *boqxiex*. In its English version, *baksheesh* means a tip; in Maltese, *boqxiex* means much, much more...

I can only quote the Slovene philosopher Slavoj Žižek in reply to the cynics:

> The position of the cynic is that he alone holds some piece of terrible, unvarnished wisdom. The paradigmatic cynic tells you privately, in a confidential low-key voice: 'But don't you get it that it is all really about (money/power/sex), that all high principles and values are just empty phrases which count for nothing?' What the cynics don't see is their own naïvety, the naïvety of their cynical wisdom that ignores the power of illusions.

Žižek clearly refers to Don-Quixote-like illusions. And he is obviously right. He is repeating what others have held before him, that ideals – or "illusions" – are powerful. They are meaningful signposts in the everyday life of people. Then again, "illusions" – ideals, ideology – are also powerful tools for those who wield power. This type is the Sancho-Panza-like illusion, which does not look up to ideals but down to instincts.

Feminism – which is clearly an "illusion" in this sense – can be of the two types: idealist and instinctual. It can also be a potent tool in the hands of the powerful. Just look at the first ideological "reform" Prime Minister Muscat wants to carry out in 2019, at least if we are to take him at his word (I'm referring to his statements made during the customary yearly exchange of wishes with the President). He intends to introduce gender quotas in Parliament.

But the illusion goes further. Ideological pressure is mounting to introduce the ultimate Women's Right: abortion. 2019 might indeed, though for the wrong reasons, turn out to be Women's Year.

Feminism

2018 has witnessed a renewed effort, by a minuscule albeit vociferous minority, to push forward the radical feminist agenda. Historically speaking, there have been different waves of feminism. I prefer to look at feminism in its radical and moderate forms. (I have recently bought, but not yet read, an Oxford University Press publication called, *Satanic*

Feminism: Lucifer as the Liberator of Woman in Nineteenth-Century Culture (2017).)

I think that in reality we are all moderate feminists. In the sense that it offends our sense of equity and reasonableness that women be treated as inferior to men. I am a staunch believer in equality, and have a very critical opinion of those chauvinists who believe that gender should imply less opportunities for personal development or different compensation for the same work, say. But this does not mean that we are radical feminists who want artificially to create equality where biology dictates that there can be none. Let us briefly analyse from three different angles the women's rights landscape in Malta.

First Angle: The Gender Pay Gap
JOSEPH MUSCAT'S GOVERNMENT FLIES THE FLAG FOR A VAGUE SORT OF FEMINISM. Using the 'Most Feminist Government' mantra, the Muscat administration has tried – once again – to be everything to everyone. Radical feminist to the radicals, moderate feminist to the moderates. Essentially, the 'Progressives and Moderates' rhetoric rehashed.

If we look at the statistics, we find that the Muscat administration has grandiosely failed on the gender pay gap. The latest Eurostat statistics I could find, published in the 2018 *Report on Equality between Men and Women in the EU* but covering up to 2016, contain an incontrovertible trend which gives the lie to Muscat's 'Most Feminist Government' pretence. The gender pay gap in Malta has actually increased under the Muscat administration, by 3.3%! The difference in remuneration between men and women was 7.7% under the Nationalists in 2011, but it rose to 10.4% in 2015 and 11% in 2016! There can be no doubt that the Muscat administration has failed to deliver on the moderate feminist front. Not only did it fail to reduce the gender pay gap; the gap actually increased. The administration is thus turning to the radical feminist agenda, enlisting a motley crew of friends and useful idiots.

Second Angle:
The Patriarchy Fantasy
PATRIARCHY IS THE IDEA THAT THE MAN IS *PADRE PADRONE*, FATHER AND MASTER (OR TYRANT). *Padre Padrone* is actually the name of a 1975 Italian novel, written by the Sardinian author Gavino Ledda and translated into 40 languages. It tells the story of a young shepherd who lives under the yoke of his father's authoritarianism, but manages to emancipate himself through education. It is a mainstay of progressive pedagogy.

The idea that the father/man is master, which has a remarkably long history, has now been appropriated by the radical feminists who claim that since the man does not own the woman's body but she owns it, she is entitled to terminate the life of the child produced with that man. The premises of this argument obviously ignore the inherent and implied aleatory contract that exists between two adults who engage in carnal relations: that the engagement can result in the creation of new life. Instead, it revoltingly adopts a property-based discourse which can be debunked by psychology, rather than philosophy.

However, one of the big mistakes committed by the radical feminists is to assume that all human societies are the same. In his *L'origine des systèmes familiaux* (2011), Emmanuel Todd has demonstrated that there are at least 15 different types of family systems in Eurasia, some of which consider the father as the source of power, others the mother, and a few others still that are based on equality. To state that there is a universal patriarchal model of exploitation of women is pure fantasy. Even to claim that patriarchy still exists today is bordering on fantasy.

There was patriarchy in the past, yes. Just consider the *ancien régime* system in France when fathers interfered in their daughters' choice of husband. People my age will remember the Japanese manga *The Rose of Versailles* (also called *Lady Oscar*) set in France in the period of the Revolution. It is the fictional story of a General who desperately wants a son and imposes on his last-born daughter to grow up as one. When the girl, Oscar, grows up, the turbulence of the Revolution (the most potent symbol of which is the beheading of the King-Father) and the turbulence of falling in love with her servant and best friend André, make her blossom into the rose she really is.

Yes, there was patriarchy in the past. The Roman Church opposed it vehemently – the Church authorities in Rome even urged French priests to celebrate clandestine marriages to avoid women marrying against their wishes. The rationale was that Mary gave her consent to become the Holy Mother; similarly, the consent of women was absolutely necessary for the validity of a marriage.

But the patriarchy of the past has now all but disappeared, except – ironically enough – in the former Communist countries where, according to the Eurostat statistics I quoted above, the perception is still prevalent of women as servants of men. Here, however, I must insert a word of caution, as the West has often misrepresented the 'liminally exotic' women of the East. A book which I have found to make interesting reading on this topic is *Vampirettes, Wretches and Amazons: Western Representations of East European Women* (2004), edited by Valentina Glajar and Domnica Radulescu.

Third Angle: Respect is to be Won not Extorted

A BIG MISTAKE MUSCAT'S ADMINISTRATION INTENDS TO COMMIT IN 2019 WILL BE THE IMPOSITION OF GENDER QUOTAS IN PARLIAMENT. This is obviously myopic. Under the present system, women are neither prevented nor discouraged from contesting elections, and women are increasingly succeeding in getting elected. Why not leave well alone?

Of course, if you don't believe in the free vote but in Whip power, you don't really need talent, just numbers. If, on the other hand, you want talent, then the system as it is allows women (as much as men) to contest elections. Why not have the best (wo)man win? Why concoct an alternative system that could permit the less talented to take the place of the more talented simply on the basis of gender? In the long run, positive discrimination is in the interests of neither women nor society in general. A real feminist – be s/he moderate or radical – is necessarily against positive discrimination.

If a woman gets elected under her own steam, she will be respected. If a woman gets a seat in Parliament because there's a quota to meet, she might be the most intelligent person on earth, but she will never really win anybody's sincere respect. The myth will be perpetuated that, at least in politics, women can make it only if given a hand. Respect, like love, can only be won, never extorted.

Having failed on the gender pay gap issue, the Muscat administration has to play these two cards: gender quotas and abortion. It has to kowtow to certain lobbies for political survival.

My Personal Library

An unintended consequence of the success of feminism has been the creation of a huge generation of aging frat boys, men who have been freed from the old tests of manhood, such as the ability to marry and provide for a woman and children. That's how author Caitlin Flanagan described the principal message of an interesting book called *Manning Up: How the Rise of Women Has Turned Men into Boys* (2011), by Kay S. Hymowitz.

How Joseph Rules Malta[31]

A COUPLE OF YEARS BACK, I VIS-
ITED BELARUS, THE ONLY EURO-
PEAN NATION-STATE WHICH DOES
NOT FORM PART OF THE COUNCIL
OF EUROPE. I sat down in a café in
downtown Minsk and somehow
ended up discussing politics with a
chap. He assured me that they are
a democratic country and, needless
to say, I was immensely intrigued
by this bold statement.

'Of course!', he lectured me. 'If
our Government raises the price of
something, people will take to the
streets and angrily air their views.
Our President will duly take note
and he will hurry to organise a
mass meeting to reassure the people that they have been heard and
that they are right. How on earth
did the price rise when he never
gave the order? The Minister surely
misunderstood, and he, the President, will right this obvious wrong.
Everything will be back to normal.
Now isn't that democracy?'

I smiled. But then last Sunday,
I listened to Prime Minister Muscat's sermon and I heard him talk
about the thoughts that cross his
mind while he's driven round the
streets of Malta. Joseph Muscat told
his congregation that sometimes he

---

31   The title of this essay is a
reference to Dom Mintoff's short
pamphlet *How Britain Rules Malta*.

is appalled to see high-rise buildings in streets otherwise characterised by two-storey buildings. He
seemed to indicate that he will look
into it, that he will right this obvious wrong. Then I remembered
my Belarus friend's description of
politics in his country. Even they
think they live in a functioning democracy. Even they think that it's a
functioning democracy when the
country's top man needs personally
to see things going astray to then
personally take an interest to set
matters right. They cannot conceive
of a self-regulating system that is
governed by laws not by men. Belgium survived for 589 days without
an elected government in 2010-11.
That's five hundred and eighty-nine
days. But then, perhaps, Belgium is
not a personal "democratic" fief.

The Women Behind the Man?

WHO ARE THE IDEOLOGUES OF
MUSCAT'S GOVERNMENT? Eddie
Fenech Adami had Peter Serracino
Inglott and others; we also know
about Lawrence Gonzi and Alfred
Sant. It was always the case that we
knew who more or less advised the
incumbent at Castille on "ideology". But – and I do stand to be corrected – it seems to me that we are
not similarly aware of who advises
Joseph Muscat.

In normal democracies, the
identity of the intellectuals close to

the top people is known to the public and is thus open to fair and legitimate scrutiny. For instance, when last summer the French newspaper *Le Figaro* interviewed philosopher Diego Fusaro, it introduced him as an ideological adviser to Italian Deputy Prime Minister Luigi di Maio and Matteo Salvini (*'l'homme qui murmure à l'oreille de Di Maio et Salvini'*). But what about Malta?

Consider when Prime Minister Muscat infamously changed his mind on gay adoption. If I have to be frank, I do not believe his story. It was obvious from day one that once he legislated gay marriage, he had no choice but to legislate gay adoption – otherwise there would have been a glaring case of discrimination. But do you remember his narrative? Since he had publicly expressed his opposition to gay adoption prior to the elections and then had to make a U-turn to honour what were probably pre-electoral pledges made to a particular lobby, he justified his volte-face by claiming that he read one book and changed his mind!

One book? How's that for a serious approach to ideological matters? One book and down the hole we fall...? What was it, a momentary lapse of reason? How can such important decisions be taken on the strength of one book? What book was it, anyway? Joseph Mus-

My "Personal" Library

While rummaging through my father's library, I chanced on the very first issue of an AŻAD publication, *Perspektiv*, published in October 1977. There's a beautiful four-page article by the late Dr Joseph (Peppinu) Cassar, called 'The Catholic Left in Malta' (pages 22-26). Let me quote one snippet:

> Many of those who still organise crusades against Communism are not aware how disgusting is a system which considers profit as the essential factor of progress, competition as the supreme law in the economic sphere, private ownership of the means of production as an absolute right without corresponding limits and social obligations. Yet all this is what is meant by Capitalism... The Christian has the duty to work for peace and for the destruction of barriers which keep the human race apart. Instead of spending billions of dollars to build their armouries to be able to destroy each other, nations should work hand in hand to destroy the misery which afflicts a large part of the world. This is not utopian fantasy. It is an ideal for which every Christian must strive... against hunger, injustice and oppression. Solidarity and fraternity should be the ideals to go by.

cat has been governing this country for almost six years, and we (or at least I) don't know for sure who his ideologues are. If you know, please let me know.

What Happened on St Valentine's Day

THE ORCHESTRATED ATTACK ON THE COUNTRY'S SOCIAL FABRIC WHICH TOOK PLACE ON ST VALENTINE'S DAY 2019 NEEDS TO BE PROPERLY ANALYSED. It was a disgusting act by *Malta Today* when it published an unsavoury piece of news on the day dedicated to 'love'. Let us be frank, St Valentine's is one big pseudo-feast meant to boost sales. That said, it is still a nice feast – in the sense that it is nice that your Loved One spends some money to remind you that you are his or her Special Person in the World.

That Matthew Vella, of *Malta Today*, saw it fit to pollute such a day with a news item promoting abortion services speaks volumes. Let us follow how the story unfolded, to analyse the underlying narrative.

February the 14th
BEFORE 0800 HOURS ON FEBRUARY THE 14TH, MATTHEW VELLA PUBLISHES THE INFAMOUS ARTICLE, INFORMING MALTESE CITIZENS THAT THERE IS A "CHARITY" SOMEWHERE OFFERING ABORTION SERVICES. Now, this in itself is pointless overkill. If it is true that there are some 400 Malta-resident women who obtain abortions abroad, why on earth is this charity needed? Are

there women who, in these days of low-cost air travel, cannot afford a trip to wherever? It all smacks of rotten ideology more than anything else does.

Peter Singer, the most dangerous philosopher in the world today
THERE IS AN AUSTRALIAN, A PETER SINGER, WHO *THE GUARDIAN*, IN A 1999 ARTICLE, DESCRIBED AS 'A PHILOSOPHER WHO EATS NO MEAT OR DAIRY AND THINKS WE'RE NO BETTER THAN ANIMALS. In fact, he thinks a chimp has more right to exist than a person, and that killing babies can be justified'.

Peter Singer's books are the vegetarian and vegan gospels. Many of the arguments you will hear from vegetarians – whether they know it or not – come directly from Peter Singer's pen. This Peter Singer is not only in favour of abortion (that is, pre-birth killing) but has even proposed a 28-day period in which parents can decide to kill their newborn babies (that is, post-birth killing).

In his book *Practical Ethics*, Peter Singer argues that: 'Human babies are not born self-aware, or capable of grasping that they exist over time. They are not persons.' But animals are self-aware, and therefore, 'the life of a newborn is of less value than the life of a pig, a dog, or a chimpanzee'.

February the Fifteenth
AND BANG ON CUE, ON FEBRUARY 15 THE SAME *MALTA TODAY* PUBLISHES AN ARTICLE ACCOMPANIED BY A VIDEO-CLIP OF AN ANIMAL-RIGHTS ACTIVIST WHO STOPS A LORRY CARRYING PIGS ON ITS WAY TO THE SLAUGHTERHOUSE, AND, CALLING THE PINK ANIMALS 'MY BABIES!', APPEALS TO VIEWERS TO ABSTAIN FROM EATING MEAT. The coincidence is too striking not to attract our attention. This is very clearly a Peter-Singer-inspired narrative. The article, called 'Animal activists "apologise" to pigs on their way to slaughter at Marsa abattoir', was about at least one animal-rights activist from a group called Animal Liberation Malta. Now, guess what one of Peter Singer's books is called? Yes, you guessed right: *Animal Liberation*!

The connection could not be clearer.

On February 14, we get the abortion services advertorial. On February 15, we get the Pigs 'My babies!' video-clip and article on the "philosophy" of animal liberation. Clearly, *Malta Today*'s editorial line seems to be that pigs have more rights than human babies.

Meat eating
AS FAR AS I AM CONCERNED, YOU CAN EAT WHATEVER YOU LIKE. I subscribe to the most liberal school

My Personal Library

The fiery, unique, kind-hearted, extraordinary Giuseppe Mifsud Bonnici, affectionately known as Ġoġò, former Chief Justice, former judge of the Strasbourg Court, a former chess champion, former professor of Philosophy of Law who sealed my views on abortion with a robust lecture way back in 1992, passed away this week. He was 88 years old.

When I met him for the very first time, I was, like almost all the other law students, 18 years old. He immediately struck me, for his vibrant intelligence, acute sense of irony, and idealism. It was his idealism which captured my imagination. I quickly made up my mind that one day I would write a book with him. Sixteen years later, in 2008, I did.

He chose the title, *Il-Liġi, il-Morali u r-Raġuni* [Law, Morality and Reason]. Except for one chapter (called 'Quorum pars minuscola fui', which he had already given me as a text), that book was the fruit of a long series of interviews I recorded with him hebdomadally. I used to go every Friday afternoon, armed with a little walkman. He would welcome me, with a huge dose of irony, as the *ritarda-tarju* [the late-comer], because each time I would be late. And we would laugh heartily, because his criticism was not mean, and there's not much I can do about my time management disability.

When the book was published, somebody told me I had been courageous because Professor Mifsud Bonnici was the irascible type. That description was partially true, but during all those hours spent with him I discovered a man who was not only extremely intelligent but also kind-hearted and deeply spiritual. While transcribing one of the interviews, it dawned on me that he spoke as though he sung. There was an inherent musicality in his way of talking. It wasn't just the baritone voice, but the delivery. It was musical – and I told him as much. He confided that he had inherited the timbre from an ancestor.

He once showed me his extensive collection of books – it is a bibliophile's dream come true. He used to read religiously the philosopher Alasdair MacIntyre, walk on his treadmill, and play chess, every single day. Once I needed to talk to him, and his wife told me he was hearing Mass at the church nearby. I went there and found him in the front row, alternately nodding, and disagreeing with the preacher. He was extraordinary. I simply loved him. During my father's funeral, he sat by my side. It was a small but most meaningful gesture.

In those interviews we covered all the topics which are now the political earthquake being delivered, with or without an electoral mandate, by Joseph Muscat: abortion, euthanasia, homosexual marriage, divorce... It was a real *tour de force* by a seasoned thinker.

as a mathematical problem severed from life and from his personal existence. No serious person can discuss problems of philosophy of law without feeling personally engaged in what he is arguing.

The parting shot in that little book of ours was a powerful statement by Peter Serracino Inglott. He outlined the great contemporary battle between the ultra- (or neo-)liberals and the traditionalists. We had twice gone to dinner, in Valletta, PSI, GMB and I, before PSI dictated that essay to me in his room at the Dar tal-Kleru in Fleur-de-Lys. Someday I will write about those two extraordinary conversations between two Catholics: an old-school liberal and a traditionalist conservative.

In that essay, PSI wrote:

[F]or Professor Mifsud Bonnici, Philosophy of Law is not some abstract subject that can be treated

Professor Mifsud Bonnici's book is a continuous argument against that sort of schizophrenia leading to behaviour which disagrees with one's beliefs.

Many people should actually ask themselves whether partisan allegiance and the chimera of personal gain disconnect them from their real values.I will sorely miss Giuseppe Mifsud Bonnici.

The last email from him was on December 24. He extended his wishes for the festive season.

His name is now added to the growing list of people I will never be able to talk to again.

In the photo: the Author and the late Giuseppe Mifsud Bonnici, Valletta 2008.

of thought where food is concerned. At the same time, yes, I do have many moral problems with the industrial process that treats animals as if they were not sentient. Animals feel pain and pleasure, and I have considerable moral qualms about the cruelty inflicted on them, not exactly at the slaughter phase but during their short and miserable lives on industrial farms. I must admit I have agonised at the supermarket wondering to myself why an animal should be brought into the world to spend a short, miserable life to then end up on my plate. I now buy the free-range product. That does not mean I will give up eating meat. (Even though I did give up eating beef and did reduce my intake of milk drastically because of the cruelty inflicted on animals in intensive animal farming.) But I am hoping against hope that moderate animal-rights activists will succeed in changing agribusinesses. We need the humane treatment of animals reared for human consumption.

A Footnote: The Green Party
Interestingly, Peter Singer was a Green Party candidate in the 1996 Australian elections. Again, *Malta Today* has followed the Peter-Singer-inspired narrative to the hilt. Salvu Balzan attacked anti-abortion former Green Party chairperson Arnold Cassola while breaking a lance in favour of the new Green Party Ewok-look-alike starlet, who coyly wants us to discuss abortion. This coy wish to have a "mature" debate on a taboo practice is the usual strategy used by those who want to introduce the taboo practice in the country. Let us not be fooled. (For the benefit of the PC-Brigade, when I say Ewok-look-alike I am referring to the hairstyle and spectacles.)

However, the attack on Professor Cassola – who resigned from his own party on the abortion issue – was unwarranted and despicable. No, Salvu Balzan. Professor Cassola is right, and the Ewok-look-alike starlet is wrong.

To understand the Ewok-look-alike starlet's way of seeing the world, she wants to be called "they". Yes, you read correctly. She wants to be referred to as *they* – at least this is what she/they said a couple of years ago during some youth event in Ottawa, Canada.

The dictatorship of the headline
Clearly, *Malta Today* thinks that it is fine to play politics while pretending to do journalism. I do not share this view. Journalists should not play politics; they should comment on politics. If a journalist wants to change the laws, he or she should contest

136

the elections and give the people a chance to express an opinion. A journalist who uses the newspaper he or she works for to promote a political agenda, going beyond analysis and commentary, is abusing the democratic system. Because in the democratic system, you give the last word to the people, who are the true sovereign. When a journalist plays the game I am referring to, the journalist bypasses and debases the sovereignty of the people, and imposes his or her own sovereignty on them. It becomes the Dictatorship of the Headline, and replaces democratic debate with propaganda.

The role of Joseph Muscat
IT IS NO SECRET THAT *MALTA TODAY* IS A STAUNCH SUPPORTER OF MUSCAT'S GOVERNMENT, WHICH IS WHY ONE FEELS SAFE TO ASSUME THAT THERE IS MUSCAT'S TACIT BLESSING TO THIS ENTIRE CHARADE. Indeed, offering abortion services to Maltese citizens when abortion is a crime in Malta, is a direct attack on the sovereignty of the country. Just like the government sent a *note verbale* to the UK on the Cambridge Analytica issue, it should also have sent a *note verbale* on the provision of services meant to make a fool of Maltese law. The only possible conclusion is that Muscat's government has acquiesced to the charade be-

cause it agrees with the provision of those services.

All said and done, it has found a crafty way of introducing abortion in the country without actually changing the laws.

This is a new record in political dishonesty.

Abortion:
Big money, useful idiots

WHENEVER A NEW INITIATIVE CROPS UP, YOU HAVE TO ASK, "*CUI BONO?*" ("WHO BENEFITS BY IT?"). Often, the supposed beneficiary is not the one being pushed forward, but somebody else who lurks in the background.

The new initiative – which Media Today's Salvu Balzan seems quite excited about – is, sadly and stupidly, abortion. Mr Balzan wrote: 'This is the beginning of a long campaign, but it is bound to endure a lot of bumpy rides and it will not be an easy campaign.' Just so that we know who the actors in this macabre play are, these are the words of someone who, despite all the attempts at hide-and-seek, gives the impression that deep down he is all out for abortion.

Mr Balzan was referring to a group of miniscule associations that have banded together to promote "women's rights". For once, Mr Balzan (whom I deeply dislike – it is reciprocated, don't you worry) expressed a thought I can easily and completely share: 'There is little doubt that the Muscat administration's progressive reforms in gay rights, gay conversion and civil unions have galvanised these women campaigners to come forward.'

Yes, all said and done, Joseph Muscat will have to foot the historical bill for the pro-abortion climate that has come to this country. The moral fibre of the country has been ruined. And, like a naughty boy who has eaten all the cookies in the jar, Muscat even seems proud of this great achievement – *L-aqwa żmien* and all that. But let's not jump the gun. Let's walk-through the analysis of the present situation.

Only fools would rush in

THIS GROUP OF VOCIFEROUS ASSOCIATIONS, WHICH REPRESENT A MINORITY OF VOTERS, AIMS TO CONVINCE THE ELECTORATE THAT THE COUNTRY NEEDS ABORTION. This when Eurostat figures for 2017 show that while France had the highest fertility rate in the EU, Malta had the absolute lowest. And these associations claim - inspired by a warped logic - that Malta needs abortion.

They also claim that the beneficiaries will be women, who can now have complete control of their bodies. One would have thought that abstinence, contraceptives, the natural method, self-control, and so on, were all different aspects of having complete control over one's body. That women who willingly engage in the sexual act and are not careful, and only when they realise they are pregnant want complete control of their bodies seems to me to be putting the cart before the horse. (*Lovin Malta* will consider this piece of advice as patronising. No kidding.)

The horse is a good metaphor. Do you remember the Greek mythological figure, the Centaur, half-human, half-horse? The Centaur's upper part is human; the Centaur's lower part is equine. The Greeks had a very clear message in mind: our human part (reason) should control our animal part (sexual instincts). We are not slaves to our animal instincts.

But, these pro-abortion campaigners will tell you, 'What about rape?' This seems to be the crucial question for these associations. Rape. A respected gynaecologist has argued that the number of rapes in Malta is inflated. This has enraged the pro-abortion campaigners whose response was that some women are raped by their partners, who want to impregnate them in order to subjugate them.

This is dangerous ground. The argument seems to be that the couple do not agree on whether to conceive a child, and the man decides to do it without the woman's prior consent not because he wants a child but because he wants to tame the shrew that is his wife/partner. What a price to pay to stay in a relationship with a headstrong, obdurate woman!

And how exactly do you put a woman in her place by making her pregnant? I remember reading a 2010 study which said that neurotic women are more fertile and have more babies than their laid-back female counterparts, but I wonder whether this is what the associations have in mind. Then again, if the woman has no intention of conceiving a child, why not teach her to use contraceptives or the natural method, or better still, use her brains and abstain from intercourse, or simply leave a man she clearly doesn't love (enough)? Why allow her to depend on the man's behaviour if there are doubts, only then to offer her abortion? Moreover, who assures us that this is not the woman's paranoia or the man's bragging about subjugating his partner? How can that be verified? It could just be nothing more than bragging to hide the shame of not having behaved in a manly fashion and exercised self-control. This type of analysis is very close to what the Italians refer to as *fare il processo alle intenzioni*, that is to say trying to discover people's motivations by reading their minds.

This is all so volatile and whimsical and not only. This is actually an invitation to open the door to abortion-on-demand because all women can argue that they have been raped. How to determine whether the couple really wants a child or whether the man "raped" her to conceive a child in order to subjugate her to his "patriarchal power"? Should they stipulate a specific contract, renewable every six months?

Mad (mind you, not madcap) liberalism opens many a can of worms; it is a labyrinth where the individual is lost in freedom and ends up devoured by the Minotaur of egotism. So far, it is all very subjective. Let's move to the objective questions we should be asking ourselves about the big money involved in the abortion industry. Where is this big money? Let's consider at least two aspects of the industry. The provision of the service and the sale of the resulting product. If one abortion costs, say, €1,000 and there are 400 abortions a year, that's €400,000 a year for the provision of the service. Who will pocket this money if it is provided by the private sector? Or, if it is provided by the public sector, why should we spend this money when the country's birth rate is so low? With regard to the sale of the resulting product, consider that in 2014 in the United States, the National Institute of Health spent $76 million on research using foetal tissue, that is, pieces of aborted babies. Foetal tissue is not used only for medical research. It can also be used in other industries, such as the soft drink industry. Check whether your soft drink contains HEK 293. HEK stands for 'Human Embryonic Kidney' cells. The flavour in your soft drink might have been obtained from chemicals from the cells of a healthy foetus legally aborted in The Netherlands. There is big money involved in the abortion industry.

Useful idiots

ARE THE CAMPAIGNERS WE ARE SEEING ON TV AND ON NEWSPAPER PHOTOGRAPHS ON ANYBODY'S SECRET PAYROLL? Are newspapers and news portals indirectly promoting the pro-abortion agenda being secretly funded? I would not know. It might also be the case that they are "useful idiots", that is people who believe the ideology and are ready to campaign for it without understanding, or ignoring the fact, that behind the ideology there is big money.

How big is this big money?

WE LIVE IN TIMES THAT CERTAIN THINKERS REFER TO AS "LATE CAPITALISM". There is big money behind many of the battle cries of the extreme liberalism of Late Capitalism. The cannabis market in Canada – the world leader in that market – is worth C$16 billion. Worldwide, pornography rakes in more or less

US$97 billion. The extent of the LGBT market in the US is estimated at $884 billion, and £6 billion in the UK. A study has calculated that doctor-assisted suicide (euthanasia) could save Canada up to C$139 million each year in end-of-life care. In 2016, the global market for assisted reproductive technology (ART) was worth US$2,210 million. With an estimated growth rate of 6.3 per cent *per annum* between 2017 and 2025, the expected worth in 2024 is US$3,779 million.

The conservative alternative

THE CONSERVATIVE IS OPPOSED TO THESE EXTREME LIBERAL "ACHIEVEMENTS". The Conservative believes that unborn children should not be killed and the dying should be taken care of. The Conservative is very sceptical about pornography, cannabis, and ART, and has many reservations with regard to same-sex marriage and child adoption.

There is clearly no money in the conservative vision, because, all told, it is essentially an anti-business stance. And if there is no business objective to pursue (this type of business I mean, not traditional business), there is no money to be made.Conservatives are usually pro-democracy. More than the extreme Liberals, who tend to get angry with them, and try to delegitimise the Conservatives.

It might be that that day will soon dawn when Late Capitalism will not require democracy any longer, and the extreme Liberals will simply take over. They will enforce the ideology that if your wife or girlfriend wants to terminate your baby, it's fine. Or if you don't feel like becoming a mother, its fine as well: it's your life, your body, your choice.

Thank you Joseph, for creating this climate. You even admitted lately, to *Politico*, that your 'recipe to get into power, and stay there, is to embrace ... capitalism'. By which you mean this Late Capitalism and its sleazy partner, Extreme Liberalism.

Bottom line

THE THING WITH ABORTION, AS WITH ALMOST EVERYTHING ELSE LIBERAL, IS THAT IF ONLY A FEW DO IT, IT'S A FACT OF LIFE AND YOU DON'T FRET ABOUT IT. But if it is normalised – like the NHS in Britain tries to do, for reasons which I cannot completely understand, by stating that almost one in every three British woman have had an abortion (why?) – then it becomes problematic. Theft happens all the time, but it has not been normalised. Private property is still considered "sacred". Once normalisation sets in, then problems begin. Mostly for one's serenity of mind.

Because once the "morality" (*mores*) changes, then the social order (*ordo*) changes too. And, as Slavoj Žižek has pointed out, 'we increasingly experience our freedom as a burden that causes unbearable anxiety'.

I try to offer a "philosophical" angle to my writings. Those who cannot understand the "serenity of mind" aspect do not need "philosophy" but other fields of knowledge.

Žižek, for instance, is not only a philosopher but also a psychoanalyst.

My Personal Library

According to the blurb on the book's back cover, Rose Holz's *The Birth Control Clinic in a Marketplace World* (2012) is the 'first book to chart the origins and evolution of the charity birth control clinic movement in the United States from the 1910s throughout the 1970s'. Rose Holz 'uncovers the virtually unexamined relationship between Planned Parenthood and the commercial marketplace sphere'. This book deals, in an intelligent way, with the way charity organisations established links with the commercial world in the United States, how 'charity clinics increasingly used commercial techniques to reach impoverished communities and adopted the language of consumer choice to make appealing the services they offered to potential clientele. In short, the lines between business and charity work are not so easily drawn, despite the birth control propaganda and the subsequent birth control historiography that often suggested otherwise' (p. 4).

Liberal Environment

Sandro Chetcuti, of the Malta Developers Association, not too long ago rightly complained about lacklustre urban planning in this country. He was quite obviously correct in his assessment, though it did not cover the entire picture.

Our urban (and by extension, natural) environment is in this state not only because of the reasons mentioned by Mr Chetcuti, but for others too. Consider the fact that there are relatively few investment opportunities in Malta. If people endowed with stamina, acumen, and foresight were to find other avenues for their investments, our architectural heritage would probably be spared the current onslaught. Instead of negotiating outside-village-core deals, the Government should encourage export-oriented business. We have formed part of a 512-million-consumer single market for 15 years now. Is it not high time our entrepreneurs start seriously availing themselves of the opportunities provided by the largest single market in the world?

Individualism

The ongoing degradation of the environment is also due to the individualism that has taken root in the Maltese collective psyche. Individualism is the centrepiece of the Extreme Liberal ideology, the dominant ideology of Late Capitalism, and capitalism is the model wholeheartedly embraced by Prime Minister Muscat (as he bragged to *Politico* a couple of weeks ago). But individualism is not just selfishness, even though the two overlap. Individualism is a mixture of selfishness, egotism, and exaggerated self-esteem. The boundaries between these three (and other) elements are neither rigid nor clear-cut.

My desire above all else

The idea that one's desire is the measure of all things allows, among other things needless to say, the ongoing destruction of our architectural heritage and the natural environment. This idea negates that the individual lives in a community; that his or her desires have to have a limit, and that that limit is set by the needs and desires of other members of the community. Incidentally, this is one of the basic tenets of the philosophy underlying human rights. My rights end where your rights begin. Vice versa, and just to make sure the ultra-egotists understand, your rights end where mine begin. It is a continuous negotiation between positions, and nobody can have it completely his or her way.

Negotiation

DO YOU REMEMBER THAT INCISIVE SKETCH BY COMEDY KNIGHTS, IN WHICH AN APPLICANT APPEARS BEFORE A FICTITIOUS MALTA NATURE AND BUILDINGS AUTHORITY AND THE BOARD MEMBERS URGE HIM TO BUILD HIGHER AND BIGGER? That was intelligent satire and not symbolically far from the truth.

But what I have in mind is something a bit different. By negotiation I do not mean the height and the façade, but the very idea of fundamentally changing the nature of a neighbourhood and a town (incidentally, a theme Comedy Knights dealt with in their sketch).

At this point, it is necessary to make a distinction between the rights of others expressed individually and the rights of others expressed collectively. Let us consider the threat posed to a two-storey neighbourhood by the application to "develop" a high-rise building. Some neighbours might individually claim that their right to sunlight and fresh air could be denied because of the new building. But for somebody who does not live in the neighbourhood, the right to a beautiful landscape or skyline is a right expressed collectively. It is a right of the community, made up of individuals. Even overbuilding town peripheries is an abuse of this collective right. Do we want our towns to be surrounded by soulless, at times Brutalist, high-rise buildings embracing a quaint core?

This collective right is protected by Article 9 of the Constitution, which speaks of the "Nation", that is the community made up of individuals par excellence: 'the State shall safeguard the landscape and the historical and artistic patrimony of the Nation. The State [...] shall take measures to [...] nurture and support the right of action in favour of the environment.' (We still labour under the wrong impression that acts going against this provision are not actionable in court. Judge Giovanni Bonello argues why action can be taken in his book *Misunderstanding the Constitution* (2018).) Instead of safeguarding the 'landscape and the historical and artistic patrimony of the Nation', the State is permitting its destruction. This is what Sandro Chetcuti complained about. This is what courageous organisations like Flimkien għal Ambjent Aħjar are fighting against.

Shift in mentality

THE PROBLEM LIES ON A DEEPER LEVEL: THE SHIFT IN MENTALITY PERMEATING THE COUNTRY'S ENTIRE CULTURE. (Switch on your irony receptors please.) The much-liked, highly respected Salvu Balzan, of Media Today (you can switch off your irony receptors now), has

144

rightly claimed that Joseph Muscat's liberal vision has galvanised a climate conducive to requests for the legalisation of abortion. This clearance of Extreme Liberal permissiveness at the moral customs house has resulted in the splurge of permissiveness in other areas. And it could not be otherwise. A dominant ideology simply diffuses throughout a community, from one field of behaviour to another, like thermal conduction from one material to another. That is why it becomes dominant. Because it is widely diffused, accepted, and followed. You cannot have permissiveness in the private lives of citizens but strict rules in other areas of their lives. People will simply approach different situations with the same thought patterns. For instance, if they can choose their own gender identification – irrespective of what society thinks – and expect society to respect their idiosyncratic choice, why shouldn't they decide to build a five-storey, narrow block of pigeon-coops-passing-for-flats in a two-storey townhouse neighbourhood?

Through the Looking-Glass, and what they found there
MALTA TODAY RECENTLY PUBLISHED A CURIOUS STORY IN WHICH, ALMOST IN ALICE-IN-WONDERLAND FASHION, A LOCAL POLITICIAN MADE THIS STATEMENT: 'BY A TRANS PERSON I MEAN SOMEBODY WHO DOESN'T IDENTIFY WITH THE GENDER ASSIGNED AT BIRTH. So, usually whenever somebody is born, the doctors go: you are male or female. I no longer identify as female. But neither do I identify as male, and that's why we use the term non-binary – to identify something that is not male or female.'

The journalist's jabberwocky logic made him conclude that 'the common pronouns we usually use for male or female – which are he or she, him or her – do not apply in this [politician's] case. At least when speaking in English, where "they" has become commonly used as a pronoun to refer to a person who neither identifies as male or female.'

'But why is it important for people to respect these pronouns?' asks MaltaToday. 'Well, by respecting somebody's pronouns, you show that you're actually listening to them. That you believe that they know who they are, and so you don't force an idea of what you think they should be on them,' answers the politician.

Using jabberwocky logic, if one fine morning I wake up and start identifying as an amphibian (even though my body is still that of a mammal), then the others should call me 'frog'.

145

Bend the rules, kowtow, and shut up
JUST AS YOU HAVE TO BEND THE RULES OF LANGUAGE TO ACCOMMODATE THE DESIRE OF THIS POLITICIAN TO BE REFERRED TO AS "THEY" (EVEN THOUGH WE ARE REFERRING TO A LADY), SO YOU HAVE TO BEND THE RULES OF AESTHETICS AND URBAN PLANNING TO ACCOMMODATE THE DESIRE OF SOME PEOPLE TO BUILD HIGH-RISE MINI-TOWERS IN TWO-STOREY NEIGHBOURHOODS. It is all inter-related, the same worldview.

And, mind you, if you do not kowtow to the dominant ideology you are punished with (for the moment) verbal violence.

Just consider two comments posted underneath my article of last week. It was an article against abortion in which I did not insult anybody; I simply argued that there is big money behind the abortion industry.

Somebody self-styled CJohn Zammit wrote, 'Even in the most polite circles, Dr. Sammut would be shown the Right Royal Finger, and told to mind his phakking business. With the correct spelling.' Somebody self-styled Anya Soldatova-Livera replied to CJohn Zammit, 'Well said. What a misogynist. Not a dumb one, but very oppressive and manipulative.'

(Could have been worse. I could have been dumb as well.)

Let me say nothing about the repeated calls for a "mature" debate. Let me just highlight that whereas the Liberals do not want 'you to force an idea of what you think they should be on them', they are ready to force their idea of what you should (or should not) be on you!

When limitless desire takes control of the individual, you ultimately get destruction of the Self and by extension, of the surrounding environment.

The imperialism of the Ego
WE ARE RELENTLESSLY AND INEXORABLY MOVING TOWARD THE IMPERIALISM OF THE EGO, THE DICTATORSHIP OF THE INDIVIDUAL, AND THE RELEGATION OF THE COMMUNITY TO A THING OF THE PAST, ALMOST A NIGHTMARE FROM WHICH SOCIETY HAS THANKFULLY WOKEN UP. Such shifts take long to materialise, mostly because they need gradual changes with each new generation.

They might even not materialise at all if something unexpected thwarts their progress.

But tendencies are always clear years in advance for those who have the foresight to see them coming.

It is up to the leaders of society to decide whether to follow the flow or to change direction. In the meantime, while we are wasting precious time discussing Liberal "Jabberwocky", Ricasoli Fort is crumbling down into the sea, the old Customs House in Valletta *ditto*, Pietà is threatened, and countless other environmental atrocities lie in wait.

My Personal Library

I will write about what there is not in my personal library, but perhaps there should be. Shamefully, I do not have a single book on the philosophy of architecture. And I think I have only read two books in my whole life on the subject; I do not even own them, I merely borrowed them from a library, and it was within the context of a university course and specifically about the Gothic architectural revival of the 19th century and its links to Tractarian currents in English Protestantism. I wonder, however, how many people involved in the industry own books on the philosophy of architecture, and whether these ideas are ever discussed, and where. One can obviously speak from intuition, but education is always better.

Shipwrecked on
Our Own Islands

LAST SUNDAY WAS FREEDOM DAY;
I AVOIDED WRITING ABOUT THE
COMMEMORATION ITSELF BE-
CAUSE I THINK IT IS FUTILE. Forty
years have passed since Malta
gained sovereignty over her entire territory, and the world today
is not the world then. The event
now belongs to historians, each
of whom will treat the past in his
or her own way in order to justify
their vision of the present.

But our relationship with past
events is something which belongs to us all. We look back at
our collective past and assign
to each event a place in our collective memory. In the past, the
dominant theory was that a nation was created by common
blood, the soil on which one is
born, and the length of time suc-
cessive generations spent living
together. Nowadays, I think it is
the collective memory of past
events that makes a nation. Now
consider the rock opera Ġensna,
written by Ray Mahoney and Paul
Abela to celebrate the attainment
of Freedom on 31 March 1979.
It is a secular nationalist rock
opera, unlike other nationalist
rock operas which invoke a religious theme, such as the Hungar-
ian István, a király [Stephen, the

King] which mixes patriotism with
religion.

The billboards put up to promote this year's performance of
Ġensna, a celebration of Maltese nationalism, were in English, the language of the Empire from which we
– a conquered, not a settled, colony
– gained our freedom... Consider
also that during the closing ultra-
nationalist ballad Tema '79, a video
of the Maltese flag billowing in the
breeze played on the big screens
behind singers and orchestra, while
the lyrics waxed lyrical about 'il-
ħamra u l-bajda nbusha' and just
a few songs earlier, somebody had
been lamenting that 'mitna ta' xejn,
mitna għall-barrani'.

(The 'il-ħamra u l-bajda nbusha'
verse always makes the crowd ex-
plode into a sincere applause, and
many discover warm tears rolling
down their cheeks. It reminds me
of that anecdote, so beautifully rendered by Sir Arturo Mercieca in his
autobiography, when one of those
shot by British soldiers in 1919 is
carried into the premises of the
Giovine Malta and somebody dips
his white handkerchief in the victim's wound and raises it for all to
see: red and white, like our flag, like
our blood. You catch the Romantic
drift.)

This was the ultra-nationalist
Ġensna and... out of the entire billowing flag, the George Cross was

given unbelievable prominence in that video!

These two instances (the billboards and the billowing flag on the big screens), ironically related to a pop-culture reflection of anti-Imperialist sentiment, are symptomatic of the cultural displacement that has been going on over long decades, leaving us culturally shipwrecked on the shores of our own islands.

Charles Xuereb's problem
CHARLES XUEREB GOT INVOLVED IN A DISCUSSION ON WHETHER THE GEORGE CROSS SHOULD BE REMOVED FROM OUR FLAG. I will say it loud and clear from the outset that I have mixed feelings on this subject. On the one hand, I can and do understand that it is a reminder of our part – big or small, I really can't fathom – in the defeat of the Nazi-Fascist regimes, the regimes which promoted eugenics and racial hatred and extermination. But on the other hand, the Cross was given to us by an Empire which also believed in eugenics and White racial superiority. To my mind, the most intelligent observation on our role in the Second World War came from the acute mind of the late Guido de Marco: we fought with the bad against the worse.

So, long story short, I am not a great fan of the George Cross on our flag, yet I do not feel it should be removed.

Not yet, at least.

Eugenics
ACCORDING TO WIKIPEDIA (MY APOLOGIES), 'EUGENICS IS A SET OF BELIEFS AND PRACTICES THAT AIM TO IMPROVE THE GENETIC QUALITY OF A HUMAN POPULATION BY EXCLUDING ... CERTAIN GENETIC GROUPS JUDGED TO BE INFERIOR, AND PROMOTING OTHER GENETIC GROUPS JUDGED TO BE SUPERIOR.' In early-20th-century America, the following individuals were subjected to eugenics methods: the poor, mentally ill, blind, deaf, developmentally disabled, promiscuous women, and homosexuals. In Nazi Germany, racial groups too were targeted, such as the Roma and the Jews.

The word "eugenics" cropped up in neither the United States nor Nazi Germany. It was an Englishman – a cousin of Charles Darwin's – who coined the term in 1883. Francis Galton got obsessed with his cousin's *Origin of Species* and cooked up the idea that the human "race" could be improved in the same way that domestic animals are improved: through breeding. In his 1869 book *Hereditary Genius*, Galton wrote, 'Let us do what we can to encourage the multiplication of the races best fitted to invent, and conform to, a high and generous civilisation, and not, out of mistaken instinct of giving support to the weak, prevent the incoming of strong and hearty individuals.'

Important British writers were enthusiastic about the improvement of the human race. George Bernard Shaw wrote, 'The only fundamental and possible socialism is the socialisation of the selective breeding of man.' Bertrand Russell proposed a system of colour-coded 'procreation tickets' to ensure that the gene pool of the élite would not be diluted by inferior human beings. HG Wells praised eugenics as the first step towards the elimination of 'detrimental types and characteristics' and the 'fostering of desirable types' instead. In 1910, Winston Churchill cautioned, 'The multiplication of the feeble-minded is a very terrible danger to the race'. Daniel Finkelstein wrote in *The Times* (of London)[32] that 'Winston Churchill was a racist but still a great man' while Professor Kehinde Andrews, who focuses on Black Studies at Birmingham City University, said[33] that Churchill was a 'racist' and that Churchill's views on India 'were so extreme, they couldn't be separated from Hitler's ... [Churchill] was someone who believed the white race was superior'. This was the *crème de la crème* of the Empire

---

32   12 February 2019.
33   www.itv.com (9 October 2018).

that gave our ancestors a collective George Cross.

Relations between races
WHEN IN 1938 HITLER MADE MUS-SOLINI INTRODUCE THE RACIAL LAWS – TO ENFORCE RACIAL DIS-CRIMINATION IN ITALY, DIRECTED MAINLY AGAINST THE ITALIAN JEWS AND THE NATIVE INHABIT-ANTS OF THE COLONIES – THE ITAL-IANS THOUGHT THERE MIGHT BE A PROBLEM WITH THE SICILIANS. The Fascist ideologue Julius Evola devised an ingenious solution: despite their ethnic origins, the Sicilians were Aryan in spirit, and part of the superior race!

Let us not be beguiled. The British Empire reserved the same treatment for its component races. Malta was one of the three "White colonies" (the other two being Gibraltar and Cyprus) and therefore, like the Sicilians, difficult to categorise. But the judgment was straightforward in the case of the other colonies, in Africa and Asia: these peoples were inferior. Just consider that a 1910s manual for British consuls specified how much money consuls should give to Canadian, Maltese, Asian, and African shipwrecks all hailing from the Empire. One need not be a rocket scientist to guess that I listed them in decreasing order of aid entitlement.

The British Empire was as racist

as Nazi Germany. Were the British responsible for mass killings? 'Between 12 and 29 million Indians died of starvation while [India] was under the control of the British Empire, as millions of tons of wheat were exported to Britain as famine raged in India. In 1943, up to four million Bengalis starved to death when Winston Churchill diverted food to British soldiers and countries such as Greece while a deadly famine swept through Bengal.'

(Read more about British atrocities in this article published by Britain's *Independent* in 2016 here: https://www.independent.co.uk/ news/uk/home-news/worst-atrocities-british-empire-amritsar-boer-war-concentration-camp-mau-mau-a6821756.html.)

This was the Empire that gave our ancestors a collective George Cross.

And now: Charles Xuereb

It is self-evident, I hope, that what I have just written does not imply that I am a Francophile! Only somebody afflicted by severe paranoia could make such a state with a straight face. And yet, this is precisely the conundrum Charles Xuereb finds himself in and seems unable to disentangle himself out of.

It is well-known that Charles Xuereb is an ardent Francophile. But this does not mean that what he is saying about the George Cross has necessarily to be understood in this Wonderland-like dichotomy! This Manichaean view of the world is over-simplistic, anachronistic and, all told, uncouth. We can't discuss things and be labelled Francophile, Anglophile, Italianate, as if we were stuck in the controversies of 200 or 100 years ago! What Charles Xuereb is saying relates solely and exclusively with being Maltese.

Obviously, Dr Xuereb does not need me, or anybody else for that matter, to break a lance in his favour. He can defend himself, and I am not out to defend him. But he is making a very important point. He is arguing about our present relationship with our colonial past. And his point deserves to be defended. It deserves to be taken out of the silly Britain-vs-France rivalry of 200 years ago and placed firmly in the 21st century. What Charles Xuereb is saying – despite the fact that he is an ardent Francophile – belongs to 21st-century Malta not the Napoleonic Wars! Indeed counterarguing that Charles Xuereb is a Francophile and *that's why* he's against the George Cross (to be read in a knowing, smug tone) is just a worthless *ad hominem* response because, objectively speaking, whether Charles Xuereb is a Francophile or not does not diminish the validity of his argument by one iota.

The post-colonial dream

Not even Dom Mintoff, in his wildest dreams, dreamt of a Malta standing alone, all ties severed. Despite the mouse-that-roared rhetoric echoed in Ġensna, Mintoff's original neutrality project aimed to involve five neighbouring countries to guarantee our neutrality and (implicitly) freedom. As things turned out, only Italy ended up standing as our guarantor.

But the post-colonial dream was not limited to geopolitics. It extended to culture. The enthusiasm of the 1960s – personified in the literary heroes of the *Moviment Qawmien Letterarju* (my father was one of the co-founders of that post-independence literary movement) – fizzled out by the 1990s. The realities of a small domestic market caught up with the idealism of the early years. The "nationalist" dew of the 1960s post-colonial dawn evaporated once the sun of economy and history rose high up in the sky. With the fall of the Berlin Wall in 1989, a new world order set in, a new world order engendered during the Cold War which the West won hands down in 1989.

The quest for national identity became first the quest for European identity and, then, for individual identity. For many Maltese who had lived under British rule, Malta's joining the European project meant that for the very first time in their history, the Maltese people could send their representatives to sit at the big European table, as equals. This had not been the case during the Vienna Congress in 1814–15, when the future of our country was being debated by the big European powers. Malta – the former British colony, though admittedly one of the three White colonies – was now fully certified as European.

And then, as post-Cold-War politics evolved into the gender identity creature they are today, Malta followed suit. But the post-independence dream has been shattered. One could almost say that there never even was a post-independence dream. It was only a dream-like mirage. Post-independence history has unfolded on a post-colonial stage. The two are intertwined, like Janus, the two-faced Roman god from whom we get the name of the month January, one of whose faces looked at the past and the other at the future, while both faces existed on the same head found in the present.

Our cultural points of reference have remained intimately related to the British Empire. Our post-in-

152

dependence dreams exist against a post-colonial backdrop.

The battle between myth (or memory) and fact
CHARLES XUEREB'S ARGUMENT IS NOT THAT WE SHOULD DEMOLISH ANY BUILDING (I STAND TO BE COR-RECTED); HE'S SAYING THAT THE GEORGE CROSS IS A SYMBOL BASED ON MEMORY NOT NECESSARILY ON HISTORICAL FACTS. Was the British Empire a good thing? Was it driven by lofty ideals? What does that Cross represent: the legacy of the Empire, namely progress for humankind in general, and for the Maltese in particular? Does it represent Maltese resilience and sacrifice in the face of Nazi-Fascist aggression? Does it make sense in today's world – when the Germans are our partners – to keep clinging to a Cross given in different historical circumstances when other ideologies held sway? Does the memory correspond to the facts and are we today happy with what those facts mean? This is what Charles Xuereb is saying.

There are no simple black-or-white, yes-or-no answers to these questions. Was the Empire good or bad? Probably it was only ugly (for most), and inevitable. The world was ruled by empires; nation-states appeared only in the long 19th century, the Age of Nationalism. Can we ascribe moral qualities to em-pires or nation-states? I would not do so. But I would say that they were inevitable – almost borrowing and adapting an idea from Hegel (hopefully without incurring Ken-neth Wain's divine wrath), namely that the State represents the will of God.

Would it have been better had we been annexed to the French in-stead of the British Empire? Who knows! That's alternative history, and I sincerely dislike such exercis-es, simply because of the numerous unknowns which render the whole exercise futile.

Did lofty ideals inspire the Brit-ish Empire? For some, certainly yes. But there was no single inspi-ration for all those who created the British Empire. Some – such as the missionaries – wanted to pros-elytise and spread Christianity and save souls. Others – like the busi-nessmen – wanted to grow rich. Others wanted a career, or simply adventure. Many did believe that they were bringing progress to backward or primitive societies. As Marx pointed out, Darwinism was a projection of the liberal-capitalist society unto nature. And Darwin-ism did probably inspire many of those who expanded the frontiers of the Empire, in the sense that they really did believe in the survival of the fittest, that British society was probably the pinnacle of human evolution and that the weak should be weeded out while the others taught how to ape the achievements of their betters just like children are taught to emulate adults.Is this anti-British? Of course not! It is a position not against a people (or a "federation" of nations, for that is what Britain really is), but against an ideology. Good people can and do live under the yoke of bad ideologies. When one criticises an ideology, one does not criticise the people who inhabit the universe it creates. When the West criticised Soviet ideology, it was not criticising the individuals who lived in the Soviet world. Likewise, when one criticises Nazi ideology, one is not criticising the individuals who lived under Nazi rule. There is a huge difference between ideology and the people who have no choice but to live under its yoke.

Norman Lowell: like Pilate in the Credo?

WHILE PEOPLE SEEM BLIND TO THE IDEOLOGY WHICH PARTLY SUSTAINED THE EMPIRE THAT GAVE US THE GEORGE CROSS, THERE IS ALSO (JUSTIFIED) CRITICISM OF NORMAN LOWELL'S IDEOLOGY. What is lacking is the realisation that what Mr Lowell is saying is not too different from what many in the British Empire believed. For some people,

Mr Lowell is raving mad when he argues that the disabled should be disposed of. He is simply quoting *Mein Kampf* and Nazi policy. If you look up in *The New York Times* of 13 September 2017, Kenny Fries' article called: 'The Nazis' First Victims Were the Disabled', you will find a chilling essay on what the Nazis did to the disabled. In Brandenburg, the first "T4 site", the Nazi authorities killed approximately 300,000 disabled people. Your eyes are not deceiving you: that's three hundred thousand people, killed because they were considered unfit to live: "undesirables".

For Mr Lowell, an admirer of Herr Hitler, this was good public policy. For me, a hopeless romantic, it was madness: tears have started to well up in my eyes while re-reading that article and writing these words and I have to stop typing.

In 1930 Britain – the Mother Country of the Empire that gave us the George Cross – Julian Huxley, secretary of the London Zoological Society and chairman of the Eugenics Society, wrote: 'What are we going to do? Every defective man, woman and child is a burden. Every defective is an extra body for the nation to feed and clothe, but produces little or nothing in return.'

During my research, I found an academic article on deafness and imperialism. The author, who hails from the University of Sheffield, argues that 'disability... not only operated as an additional "category of difference" alongside "race" as a way of' marking differences between the colonisers and the colonised, but was 'part and parcel of the same cultural ... system'. In other words, in the British Empire, race and disability were two ways of distinguishing the superiors from the inferiors.

To put it bluntly, those who (rightly so) chastise Mr Lowell for his appalling support for the Nazi policy of eliminating the disabled, should also be aware that the British Empire also saw the disabled as "different", as a category of inferior people. And so on.

Decolonisation of the mind

DECOLONISATION IS NOT JUST A POLITICAL PHENOMENON, IT IS ALSO INTELLECTUAL. This too, I believe, is something Charles Xuereb is trying to convey but he keeps encountering irrelevant "accusations" of Francophilia. One really starts despairing.

The problem for us Maltese is that we belong to a small nation, with limited intellectual resources and a small domestic market. When a Maltese intellectual writes in Maltese, they are risking oblivion. Or – in the same incredible way that Dr Xuereb's valid argument gets the Francophile flak when a love for France and things French has absolutely nothing to do with the argument – those who write in Maltese are tacitly charged with choosing Maltese because they are afraid of scrutiny by the wider world.

In part this could be true. Then again, there are some topics in which foreigners need not poke their nose: topics we refer to as Melitensia. Be that as it may, we have a strong limitation and this is a real hurdle for the decolonisation of the mind.

* * *

I STARTED OFF THIS ESSAY WITH SOMETHING I NOTICED WHILE WATCHING A VIDEO RECORDING OF THE PERFORMANCE OF THE ROCK OPERA ĠENSNA. The lyrics spoke of dying in vain, for the foreign master ('*mitna ta' xejn, mitna għall-barrani*') and of kissing the white-and-red flag ('*il-bajda w ħamra nbusha/ bħalha m'hemmx/ din ma tintemmx*'), while prominence was given to the George Cross on the flag billowing in the breeze on the big screens behind the orchestra.

Meanwhile, public thinker Charles Xuereb has been involved in a public debate on the not-so-new question of whether to keep the George Cross on the flag, or remove it. The debate highlighted the tensions between (popular or cultural) memory, or myth, and historical fact. I tried to make the point that if the George Cross is a symbol reminding one and all of the Maltese contribution to the defeat of the racist Nazi-Fascists, we should still not forget that the same Empire which gave us the cross was racist too. This necessarily led to the question whether we want to identify with a symbol recalling times when racist ideas and policies were accepted and implemented.

While having no strong opinion either way on the George Cross issue, these questions did lead me to consider whether we have emancipated ourselves from the colonial mindset. Has political decolonisation triggered decolonisation of the mind? Are historical facts slowly but surely managing to encroach on popular or cultural memory and myths?

This is politically important because the country's symbols are officially sanctioned: they represent the State of Malta locally and internationally. What is the self-image our little State wants to portray to the world?

If politics followed logic, the George Cross would have been removed on May 1, 2004. But the logic of politics dictates otherwise; it follows emotion and economics,

objectives and considerations kept hidden from the public (security, corruption, legitimate and/or illegitimate commercial interests, soft imperialism, etc).

But this discussion on who we are and what to do post-Empire, is equally important on the societal and personal level. It is in part dependent on our traditions and collective memory. But also on the rain of new ideas brought to us by clouds formed elsewhere. This tension electrifies the debate between the liberals – the partisans of "new" ideas – and the conservatives, who are for tradition and memory. Both approaches have their inherent risks. For the conservatives it is the risk of thinking that things were always done in a particular way. If the conservatives accept that change happens over time, they would experience less anxiety. The liberals' major risk is to assume that all that is new has to be good solely on the basis of it being new. They forget that revolutions are costly because they embrace untested novelties. If the liberals accept that slow reform is wiser than rash revolution, they would cause less anxiety, for themselves and others.

Attack of the clones?

BEING A VERY SMALL COUNTRY, WE CLONE ALMOST EVERYTHING, INCLUDING IDEAS. Professor Ġużeppi

Schembri (Bonaci) opened his 1989 book on the common heritage of mankind by quoting, if I remember well, the Russian thinker Vernadsky: a people that only imports ideas is a dead people. This might apply to huge nations – like Russia – but not to micro-nations, as new ideas arise where there is experimentation not in backwater communities.

This is the big identity challenge: how to find ourselves in the meanders of post-Empire cultural imperialism. Whether we like it or not, our only real communication channel with the outside world is the English language. Whatever seeps through from other linguistic worlds does so through the mediation of English and of British culture. We read mostly in English, and mostly British and American authors. Our students study from books written in English for their exams, our professionals depend on books written in English for their work (apart from the legal profession, which still refers to old Italian books in certain fields). Those who study foreign languages, usually study literature, nothing else. We therefore still inhabit the world of ideas of the former colonisers, and, now, their senior partners. This is not decolonisation of the mind.

Real emancipation can be achieved through the acquisition of knowledge in other languages, to open ourselves to other approaches to knowledge.

A phantom menace?

WE NEED TO STEP OUT OF THE NEO-COLONIAL COMFORT ZONE, POSSIBLY THROUGH A GRADUAL REFORM OF THE EDUCATIONAL SYSTEM, INTRODUCING, LITTLE BY LITTLE, THE STUDY OF CERTAIN SUBJECTS AT SECONDARY AND TERTIARY LEVELS IN OTHER LANGUAGES. I have French, Italian, and German in mind, allowing future citizens to acquire skills in specialised disciplines in these three languages in addition to English, thus accruing not only intellectual but also economic benefits. The country needs to master these three languages in addition to English, to achieve three parallel objectives: emancipation from the neo-colonial mindset, penetration of the Italian, German, and Francophone markets not only in tourism but also in other profitable economic sectors, and adjustment to the post-Brexit European environment.

Depending intellectually on only one country is, to put it in a circular fashion, intellectual colonisation. What do we stand to gain by chasing the ghost of a Britain that no longer exists? Why should we feel menaced by the prospect of finding ourselves in a wider context?

A force awakens?

THE IRONY IS THAT EVEN A DEBATE ON POST-EMPIRE GETS CAUGHT UP IN EMPIRE TERMS, AS THE EMPIRE AROUSES NOSTALGIA AND CRITICISM IN PRESENT-DAY BRITAIN. The only way to leave Empire is to open up to other cultures, because our own resources are too limited for cultural self-sustainment. We need to import ideas and to aspire to an intellectual cosmopolitanism.

The Maltese can forge their own identity by savouring different cultures while avoiding slavishly to limit themselves to one, dominant culture they encountered by happenstance 200 years ago or so.

The new identity would then percolate to the rest of society in a long-term project. It would be the awakening of our force.

The Empire struck back

WE ABOUND IN CONTRADICTIONS IN MALTA. For instance, we declare that Maltese is the national language of our Nation-State and yet the fundamental law of the Maltese State, called *The Constitution of Malta*, is in Maltese and English, as if anybody outside of Malta really cares what our Constitution has to say or those who are interested cannot obtain a certified translation. It is our Constitution, the Constitution of the Maltese, so why should it be in two versions, one of which is not the national language? Other former British colonies have their equivalent documents in English either because English is their "national" language or because their "nation" is made up of so many tribes that they need English as a "national" *lingua franca*.

Then there are the George Cross contradictions. We keep a reminder of the Allied victory over the Germans and the Italians on our flag when these are now our partners in the European Union, Britain is leaving, and France and Germany have been best friends for decades.

We commemorate the *Sette Giugno* incidents – when British troops opened fire on the protesting crowds, killing four Maltese, on June 7, 1919 – and yet we keep the George Cross. This year will be the centenary of that event. Completely oblivious to the irony and the contradiction, we shall probably fly the George-Cross flag during the ceremony to commemorate the Empire striking back and killing four of ours.

In that same year, the Empire had stricken back, in India, on April 13, when, to quote *The Guardian* of a week ago, 'Hundreds of civilians were massacred by a British general who was later treated as a hero'. The British newspaper was commemorating 'the centenary of a British general gunning down unarmed

Indians who had gathered peacefully in a park in Amritsar'.

On April 13, 1919, 'without any warning, and just 30 seconds after he entered the park, [General Reginald] Dyer ordered his soldiers to fire. They fired for 10 minutes and stopped only because they had run out of ammunition.

By then 337 men, 41 women and a baby of seven weeks had been killed, with another 1,500 injured.' *The Guardian* continued: '[General Dyer's] admirers ranged from Ulster politicians such as Edward Carson to the Archbishop of Canterbury, who called him a 'brave, public-spirited, patriotic soldier.'

More astonishing was the reaction of the House of Commons. With Edwin Montagu, the Secretary of State for India, portrayed as anti-Dyer, the House debated a motion to reduce Montagu's salary, a severe form of parliamentary censure.

Among Tories at the time it was not what Dyer had done, but Montagu's Jewishness that became the central issue. Austen Chamberlain, then Chancellor of the Exchequer, wrote, 'On this occasion all their English and racial feeling was stirred to a passionate display ... A Jew rounding on an Englishman and throwing him to the wolves – that was the feeling.'

This was the Empire that gave us the George Cross, which we claim helps us remember our victory on the Nazi-Fascist regimes (that, among other things, hated the Jews).

My Personal Library

John Darwin's *Unfinished Empire: The Global Expansion of Britain* (2012) is an excellent introduction to the British Empire. The blurb more or less sums up the debate:

> For perhaps two centuries its expansion and final collapse were the single largest determinant of historical events, and it remains surrounded by myth, misconception and controversy today.

Sir Arturo Mercieca's *The Making and Unmaking of a Maltese Chief Justice*, republished in English in 1969, is not only an autobiography but also a valuable commentary on a big chunk of 20th-century Maltese history by an acute intellect. Just consider what he highlights about the new, 1961 Constitution: the creation of a Constitutional Court.

For the uninitiated this is of little import; but for somebody who loves law and history, the observation gives away a sense of understated excitement at something new not only for Malta but for a British colony, given that the English legal tradition did not admit of a Constitutional Court.

Equally beautiful is a 1994 book called *Malta: Culture and Identity*, edited by Henry Frendo and Oliver Friggieri. It is a collection of essays that attempt to capture our culture and identity from diverse angles on the occasion of the 30th anniversary of Independence.

On my shelves there is a copy of Pimlico's edition of Hitler's book *Mein Kampf*. I bought it from a bookshop in England and started reading it 10 years ago. I admit I had to stop: it nauseated me so much that I could not bear it any longer. It wasn't just the thematic monomania; it was the themes themselves: anti-Semitism, mostly, but not only.

That said, Hitler did read a lot (of cheap pamphlets) and he understood perfectly the Darwinian subtext of the world he lived in. He was a politician, not an intellectual, more clever than intelligent. What struck me most, however, was that many of his observations can still be heard on the streets, from the working classes and some elements of the middle classes.

Look Who's Back, a novel by Timur Vermes, published in 2012, proposes the thesis that if Hitler were to come back, he would find considerable support in today's world. The book was made into a film, inspiring another film on Mussolini (*Sono Tornato* [I'm

Back]), which proposed an analogous thesis.

If the Extreme Right does return, I will blame it exclusively on the Socialists, who abandoned the working classes and jumped on the liberal-libertine wagon with their fancy ideas of men wanting to become women, men marrying men and hiring women's uteruses to have children while other women abort the children they wilfully make with men, and other such chaotic thinking that renders ours the Age of Madness.

In his *The Gentle Civilizer of Nations: The Rise and Fall of International Law 1870–1960* (2001), Martti Koskenniemi argues that many newly-independent former colonies chose of their own accord to import wholesale the practices and systems of their former colonisers.

In a sense, imperialism succeeded in civilising the "backward" and the "primitive". Charles Xuereb has called it a 'Stockholm Syndrome' of sorts. I would agree only in part, because the Stockholm Syndrome is usually linked to captivity.

In our case, I would not say we were captives on our own islands; I would say that we ended up shipwrecked – though not necessarily marooned – on our own islands, having lost the ship of our identity during the tempest that was colonialism and Empire.

The Abortion Charade

THE ABORTION QUESTION IS GETTING HOTTER BY THE DAY. Prime Minister Muscat claims that the government has no intention to legalise abortion, and yet pro-abortion activists (euphemistically and deceitfully calling themselves pro-choice) feel emboldened to request the legalisation of the right to terminate the life of the unborn. Nobody felt thus emboldened under any other Prime Minister.

What I think the Muscat means is that there are many among his MPs who are good people, and wouldn't want to have the blood of the innocent killed under such barbarous legislation on their hands. Yes, I am sure he is right; the majority of Labour MPs do not want to have their name associated with the introduction of such a law in Malta. And whereas they understand that they owe everything to Muscat, they also understand that there is a limit which neither Muscat nor the lobbies that support him, can overstep.

Doctors and the giving of moral advice
THERE ARE SOME DOCTORS IN MALTA WHO THINK THEY SHOULD ADVISE WOMEN TO TERMINATE THEIR PREGNANCIES AND FEEL EMBOLDENED TO ASK TO DO SO IN BROAD

DAYLIGHT. They are politically savvy and understand the political subtext of what's going on. Needless to say, they ignore two facts: when the real medical need arises, the law allows terminations in an indirect way, and all practising doctors know this. It's a fact of life, and one accepts it as such. Instead they emphasise the other cases, when it essentially boils down to abortion on demand. I want to tell them loud and clear: We, the majority of the Maltese people, are against legalising abortion, and that's the way we want it to stay.

My own opinion is that, with all due respect, very few medical doctors are equipped to give moral advice on terminating the life of an unborn child. This young doctor who feels emboldened by the current political climate to ask for the legalisation of abortion thinks he can follow his conscience, but he should think twice. Mostly because he is probably not following his own conscience, but unconsciously following ideology.

Ideological shift
IDEOLOGY IS A SUBJECT I HAVE OFTEN TACKLED IN MY WRITINGS. I follow Slavoj Žižek's teachings on the subject (which he bases on other philosophers, etc); he usually refers to a 1988 movie, John Carpenter's *They Live* – I suggest watching it as it explains how ideology works, and why people turn violent when you criticise their ideological beliefs.

Whereas in other times the dominant ideology was that humanity is created in the image of God (*imago Dei*), an important ideological shift took place in the nineteenth century. The ideology of humanity being created in the image of God was replaced by the ideology that humanity evolved from lower animals. And, therefore, humans are simply higher animals. The divine (what makes Humanity special) was removed from the equation; its place was taken by the "pragmatic" consideration that Humanity belongs to the animal kingdom and that there is no Heavenly Kingdom to aspire to. Christianity had found an equilibrium in the figure of Christ, the point of convergence between divinity and humanity when *The Word became flesh*. This equilibrium was wiped out by the ideological shift of the nineteenth century. Our earthly, animal qualities were declared sovereign while our divinely-inspired "soul" was banished out of the collective consciousness as something childish, naïve, superstitious, and "medieval".

This was, of course, one big travesty of history and philosophy. But let's not get into that. What is important for our purposes is the ideological shift from humanity as image of God to humanity as simply another animal species. This is one of the essential elements of Darwinism.

It is clear, I believe, that this ideological shift makes it easy to accept abortion. If people are simply higher animals, then killing them can be excused and tolerated. Thus when they are still not useful (when they are foetuses) or no longer useful (when they are old, frail, and unable to take care of themselves), they can be eliminated. This is one of the political implications of Darwinism.

The link with neo-liberalism
DARWIN NEVER USED THE PHRASE 'SURVIVAL OF THE FITTEST'; IT WAS COINED BY HERBERT SPENCER (1820-1903) WHO INITIATED THE PHILOSOPHY CALLED "SOCIAL DARWINISM", THAT IS THE POLITICAL APPLICATION OF DARWIN'S SCIENTIFIC THEORY. At this point, I have to relate a personal anecdote. In autumn of 2017, I visited Senegal, in Western Africa. It was an incredible experience; I could see with my own eyes the social ravages of the slave trade. I visited the island of Gorée, from where slaves were shipped off to the Americas, and I cried. You have to be there to feel the intensity and oppressiveness; the air is still heavy with the living memory of the inhuman conditions these poor souls were detained in, the cramped rooms where the male slaves were fattened and the females raped by their white keepers... The island has become a veritable monument to human beast-like behaviour toward fellow humans. But in Senegal, I also had what I shall refer to as a "Galápagos moment". You know, Darwin "saw" the evolutionary process when he observed the beaks of birds on the Galápagos Islands, and compared them to the beaks of birds on the South American continent. In Senegal, we visited the *Langue de Barbarie*, the estuary of the Senegal River. While crossing on the boat rowed by an old Senegalese and his grandson, I looked at the birds perched on the shores. I saw no competition there, no "survival of the fittest". What I saw was beauty. The birds seemed to me aware of their beauty, they were sort of showing it off, to each other mostly. (In January of this year, I read in *The New York Times* an article called 'How Beauty Is Making Scientists Rethink Evolution'.)

As I observed those beautiful birds, a little voice inside me said, 'There's no brutal competition here! There's beauty and a way of life in which beauty plays an important role!' And then it dawned on me! Darwin had projected the brutal competitiveness of the economic *laissez-faire* characterising the political world of his times unto an unsuspecting natural world! But the story does not end here.

In 2018, I started reading Enzo Pennetta's 2017 *L'Ultimo Uomo: Malthus, Darwin, Huxley e l'invenzione dell'antropologia capitalista* [The Last Man: Malthus, Darwin, Huxley and the invention of capitalist anthropology]. Pennetta quotes a letter Marx wrote Engels in 1862 in which he explains Darwinism in more or less the same terms: Darwin projected unto nature the capitalist desire to dominate the market and the Malthusian idea of the struggle for survival. This is the explanation of why abortion is now tolerated (and even, somehow, in a perverse way, promoted). It is the liberal philosophy of economics (capitalism) being imposed on nature while posing as science. But it is pseudo-science!

What is real science?

REAL SCIENCE IS SOMETHING YOU CAN MEASURE AND DETERMINE EMPIRICALLY. In other words, something you can replicate in a laboratory. For something to be scientific, you have to be able to repeat it under the same conditions. Let's consider one of the simplest scientific facts: the evaporation of water. Wherever you go in the world – anywhere – if the atmospheric pressure is 0.101325 MPa, water will always boil at 100°C. There's no way that at that atmospheric pressure and at that temperature, water will not boil: it always becomes vapour.

Why am I saying this? Because there is the attempt to justify abortion on scientific grounds. The most powerful pro-abortion argument is that the foetus is still not a person, not an individual, and therefore should not enjoy protection at law. Proponents of this argument claim they can determine when somebody becomes a person!

In his book *A Defense of Abortion* (2002), David Boonin argues that measurable cortical movement in the brain determines when one becomes a person.

And yet, this is simply not true. If it were true, the different specific laws that regulate abortion in Europe, say, would not be so diverse, they vary from 10 weeks (in Portugal, for example) to 24 weeks (in the UK and the Netherlands, for example). If this were a real scientific issue – as opposed to it being an ideological one – then it would be like all scientific facts: the same everywhere, just like water boils everywhere at the same temperature (if the atmospheric pressure is the same).

But whereas in real science, the change from one state to another (from water to vapour, say) is truly measurable, in the case of pseudo-science, the change from one state to another (from foetus to person) is arbitrary. And therefore, ideology, not science.

Every human being belongs to humanity
A COMMON MISCONCEPTION IS THAT CHILDREN *BELONG* TO THEIR PARENTS. Capitalist/neo-liberal thinking embraces the idea that children are property. But no human being is property (one reason why slavery was abolished). All human beings are human beings and they belong (in a metaphorical, spiritual sense) to all of humanity. Thus every human being conceived belongs to humanity, not to their mother.

Why is this? Because in every human being there is the potential to solve one of the myriad problems facing humanity. Upon growing up, a child can follow any calling – from science, medicine, law, architecture, engineering, to anything else – and improve the common good. Leonardo da Vinci and Franco Zeffirelli were both born out of wedlock. Pro-abortion preachers would tell you that their mothers could have aborted them, to avoid scandal, to go on with their lives, and so on. They would have deprived us of their geniuses. Andrea Bocelli too – doctors suggested his mother to abort him. This in the name of an ephemeral right to choose, of the unfounded and illogical claim that you can do whatever you like with your body. We know that this not to be true.

You cannot do whatever you like with your body. We hospitalise certain patients to avoid them harming themselves. The State runs anti-to-bacco and anti-alcohol campaigns because no, you can't do whatever you like with your body. Tellingly, whereas you can use your body to knife somebody who's making your life hell... well, actually you can't do that.

So, no, the arguments in favour of abortion fall flat. They are based on pseudo-science, on philosophical misunderstandings, and on the selfishness of some who do not understand their role in the wider world, who think that the entire world spins around them, who think only what their country can do for them rather than what they can do for their country, the world, and humanity.

Let's stop this abortion charade and concentrate on the serious things: like corruption, air quality, overbuilding, and the many other problems which Joseph Muscat's neo-liberal Government is allowing to plague our country.

My Personal Library

YOU CAN FIND VIDEOS UPLOADED BY THE ITALIAN INTELLEC-
TUAL ENZO PENNETTA ON YOUTUBE AND FACEBOOK. In his 2017
book, *L'Ultimo Uomo: Malthus, Darwin, Huxley e l'invenzione
dell'antropologia capitalista* [The Last Man: Malthus, Darwin, Huxley and the invention of capitalist anthropology], Pennetta discusses
the theory of the overpopulation of the world presented by Robert
Malthus (and now considered to be wrong), the Darwinian idea
of the survival of the fittest (which justified the Nazi ideology of
exterminating disabled people), and the eugenics of Aldous Huxley's *Brave New World*. Though dealing with political philosophy,
the book is written like a thriller, exposing intrigues, discoveries,
hypotheses, and manipulations. It also describes the rise of progressive ideology, starting with the utopian ideas of Francis Bacon and
August Comte and reaching our times marked by social engineering: birth control and gender theory. It all boils down to social control and domination, the creation of a new anthropological model.
As Žižek teaches: *cui bono*? Who will benefit from all of this? The
people? Or the "élites"?

In his little book – just 195 pages long – Pennetta, whose tertiary education revolves around biology and pharmacy studies, summarises and explains some of the tenets of contemporary ideology.
Let's see what Pennetta has to say about the Australian philosopher
Peter Singer. The reader could ask: Why should I care what an Australian philosopher has to say? Well, you should – because Singer's ideas percolate down into the cracks of public discussion and
are then taken up by campaigners and the journalists who support
them. These people will subsequently regurgitate these ideas and
present them to you as if they were the Truth, not as the premasticated ideology that they in reality are. And your life ends up being
shaped by them.

Pennetta summaries Singer's take on politically corrected ideas
according to the Darwinian approach thus:

1. Reject the idea that parents have any authority over their own
children

2. Contest the contents of the Bible

3. Refute the idea that human beings are superior to animals .

How are these principles being applied around us? Recently, worried parents were told essentially to shut up when they expressed their concern at what their young children are being taught at school as "sexual education".

1. Certain Maltese newspapers alternate pro-abortion articles with faith-based articles. The strategy is to build the case for abortion and discredit those who oppose it, as if the debate on abortion was simply religious and those who prefer a religious approach are cut off from reality, fanatical readers of holy books. Clearly this latter image is a caricature, as in reality we have a very moderate Church and a very fanatical (neo-)liberal lobby.

2. Not too long ago, a solitary animal-rights campaigner tried to whip up support for putting an end to slaughtering pigs. This was given a lot of publicity by one particular newspaper, which also supports pro-abortion arguments. Let's not forget that, according to the philosopher Singer, a pig should enjoy more rights than the unborn human child.

The pattern described by Pennetta is clearly applied and adhered to. But Pennetta also discusses tricks used in the campaigns for the acceptance of neo-liberal ideas, such as Singer's. He analyses the strategies used by the American Civil Liberties Union which, you will find, have many elements in common with strategies used by civil-liberties lobbies in Malta:

1. Dispose of big sums of money, the origins of which are not always transparent

2. Find political support

3. Their origins are at times tied to personalities who acquire icon status

4. Enjoy credit with the media

5. Have important contacts within the academic, industrial and financial worlds

Their plan of actions usually involves:

1. Choosing a field of action

2. Creating interest in their objectives

3. Mobilising political and legal support

4. Obtaining social, or even just media, consensus for their objectives.

The obvious question is: who is behind these structures, and who stands to benefit from them? *Cui bono?* – who stands to gain?

Is Muscat Invincible?

LET'S KEEP IN MIND THAT IN POLI-
TICS, APPEARANCES ARE OFTEN
MORE IMPORTANT THAN REALITY.
Many people, mostly those who
are in business, are increasingly
concerned with the perception that
Muscat is invincible. They realise
that if this perception continues
growing, it will give rise to the sort
of government that business abhors
– one that is so sure of itself and its
eternal popularity that it starts encroaching on the freedoms business
needs to survive and thrive.

Needless to say, nobody is invincible. Shrewd politicians intuit
that they are instruments of history,
that they are not completely in control but ride the wave of social and
economic currents and undercur-
rents. The successful politician can
read the mood and the signs of the
times, and knows how to manipulate the sails of his/her party boat
so that the wind of history pushes
it through the water of politics. But
once that wind stops blowing, their
boat stops as well.

Joseph Muscat does not only sail
his boat according to the way the
wind blows. (As a matter of fact, he
is not the only one who has mastered this technique. Others did it
before him, and many others will
do after him as well.) What Joseph
Muscat has, that others might not

have, is a party past. When he started militating in the Labour Party
in 1992, Muscat was not the only
youngster who accepted Alfred
Sant's invitation to help the Party.
But he was the only one who approached the Party as if it were a
family, as if it were his family. For
many Labourites, Joseph became
the star of the Labourite Family,
and thus the star of each Labourite family. (No wonder he founded
the now-defunct news portal called
Malta Star – he aimed to become
Malta's Star.) He worked assidu-
ously to become a 'member' of each
Labourite family. At a time when
only Labourites listened to Super
One – and Labourites listened only
to Super One, Joseph was there,
talking to them in their kitchens,
sitting rooms, and cars as if he were
their favourite nephew or grandson
who, despite their working-class
background, went to university and
was learning stuff.

Joseph spoke to them in a familiar, loving, and matter-of-fact tone
of voice, entering their homes...
and their hearts. Nobody else succeeded in this, even though Super
One Radio pullulated with political preachers. Joseph was not a
preacher: he was a member of each
Labourite family.

This strategy found its culmina-
tion in 2008 – 16 whole years after
it had begun – when, as freshly-

elected Leader of the Labour Party, he made a request to all Labourites. He introduced them to his wife and told them, in his endearing village accent marked by diphthongs (ħobbuwha instead of ħobbuha): 'This is my wife Michelle: love her (ħobbuwha) because she loves you!' It was the graduate son of the working-class family who brings home his sweetheart and, introducing her, asks them to accept her because she has accepted them. The dynamics of this psychological game are impressive.

At the time, the satirist Joe Demicoli had compared Joseph Muscat to the Messiah and, in part, he was right. But Mr Demicoli's satire had completely overlooked this homely aspect of Muscat's ascension to power.

By acquiring this symbolic membership in all Labourite families (the building blocks of the One Labourite Family), Joseph Muscat acquired immunity from criticism. This explains why, despite the glaringly obvious malfeasance of two of his closest collaborators and his equally glaringly obvious unconditional defence of them, criticism has left him virtually unscathed. Just imagine a member of your family being accused of committing a serious crime. Unless you are the victim, you will passively accept it. The reason: all the love you have

invested in that relative. Muscat is benefitting from the love that Labourites have invested in him over long years. 'Love her' also meant: 'love her as you love me'. 'Because she loves you' also meant: 'because I love you'. In this campaign, he cashed in on that love again: 'Be with me again.'

The language might sound messianic and, in part, it is. But mostly it is the love one has for one's relatives. Family – the very unit which, ironically, Muscat's policies are destabilising and debilitating – is what makes Muscat's political fortune.

Greener pastures

THE SHREWD POLITICIAN UNDERSTANDS THAT THE WIND OF HISTORY WILL ONE DAY SUBSIDE AND HE TRIES TO LEAVE ON THE EVE OF THAT DAY. It is only logical that Muscat should be planning his exit from politics by looking for pastures where the grass is greener. But to get to there, he needs to demonstrate that he is not a retrograde. In comes the abortion charade we have been witnessing for some time now.

While insisting that the Labour Government has no intention of legalising abortion, certain "useful idiots" known to be close to certain centres of power, have been pumping up the volume on abortion, feeling sufficiently emboldened to ask for its legalisation. Naturally, all pro-life elements in the country have stood up to resist the onslaught on one of the fundamental values of Maltese society.

During discussions on his transition to greener pastures, Muscat will undoubtedly tell his friends: 'You see, there were even the usual useful idiots clamouring for abortion. But it could not be done. For many reasons.' Only time will tell if Muscat's friends see or don't see through his stratagems.

The fact, however, remains that much of the Maltese political game is being played to further personal interests, rather than the common good.

Muscat's fortune
JOSEPH MUSCAT SPENT 16 WHOLE YEARS STUDYING ALFRED SANT. Dr Sant's tenacious hold on power not only supplied Muscat's apprenticeship but also turned the wheel of fortune in favour of the young Muscat.

Machiavelli observed that a prince's success depends on both his Prowess and Fortune. What Machiavelli said about the 'civil principality' applies to Muscat. In the civil principality, a citizen comes to power 'not through crime or other intolerable violence', but by the support of his fellow citizens.

This, says Machiavelli, does not require extreme prowess or fortune, only 'fortunate astuteness'.

Muscat's prowess comes from his observation at close range of the mistakes committed by his predecessor as Prime Minister and Leader of the Opposition. Dr Sant was an austere Prime Minister, and – to use a metaphor from Maltese history – many Knights had no time for Lascaris. As Leader of the Opposition, Dr Sant preferred principle to pragmatism, the price for which was hefty. All those characteristics which, in theory and an ideal world, were good (such as principled inflexibility, etc.) turned out to be completely disastrous in practice and the real world. Joseph Muscat saw all of this unfold before his eyes and took copious notes. The lesson was this: if a politician upholds principles during political storms, s/he will end up smashed on the rocky coast of defeat.

At the same time, Muscat's fortune was made by Dr Sant's tenacious hold on power. By remaining at the helm of the Labour Party for 16 years, Dr Sant allowed Joseph Muscat not only the opportunity to build an intimate rapport with Labourites, to learn the ropes and to conceive the Machiavellian notion that in politics no principle is sacred, but also – once the Sant years were over – to enjoy the gratitude for the "liberation". In a paradoxical way, Muscat benefitted from his predecessor's overstay and overdue departure.

According to a certain source, Muscat played a trick during the 2008 election by alerting certain elements in the Nationalist Party to the ace Labour had up its sleeve: the Mistra Bay Scandal. If this is true, then Muscat deliberately derailed his own Party's campaign, wrong-footed Alfred Sant and paved the way for his own ascension to power. Upon acquiring it, he made a point of avoiding his predecessor's "mistakes": principles not to be held sacred, naughty behaviour to be tolerated and brazen-facedly defended, political positions to be constantly considered as malleable. Machiavelli also says that at times the Prince has to be a lion and at others a fox. Though with certain individuals, he has behaved as the lion, Muscat usually behaves like a fox. I think it did help that Muscat's father was self-employed, selling fireworks. This trade must have taught Muscat how to negotiate and sell (what ends up in) smoke.

In sum, all these ingredients – long-term rapport with Labourites, long-term apprenticeships, perfect timing and fox-like behaviour – have made Joseph Muscat what he is. Whoever wants to beat him at the polls has to keep this in mind.

Whoever wants to succeed him in the Party, *ditto*.

Gender quotas
THE 2019 EUROPEAN PARLIAMENT ELECTION RESULTS SHOWED BEYOND THE SHADOW OF A DOUBT HOW USELESS – EVEN PERNICIOUS – GENDER QUOTAS ARE. The electorate had to choose six representatives and, without any State intervention – no quota, no imposition, no interference – chose three ladies and three gentlemen. The electorate chose – spontaneously, without being forced – to spread equally among the two sexes.

It is obvious that the only requisite to see women in high places is equal opportunity. The electorate will then assess each candidate on merit. Almost inexplicably, just as when you do not mess with populations half the babies are born male and the other half females, so the electorate – when not messed with – chose women as one half of the elected representatives and men as the other half.

Fascism is when the State does not trust the individual with important decisions and substitutes the ideological conscience for the individual's conscience. Fascism is not an ideology – it is a mode of governing. Mussolini's and Franco's were conservative Fascisms. Now we have liberal Fascism, where certain States impose a liberal conscience on the individual: the individual does "the right thing" because the élites so dictate. But, as we have seen, there is no need for such brutality.

When the liberal principle is just and fair (because, let's be clear, not every liberal principle is just and fair), people will spontaneously implement it. Equal opportunity for all is just and fair; that women, being inferior, are incapable of running for office is ideological rubbish. Because equal opportunity is a just and fair principle, people will implement it.

State intervention is clearly useless – but also pernicious. If a woman is elected on the strength of an imposed gender quota rather than elector trust, then that woman has to deal with the implied negative assessment of her abilities over and above the bitterness of males who, had it not been for the ideological imposition of gender quotas, would have been elected but were instead left out in the cold. Indeed, *vox populi, vox dei*. If you give them the right opportunity, the people will vote well. There's no need for interference, for the (Fascist) imposition of (liberal) values.

If Modernity is indeed the daughter of Reason, then there is no need to apply Force. Contra-riwise, where "Modernity" needs Force, then it is a False Modernity. Let Reason take its course.

Reason is intimately related to Justice, and Justice is a sentiment common not only to humans but to most creatures, as Darwin himself observed. It is innate in us and is then shaped by nurture. If Justice is the obverse of the coin, then the reverse is our moral sense.

In *The Descent of Man*, Darwin wrote that 'our moral sense' originates 'in the social instincts, largely guided by the approbation of our fellow men, ruled by reason, self-interest and, in later times, by deep religious feelings, and confirmed by instruction and habit.'

It is extraordinary how something like Justice – which makes the electorate choose with exquisite equality – is something that transcends individuals and is exercised as if individuals are acting together like one organism.

In a twisted way, many of our misconceptions on gender – essentially that women are inferior to men – could be due to a (deliberate?) misinterpretation.

In the turbulent years of the French Revolution, French women asked that *Les Droits de l'Homme* (The Rights of Man, *I Diritti dell'Uomo* – which we Maltese instinctively translate as *Il-Jeddijiet tal-Bniedem* not as *Il-Jeddijiet tar-Raġel*) be extended to the female sex. This was – incredibly enough – denied to them because the rights were understood in a literal fashion, as the rights of men!

One particular 20ᵗʰ-century philosopher argued that our language is our limitation. In this case, the English language (but also French, Italian and Latin) served as a limitation, because of the double meaning of "man" as both "male" and "human being".

In the case of Maltese, there is no such limitation. When we say *bniedem*, we know that it refers to "humanity", not "the male". We know because the sense is alive in the word "*bniedem*", which we have inherited from our ancestors. We feel that sense because we are native speakers. All words carry within the germ that beget them.

This hidden life of the word found its natural expression in the vote of the electorate last week when, voting for its six representatives, it chose three women and three men.

Was it a matter of chance? I think not. But let's see what happens in five years' time. In the meantime, the evidence we have so far indicates that there is no need for gender quotas. Let the will of the people be freely expressed, and that freedom will rake in huge profits in terms of equality. There's no need for ideology.

Ideology
PRO-ABORTION READERS WHO LEAVE COMMENTS ON NEWSPAPER WEBSITES AND, INDEED, EVEN PRO-ABORTION CAMPAIGNERS, MERELY REGURGITATE IDEOLOGY, PREMASTICATED THOUGHTS SPEWED OUT OVER AND OVER AGAIN UNTIL THEY START REPRESENTING A (CONSTRUCTED) REALITY. Ideology is a set of ideas promoted to support the (usually economic) interests of certain groups of people. These ideas are repeated from different angles, in different fashions. Many people either do not have the time or the wherewithal to filter these ideas, which then soak in and build up into a self-image, or a self-perception. This explains the violence with which people defend the ideology to which they adhere, as it becomes a integral part of how they view themselves as individuals and as part of a community. If you disagree with their ideology, they take it as an attack on their psychological integrity and identity, and react with violence.

Many of the ideas making up an ideology are, in reality, a selection of intuitions buttressed into a moral certainty. Consider the case of abortion. There are different intuitions connected with the termination of a pregnancy: that it is morally good to "save" a mother-to-be who feels she is in distress, or that it is morally good to save the life of the unborn child. Ideology will favour one intuition over the other. At times, the Law Courts confirm an ideological stance, by endowing it with the semblance of impartiality. It is a part of our dominant ideology to think that judges are impartial in matters of morality. In fact, this is not true. Judges will follow their own conscience, or intuition which, again, and in a circular way, is influenced by the dominant ideology.

Now let me make Kenneth Wain (one of our 'major philosophers', according to Wikipedia) happy. You might recall that, a couple of years back, Professor Wain attacked me sharply and uncivilly for criticising the PSCD syllabus, as I (and others) saw in it a pro-abortion/pro-choice stance. Let's see how he reacts this time as I quote his favourite philosopher, Richard Rorty:

> We think that the most philosophy can hope to do is summarise our culturally influenced intuitions about the right thing to do in various situations. The summary is effected by formulating a generalisation from which these intuitions can be deduced... [T]he US Supreme Court's construction, in recent decades, of a constitutional

'right to privacy' [is an example] of this kind of summary. We see the formulation of such summarising generalisations as increasing the predictability, and thus the power and efficiency, of our institutions, thereby heightening the sense of shared moral identity which brings us together in a moral community.

To make Professor Wain even happier, I will quote another titbit from Rorty. Rorty is quite explicit that ideology is essentially a selection of ideas, and that young people can be converted to it:

> it is not very hard to convert [students] to standard liberal views about abortion, gay rights, and the like. You may even get them to stop eating animals. All you have to do is convince them that all the arguments on the other side appeal to 'morally irrelevant' considerations. You do this by manipulating their sentiments in such a way that they imagine themselves in the shoes of the despised and the oppressed. Such students are already so nice that they are eager to define their identity in non-exclusionary terms... Producing generations of nice, tolerant, well-off, secure, other-respecting students of this sort in all parts of the world is just what is needed – indeed all that is needed – to achieve an Enlightenment utopia.

You can clearly see that Rorty is

saying that 'standard liberal views' can be manipulated into self-identity for young (and therefore impressionable) people. Among such 'standard liberal views' is abortion, and any opposition to abortion is an 'appeal to "morally irrelevant" considerations'. All told, the technique Rorty describes, is actually quite simple to execute.

The problem, of course, is the utter rubbish being presented as 'standard liberal views'. That a mother-to-be can kill her own unborn child because that unborn child is still not a "person" (however "person" is defined) is utter rubbish: ideological rubbish. It reminds us of other ideological rubbish from the past, now consigned to the dustbin of history. Ideological rubbish such as the consideration of slaves as three-fifths of a person in antebellum America. This fraction was based on the other ideological rubbish that blacks are inferior to whites.

But here's an example of ideological rubbish from the past intimately tied to us Maltese.

The famed English poet Samuel Taylor Coleridge (1772-1834) had this to say about us: 'It is interesting to pass from Malta to Sicily: from the highest specimen of an inferior race, the Saracenic, to the most degraded class of a superior race, the Europeans'. The utter rubbish of race was the ideology of Coleridge's times and even a brilliant man like him succumbed to it.

In our times, other ideological rubbish is shoved down our throats.

My Personal Library

Niccolò Machiavelli (1469-1527) is mostly known for his *The Prince*, first distributed in 1513, but published in 1532.

Machiavelli's principal aim when writing this book was to exhort a prince to unite Italy – at the time a territory divided into several states and statelets, some of them under foreign domination. He looked to Lorenzo the Magnificent, of the de Medici family, to be the leader who could unite Italy.

In *The Prince*, Machiavelli discusses whether a Prince should be generous or parsimonious, cruel or merciful, in what way he should keep his word, how he should avoid contempt and hatred and similar topics. I might one day write an analysis of Joseph Muscat's government from a Machiavelli (not Machiavellian) point of view.

If you have seen the mafia movie *A Bronx Tale* (1993), you might remember the scene in which Italo-American mobster Sonny LoSpecchio lectures his young *protégé* Calogero (originally named Lorenzo ... for The Magnificent?) Anello about Machiavelli.

LORENZO: What do you read?

SONNY: You know... things... you know. I read philosophy.

LORENZO: Philosophy? You read Philosophy? Come on, Sonny.

SONNY: Sure. You ever hear of Machiavelli?

LORENZO: Who?

SONNY: Nick Machiavelli, believe me, this man had it together. If he was around today, he would be my Consiglieri.

LORENZO: So what about this guy Machiavelli?

SONNY: Availability, that's what he always said.

LORENZO: What do you mean?

SONNY: I could live anywhere I want to. You know why I live in this neighborhood? Availability. I want to stay close to everything. Being on the spot you can see trouble start and deal with it immediately. Trouble is like a cancer. It's easy to cure when it's small, but if you wait too long, it grows and then it kills you. So you gotta cut it out early. Availability. That's what it comes down to. The people in this neighborhood, that see me every day that are on my side – they feel safe and that gives them more reason to love me. But the people that want to do otherwise, they think twice, because they know I'm close. And it gives them more reason to fear me.

LORENZO: Is it better to be loved or feared, Sonny?

SONNY: It's nice to be both, but

it's very difficult. But if I had my choice, I would rather be feared because fear lasts longer than love. Friendships that are bought with money mean nothing. You see how it is around here, I make a joke and everybody laughs. I know I'm funny... but I'm not that funny. It's fear that keeps them loyal to me. But the trick is, not to be hated. That's why I treat my men well. But not too well. I give them too much, then they don't need me. I give them just enough where they need me but they don't hate me.

In the following scene – one of American cinema's most iconic – a group of Germanic-looking Hell's Angels bikers walk into the mafia-owned bar and misbehave obnoxiously and roughhouse. Irked, Sonny and his Italo-American mobsters then beat the living daylights out of the bikers and kick them out of the neighbourhood: the realisation of Machiavelli's dream – the Italians driving the Germanic invader out of Italy.

Legend has it that Mussolini kept a copy of *The Prince* on his bedside table for bedtime reading.

***

WRITTEN IN MIDDLE ENGLISH,
CHAUCER'S *CANTERBURY TALES* (1387-1400) ARE A CLASSIC, A JOY TO READ, PREFERABLY, HOWEVER, WITH A MODERN ENGLISH PARALLEL (OR EVEN INTERLINEAR) TRANSLATION. I love *The Nun's Priest Tale* in particular, because in that little tale the cock Chauntecleer gives a two-limbed answer to the perennial question of Woman.

While arguing with the hen Pertelote, one of his seven wives, the cock Chauntecleer tells her – in Latin – to underline her lack of knowledge – '*In principio / mulier est hominis confusio*' which he mistranslates (on purpose) as '*Womman is mannes joye and al his blis*'. The hen Pertelote is obviously ignorant of the real meaning of the Latin phrase, but very happy with the (mis)translation.

With this little piece of verbal trickery, the cock Chauntecleer explains to us that 'In the beginning, woman is man's downfall (or ruin)' and at the same time she is 'a man's joy and all his bliss'.

Wise words indeed. Then again, these are a hen and a cock talking, and their conversation must necessarily be understood in the light of the old adage, 'It is a sad house where the hen crows louder than the cock'.

Creating a New Constitution

TRADE UNION REPRESENTATIVES HAVE RECENTLY BEEN INVITED TO PARTICIPATE IN DISCUSSIONS ON A NEW CONSTITUTIONAL DOCUMENT. Will they propose economic human rights, the human right not to be poor?

In our political-economic system, isn't wealth a choice? That is to say, isn't one free to become rich if one wants to? Isn't this the basic notion of capitalism? Doesn't capitalism assume that all men and women are born free from legal shackles and therefore free to become rich if they work hard enough?

These are, in their crudest form, the basic philosophical principles underlying a liberal democracy – liberal in the sense of the freedom to become rich if you work hard enough. This would also explain why our republic is built on work. You are free to work for yourself and therefore free to become rich. This necessarily means that if you do not become rich, then it is your fault: you did not exercise your freedom, the freedom that a liberal democracy ensures you are entitled to and can enjoy if you so wish, and this from the moment you are born.

All human rights can be understood as corollaries to this implicit basic principle. This is why the Civil Codes of the 19th century were called *Liberal* Civil Codes, and were understood as implements for constitutional principles because, unlike the civil laws of the former system, the Liberal Civil Codes contained laws that ensured that everybody – irrespective of one's birth – was free to become wealthy. The poor, therefore, are poor because of their own choice; they fail to exercise the freedom given to them by the system and to become rich.

Socialism was the retort to this philosophy and trade-unionism one of the reactions to raw capitalism: if they unite, workers can obtain better working conditions from employers.

However, the trade union movement could not overcome the basic philosophy of capitalism, namely that you are free to become rich.

Obviously, as opposed to the former system in which the nobility and other notables enjoyed advantages which the commoner did not. For instance, a nobleman could pay back his debts under less onerous conditions than the commoner, giving the former an unfair advantage over the latter. Liberalism brought a level playing field: all economic actors would be subject to the same laws, and privileges barred. In this philosophical outlook, everybody has the right to become wealthy.

In theory, everybody can start a business and, if they are smart and lucky, become rich. In this logic, it follows that the poor are poor because they do not avail themselves of the freedom to become rich.

But we know that this is not entirely true. It is not the case that all the poor are poor because they are lazy.

Some poor people are simply unlucky: their business might have been wiped out by an economic crisis; they might have been victims of a mental or physical disease; they might not be particularly bright; their business idea or model might be wrong... All this is already envisaged by capitalism: it is ultimately 'the survival of the fittest'. The obvious question is: so what happens to the less fit; do they disappear?

For these and other reasons, I really wonder what the trade unions can bring to the table. If they argue successfully that economic human rights should be introduced – the fundamental right not to be poor – then they will have scored an enormous victory to reduce poverty in this country.

Will they ask that the new Constitution contain provisions to protect workers from further automation? A few days ago, the BBC reported that 'up to 20 million manufacturing jobs around the world could be replaced by robots by 2030, according to analysis firm Oxford Economics'. As the current Administration has wholeheartedly embraced neo-liberalism, I am sceptical.

Neo-liberalism has seduced the Left. The Left espoused identity politics causes, now even to nauseating extremes. For instance, now that homosexuals can marry people of their own sex (homosexuals could always marry people from the other sex; it was never prohibited), do we still need the Gay Pride? This is an exaggeration meant to divert society's attention from the needs of the poor – and of the workers, who are not exactly in the category of 'the poor', but might soon slide downwards.

And it could not be otherwise. If you look at recent history you will realise that two things have happened in the post-1989, post-Berlin Wall world.

Before I continue: I was – and still am – no fan of the USSR. It's a good thing that the Soviet Union is no longer but it's not an entirely good thing. There have been side-effects which, I believe, have not been properly tackled by the West. The demise of the Soviet Union meant that any brake on neo-liberal tendencies in the West ceased to exist. These tendencies did not sprout overnight – they had been maturing over many years – but the end of the USSR meant that they could now blossom unhindered, which they did. Then when the Communist bloc disintegrated, and the new markets of Eastern Europe opened up to the West's capital, there was a clear need to pay for the (re)construction of the East, diverting over there the wealth of the West. It was clear that the post-WWII boom was destined to end: the workers had to pay for the West's victory in the Cold War. As if purposely to keep the workers distracted, the 1990s saw a crescendo in identity politics.

Not only gay rights, but also the transgender agenda started encroaching on public discourse, little by little replacing the worker-rights agenda. The dominant ideology started to promote the transgender agenda, whereas workers' rights fell to second – if not third – place.

It is no surprise, therefore, that a pro-worker philosopher such as Slavoj Žižek, who has also studied psychoanalysis, should recently argue that from a Freudian point of view, trans-genderism makes little psychoanalytical sense. Indeed, there is a problem with having to accept the self-perception of a person, when that self-perception does not tally with reality. A (wo)man feels (s)he is a (wo)man, and society should humour him/her. So if somebody feels they are a cat, a dog, a Martian, Napoleon, should society humour him/her as well? A lot of energy is being diverted toward these "studies" at the expense of workers' rights.

The environment
THE PRESENT CONSTITUTIONAL DOCUMENT DID FORESEE A LIMIT TO THE IMPLICIT RIGHT TO BECOME RICH: IT IS FOUND IN THE STATE'S DUTY TO PROTECT THE ENVIRONMENT.[34] Capitalism is based on the exploitation of the environment, which is why the Greens sit on the Left in a typical parliamentary assembly. The Greens might not necessarily be interested in workers' rights, like the Socialists, but like the Socialists they dislike capitalism because, from their perspective, it destroys the environment.

Among other things, liberalism means the economic freedom to exploit the environment and natural resources. This freedom is so basic to capitalism that governments cannot get themselves to act effectively to curb CO_2 emissions.

My own opinion is that climate change is partly caused by industrialisation and partly by natural causes. I hold this opinion because there have been numerous ice ages in the past, before industrialisation. Still, it is clear that the burning of

----
34 Chapter 2 of the current constitutional document.

fossil fuels does contribute to the planet's warming and this has to be remedied. How to remedy it, when capitalism is the economic system, based on the exploitation of the environment? Even the Communists have become capitalists! (China.)

In the case of Malta, if you expect to see pro-environment action from Joseph Brancaleone Muscat, forget it! (Brancaleone is not a reference to the surname, but to a vintage Italian movie, which has now attained cult status – *L'Armata Brancaleone* [*For Love and Gold*].)

Just look at the construction "industry" debacle to understand Muscat's environmental credentials. First he allowed all-out exploitation (even promising a probably-useless Gozo-Malta tunnel to have enough material for land reclamation) and now he wants to introduce discipline overnight because his *laissez-faire* free-for-all ultra-neo-liberalism has caused a veritable national cataclysm![35]

Historical/ironic parenthesis. Many have noted that the family that lost their home because of the wall that collapsed, had a photo of Joseph Muscat in their kitchen. This seems to be an old tradition: when Samuel Taylor Coleridge was secretary to Alexander Ball's gov-

---

35   This was written before the tragic death of Miriam Pace in her Ħamrun home in early 2020.

ernment in the early years of the British occupation, he remarked that the simple folk kept a picture of the Virgin Mary and a sketch of Captain Ball in their kitchens. This prompts me to speculate whether the Maltese still view the Prime Minister as the heir of the Governor, who in turn was the heir of the Grand Master.

Neutrality
SOME 20 YEARS AGO, WHEN HE WAS STILL LABOUR DEPUTY LEADER, NOW-PRESIDENT GEORGE VELLA PROCLAIMED A BEAUTIFUL PHRASE: '*MALTA SUPPERVA!*' [PROUD MALTA!] – *MALTA SUPPERVA* IN THE SENSE OF HER NEUTRALITY. Now, some years back Joseph Muscat toyed with the idea of doing away with neutrality. Then he stopped playing. Will the new constitutional document retain the neutrality clause? My question is not airy-fairy. As a matter of fact, our neutrality is of the pragmatic type – our safety is guaranteed by Italy. I believe that the politico-military implications are clear.

However, our neutrality is not only in our interests (it would avoid the destruction we experienced in the early 1940s – even though what the Luftwaffe bombers *non fecerunt, fecerunt* the "developers"). Our neutrality is also in the interests of the big powers. Small states such as ours should not exist in a logical world. But in a world of *realpolitik*, small states exist for the benefit of the big ones. A small state that is also neutral is useful to the big states as it can serve as an intermediary and/or interlocutor.

The other alternative is to become a naval base again. Our ancestors fought against this tooth and nail. The Maltese were never happy with the "Fortress Colony" role imposed by the British; we would not be happy to become a Fortress again. Neutrality is a much more intelligent path to follow, with benefits for us and for the big powers.

When I look at Muscat's foreign policy, however, I am utterly not impressed. Look at the dog's breakfast he's made of our relationship with Italy. He put all of his eggs in one basket – he befriended Matteo Renzi and when Mr Renzi's stint came to an end, Muscat found it difficult to find common ground with Mr Renzi's successor, Matteo Salvini. I am sure that Muscat did not follow the advice from seasoned advisers who, following Italian politics, know they are volatile. If he followed Keith Schembri's advice, it shows shallowness of judgment. If he followed nobody's advice, then it's even worse. Muscat's foreign policy has probably been his weakest point, even weaker than

his record on the environment and traffic management, national image management, and other debacles. Indeed, apart from so-called 'civil rights', Muscat's legacy will be quite mediocre, not to say depressing.

The country needs neutrality. It would be stupid to let neutrality go.

He was *So* Close

THERE WAS TALK ON THE STREET, IT SOUNDED SO FAMILIAR. Great expectations, everybody was watching him. People he met, they all seemed to know him; even his old friends treated him like he was something new. Everybody loved him, so he couldn't let them down. There's talk on the street, 'twas there to remind him... doesn't really matter which side he's on. He's walking away, and they're talking behind him. They'll never forget him 'til somebody new comes along.

Shallow judgment
THAT HE EVEN THOUGHT HE COULD MAKE IT BETRAYS THE SHALLOWNESS OF HIS JUDGMENT. How could he ever think he would be taken seriously when he simply ignored the obvious implications of pigheadedly (and big-headedly) protecting his closest aide who had created a secret tax-avoidance (if not even a tax-evasion) scheme? Others stepped down; he dug his heels in. His stubbornness demonstrated not resoluteness and strength of character in the face of strong criticism, but shallowness of judgment coupled with a serious character flaw.

Shallowness of judgment because he let others see that he is unable to extrapolate, to foresee the unavoidable future consequences of his present actions. He might be good when he's playing in the local, amateur league; but as soon as he tried to prove his mettle in the overseas, professional league, he discovered he was out of his depth. As was inevitable, he was cut down to size. And it was not only because he demonstrated a clear shallowness of judgment, not only because he displayed a telling inability to understand that non-locals (that is to say, people who do not depend on him for their business, careers, or what have you) would be evaluating his behaviour according to higher standards set by the exigencies of world-power status; he thought he could play the big-league game according to the rules of petty parochial power.

He was cut down to size because of a serious character flaw of his: he thinks that he is the perennial new kid in town. This deluded self-perception – possibly validated by small-scale communities but certainly derided in large-scale ones – could never bear the stress and strain of a different milieu, one where raw talent on the one hand and powerful, oft concealed political connections on the other, are the key factors that unlock a situation, not the herd-like support of blinkered supporters. Yes, he was almost there. But that's practically of no importance. What matters is that he is not there. The skeletons in his cupboard were too many. He had closed his eyes to the skeletons in the cupboard of some of his favourite acolytes, while believing that nobody had realised this or that his own skeletons in the cupboard would be similarly disregarded. Instead, he was "punished" for breaking rules that are not written – because they are not legal – but are perhaps even stronger than written rules: the unwritten rules of civilisation. He was not aware that there's more to civilisation than meets the eye, possibly because, whether one likes it or not, the truth is that the more subtle aspects of civilisation remain unseen by people who lack a certain background.

Though this might sound elitist, it is not, for elitism is something else altogether. But the elite do partake of this civilisation. However, whereas all the elites partake of it, it is also shared by others who do not belong to the elite. He seems unable to read the unwritten rules of civilisation, and this is quite apparent to those who can actually read them. He was the small-town wonder boy who owed his success more to luck than talent, who went to the big city to audition for a part in the big show. They did not turn him down. They simply ignored him.

He massively misread civilisation. He reckoned that abortion is the in-thing in the civilised world. So he cajoled certain people to speak out. True, not all those who support abortion spoke out because of his cajoling – some of them simply joined the bandwagon when they realised that the climate was favourable. He aimed to be perceived as trying to civilise his own backward people. He thought that by distancing himself from pro-life retrogrades, he would score points with the civilised ones he so wished to impress. But the game was too obvious to impress anybody with the very level of civilisation of those whom he wished to impress. Again, his shallowness of judgment made him think that playing according to local, amateur rules would secure victory in the game played according to professional rules. At the same time, his delusion – that he's the perennial new kid in town – made him oblivious to the obvious fact that the people he wished to impress usually have unusually high IQs.

So he came back from the playground, his shirt hanging out, his trousers soiled, his overall appearance unkempt and shabby. When he played football with his classmates, he usually won; now he had played with the professionals of the Premier League, and just came back. Cut down to size, his head hanging. His friends tried to cheer him up, ironically by emphasising that he had been very close to succeeding. They too displayed shallowness of judgment. Why highlight the near miss? The fact that he surrounded himself with people who, like him, display shallowness of judgment further confirms his own shallowness of judgment.

Once a friend told me that there are places, like India for instance, where bachelors place adverts in the papers to find a bride. Some of them advertise themselves as "Admitted to Oxford" or "Admitted to Cambridge". Their selling point would be that they are so smart that they were admitted to top-notch universities. But they're not as smart as they think. The classy girls whom these chaps try to impress would ask the obvious question. 'Good, you were admitted. But did you finish the course?'

That cafone, again

THERE IS A WORD IN ITALIAN, CA-FONE, WHICH HAS SOMEHOW PER-COLATED INTO AMERICAN ENGLISH SLANG. I do not know how this happened – I can only guess that it was the Italo-Americans who brought it with them.

Originally, in the dialects of southern Italy, the word *cafone* had a neutral meaning: a poor peasant.

In Ignazio Silone's beautiful novel *Fontamara*, there is a description of the structure of early 20th-century rural Italian society given by one of the characters:

> God is at the head of everything. He commands in Heaven. Everybody knows that. Then comes Prince Torlonia, ruler of the earth. Then come his guards. Then come his guards' dogs. Then nothing. Then more nothing. Then still more nothing. Then come the peasants (*i cafoni*). That's all.

But over time, the Italian word came to mean an uncouth, boorish, ill-mannered person. A mid-20th century dictionary has entries such as *scafonizzare*, meaning 'to civilise a barbarian or primitive people'. One also finds *motocafone*, meaning 'a rude driver'. And one finds the hilarious *anglocàfoni* – the accent has to follow the model of *anglosàssoni*. The *anglocàfoni* are 'Italo-Americans that are more attached to Italian culture than their Americanised fellow Italo-Americans'.

But the primary meaning in Italian is 'boorish, uncouth, ill-mannered' and it is with this meaning that *cafone* has managed to insinuate itself into American English slang.

It came to my mind while watching Salvu Balzan's latest videoblog. The man is, unfortunately for this little country of ours, a wonderful specimen of one particular subspecies of the species *Cafone*.

There are different subspecies, I believe: *Cafonis italicus meridionalis*, *Cafonis italicus septentrionalis*, *Cafonis americanus septentrionalis*... and, for our sins, *Cafonis melitensis*. Salvu Balzan is a museum-quality specimen of *Cafonis melitensis*.

He did speak of how he would like to be remembered when he goes to the next world ('if a next world there is', he hurried to console us).

He would like to be remembered for both his good and not-so-good qualities. He shared this profound thought while denigrating the memory of Daphne Caruana Galizia and the BBC for airing a drama about her. He said a lot of things about her which I will not repeat.

But one thing struck me of what he said, and I'll to refer to here; it actually drove me to write about our *cafone*. It betrays a profound lack of self-awareness, the unmistakable characteristic of the true *cafone*. This gentleman spoke of the truth, of the devotion journalists should show toward the Truth.

He seems to delude himself that he's a Servant of the Goddess Truth, probably even the Chief High Priest of the Roman Goddess Veritas, or her Greek counterpart, Aletheia. Mr Balzan repeatedly tried to enter the Temple of Aletheia; each time he was solemnly kicked out and told in no uncertain terms not to trespass again. Or else.

Imagine a Monty-Python-like movie peppered with elements from *The Exorcist* in which Mr Balzan approaches the Temple of Truth, and the High Priests – a hybrid between the Knights Who Say Nee and the monks of the Holy Hand-Grenade of Antioch – warn him that if he dare approach the Temple, they would throw the Holy Water of Truth in his general direction and it would first burn his skin, then him.

Salvu Balzan for the Truth. That sentence promises to collapse like those walls whose foundations were excavated by the greedy developer building a block of flats where the house next door once stood. Such are the fragile foundations of such a sentence.

My Personal Library

My attention was recently caught by a book called *Decadence, radicalism, and the early modern French nobility: the enlightened and depraved* by Chad Denton (2017). The author proposes the thesis that sodomy and adultery played a primary role in the decline of the French nobility. He argues that, impressed by the ideas of the Enlightenment, the nobles "evolved" from a warrior class into an educated class. They embraced libertinism, as a pragmatic and secular ethic of sexuality, and sceptically rejected Catholic moral orthodoxy. They saw it as a means to reassert their privilege: only the educated high nobility could practise sodomy and adultery and not risk either the death penalty or ostracism.

The French nobility thus acquired the image of being parasitic and corrupt, rendering the entire class obsolete in the eyes of contemporaries. In Denton's opinion, this led to the political and social decline of the French nobility. The book makes fascinating reading, even though one has to ask whether Denton's thesis – which seems to exclude other causes – can be accepted in its entirety.

The Fireworks Vendor's Son

YEARS LATER, AS HE FACED THE NEWS OF HIS FAILURE, HE WAS TO REMEMBER THAT DISTANT AFTERNOON WHEN HIS FATHER TOOK HIM TO DISCOVER FIREWORKS. From that childhood discovery, a life philosophy was born which was to grow into an approach to politics.

As a boy, he was mesmerised by the beauty of the colourful patterns that looked like prehistoric eggs on a riverbed, by the peony that make a spherical break of coloured stars and the chrysanthemums that leave a visible trail of sparks, by the fish that burst and little squiggles of light squirm away from them, by the palm that produces long, thick streams of light, by the crosette that crosses squiggles of light over each other haphazardly, and by the kamuro that has a dense burst that leaves a large, glittering trail.

As a man, he was seduced by the fireworks philosophy. You work hard to sell the lot, you promise the best spectacle this side of the Great Sea, and once it all literally goes up in smoke you face no further responsibility. Your job is done and you move on.

The fireworks mentality permeated much of his political activity.

Two people living together
CERTAIN LEGISLATIVE CHANGES

HAD TO BE MADE: IT WAS CLEAR THAT TWO PEOPLE LIVING TOGETHER – AND THUS HEAVILY INVESTING IN EACH OTHER – HAD TO HAVE THEIR STATUS SOMEHOW RECOGNISED BY THE LAW. In the past, siblings for instance could make an *unica charta* will, that is a joint will between two people. (The law was changed in the beginning of the 1980s, disallowing everybody except spouses to make *unica charta* wills.)

Whereas it cannot consider "love" as an element on which to base its provisions – love cannot be objectively determined – the law can envisage rights and obligations based on factual situations, such as sharing one's life with another person. It is reasonable to suppose that in such factual situations protracted over time, individuals develop a vested interest in each other's welfare and inheritance. Reforming the laws to reflect these situations is an inherent quality of the political system we inhabit.

In the distant past (the period we refer to as the "Middle Ages"), when the State was weak or even primitive, decisions of this type were taken on a discretionary basis. Somebody in authority would assess a situation and take ad hoc decisions. This, of course, led to the usual problem associated with discretion: discrimination. It was not necessarily a question of a priori discrimination, that is to say discrimination stemming from a policy. Instead, the discrimination would be the result of the different views and values espoused by different office-holders.

One of the promises of the Modern State was to eradicate this discrimination, by removing discretion. The judge, for instance, became a State official whose job was to apply the law, not to make the law. This new system has been called, by Paolo Grossi among others, juridical absolutism. Only the State Legislature can make law; neither its functionaries nor its judges, and not even other "informal" sources of law. In other words, reforming legislation is part and parcel of the modern political system. Since the State is the only recognised source of law, State legislation has to be reformed every so often as no factual situation is static. Celebrating what should be a routine legislative reform as some great political achievement – therefore reflecting an ideological victory – is not only silly: it is pernicious. It distracts from the real function of the law-making branch of the State, that is the level-headed reform of legislation. It is the fireworks syndrome: keeping the populace happy with colourful patterns in the sky and lots of din in the air, while other, possibly equally important reforms slide away into oblivion, into the less exciting realm of forgetfulness.

Two instances, both reported by the press, come to mind among the multitude of reforms that are needed.

One, the need to update our laws to reflect discoveries made by psychology in the field of coparenting. Psychological research has found that children need and want co-parenting after their parents separate. This cannot be left to the Courts of Law – the Courts cannot and shouldn't create the law. This change has to be made through legislative reform. What has the Minister for Justice[36] done about this? Nothing.

---

36   Dr Owen Bonnici.

The Minister's only aspiration in life is to metaphorically lick his master's metaphorical backside to metaphorically make up for his metaphorical incompetence. It metaphorically makes a Metaphorical Minister of him.

Two, the need to update our laws to enforce proper traffic management when an ambulance is rushing to save a life. Not too long ago, the press published a story about doctors being concerned that people don't know what to do when an ambulance needs to pass. Or rather, people either don't know what to do or else they can't do much because of the mess our roads are in. In either case, legislative reform is needed to punish the irresponsible who don't cooperate with ambu-

The Author with Paolo Grossi, Florence 2006.

lances and to create new rules for the decent who are hampered by the chaos reigning on the roads.

What do we get instead? Fireworks-like celebrations of ideological legislation while other legislative reforms are left to pine away like whales dying on a beach. When the Nationalists reformed the so-called Family Law in 1992 and 2004, I can't remember such fireworks-like celebrations. The reforms were necessary and part of the normal government of a democratic State, and were treated as such.

It's all about him

But the fireworks vendor's son is not so much interested in State and Country as in his own (now botched) career advancement. According to a story that appeared on an online news portal and has not been denied by Castille, the fireworks vendor's son employed State resources to lobby for his own appointment to high office. This is nothing short of scandalous. In a normal democracy, he would have had to resign. Instead he wants to go back to his "work" with more vigour, whatever that is code for. If he were toiling for State and Country, rather than his own personal ambitions, he would solve the two biggest problems of the country: chaotic traffic and chaotic, destructive urban development.

Professor Alex Torpiano, the new president of Dín l-Art Ħelwa, gave an interview in which he blamed the Planning Authority and politicians for the mess the country is in. I could not agree more. And the fireworks vendor's son is the prime culprit. We need a present mindful and respectful of the past, that tries to secure the wealth and well-being of the future. We do not need chaos and short-term "development" which poisons any chance of long-term wealth and well-being. Had the fireworks vendor's son been doing his job properly, he would have found a solution to these problems. After all, the right to private property is not absolute. It is limited by the *Pjan Regolatur* from time to time; but it is always limited by the Constitution which imposes the obligation on the State to protect both landscape and historical heritage.

If the fireworks vendor's son were good at his job – as he claims to be ("Best in Europe" and all that) – he would have struck the balance between the individual's right to private property and the constitutional obligation to safeguard the environment. Instead, he threw his hands up in the air and threw in the towel. His political philosophy – every politician has a philosophy, even if it is shallow – is short term. It only promises ephemeral excitement based on the deeply-held notion that either there's no tomorrow or if there is one, there will be somebody else to face the consequences of the short-termism. This is not the philosophy of a statesman, but of an amateur. Yet, his genius has been to transform the fireworks philosophy into a political style. He identified his clients and sold them the political equivalent of fireworks. It worked.

(In the *festa* country, that is; up north, where things are done differently, it failed miserably.)

These two problems – dense traffic and chaotic construction – are destroying not only the quality of life of this country's citizens, but also the most important product it can offer to the outside world: tourism. Malta simply does not have uncontaminated spots. Everywhere is either a building site or spoilt by some aesthetically-challenged construction. As to mobility: choose any two points in the country and you will realise that it takes ages to get from one point to the other. No efforts are made to study what's done in other countries, to emulate good practice.

France, the number-one tourist destination in Europe, could be a model to learn from. Is anybody even aware of how the French conserve their heritage? A visit to the Bourgogne-Franche-Comté region would open some eyes as to how a top-notch tourist destination should be managed. You don't see cranes and *bajliet tal-konkos* everywhere. One hot spot in that region is the Abbey of Cluny (or what remains of it – it was partly demolished Malta-style, *avant la lettre*, in the late 18th century). The Abbey itself is the main attraction, but the Cluny experience is cemented by the overall architectural ambience of the town. You depart with your spiritual lungs full of the air you just inhaled – the oxygen of beauty.

This cannot be said of Malta. We have a few (admittedly very beautiful) buildings here and there, a gem (Mdina), and then... chaos. A chaotic product which lacks identity and focus. A mishmash of the beauty of bygone years and the banality of today's greed. In Cluny, one attraction which particularly struck me was La Malgouverne. For the name more than anything else. If I'm allowed a pun, Malgouverne is one characteristic we surely share with Cluny.

Professor Mark Anthony Falzon opined that 'it's really all about Joseph'[37] – an opinion that echoes mine and that of the majority of the thinking public. If this were an absolutist State, it would be fine. But in a democracy, nobody is the State, nobody can behave as if he were

---

37   "Joseph über alles", *The Sunday Times of Malta*, May 26, 2019.

the *Roi Soleil*. In a democracy, office-holders administer the State on behalf of the people, not for their careers or other personal objectives. And while chaos reigns and resources are employed to promote individual careers rather than to nurture the Country and its needs, the fireworks vendor's son's best friend – the Panama one – allows his own bald sidekick to boldly go to Libya to conclude only God knows what business.

It is becoming clear even to the less bright, that Malta has become a kleptocracy.

Chronicle of Tragedies Foretold?

HE IS CLEARLY UNDER PRESSURE.

After the botched attempt to attain high office – a foolhardy ambition given his internationally-known blunders, which shows all-round shallowness of judgment – he himself has to face the music. In the sense that everything now seems to indicate that his style of ruling was based on the assumption that he would soon be leaving for greener pastures, and his successor from his own party would clean up the mess.

Now that the cunning plan has failed, he must see how to find the way forward in the mess he himself created.

His knee-jerk reaction has been to spray outlandish claims all around, such as that the people never had such a good quality of life.

But many – including his own supporters – are beginning to see through the buzzwords, to make their own calculations.

They are realising that the impersonal economy might be doing well, but that their personal situation has not really improved. It has actually deteriorated.

After all, only a small percentage of the population is raking it in from the wanton destruction of the environment, but it is the vast majority that's paying the price for this "economic growth".

It is very much private (minoritarian) profit at the cost of public (majoritarian) welfare.

This is probably the hallmark of his legacy.

That a tragedy is in the making is very clear.

The economy works in cycles, and he knows it.

It would seem logical to suppose that he was preparing his exit from local politics to coincide with the downturn in the economic cycle.

Not too long after I published my book *L-Aqwa fl-Ewropa. Il-Panama Papers u l-Poter*, an economist got in touch and told me that the economy would start cooling down in 2018/19.

Finance Minister Edward Scicluna himself – who, of all people, now seems to be embroiled in financial bamboozling – had acknowledged this some time ago.

This abuse of public office is nothing short of obscene.

Public office is not there for private ambitions. It's there for public service.

But this sense of self-abnegation seems to be alien to the left-liberal worldview, which rewards pleasure and regards with suspicion those who apply self-restraint in their dealings with themselves, the others, and society as a whole.

This week, two important Italians passed away: Andrea Camilleri (about whom further down) and Luciano de Crescenzo.

Both were over 90 years old and both were from the Italian South, which is supposedly backward and less civilised than the North.

Luciano de Crescenzo was a Neapolitan engineer who, somewhat late in life, became a philosopher-novelist.

His most famous novel is *Così parlò Bellavista* (obviously a pun on Nietzsche's *Thus Spoke Zarathustra*) and when it was published in 1977, it sold more than 600,000 copies.

In it, the protagonist – a retired philosophy teacher – explains the difference between the Love Peoples (Italians, Spaniards, Poles, Irish, Greeks) and the Freedom Peoples (Britons, Scandinavians, Germans) and those in-between.

But he also speaks of the difference between the Stoics and the Epicureans.

The Stoics are those who are ready to forgo pride and pleasure because they believe in something bigger than themselves. The Christians, for instance, are Stoics because they believe in eternal happiness and are therefore ready to suffer on this earth to acquire happiness in the next. The Epicureans are those who seek pleasures in the here and now. To my mind, de Crescenzo's explanation of this categorisation applies to politicians.

The Stoic politician applies self-abnegation because s/he is a wo/man of State and the interests of the State inspire his/her actions. The Epicurean politician could not care less, and thinks only of how occupying a State office can serve his/her own ambition, be it political, financial, or God knows what else (remember, only two things are infinite: the universe and human imagination, be it intelligent or stupid).

By applying this categorisation, we understand that we are currently ruled by an Epicurean, for whom instant gratification is more important than long-term planning. We can clearly identify the ingredients of tragedies foretold.

Indeed, all tragedies are foretold – it only takes men and women endowed with judiciousness, whose judgment is not shallow, to read the signs. It then takes men and women of courage to act on those signs, even if in the short term they might encounter the backlash of unpopularity.

But he feels the need for popularity more than the need to do the right thing. The real tragedy is that the price will be paid by the nation, not by him.

All tragedies are foretold.

Do you remember the Genoa bridge that collapsed last year?

An inquiry has now established that safety problems had been apparent for at least the last 10 years before the disaster.

Did anybody do anything about them? No.

The tragedy – unlike the concrete of the bridge – did not fall from the sky.

It had been in the making for a number of years; people with "second sight" (the "prophets" of the past) could extrapolate from what they saw but, like all "prophets", they were ignored.

And then the tragedy that had been foretold, happened, and left 43 dead.

The country as it is being managed at the moment has all the ingredients of a tragedy foretold.

When the tragedy happens, however, we will only have ourselves to blame.

In the environmental sector, it is abundantly clear that it's "abandon ship".

In the reputational sector, the damage done is huge.

And on it goes: a litany of tragedies foretold, but whitewashed by sparkling buzzwords and linguistic bravado.

He is a like the Wizard of Oz.

He gives diplomas to Scarecrows, medals to Lions, and heart-shaped watches to Tin Men.

But as yet, he has not admitted that he is a humbug, though intelligent people are realising that he's not administering our Oz in the interests of Oz.

The cracks in the Wizard's palace are beginning to show, and clearly so.

Here I'm not referring to the long-term tragedies which can be extrapolated from the way things are managed at the moment.

I'm referring to strange contradictions which I must admit I cannot fully understand as yet.

Consider this contradiction, for instance. We are being told that the population has to keep increasing, and yet the property market has slowed down – as admitted by the President of the Malta Developers Association.

Does this mean that there is now enough housing for the expected (artificial) increase in population?

An aside: the artificial increase in Malta's population comes mostly from immigration from the East of Europe, where populations are ageing and the younger generations are being depleted.

In the not-too-distant future somebody will have to foot the bill for Eastern Europe's pensioners, their healthcare and so on.

Consider something else that is happening.

Tourist bed nights have dropped for the first time in four years – under the Panama Papers Minister for Tourism.

At the same time, the same Minister – who it seems was embroiled in the hospitals mess – has negotiated the creation of a new, third-class-travel passenger airline.

Is this a new trend?

Will tourist arrivals increase while tourist bed nights keep dropping?

If indeed this is a new trend, what will the consequences be?

Let's be honest with ourselves.

First, the picnic can't go on forever.

Second, picnic's over – you have to clean up.

Third, if during the picnic you're not careful when you light your barbecue, you can even set the woods on fire, and there won't be any more picnics in the future. This is what we're talking about here.

Do you remember *The Wizard of Oz* movie?

At the end, the Wizard climbs on an air-balloon and leaves Oz.

The movie ends with the girl Dorothy exclaiming, "There's no place like home!" – indeed, there's no place like home(land).

And we're ruining it.

My Personal Library

On Wednesday 17 July, 2019 Andrea Camilleri passed away. He was perhaps the most prolific and widely-read Italian author of the last 30 years. I had the good fortune of meeting and interviewing him 19 years ago, in his Rome apartment, upon his invitation. I cannot here do justice to the more than 100 books he wrote and published. But I can make three observations about his work and life.

One. Many readers loved his Montalbano stories for their astute plots and insightful characterisations. I have loved Camilleri for another reason. It is not because Camilleri was highbrow literature – he was not. But his novels and short stories lend the reader – particularly if the reader is young – the vantage point of the old raconteur. Camilleri's stories are powerful because they are distillations of memories, left to mature in the casks of old-age wisdom. In a society which reduces its old folks to recluses in homes for the elderly, a national grandfather who wants to narrate about his youth through the microphone of the wisdom that comes with old age, has necessarily to become a best-seller. To my mind, Camilleri is more of a sociological than a literary case. Very much like Bud Spencer, who fulfilled the role of father to a number of generations brought up in a fatherless society, a society seemingly made up of sons and daughters of widows. It is not just a matter of feminism. The slow disappearance of the father figure has been observed in literature, starting more or less with the beheading of the French King during the Great Revolution in France. Camilleri seems to me to have been to the Italians, and perhaps even to others, the grandfather they lacked, as everybody locks their elderly away in homes just as everybody entrusts their children to day care centres and nobody has time for family anymore. The ongoing attack on the family is dictated by the dominant mode of production, which does not need the family as economic unit to function properly.

Two. Camilleri's historical novels, all based on or inspired by true historical events, are narrative gems. Style, characterisation, plot are handled in a masterly fashion. The theme is almost always "Sicilianity" – *sicilianità* – and mostly in the context of Sicily as part of something bigger not Sicily taken as an entity separate from any other, a "stand-alone" polity. Take his *La mossa del cavallo*, a veritable tour de force in psychology, a treatise in strategic thinking. It is the story of a police officer who gets arrested for a murder he was about to report to his colleagues. The central idea of the novel is that the officer was originally Sicilian but his family had moved to Genoa, and he thus needs to rediscover his roots, start thinking again in Sicilian and unravel the hidden threads determining his situation. In a sense it is interesting for us Maltese as we think that because we sort of communicate in English, then we sort of participate in the English world. Pure fantasy, needless to say. Then, I found Camilleri's *Il re di Girgenti* to be his masterpiece – the maestro depicts and criticises superstitious Christian ideology (and stupidity). Yet, over the years, Camilleri too succumbed to the left-liberal ideology. I found this contradictory.

Three. Camilleri's success came late in life. He had published his first novel in the 1970s, but made no inroads in the national book market. In the late 1990s, Camilleri benefitted from the same fortune that had shone on the brave Luciano de Crescenzo: he was endorsed by Maurizio Costanzo during his highly popular talk show and from then onward he never looked back. This says a lot about luck and perseverance, in the sense that it is perhaps never too late for Lady Luck to smile at you.

Camilleri's life-story imparts a lesson in hope, in never giving up. Then again, you have to live long enough eventually to reap the fruits of your encounter with the Lady and of your perseverance.

In the photo: the Author with Andrea Camilleri, Rome 2000.

A Decade of Decadence

I AM NOT A PSYCHOLOGIST, AND DO NOT PRETEND TO BE ONE.

But, simply out of empathy and common sense, I can understand how he must be feeling now.

After the international fiasco – even though he keeps wearing his cool, smart-aleck mask – deep down he must feel distraught.

"Distraught" not as in Shakespeare's 'as if thou wert distraught and mad with terror', but in the sense of 'agitated with doubt or mental conflict or pain'.

Obviously, this must be his state at the moment, and one can fully empathise.

Then again, despite all the empathy, one has to ask: what on earth possessed him to persevere in his quest for an international office when his local shenanigans had been exposed all over the world?

This tunnel vision says a lot about his judiciousness.

If he couldn't work out the simple equation that protecting Panama-Papers people equals no chance of attaining high office abroad, how can he then work out the consequences of the policies his administration pursues and will be pursuing at home?

One downside to public office is that when you voluntarily aspire to and attain it, you implicitly give up your "right" to be shielded from criticism that could increase your agitation, mental conflict or pain.

The public needs to be aware of the anguish caused by a major career setback because that anguish will necessarily affect your psychology, particularly if you happen to have the power to take decisions that impact the entire nation.

Policies pursued

LET'S CONSIDER THE NEW RULES FOR BANK LOANS: IT SEEMS THAT THE CENTRAL BANK WANTS TO REIN IN THE BUY-TO-RENT SECTOR.

What does this mean in relation to population growth?

Last April, during the Labour Party General Conference, the Prime Minister asked,

> Can someone explain how it is
> a problem that EU [citizens] are
> coming to work here instead of
> the other way round? ... I would
> much rather have an international
> company to stay in Malta but bring
> in foreign workers than shut down
> and leave.

This was last April, a mere three months ago.

So why is the Central Bank now changing the rules for buy-to-rent loans?

What's going on?

Government and bedrooms

GOVERNMENT POLICY AFFECTS

BEDROOMS NOT ONLY IN THE SENSE OF ACCOMMODATION.

In an article published in 2010 called "The state and the bedroom", Mario Vella – the current Central Bank Governor and author of one of my favourite books ever, *Reflections in a Canvas Bag* (1989) – had criticised Nationalist MP Edwin Vassallo for saying that, 'What happens in the bedroom is, up to a point, the government's business because it often had to resolve problems caused there.'

Mr Vassallo had sensibly cited 'single parents and teenage pregnancies' as examples of the sort of problems arising from 'what happens in the bedroom'.

Nine years on, I still cannot understand Dr Vella's criticism.

Wasn't Mr Vassallo right?

Don't these cases create problems the State then has to solve?

Shouldn't the State open people's eyes to the consequences of their actions?

Dr Vella had contended that these concerns reflect 'bigotry, prejudice, intolerance and sheer ignorance'.

Again, I cannot understand how discussing the public consequences of private decisions could ever add up to these accusations.

Dr Vella promised to articulate his criticism in his next article ('More next time' he had promised),

but I couldn't find it. Most probably, he changed his mind. Possibly because it was politically expedient to make illogical criticisms without backing them up with... logical clarifications.

During a PL activity in Żurrieq in January of this year, Prime Minister Muscat referred to the same theme. In the civil sector, he said, ten years ago divorce didn't exist and the Government would go into everyone's bedroom, while today the country is at the forefront of civil rights.

Civil rights, or so it seems, are equal to sexual "liberation".

Which must therefore imply that the 'bigotry, prejudice, intolerance and sheer ignorance' of Dr Vella's article referred to what many of us consider as the responsibility inherent in sexual activity. But this sense of "responsibility" is – in the eyes of the liberal-progressives – nothing but a manacle.

Nine years have passed. The supposed 'bigotry, prejudice, intolerance and sheer ignorance' have remained unexplained by that part of the political spectrum that issues these "fatwas". As Muscat himself admitted, in this decade Malta has become a radically progressive country, despite the pre-2013 electoral pledge that the project was to be progressive with moderation. (The Minister responsible for this project has now been rewarded with higher office.)

What worries me and those who share the same ideas, is that nine years have passed and the State still makes no visible effort to inform the people of the consequences of their private choices.

It grants so-called civil rights but imparts no education. There are no pro-family, pro-life, pro-higher values educational campaigns.

Instead the dominant ideology seems to be pleasure, the here-and-now, living life like there's no tomorrow.

G.K. Chesterton called it 'the *carpe diem* religion' and warned that it is not the religion of happy people. He was talking of decadence.

*Civil rights can make
civil hands unclean*

NOW LET US SAY THAT FOR A BRIEF MOMENT OF INSANITY, I AND A FEW LIKE-MINDED FRIENDS OF MINE DECIDE THAT NOBODY SHOULD DECIDE FOR US WHAT WE PUT IN OUR BELLIES, THAT WE WANT FREEDOM TO CHOOSE WHETHER TO WORK OR NOT, AND THEREFORE THAT WE WANT TO DISPOSSESS OTHER PEOPLE OF THEIR BELONGINGS AND START LIVING OFF THEM. We create a pressure group to campaign for the abolition of private property. We want everything to be commonly owned, each to be given according to his/her needs. We proclaim our freedom to co-own whatever we like, to put in our bellies whatever we want. The Criminal Code – a bourgeois piece of legislation which penalises theft – should be amended for us to enjoy the freedom we proclaim. What would the authorities do? Would they let us campaign and spread this most subversive of philosophies, or would they take action against us?

Let us say that in a second, equally brief moment of insanity, I and some other, also like-minded, friends of mine proclaim our freedom to marry two or more, even five, spouses at the same time (like some African tribes do – multiculturalism and all that). After all, it's our bodies, our choice. The Criminal Code – a collection of bigoted Medieval laws which penalise bigamy – should be amended for us to enjoy the freedom we proclaim. Furthermore, a State Agency should be set up to help us with the expenses related to five spouses and their children. Again: what would the authorities do? Would the State in this case poke its big fat nose in our bedrooms, on the pretext that being married to five spouses goes against public policy? Would it stop us from campaigning for the legalisation of theft because it goes against public policy?

That the State does not stop those campaigning in favour of abortion, on the simple basis that abortion violates public policy, shows that he thinks that public policy should allow abortion. Only an idiot wouldn't see this.

For the benefit of the "Where's the proof?" brigade: the Labour-leaning news portal iNews published "subtle" pro-abortion propaganda in the form of a story about a British mum regretting not aborting her Down's syndrome baby.

The confusion in a few people's minds stems from reading British authors on morality and studying in British universities – doctors in particular. They fail to see that Britain is going through "managed decadence".

In the brilliant book I mentioned above, *Reflections in a Canvas Bag*, a young Mario Vella, despite having studied at the London School of Economics and Political Science, claimed that British universities are, essentially, amateurish and over-rated.

The youthful Mario Vella might or might not have been right, but some people would do well to ruminate over his observation.

Many of the observations in that book are insightful.

I wonder whether he heeds Dr Vella's advice.

Environmental decadence

ON THE ENVIRONMENT, LET US SAY. Whereas Environment "Minister" José Herrera bumbles about, mumbling things about "false nostalgias" while trees are being felled con mucho gusto, the overall impression one gets of this government's environmental policy is that... it's practically non-existent.

'The past was not as rosy as imagined,' claimed the "Environment" Minister. (Yes, you can play around with the inverted commas – after all, Dr Herrera is either the "Minister" for the Environment or else the Minister for the "Environment". Whichever you choose, you're right. You could also decide he's the "Minister" for the "Environment".)

Now, let's dissect the "Minister"'s logic. To me it seems to be along these lines:

Premise A: There weren't so many trees in the past (it's 'false nostalgia').

Premise B: We need progress.

Conclusion: Therefore, it's ok to fell trees.

The country has the highest rate of air pollution in the Union, and the "Minister" for the "Environment" waxes lyrical about 'false nostalgia'. Or waxes indignant. Again, you choose, use inverted commas, and all that.

It's becoming so Orwellian that words fail me.

It's as though "Minister" Herrera were a washing machine mumbling to itself, and the colours of words run in his speech.

What is this madness?

What have trees got to do with progress?

Real progress is achieved when more trees are planted, when trees become an integral part of any project, of the Environment. But – as Anthony Ellul of the Malta Chamber of Planners has stated – 'we have now reached a situation where there is no planning at all.'

Thing is, you cannot separate private morality from public behaviour.

The way people behave in their private lives will flow over into the public sphere.

The etymology of the word itself indicates this.

Morality derives from *mores* which means *custom*, "the way of doing things".

When the dominant ideology promotes a morality of "everybody mindlessly minding their own business", this permeates the bedroom but also flows outside, into society.

So, in this decade of decadence we see no planning in the bedroom (because the ideology does not promote thinking about the consequences) and no planning in the natural environment (for the very same reason).

This intimate psychological relationship between bedroom and natural environment is so deep that commenting on the reigning chaos, architect Richard England condensed his frustration and that of many thus:

'I remember Malta as a virgin.'

My Personal Library

In December 2016, I visited Marcello Veneziani in his Rome loft. I thought that *I* had a lot of books! I had to recalibrate my self-perception... each and every wall of Veneziani's residence was covered with shelf upon shelf, and the air was saturated with the sweet smell of lignin.

Veneziani can be classified as a populariser of philosophy. The first book of his I read, which I consider his best, is called *Comunitari o liberal: La Prossima Alternativa* [Communitarians or Liberals: The Next Alternative], 1999. He uses the English word "liberals" to distinguish these "new" liberals from 19th-century liberals.

Veneziani claims that liberals believe in emancipation, in liberation from ties, in the project of Humanity. They believe in overcoming frontiers and boundaries, and in universalism (or cosmopolitanism).

Communitarians, on the other hand, give importance to the feeling of community, to rites, to the usages and customs of a people. This is not a sociological or folkloristic importance, but one intimately related to life – these should serve as points of reference for one's orientation in life. Communitarians are children of a fatherland; the motherland of the liberals is time. Communitarians love variety and distrust precarity; the liberals prefer variability and dislike differences. Variety is diversity in the spatial sense, argues Veneziani; variability is diversity in the temporal.

In the photo: the Author with Marcello Veneziani, Rome 2016.

Impressing the Uncouth

HE HAS TRIED TO CONVINCE LA-
BOURITES THAT HE IS THE NEW
MINTOFF, OR A REINCARNATION OF
HIM. A little psychological ploy that
has so far paid handsome dividends.
Had he been a woman it would not
have worked. Apparently, science
has established that women are at a
disadvantage. A woman who seeks
to be trusted with a job or an office
needs to prove a solid track record;
a man can get away with promises
for the future.

So he was lucky from this point
of view. He simply made promises.
Tons of them. On the fourth floor
and elsewhere. However, it is now
becoming apparent to one and all
that he is no New Mintoff. One
might agree or disagree with Mintoff's ideas and plans, but I think all
can agree that Mintoff was of a different calibre. He is something else
altogether. In one thing alone he has
surpassed Mintoff: grandiloquence
directed at the less educated. He is
better than Mintoff in impressing
the uncouth. As to the other classes,
I think they took Mintoff more seriously than they take him. He owes
his success with these other classes
to his laissez-faire, nonchalant attitude – clearly the "nonchalant"
qualifies the "*laissez-faire*" as negative. His attitude is "let everybody
do more or less what they want"; it

is based on the ideology that 'every
man for himself (and the devil take
the hindmost)' – in Malta's case the
'hindmost' are those who are not
"in business" and have to pay the
price for the profits of the few. It is
also becoming clear that there is actually no really plan – there is just
a series of short-term leaps and all,
but really all, fingers crossed.

Let's consider the population issue. Has a figure really been established to reflect the maximum population these two little islands can
support? Has the breaking point
– the point of no return – been defined and identified? If yes, what
methodology has been used? What
measures have been and are being taken to avoid reaching breaking point? Has there been any cost
analysis? Not just in terms of the
physical environment but also in
terms of social cohesion, national
identity, and overall manageability
of the country.

On July 31, 2019, *The Malta
Independent* reported that the
Minister for Home Affairs and
National Security cautioned that
Malta 'is still in need of foreigners
to take up job opportunities', and
'ways must be found to encourage
legal migration, even from Africa'.

In other words, the plan is to
keep increasing the islands' population. This necessarily means that
more virgin land will be taken up

for infrastructural and residential projects, more buildings will be demolished for more soulless, badly-constructed blocks of flats to be erected, more roads will be widened for more cars to circulate the few square kilometres we inhabit, more trees will be chopped down to ease traffic congestion (!), more air pollution will ruin our lungs and noise pollution our serenity, more criminality from frustrated foreign males will increase social tensions, and the brush of shabbiness won't stop painting this entire country in opaque ugliness. That's not all.

The symptoms of overpopulation will not be limited to the bigger island but, thanks to the proposed tunnel, will extend to the smaller one too.

Everything will be engulfed in a mad bid to increase the population to enlarge the economy. And Malta and Gozo will be buried alive under the shadow not of the cypress trees but of blocks of apartments. The economy might be growing but whether this is really accompanied by a just distribution of wealth is another story. Just distribution of wealth is Socialism's strong point, but also one of the strong points of Christian Democracy.

In this country, under this administration, we have neither Socialism nor Christian Democracy. We have an ultra-liberal government that is happy to please the few at the expense of the many.

Worth his salt

A FEW DAYS AGO, BUSINESSMAN FRANK SALT WROTE AN OPINION PIECE IN THE PRINTED MEDIA, AND I FOUND A LOT IN IT WHICH I AGREED WITH. Among the points raised by Mr Salt, I found a few I can repeat without hesitation: 'our economy is booming, but at the expense of Malta losing its identity. Since our islands are full of foreigners living and working here, there is much more wear and tear to our environment, especially in the urban sphere. The sad thing is that very little effort is made to address this problem, and so, our towns – especially those which are supposed to welcome our foreign visitors – are getting more and more unkempt and tatty looking.' Malta is indeed becoming shabbier and shabbier.

Even small details. Consider for instance the floodlights that should light up Valletta's bastions. If you have time, take a walk along the rocky coast round Fort St Elmo: you will see that the floodlights that once lit up the imposing walls of the City have disappeared. In their place, rusty pillars with ncovered (live?) wires dot the coastline at uneven intervals, a tangible memory of past, discontinued efforts to highlight the beauty of the fortifications. The Best in Europe cannot even bring himself to carry out a proper upkeep of floodlights. Had he been the administrator of a block of flats, he would have been summarily fired by the flat owners in no time. But he keeps impressing the uncouth and seducing the easily seduced, derailing the entire democratic mechanism in the process.

Another General in His Labyrinth

IT IS CLEAR THAT HE IS TIRED: TIRED, AND BITTERLY DISAPPOINTED BY HIS DEFEAT ABROAD. Invincible though he thought he was, the dour reality is that, like everybody else, he is subject to failure. But there are people who do not see it coming, and when it hits them, they feel doubly distraught and shattered. He is tired and disappointed and should call it a day.

Gabriel García Márquez describes his General, the Liberator of his Continent, in his labyrinth. Our own 'General', the 'Liberator' of our little Islands, might be living the agony of the eve of his labyrinth. He is tired and disappointed, and, even though the people cheer him and prepare metaphorical banquets in his honour, in reality he is beginning to slip away from the centre stage of history. History also seems to be have tired of him, and to be disappointed in him. Signs abound everywhere now that he is beginning to lose control, his power is waning and the sun that radiates his will to govern is setting behind the distant hills. His ability to take decisions around the clock is quickly fading into a pale shimmer of moonlight.

The true leader overcomes failure by turning it into an opportunity. But then there are others who are elected "leaders" who are nothing but the product of a process described thus by Aldous Huxley in *Brave New World*: 'All that is needed is money and a candidate who can be coached to look sincere; political principles and plans for specific action have come to lose most of their importance. The personality of the candidate, the way he is projected by the advertising experts, is the things that really matter.'

The Pursuit of Happiness

ELSEWHERE, HUXLEY ALSO OPINED THAT 'THE PURSUIT OF HAPPINESS IS ONE OF THE TRADITIONAL RIGHTS OF MAN; UNFORTUNATELY, THE ACHIEVEMENT OF HAPPINESS MAY TURN OUT TO BE INCOMPATIBLE WITH ANOTHER OF MAN'S RIGHTS – NAMELY, LIBERTY.' Our Little General, our "Liberator", promised to usher in a Second Republic. It seems that the project will start now, with the drafting of a new Constitution.

A Constitution is a legal document that sets up the State, it is the political and administrative mechanism that manages our lives. The State is almost a god – it determines whether we live or die, whether we thrive in riches or strive through poverty, the taxes we pay, the benefits we get and so on. It can be said that the origins of the State are outside the Law, that they are "mythical", almost "divine". The American insistence on 'In God We Trust' could be understood in this sense.

Then again, whereas in the Middle Ages it was the Pope who crowned the Emperor – meaning that the latter's power came from God – in modern times we have forgotten from where the State derives its power and it seems that the State derives its power from a so-called basic – or fundamental – law (that is, a law which lies at the base – at the foundations – of the system) which in turn derives its power from "the people".

The American constitutional system is built on the idea that it is 'self-evident, that all men are created equal, that they are endowed by their Creator with certain unalienable Rights, that among these are Life, Liberty and the pursuit of Happiness'. I think these principles guide many, if not all, of the enlightened constitutions of the contemporary world.

And yet Huxley pointed out a possible contradiction: the pursuit of happiness may come at the expense of liberty. One could extrapolate that we could argue the opposite way too: liberty comes at the expense of the pursuit of happiness.

The fundamental question thus becomes: what is "happiness"? Is it 'prosperity, thriving, wellbeing' or does it go beyond that? Is it the unending search for pleasure?

In his *Civilization and its Discontents*, Sigmund Freud tells us that

> what we call happiness in the strictest sense comes from the (preferably sudden) satisfaction of needs which have been dammed up to a high degree, and it is from its nature only possible as an episodic phenomenon. When any situation that is desired by the pleasure principle is prolonged, it only produces a feeling of mild contentment. We are so made that we can derive intense enjoyment only from a contrast and very little from a state of things.

Another Sigmund, but this time his name is written in Polish – Zygmunt – Bauman, said this about happiness:

> happiness can be defined solely in negative terms, as overcoming, defying, defeating or putting paid to, and all in all denying, the state of unhappiness ... Happiness is the driving force of life pursuits, but like the rest of guiding, lodestar-type utopias, its 'materiality', indeed its human/social significance, is entirely entailed in stimulating its searching and the durable – though all too often serendipitous (unanticipated, unintended and unplanned) – effects of that search.

In other words, the advert-like form of happiness does not exist, according to two of the most important intellectuals of our times. Happiness cannot be bought at the supermarket of politics. Happiness is the moment we solve a problem, the moment we realise we have been treated fairly, the moment we understand that we are being given chances in life like everybody else.

He promised happiness as if he were selling toothpaste. Vote for him and the whiteness of your teeth will shine as never before, the cavities will fill themselves by themselves and the pain in your gum will disappear. This was pure, beautiful marketing, aided by advertising experts, bereft of political principles and ambiguous with regard to political action. But when you come to reality, you find another story. Let us consider the equality that any modern state should deliver – not just promise – to its citizens. Let's consider this example. Malta signed and ratified the Twelfth Protocol to the European Convention on Human Rights in December 2015 and the Protocol came into effect the following April.

In this Protocol you will find the principle of non-discrimination applied not just to the rights found in the Convention itself but – and this is extremely important and innovative – to all the rights found in our national law. In other words, Protocol 12 should protect Maltese citizens from discrimination under not only the Convention but all our national laws. But don't start celebrating yet! Despite the signature and ratification four years ago, the Protocol has still not been incorporated into the First Schedule of the European Convention Act.

What does this mean? It means that if anyone feels that they have been discriminated against, they cannot go to the Maltese Courts because, to quote a former Chief Justice: 'that article is not part of the definition of "Human Rights and Fundamental Freedoms" for the purposes of [the European Convention Act]'. 'The person would have to have direct recourse to the Court in Strasbourg, with all the expense that that entails,' the former Chief Justice concludes.

The bottom line is this. The Government of Malta has signed and ratified an international Protocol giving you, the citizen, the right to seek a legal remedy if you feel that you have been discriminated under any Maltese law (not just the Convention). You can frame this document and hang it on the wall because, by not including this Protocol in the European Convention Act, the Government has denied

you the legal mechanism to avail yourself of the protection the Protocol gives you. This is a clear example of how he works.

He advertises big and delivers either little or nothing. The advertising is more important than the delivery. Fireworks (colour, din and sulphur-smell) are his forte, not proper ways to deal with life's problems.

People are expecting a fresh start with this new Constitution, possibly less government and more governance.

I'm sceptical but hope to be proven wrong.

Then again, I'm not holding my breath.

My Personal Library

Bruce Dickinson's official autobiography, *What Does This Button Do?*, was a No.1 *Sunday Times* (UK) best-seller.

Mr Dickinson is mostly known for his role as vocalist in the most obstinately successful heavy metal band of the industry, Iron Maiden. I chanced on him at a Valletta eatery in 2006, when he was on Malta for an aviation competition. When I told him I considered him the best vocalist in the industry, his smile stretched from ear to ear: he's good and he knows it.

A University of London graduate in History, Mr Dickinson has enjoyed relentless business success. Naturally, his singing talent has been his greatest source of income and fame, but he's also talented in proper business. Amongst his numerous ventures, one finds beer-brewing and aviation. He even operates an airline for Djibouti, through a Maltese company. In August 2016, the Maltese media reported that 'in an unlikely combination of elements, Iron Maiden singer Bruce Dickinson is hoping to leverage Malta's aviation expertise to support a fledgling airline in the east African nation of Djibouti while helping to foster a relationship between the two countries.' I've no idea how this initiative eventually developed. Long story short: Mr Dickinson's life story is the story of a successful man who never succumbed to hubris but has consistently kept his ego under control, despite the business triumphs that have marked his life.

To my mind, Bruce Dickinson's Iron Maiden is one of the best examples of intelligent and successful branding and marketing one could cite. Mr Dickinson – more than any of the other band members – is a brilliant entrepreneur and businessman to be emulated. He has talent, guts, foresight, perseverance and a never-say-die attitude. Or at least: 'If you're gonna die, die with your boots on'!

In the photo: the Author with Bruce Dickinson, Valletta 2006.

A Constitutional Premiership

WHY THE NEED TO REFORM THE CONSTITUTION? This is a fundamental question which we, The People, need to answer.

Do we need to reform it to ensure the citizens' pursuit of happiness? To overhaul the balance of powers among State organs? To update our State to the post-Cold-War, globalised world? To redefine our democracy? To reshape the political class?

None of the above?

The Language Question
IT IS IMPOSSIBLE TO DO JUSTICE TO THESE POINTS IN A SHORT ESSAY. If we are to own up and confess the truth, then we have to admit that the Language Question has never been satisfactorily solved. We still use Maltese to convey messages meant for a certain social class, and English for other classes. It could be argued that the British do something similar: they use different language registers for different classes. The tabloids that used to publish topless models on their page three probably use a different type of English from those that refrained from this 'British institution'. (Incidentally, *The Daily Star* discontinued this 44-year-old tradition last April; *The Sun* four years ago.)

But if we really use written Maltese to pontificate to one social class and written English to sort of debate within others (and then spoken Maltese to pontificate and debate "nationally"), I wonder what type of debate we are really engaging in in this country. Particularly when the Constitution has to be the Constitution of the entire nation. It seems like we are deliberately leaving a segment of The People out. Why? You might ask me: why do you write a newspaper column in English? There are three answers to that question.

One, there is no Maltese-language newspaper that is not the mouthpiece of an organisation.

Two, I like this newspaper. (I particularly dislike Salvu Balzan's gutter-press paper, mostly because of the lack of ethics repeatedly shown by its editors, present and past.)

Three, I have written two books on politics in Maltese, so I write in both languages. In those two books, I did not pontificate, but tried to engage in debate with my reader. Be that as it may. The big problem, which we as a nation haven't solved and seem to have given up on, is that English still enjoys the prestige associated with the colonial administration. The implications of this psychological phenomenon are numerous, far-reaching and beyond the scope of this piece. But they do deserve to be identified and discussed.

Small Nation Problems

WE ARE A SMALL NATION, AND AS SUCH HAVE PROBLEMS THAT BIGGER ONES DO NOT. Or else we have them, but their expression is different, again because of our size. There was a series of Italian books – a collection of TV shows punch lines – called *Anche le formiche nel loro piccolo s'incazzano* [Ants too, in their small way, get pissed]. We Maltese are like those ants. So, do we Maltese need to change our Constitution to find, in our small way, our solutions to the problematic State-citizen relationship? Or does the need lie elsewhere?

Late last year, Giovanni Bonello published a book called *Misunderstanding the Constitution*. When I reviewed it, I hailed it as the most important book of the decade. In that book, Judge Bonello points out that the present Constitution could be really useful in the citizen's pursuit of happiness and the reigning in of political arrogance, if only the Constitution were properly understood. If this is indeed the case, and the present Constitution is indeed useful if properly understood, why re-write it? Why not implement the provisions of the current Constitution? (During a radio programme, Judge Bonello said, 'better a wretched Constitution in the hands of good people, than a good constitution in the hands of scoundrels.')

The Pursuit of Happiness

'THE PURSUIT OF HAPPINESS' IS PHRASE IS A CORNERSTONE OF AMERICAN CONSTITUTIONAL THINKING THAT – DIRECTLY OR INDIRECTLY – INSPIRES ALMOST ALL NATIONS AROUND THE WORLD. Who wouldn't want to live in a happy nation and be given the opportunity to seek (and find) individual happiness in this world?

I have previously drawn inspiration from the late Italian philosopher Luciano de Crescenzo and the distinctions he pointed out between the Epicureans and the Stoics. The former seek happiness in this world; the latter are ready to postpone happiness in this world, to then attain it in the next. To my mind, the Epicureans have won the day in Western constitutional thinking: the pursuit of happiness refers to this world. (The solitary exception might be Britain. Britain's constitution might not actually promote the pursuit of happiness. Though it's difficult to say because their Constitution is not written, the subtext to much of the Brexit discourse seems to indicate a craving to be allowed to pursue happiness in a country fraught with privilege and class.) So will the pursuit of happiness be the lynchpin of the new Constitution project? But, if affirmative, aren't the provisions against discrimination found in the current Constitution already a guarantee that happiness may be freely pursued in this little Republic of ours? Why re-invent the wheel?

The Prince

OR WILL THE OBJECTIVE BE TO SHOW THE PRINCE OUT AND SHOW A REAL PRIME MINISTER IN? What do I mean by this? According to the written provisions of the current Constitution, the Prime Minister is *primus inter pares*, a Latin phrase meaning that the Prime Minister is First among Equals. But is this so? Does our constitutional system treat the Prime Minister as a First Minister who leads the other Ministers? Or does the system look at the Prime Minister as a Prince served by Ministers who carry out his will? Or is he somewhere in between these two positions?

To my mind, the *primus inter pares* notion is a dead letter, an ideal never achieved, a model imposed by the foreign master and dutifully binned by the local obedient servant. The country's real constitution – the living, historical, unwritten constitution – lays down that the nominal Prime Minister of Malta is, in terms of realpolitik, Prince of Malta.

Le roi de France est empereur dans son royaume

IN THE MIDDLE AGES, FRENCH LEGAL SCHOLARS CAME TO THE CONCLUSION THAT 'THE KING OF FRANCE IS AN EMPEROR IN HIS OWN KINGDOM'. By this they meant that the king enjoyed the absolutism that the Roman Emperor enjoyed under the Code of Justinian. French scholars elaborated another constitutional principle: *Rex solutus est a legibus* [The king is released from the laws]. Or, to put it differently, the king is above (and therefore released from) the law.

"Absolutism" means that the powers of the monarch were, more or less, unchecked. This was the ideal to which the French king aspired under the ancien régime. In reality, there was always a tug-ofwar between the king and other political institutions in the country, but that would be political analysis.

What we are trying to do here is constitutional analysis, that is the theoretical framework within which the political system should exist and function.

The Order of St John – which ruled over our forefathers from 1530 to 1798 – was heavily influenced by France. It was only natural that the Prince Grand Master should model his government on that of France, and thus live and rule by the notion that the Prince of Malta is an emperor in his own principality.

The Prime Minister of Malta seems like a continuation of the Prince Grand Master, of the *Sultan* as the Maltese used to refer to the Grand Master. The power to hire and fire that the Prime Minister currently enjoys, makes the holder of that office extraordinarily powerful, consequently threatening the balance of powers between the different organs of the State. I once personally heard Dom Mintoff himself make this comparison during a public meeting in 1995, when he explicitly said that as Prime Minister he always kept the Grand Masters as his political yardstick. I believe many observers had already made that connection before Mr Mintoff owned up to it himself.

Modern ideas on constitutions are the result of the battles – not only ideological but also physical – fought two/three centuries ago between absolutist monarchs and those among their subjects who sought to contain the powers of the monarch. Hence the term, "constitutional monarchy". We are – again I have to use the same words – nominally a Republic, but in reality a sort of very weak constitutional monarchy. Our Head of State, the President, is "elected" by the People's Representatives and does not hold the office for life. But that's only nominal. Our State, I contend, is in reality an ancien régime quasi-absolutist monarchy that, influenced by Modernity, has become a (weak) constitutional monarchy, and in which the monarch is not the President, but the Prime Minister.

Nominal versus Real
MANY YEARS AGO, SOMEBODY TOLD ME THAT DESPITE THE PROVISIONS OF THE 1973 LAW THAT REGULATES MERCHANT SHIPPING, PEOPLE IN THE SECTOR BEHAVE ACCORDING TO "UNWRITTEN RULES" AND "TRADITION". I don't know if this really was or still is the case. But the analogy fits like a glove. The law might say one thing, but the people do something else. Which obviously leads to the question: why have a written law if it is flouted?

The answer could be: enforceability. As long as there are no disputes, the unwritten rules can effectively hold sway. But if a dispute does arise, then the codified, written law will (or, in theory, should) determine the outcome. Our current Constitution might have the correct provisions in it to avoid having the Prime Minister rule as though he were an ancien régime, that is to say absolutist, Prince. But, because of tradition and the living constitution of the people, the written Constitution is not understood. (This consistent misunderstanding

My Personal Library

Let's take it easy for once. *Anche le formiche nel loro piccolo s'incazzano* [Ants too, in their small way, get pissed] is a series of seven books published in the nineties, a veritable encyclopaedia of TV show jokes and wisecracks. The authors, Gino Vignali and Michele Mozzati (a.k.a. Gino & Michele), have scripted TV shows such as *Drive In* and *Zelig*, and worked with big names in Italian entertainment, such as Antonio Ricci, Aldo Giovanni e Giacomo, Antonio Albanese, Checco Zalone, Enrico Brignano, and Claudio Bisio.

Some of their jokes are language-based and would lose their comedic effect in translation. For example, 'My father used to tell me, My son, you're not a ball. You're the other.' It's gibberish in English, but cracks you up in Italian. A handful of translatable wisecracks from the books (translated for your delectation by yours truly):

'A beautiful showgirl broke up with Berlusconi the first time she saw him naked. She was disgusted at the sight of him without his wallet.'

'In Russia things are really changing. I've seen children eat Communists.'

'This weekend I went to a disco and saw the most beautiful girl ever. Our eyes met and twenty minutes later we were in bed. Yes, she in hers; I in mine.'

'Pure-breed Lombards are gaunt, to the point, precise. They are meek but tireless workers. They are a tough people, a people who, to avoid paying even a lira of tax to the central government in Rome, would rather buy a Porsche Carrera.'

is Judge Bonello's thesis in that very important book I referred to above.) Re-writing the Constitution might help to achieve the implementation of the principles needed to evict the Prince from the Prime Minister's office. Then again, this is revolutionary and it might be that the incumbent's heart is not in it. Unless, that is, he wants to bequeath this particular legacy to his direct successor: a less powerful – a constitutional – premiership. He will bequeath this legacy with the same mindset a pampered child grudgingly hands over his preferred toy to another child in the kindergarten, when his/her time to play with it is up.

Getting Away with Murder

LAST WEEK, MALTA TODAY PUBLISHED AN ARTICLE WHICH SERVES ONLY TO ILLUSTRATE THEIR LACK OF ETHICS. That newspaper – which already has a tainted image – decided to live up to its reputation and "expose" a magistrate. This is beyond scandalous! This is an attack, pure and simple, on the institutions of the country. It is nothing short of abuse of the freedom of the press. What bewilders me is the sombre silence that has accompanied it.

It is not necessary to enter into the merits of the case. What is pertinent is that the magistrate appeared in front of the Commission for the Administration of Justice and that the Commission forbade the publication of its decision. Despite the crystal-clear forbidding, MaltaToday, in its infinite wisdom, decided it knows better than the Commission and went ahead gleefully to publish the decision. It benefits us to remember that on the Commission sit members of the judiciary, representatives of the Executive, etc. In other words, this is not a club where idle people meet to share idle talk. This is one of the most important institutions of the country, and its members are among the more experienced in the legal profession. Their decision to forbid the publication of the decision was therefore not a foolish decision taken rashly – there were undoubtedly serious reasons behind it.

But then *Malta Today* rushes in where angels fear to tread. It put aside the decision of the Commission because it thinks that the public should know! But who exactly is at the helm of this silly newspaper? What understanding do they have of the Constitution, of how the law and the legal system work, of the why and wherefore certain decisions are best kept outside public knowledge? Don't they intuit the prudence which inspired the Commission to forbid the publication of the decision? *Malta Today* wrote, 'In the decision taken by the Commission for the Administration of Justice, the judiciary's watchdog decreed that its admonition should not be published. But *Malta Today*, which has seen details of the decision, has decided such a reprimand is in the public's interest to know.' On what basis does *Malta Today* think it knows better than the Commission? Under what kind of delusions do they labour?

If the law allows the Commission the discretion to forbid publication, there must be a good reason. If the Commission employs the discretion the law grants it and forbids publication, there must be a good reason too. That *Malta Today* thinks that its own judgment is superior to that of the Commission for the Administration of Justice and the law betrays two things. One, a sense of entitlement completely detached from reality. Two, an utter lack of understanding of how the State works and why it works that way. *Malta Today*'s silliness in defying the Commission's decision shows nothing but bravado and bravado also implies "intimidation". This is the reason why I contend that *Malta Today*'s silly decision to defy the Commission amounts to an attack on the institutions of the State.

Granted, few people care about the State in this little Republic of ours. The umbilical cord with the colonial mindset has never been really severed – many in Malta today still think that the State belongs to some foreign power distant from Malta, not to the Maltese people. *Malta Today* rides this wave of political ignorance – political in the philosophical not partisan sense. In the partisan sense, it rides another wave, based on certain arrangements. Those in the know need no more details; for the others, the details required are so many that neither this column nor this entire newspaper would suffice.

The point I want to make is that *Malta Today*'s decision to publish, despite the Commission's forbidding, constitutes – whether knowingly or unknowingly – an attack on one of the most important institutions of the country: the judiciary. I shall enumerate a few reasons why.

First of all, the magistrate concerned cannot defend himself in the media. If the newspaper report gave a particular slant to the story which does not necessarily reflect the truth, the magistrate cannot respond and the public will never know. So the public will only know what *Malta Today* wants it to know! The basic principle of justice that both parties should be heard, has been pulverised by *Malta Today*'s bravado. The newspaper has kicked and punched hard, and the magistrate can only take. This is unacceptable. Why should any member of the judiciary be subjected to such treatment by the supposed fourth organ of the State – the media? The media is afforded ample freedom to carry out its duties, not to abuse of it and intimidate the judiciary. The media is permitted a whole host of privileges to serve as watchdog on the three organs of the State on behalf of the public. A watchdog is not a war dog.

Secondly, there will always be leaks: newsrooms receive dozen of leaks and tips on a weekly, if not, daily basis. And yet, most editors exercise judiciousness and, having a proper understanding of the big-

ger picture, overcome the temptation and refrain from making public details that score points in the here and now but damage democracy's entire edifice in the long run. Indeed, the public need not know a newsroom's opinion about everything. Much of this gossipy news would not in reality represent facts – it would only be the newsroom's opinion on a particular happening. There is a fine line between newsworthiness and rubbish which a newsroom should be aware of and never knowingly overstep. *Malta Today* are aware of this line, but they knowingly overstep it, with much gusto and fanfare, to boot. In a way, they are like irresponsible adolescents.

That *Malta Today* couldn't restrain itself and understand that certain "news" is not news, is a clear sign that certain people should not occupy the post they're occupying. Self-censorship is necessary. Not because of fear or favour, but because it is necessary to filter the filth out. Freedom of the press is like a canal. For the stream to remain clean, you have to refrain from throwing rubbish into the water and to filter all the effluents that flow into the canal. Otherwise, the potable water of freedom of expression becomes the murky sewage of freedom of excretion.

Unlike other Maltese newspapers, *Malta Today* seems unable to weigh the pros and cons of its decisions to publish or not to publish. They seem unaware of the bigger picture, their only aim being to score points or indulge in some blind vendetta at the behest of the people at the helm. Lou Bondì had perspicaciously called *Malta Today*, 'a public vehicle for private envy', and Daphne Caruana Galizia had echoed that observation. I think they were both very close to the truth.

This leads me to my third consideration, namely how the judiciary would have reacted to *Malta Today* defying the Commission for the Administration of Justice's forbidding, and publishing the Commission's decision come what may. It is clear that after this incident, neither *Malta Today* nor people associated with it will appear before the magistrate involved, as they would invoke partiality and so on. Whether *Malta Today* intended this is a consequence of the publication, we shall never know. But nobody can eradicate speculation, and speculation is pernicious to the very ethos and bases of the State's judicial organ.

Furthermore, it is reasonable to presume that other members of the judiciary will be worried or alarmed by the flagrant disregard for the implications and consequences of publishing such a decision. We will never know the truth, because the judiciary cannot engage in public debate, but I think it is reasonable to make this presumption. Similarly, the members of the Commission for the Administration of Justice will feel uneasy. If its decisions are published, despite its forbidding such publication, how can the Commission work serenely? It is now reasonable to expect the members of the Commission, or at least some of them, to be extremely careful as to what they say or decide, even behind closed doors, because the rules have been broken and an ugly precedent set. The question now is: will the breaking of the rules go unpunished?

The scandal is that the decision of *Malta Today* to publish despite the Commission's express forbidding is, in a way, a threat to the judiciary, the only State organ on which impartiality is imposed as it is crucial for the orderly functioning of society. *Malta Today*'s decision is a sort of blackmail – I am sure this is not the first time the judiciary has felt blackmailed by *Malta Today*. The question now is: will the State react or will it turn a blind eye and let *Malta Today* get away with murder?

Malta Today is a newspaper that respects no bounds. For instance, quite a number of years ago, they invented a story about an individual and faxed him questions about the invented story. The individual concerned replied that the story was nothing but an invention, and that if they went ahead and published it, he would sue them. At the time criminal libel was still on the books, so he warned them he would sue criminally. So they didn't publish the news – meaning that they could not prove their invention. But then, many years later, during legal proceedings lodged by a relative of that individual against them on something completely unrelated, they published a news item stating that, years before, the individual had threatened legal action if they published the story they had invented! The subterfuge can be efficacious.

The intelligent reader will understand that there is no truth in the story, otherwise they would have published the story immediately instead of waiting for so many years and then hiding behind the libel threat. The less intelligent reader (and the average reader of *Malta Today* is less intelligent than the average reader of other English-language newspapers – just read the comments posted beneath *Malta Today* articles in general) would get confused and take the story at face value, getting hold of the wrong end of the stick.

Malta Today is a rogue newspaper. One would expect the journalists' associations to rebuke and condemn them for attacking the judiciary. In other countries, rogue journalists are expelled from the profession. In the *Gżira Taparsi*, as Oliver Friggieri called Malta, everybody can do whatever they like, because of a hillbilly understanding of the concept of liberalism. Liberalism is understood as free-for-all anything-goes "whore-in-a-bacchanal" way of doing things.

If *Malta Today* succeeds in getting away with murder, then we shall be fully justified to support a new constitutional document the first article of which would read, 'Malta is a *taparsi*-democratic republic founded on impunity and on the abuse of the freedom of the press'.

The need of the public to know

WHY THE PUBLIC SHOULD NOT KNOW WHAT GOES ON BEHIND CLOSED DOORS WHEN THE COMMISSION FOR THE ADMINISTRATION OF JUSTICE (CAJ) MEETS AND DELIBERATES? Perhaps to get close to an answer, a thought experiment based on two points would be in order.

First. What would happen if the CAJ were not to adhere to *in camera* proceedings? What would the practical consequences be? Would the system survive the stresses and the strains? Does the need for having an orderly society outweigh the public's perceived right to know? What is more important: that the public knows everything or that the system works well? When the CAJ is composed of members hailing from so many different places in society, why sow doubts in the public's mind? It is in the common interest that there be special officials entrusted with the oversight of such structures, but that this oversight be not made public.

Second. The thought experiment should include the possibility, envisaged by the law, for Parliament to discuss the future of a member of the judiciary. If Parliament decides that such a member has committed an act which is serious to a degree that necessitates removal, then Parliament can remove such member. It is therefore difficult to understand the need to demand that CAJ proceedings be public, even on a selective basis, as *Malta Today*, in their warped vision of the world, seem to think.

There are very good reasons to keep the system as it is. Do they need to be spelled out?

In the book *Il-Liġi, il-Morali u r-Raġuni*, the late Giuseppe Mifsud Bonnici said (my translation):

For the Commission to succeed in its mission, disciplining magistrates and judges should be a confidential matter, confidential to the Commission, that is, and not exhibited in public, as has happened in certain cases. ... Why should a judge or a magistrate be publicly accused? Except in extreme cases, needless to say, where the misbehaviour keeps dragging on. ... Proceedings should be in camera, not public. There should be dignity, not shows (pp. 168-69).

The wisdom of Professor Mifsud Bonnici's words lives on. Because ultimately, the judge and the magistrate represent the State not themselves.

My Personal Library

Robert Thake's *A Publishing History of a Prohibited Best-Seller: The Abbé de Vertot and his Histoire de Malte* (2016, US), is a book about a book called *Histoire de Malte*. It's a history of the Order of St. John which took more than ten years to finish and publish, with the road leading to its publication a long and winding one. But similarly fascinating was the road that led to its inclusion on the list of prohibited books. Dr Thake's account is a must-read: the style is flowing, the research top-notch, the material unexpectedly absorbing.

What struck me most is the Abbé's public protestation that the publishers had tampered with his text. This part of the plot captured my attention more than anything else. There was a time when the author lost all authority on the text once the publishing deal was sealed. There must be some arcane relationship between the words *auctor* and *auctoritas*.

* * *

It is ironic that the UK itself does not have a written constitution, given that it imposed codified constitutions on its colonies at the time when they were transitioning to independence. S.A. de Smith's *The New Commonwealth and Its Constitutions* (1964) presents a general survey of constitutional developments in what were then the newly self-governing and independent countries of the Commonwealth. In the chapter called 'The Advantages of Being Explicit', Professor de Smith admitted that 'there are great practical difficulties in codifying the conventions on such matters as the dissolution of Parliament and the dismissal of Ministers'. But he also warned that 'flexibility implies a high degree of uncertainty' – 'uncertainty not only as to what rules should be applied but also as to how in any particular case they should be applied.' He also added a presage:

> Residual discretions which become exercisable in an atmosphere of political crisis inevitably expose the person who exercises them to partisan criticism; and a Governor-General or a 'constitutional' President is clearly more vulnerable to such criticism than the occupant of the throne.

As an expert, de Smith could not foretell the future but he knew the system so well he could see its pitfalls, weaknesses, and risks, and could extrapolate. A layman would not necessarily follow de Smith's intuition, and this is another reason why experts have to be overseen by other experts.

Quoting Roger Waters

MY MOTHER – REFERRING TO NO-
BODY IN PARTICULAR AND TO EVE-
RYBODY IN GENERAL – LOVES RE-
PEATING THAT 'THE CHILD IS THE
FATHER OF THE MAN', AND I THINK
SHE IS RIGHT. They spoil you as a
child, you're spoilt for life. A spoilt
boy usually grows into an irrespon-
sible man, who misquotes Roger
Waters, 'I was a child then, now I'm
only a man'...

He, the Invincible, is irresponsible. Irresponsible for having seduced
a foreign real estate developer with
promises of swathes of virgin land
and undefiled sea views made in a
conversation that lasted five minutes – and now even his *fedelissimo*
is criticising the utter disrespect the
developer (like some of his Maltese colleagues, mind you) has for
our historical heritage. Irresponsible for allowing the few to grab the
cash with both hands and make a
stash, while the many can only look
on. Irresponsible for deluding the
LGBTI community while now the
children they are raising are being made to feel different by their
schoolmates, as flagged by a President *Emerita*. I call it "delusion" on
purpose, because children will always point out that the emperor is
wearing no clothes.

Irresponsible for not resigning.
For proclaiming to the four corners
of the world, upon embarking on
the journey, that he would spend
one term opposing and two terms
governing, so that he would only
amuse himself playing games only
for a while. And now that speculation on his departure date is rife, he
won't care about the implications
of staying on, as practically a lame
duck, while governance runs amok.
But – to quote Roger Waters again,
correctly this time – 'Why prolong
the agony? All men must die'...

I'm not advocating a palace *coup*
- but certain people within his Party should take action for the sake
of the nation. Just tell him, politely
and nicely, or even a tad emphati-
cally if need be, to leave, and let his
Successor take his place to impose
some order on this country that,
truth be told, though never quite
orderly, has now descended into
unprecedented depths of chaos.

This irresponsibility of his is
pernicious. It is rare that we immediately face the consequences
of myopic, irresponsible strategies.
Indeed, the evil that men do lives
after them; when a politician's political life is over, the good is oft
interred with his bones. And someone else has to clean up the mess.
But, whether we face the consequences immediately or over time,
face them we must.

It is true that the Successor of the
Invincible will have to contend with

a legacy difficult to match in terms of political largesse. Many items on the to-do list of so-called "civil rights" have been ticked off, and the cornucopia is now practically empty. (Which is why Helena Dalli's services are no longer required.) The last two taboos will stand for the moment, as it is clear that the vast majority of the Maltese oppose abortion and euthanasia, even though they accepted to tolerate other "civil rights". After all, many people harmlessly pass their time in the grassland away, only dimly aware of a certain unease in the air. So the Successor will not enjoy the privilege of portraying him/herself as a generous liberator.

But then the Successor will have also to face the consequences and implications of the sudden population boom. There are no guarantees that the political conditions which have allowed the current economic rhythm will last – if they do change, the population might shrink, making much of the current infrastructural investment redundant.

On the other hand, if the population reaches a plateau or growth continues (at whichever rate), the Successor will have to face the implications and consequences of this and will have to find a solution to the accompanying distribution of wealth problems.

These are issues that will have to be addressed by the successor in what remains of this legislature and, also, the successor in the next.

Which is why the Invincible should accept the destiny he freely willed for himself and allow his immediate successor to start taking stock of the situation without further ado, and rein in the wraiths of good governance haunting the country and spreading chaos, bringing pots of gold to the few who are out to get rich quick and frightening the many who want to safeguard the environment, the population's health, and (some of them) simply to achieve basic goals, such as making ends meet every month.

Indeed, 'Why prolong the agony? All men must die' ... The Invincible is approaching his political demise.

Why prolong the agony?

For the sake of the nation, this Invincible must leave.

He must stop taking public decisions to further personal interests.

My Personal Library

When in 1967, the psychoanalyst and musicologist Hans Keller interviewed The Pink Floyd (they later dropped the "The") for the BBC, he was not much impressed. He considered their music loud and repetitive, 'a little bit a regression to childhood', even though he added, 'but, after all, why not?' In his opinion, 'They have an audience, and people who have an audience should be heard'.

That was in 1967.

Two years later, Pink Floyd had consolidated their position as a popular cultural phenomenon. When the BBC broadcast the landing on the Moon, Pink Floyd supplied the musical background. Later on, Pink Floyd – or should I say, Roger Waters, their main lyric-writer – dared proffer something a little bit "deeper" to the public... albums such as *The Dark Side of the Moon*, *Animals*, *The Wall* and *The Final Cut* contain a "philosophical" element.

Many years ago, I used to host a radio show with Ray Azzopardi (Malta's current ambassador to Belgium and Luxembourg) and we once dedicated a programme to Pink Floyd's *The Dark Side of the Moon*. I translated the lyrics to Maltese and then Ray and I commented on their meaning and relevance to the problems of everyday life. It was an unforgettable experience, and we received fantastic feedback from listeners.

Now, there's a current in the American publishing industry that tries to capitalise on popular culture. There's a book on *The Sopranos* and philosophy, and another on *Doctor House* and philosophy, say.

So you will not be surprised to learn that there's a book on Pink Floyd and philosophy called, as you might have already guessed, *Pink Floyd and Philosophy: Careful with that Axiom, Eugene!* published in 2007.

A number of professors of philosophy teamed up to discuss philosophical themes in Pink Floyd songs. There are essays with titles such as, 'Dragged Down by the Stone: Pink Floyd, Alienation, and the Pressures of Life' and 'Theodor Adorno, Pink Floyd, and the Dialectics of Alienation'.

This does not mean that Roger Waters, or any other member of Pink Floyd for that matter, is a "philosopher" in any sense of the word.

What it does mean, however, is that artists – irrespective of the idiom they express themselves in – experience the same phenomena that give rise to philosophical speculation and analysis.

Hans Keller was right when he said that if somebody has an audience, then they deserve to be heard. Keller was referring to the bi-directional communication flow between the artist/philosopher/ public thinker/politician and the public.

Thus, if Roger Waters experienced alienation or other modern-day pressures of life, he expressed them in his own way, in words meant to be sung, like Church hymns. As a hymn is not a theological treatise, even though it conveys a message about Man's relationship with God, so a good popular music song is not a philosophical treatise, even though it conveys a message about the problems that philosophy and "serious" thinking too treat (albeit according to a methodology and within certain parameters and a certain system). The reason is quite self-evident.

All said and done, everything under the sun is in tune. You might add, even tongue-in-cheek, 'But the sun is eclipsed by the moon'... and we could go on talking about it all night long.

Invincible, the Soap Opera

THE INVINCIBLE IS BEGINNING TO CRACK. No, I am not talking about the First World War ship, but about he who – it would seem – has a number of tattoos all over his body, one of which reads, *Invictus*. Now, truth be told, *invictus* does not really mean *invincible*; it means, the one who has not been beaten, the "unconquered". But, as the humble satirist that I'd like to be, I find "the Invincible" to be more mouth-watering than the "unconquered".

Every night, before he goes to sleep, while he's brushing his teeth, he looks proudly at himself in the mirror, and recites to himself – while he hears his wife grumbling in the background that he always stays too long in the bathroom – a poem by 19th-century poet William Henley, called *Invictus*:

> Out of the night that covers me,
> Black as the pit from pole to pole,
> I thank whatever gods may be
> For my unconquerable soul.
>
> In the fell clutch of circumstance
> I have not winced nor cried aloud.
> Under the bludgeonings of chance
> My head is bloody, but unbowed.
>
> Beyond this place of wrath and tears
> Looms but the Horror of the shade,
> And yet the menace of the years
> Finds and shall find me unafraid.

> It matters not how strait the gate,
> How charged with punishments
>   the scroll,
> I am the master of my fate,
> I am the captain of my soul.

This is one of the techniques of Positivity: day after day, you repeat some positive mantra to yourself till you start believing it and it permeates your life. And yet, he had to rein in those closest to him who are preparing to pave the way for his succession. It was the holiday season and his would-be successors were working their butts off to show him out. But he is the master of his fate, he is the captain of his soul.

Or so he thinks. Isn't it clear, though, that it has now become a farce? Isn't it clear that every day something is slowly eroding his moral authority? He was too cocky when he announced to the four corners of the world that he would govern for only two terms. He cockily sowed the wind and now he's reaping a veritable whirlwind. His tendency for shallow judgment keeps haunting him, like the ghost of Banquo haunted he whose hands the seas incarnadined.

This leads me to two considerations. First, that despite the hype, the Invincible is a man troubled by shallow judgment. When the hype will be over (as it will sooner or later be), history will judge him for what he really is, a man whose judgment is consistently shallow, for whom short-term gain is a greater achievement than long-term well-being.

Second, this silly idea that has taken root in Malta that politicians should not stay on for long periods. It betrays our inability to do politics for principle rather than power. The Invincible adopted neo-liberal principles, but again for short-term gain, simply to achieve power (and God knows what else), not to implement a vision.

True, we have a duopoly instead of a spectrum of political positions represented by different parties. Where a political spectrum exists, a politician stays on, because working for a political vision is a lifelong commitment, at times even flowing from one generation to the next.

My Personal Library

Lewis Carroll's fantasy novel *Alice's Adventures in Wonderland* (1865) is considered a children's book, but anybody who's read it knows that in reality it's engaging for adults too.

It is my considered opinion that in times like ours, reading books like this one and its companion *Through the Looking-Glass, and What Alice Found There* (1871), helps to understand the "wonderful" games politicians like the Invincible are good at playing, and possibly winning.

Cheshire-Cat
Prime Minister

SOME PEOPLE DOUBT THAT STUDY-
ING LITERATURE IS USEFUL AND
WONDER WHETHER IT SHOULD BE
DISCONTINUED. I dislike utilitarian
defences of learning but if I were
with my back against the wall, I
would say that one reason to teach
literature is for intelligent students
to learn how to analyse complex
real-life situations, such as politics
and its *dramatis personae* – the
characters who inhabit its theatre-
like world.

If we were to consider the current developments in the local political scene as a tragedy (or a comedy, or even a tragi-comedy), we
could then apply literary criticism
methods to look into, dissect and,
ultimately, understand what is really happening. Politics is – more
often than not – a sort of stage, with
actors wearing masks. Many people
just accept the action at face value,
simply accepting what the masks
tell them. But a few others look behind the masks.

Theatre is a simplified explanation of real life; masks and make-up
are meant to simplify and bypass
long explanations. Real life, on the
other hand, is complex in that the
actors on the political stage wear
masks for the public, make-up for
their colleagues (on both sides of

the House) and beneath all that – if
anything actually remains – there is
their real self. Very few politicians
manage to bring their real self before the people and those who do
establish an incredible rapport, an
unbreakable bond, with the people.
Some of the most beloved politicians were/are beloved because of
this. The others were/are simply actors wearing masks and make-up.

So, we who comment on politics have to present our analysis
on three levels. One: we try to
explain the mask; two: we invite
readers to look behind the mask,
to see the make-up worn for the
other politicians and, three, we
try to ascertain if there is anything
beneath the make-up. Sometimes
we find nothing – it would be just
an empty *vol-au-vent*.

Thus, we could say that studying
literature at school prepares tomorrow's intelligent voters for this tri-
partite exercise. Let us take a recent
statement made by Robert Abela, a
Labour MP who is also a consult-
ant to the Prime Minister. This consultancy was described last June as
'fundamentally wrong' by Commissioner for Standards George Hyzler.
In a sense, Robert Abela was given
the same post as his father during
Alfred Sant's stint as Prime Minister. Are there a mask and make-up
in the case of Dr Abela? It is common knowledge that, like his father

before him, Dr Abela is ambitious. He is one of the hopefuls who aims to fill the vacancy once the incumbent (The Invincible) decides to do the honourable thing and call it a day.

But whereas other hopefuls do not carry much political baggage, Dr Abela is a politically complex figure and his role in the play (this *pièce de théâtre*, this *teatrin*) that is the current political situation requires some analysis. Last week, *The Malta Independent on Sunday* reported that Dr Abela asked an important question: 'Are we living our socialist principles, or do we feel ashamed to even mention them?' The 'we' refers to the Labour Party. The question was most probably rhetoric. Is it not common knowledge that Labour, in its current incarnation, has thrown away its last vestiges of socialism? It has unashamedly distanced itself from social democracy and brazen-facedly striven to achieve neo-liberal objectives. The poor and the vulnerable have been swept aside and their place has been taken by a certain category of businessmen, opportunists and proponents of identity politics.

I argued as much in my 2016 book *L-Aqwa fl-Ewropa*, and I quoted numerous Labour exponents to support my argument. The fact that, only now, has Dr Abela felt

the need to ask his question raises a number of issues.

His political conviction is not one of them. I actually believe that, like his father, Dr Abela Junior truly wants to be a socialist politician. So I certainly do not view him as a hypocrite. Drs Abela – father and son – are both socialists: there is no doubt in my mind about this. The salient political characteristic of Robert Abela, as a character in the play we are analysing, is another. It forms part of the political legacy bequeathed to him by his father, George.

George Abela, known as *The Switch* in his University days, was always popular, mostly because he is endowed with two qualities: charisma and cold-bloodedness. But the admixture of these two qualities must have created in him a sort of recklessness, a sort of belief that he can get away with anything.

Let me take you back to 1998: Dom Mintoff is quarrelling with Alfred Sant who, despite the advice he is being drip-fed, cannot find how to appease his feisty predecessor. The quarrel escalates and Dr Sant sees an early election as the only way out; to many in the Labour Party it is as clear as day that this is suicidal. I can still remember two old-school politicians arguing in the Executive Committee against such an unwise decision: the thunderous Joe Debono Grech and the suave Freddie Micallef. Their styles were different, but their message was the same and, deep down, everybody knew that they were right. Theirs was a position based on commonsense and long years of political experience. But, ultimately, they were echoing the mood among the grassroots. The electorate had decidedly turned against Labour, mostly because of the water and electricity bills and, more importantly, because the people felt betrayed that the cash registers introduced by the VAT innovation had not been removed. It is true that Labour had promised nothing of the sort but, on the other hand, it had done next to nothing to dispel the "misunderstanding". Playing such games with the electorate is like playing with fire – you are sure to burn not just your fingers, but more.

George Abela also opposed the idea of an early election: but he went a step further. His self-confidence was boosted by his undeniable charisma and his misguided cold-bloodedness which led him to pronounce the fateful statement that if Labour went for an early election he would 'stop there'. That statement broke the unwritten holy rule of loyalty.

From a stalwart who disagrees but is loyal, he suddenly transmogrified into a stalwart who disagrees and stopped being loyal. He failed to foresee the consequences of his actions, to understand that his decision would – in the final analysis – be viewed as a contributing factor to the ensuing defeat at the polls.

This is the political legacy that Dr Abela Senior bequeathed to Dr Abela Junior and this situation makes me suppose that Abela *fils* is haunted by the political ghost of Abela *père*. To my mind, the political legacy of the father conditions the political action of the son. If Dr Abela Junior really believes the question he asked about Labour's distancing itself from socialism – and there is no reason to doubt the sincerity and relevance of his question – he should either have not contested the general elections with Labour or else he should now leave. It's an almost universal verdict – one that was emitted quite some time before the last elections – that socialism and social democracy are the North Pole to Joseph Muscat's Neo-liberal South Pole. My analysis is that Dr Abela Junior cannot leave because of the long shadow Dr Abela Senior's political history casts on him.

Dr Abela Senior left Labour in 1998 for strategic purposes, which came to the fore 10 years later when he ran for Labour leader and lost to The Invincible. In 1998, Dr Abela Senior did not leave Labour on a point of (political philosophy) principle. His mistake had far-reaching consequences, and he paid dearly for it in the Labour Movement. Had Dr Abela Senior been more realistically self-confident and less cold-blooded, he would have expressed his doubts about the wisdom of an early election but kept his position at the frontline, as did George Vella, the other deputy leader. Dr Vella wisely garnered everybody's respect; Dr Abela foolishly squandered it.

Fast forward to 2019: Dr Abela Junior should have left on a point of political philosophy principle, because really The Invincible is a shameless neo-liberal for whom the vulnerable mean very little, if anything. Instead, Dr Abela Junior has decided to stay on, opening his (undoubtedly sincere) philosophical statement to justified accusations of opportunism.

Knowing and having studied literary works of art helps to understand the dilemma Robert Abela is facing. To me, he is philosophically motivated but experientially blocked. He probably understands that he will be perceived as an opportunist who is pandering to the old-school socialists in the Labour Party and I am sure he does not like to be perceived as an opportunist. On the other hand, if he distances himself from the neo-liberal Prime Minister, he is afraid he will be compared to his father, with all the bad memories such a comparison would evoke. So he stays on, criticising the Prime Minister for abandoning the vulnerable but not doing anything to help the vulnerable for whom his heart bleeds.

This is the tragedy of Robert Abela on the stage of Maltese political drama. But Robert Abela would make a compelling secondary character in a play called *The Invincible: the Tragedy of Lust for Power* – a secondary character because he would not be as compelling as the main character: The Invincible. Now even neo-liberal Martin Scicluna – writing in the printed media – has made the effort (politely) to remind The Invincible that, because of his tactical mistake of pre-announcing his own political death to the four corners of the world, he has to leave – and by not later than six months from today, underlined Neolib Martin. If even Neolib Martin is saying it, then it means that yours truly and many others are right: for the sake of the nation, The Invincible must go.

For The Invincible it won't be easy. Admitting (even implicitly) the tactical mistake carries a price he cannot psychologically afford. On top of that, it is clear that he enjoys taking the nation for one ride after another (probably more than he enjoys governing). His mind-set is such that he enjoys being the sharpest knife in the drawer, the smartest kid in Form 2C, and so on. His Cheshire-cat grin attests to this. It will not be psychologically easy for him to get down from the political rollercoaster that has provided him with an endless supply of kicks. But he needs to come to terms with the fact that all ego trips end one day. As his wife tells their children – and clearly Mother Michelle is endowed with more commonsense in her head – he will not be Prime Minister forever. She is self-evidently right. But her mistake is to limit her words of wisdom to the children who are, for the record, two adorable girls who must really make their parents proud. It is the husband who does not make the wife proud, because he should pay heed to her words. It is not for his own sake (though also) – it is mostly for the sake of the nation which, as I have previously written – and Neolib Martin has echoed me – does not need a lame-duck Prime Minister.

My Personal Library

If you are interested in theatre and masks, why not read about the *commedia dell'arte*? Two good books on this Italian tradition are Allardyce Nicoll's *The World of Harlequin* (1966) and Pierre Louis Duchartre's *The Italian Comedy* (1963).

I bought them second-hand when I became fixated on Sergio Leone's movies.

As Leone's first Western was inspired by an Akira Kurosowa movie which in turn had been inspired by a Dashiell Hammett pot-boiler novel, itself inspired by Carlo Goldoni's *Harlequin Servant of Two Masters*, I read these two books before going to Milan's Teatro Piccolo to watch Goldoni's play.

Abortion Din, Again

IS THE ABORTION DEBATE A SIDE IS-
SUE BEING BLOWN OUT OF ALL PRO-
PORTION? Does legalisation matter
only to a very small minority and of
no priority at all to the population
at large?

All told, I think that for the vast
majority of the Maltese the issue
is not a priority. In 2019, the overwhelming majority of the Maltese
are against the legalisation of abortion. Will it be like that in 2029,
say? It's difficult to say. My impression is that the younger generation
are being heavily influenced by the
media and by the propaganda the
Hollywood volcano keeps spew-
ing out. If you keep count of all the
Hollywood stars and starlets who
come out in favour of abortion, it
becomes abundantly clear that Hollywood – possibly the world's greatest ideology factory – is pro-choice.
This has been going on for some
time now. I remember watching a
movie starring Liam Neeson some
5 or 6 years ago, in which the protagonist saves his daughter from
kidnappers, or something like that.

At the end of the movie – which
had been rated "13" – his daughter
tells him that she's pregnant, and
he tells her that he will support her
whatever she chooses. The abortion option has been normalised to
such an extent that it's presented as

a normal option to an audience that
includes very young teenagers.

With such a barrage of pro-
choice ideology, it shouldn't surprise anybody that the younger
generations will support such an
ideology. They won't even know
why, and if you poke them they'll
turn aggressive. Because you would
be attacking a belief built on brain-
washing, not conviction. This week
I tried a social experiment. There's
a satirical page on Facebook which
usually comes up with intelligent
comments on contemporary Maltese politics and society. But this
week, it commented on the pro-life
demonstration and poked fun at
the speakers. I observed that abortion is not something to joke about.
The reactions I got were quite sarcastic... When I asked for the reasoning behind the sarcasm (a veiled
sort of aggression, to be sure), I got
no answers.

This is not surprising. Ideology
is a set of ideas that we know, but
we don't know that we know, and
we don't know why we know them.

It's like gravity. We all know
gravity, but few of us know (or are
aware that they know) gravity, and
even fewer of us know why there is
gravity.

Ideology is like the water in an
aquarium. All fish know there is
water, but they take it so much for
granted that they don't know that

they know and probably don't know why they are in the water.

Ideology depends a lot on media manipulation. Dr Goebbels, the Nazi Propaganda Minister, was the prime but not sole expert of this mode of public opinion control. Goebbels simply made use of techniques that were coming to the fore in the early 20th century. Many of them, however, had already been used for centuries. What happened in the 20th century, and is certainly happening now with ever-increasing momentum, was that the level of technology grew to such an extent that manipulating more people with more ease became an attainable goal.

In Malta, this is happening without compunction. During this week, the State television station has been broadcasting suspicious news items. On September 26, the important news was broken to us that 'Abortion in New South Wales is no longer illegal'. No hidden messages here? On October 1, we were informed that a 'Moroccan journalist [was] jailed on charges of an abortion that never happened'.

Needless to say, this would be an abuse even had the charge been another – but in this suspiciously pro-choice climate, the relevance of the news item seems to me to shift from the false charge to the false charge being abortion. But let's give TVM

the benefit of the doubt. After all, this is a newsroom which considers 'Shop in Auckland screens porn, after being hacked' (September 30) as a juicy news item to serve its audience under 'Foreign Affairs'. It was even updated! With all that's happening around the world, this was deemed a news item to be broadcast on the State news outlet!

Point is, these are attempts to sexualise the culture, to impose the idea on the population that sexual freedom is the highest goal to which one should aspire. This is nothing new. It's the neo-liberal ideology in the West, the subtext being: sexual freedom is the only freedom you can aspire to, otherwise you've got no freedom at all. Your political rights are being eroded (fake news on the internet, artificial-intelligence sieving of data to manipulate elections, etc); your social rights are being eroded (precarious work, irregular immigrants to dilute any sense of cohesion among the workers be they blue- or white-collar); your consumer rights are being eroded (Big Brother watching your buying patterns to cajole you into buying more useless stuff, planned obsolescence of products, etc) – but you enjoy sexual freedom. And they keep harping on this particular freedom (which is a freedom to be taken with more than a pinch of salt – what freedom is it that allows you to kill your own children? is it freedom or desperation?) so that they hide from you that they're taking your other (more tangible) freedoms. If they give you the freedom to kill your own offspring so that you can be a career woman, unless you're self-employed that career is more to the benefit of your employer than yours. Who are "they"? All those who stand to gain from this ideology. All those who stand to gain from precarious work, from blurring the line between family life and work, from having governments that open the doors for Big Business while keeping SMSs and workers out in the cold. Who are they? Their name is Legion. One of those who stand to gain from the pro-abortion debate is The Invincible. His track record on good governance is so dismal, and – more importantly – his passport scheme is so dangerous (keep in mind the recent reportages we are all aware of), that he is risking a lot. Already his bigger ambitions were thwarted because of his passport scheme and his irresponsible shielding of his Chief of Staff and favourite Minister when it was discovered that, just after a few days in office, they opened secret Panama-registered companies. If he is not careful, he'll be further undermined because he has still taken no corrective measures.

Let us not be naïve. The reportages about the passport scheme did not come out of thin air. Or if they did, they certainly did not go unnoticed. These media attacks usually have serious repercussions, which are not necessarily apparent to the public. They are like torpedoes and there is usually a shock wave. Giving the impression that he is an ardent neo-liberal, a committed missionary trying to convert this heathen population to neo-liberalism, could help him save his skin. This is why a topic like abortion, that certainly has no majority support in 2019 Malta, is given such prominence on the State TV broadcaster. It is a tactic to keep The Invincible from sinking after the torpedo attacks.

* * *

THE PRO-CHOICE LOBBY MAKES LITTLE SENSE TO ME. Their arguments are intellectually weak, emotionally charged, and mostly based on hysteria. Up till a short while ago, the pro-choice lobby was arguing that abortion should be legalised because many pregnancies are the result of rape. This seemed an absurd claim to make, as the statistics do not show a noteworthy rape rate. Then they clarified. They argued that men rape their wives or partners. The accent was therefore shifted toward marital or quasi-marital rape. I have argued that this too is absurd. If indeed marital rape takes place, then there should be a trial and only after a trial should there be legal consequences. If women are allowed to abort because they think there was rape, then the entire judicial edifice would be demolished. It would pave the way for State-sanctioned vendettas, doing away with the judicial remedy to criminal offences. Why do we have trials? To ensure that (1) a crime was indeed committed, (2) the real offender is identified and the degree of guilt determined, and (3) the just punishment is meted out. Allowing women (the purported victim) to determine that a crime was committed by their partner, and then to self-apply a remedy (destroying the new life conceived), would mean bypassing and short-circuiting the judicial process and the rule of law. Luckily, they stopped promoting this silly argument. Now, they seem to be insisting on 'My Body, My Choice'.

At first blush, this seems to be a reasonable argument. After all, why should a woman carry in her body a new life if she does not want to? Upon further reflection, this battle cry is like hysteria. There is, in motherhood, an ethical contract as well as a set of rules imposed by law: the contract between the par-

ents and the new life. As it is a donation, it is a unilateral contract: the parents donate life and care. (The child would then accept, making the situation two unilateral deeds: the parents unilaterally donate, the child unilaterally accepts.)

Donating care is a corollary of donating life. Can life be taken away, once donated? This is the crux of the matter.

There can be no doubt (even though some crazy philosophers don't agree) that after birth, life cannot be taken away. The doubt (that the pro-choice lobby is trying to instil) is that life donated can be revoked before birth. For them it's a sort of cooling-off period, like the right given by the law to change your mind after you buy something, or to return it if it is defective. The obvious difference is that when you buy something, it is inanimate, whereas a child, though unborn, is alive. The analogy – be it explicit or implicit – is therefore wrong, as it equates a donation (of life) to a purchase (of an inanimate object). The fundamental questions thus become: When should the contract of care start, from inception or from birth? Should there be a cooling-off period in a pregnancy, and why? You will receive no answers from the pro-choice lobby, because the answers, if sincere, would clearly show the cracks in the case for abortion. The essential point is that Life is so precious it cannot be meddled with. Unfortunately, the West has accepted that Life can be meddled with, accepting abortion and euthanasia... I have recently discovered a Swiss philosopher, Barbara Bleisch, who is even arguing that there's no case for filial care of ageing parents.

It's a return to Roman times, when the old were left to die in a cave, unwanted children exposed to the elements, and the disabled thrown off a cliff.

We have to ask ourselves what kind of world this is.

My Personal Library

Modernization, Cultural Change, and Democracy: The Human Development Sequence by Ronald Inglehart and Christian Welzel (2005) explains the background to this discussion. Chapter 5 deals with family values and sexual norms. Let me quote:

> Traditionally, the family represents the basic reproductive unit of any society. Consequently, traditional cultures tend to condemn harshly any behavior that seems to threaten reproduction and child-rearing within the family, such as homosexuality, divorce, and abortion. But in post-industrial societies with advanced welfare institutions, a strong family is no longer necessary for survival. These rigid norms gradually lose their function, and more room is given to individual self-expression.

In other words, the welfare State (a Socialist ideal) has given birth to circumstances which are being exploited by Big Business (hardcore right-wing supporters). The Left has become liberal because it suits Big Business. There's nothing in Malta which comes close to multinational Big Business. In the grand, international scheme of things, Maltese businesses are small-to-medium.

A Cynical Government

'IMMATURE CYNICISM', A PHRASE USED BY JORDAN PETERSON, CAN BE USED TO CLASSIFY MOST OF THE REACTIONS TO PRO-LIFE ARGUMENTS. Particularly those arguments that try to ascribe religious thinking to the anti-abortion position. If I were an atheist (which I am not), I would still think the same. Because the anti-abortion position can be adhered to even on non-religious grounds.

Human life is the most precious "asset" in the world and as such is inalienable. The truth of this ontological statement being self-evident, it needs no further articulation.

Elective abortion destroys this self-evident truth, and reduces the existence of a human being to the object of the will of another human being. This is of great prejudice to the individual. By placing the offspring's life at the mercy of the mother's will, elective abortion pollutes communal life, as it legitimises the idea that one human being's life can actually depend on another human being's will. This pollution is of great prejudice to society, as the ideology that life has no intrinsic, inalienable value overflows into other sectors of communal life, despite what Catherine-wheel-like pundits and ideologues keeping repeating. Elective abortion undermines logical thinking, by introducing the absurd idea that only from a certain moment onward does biological life become political life and thus starts deserving the State's protection. The fact that different States allow abortions at different stages of pregnancy demonstrates that there can be no agreement on the moment when biological life becomes political life, because this transformation defies measurement – it is not physical, it is metaphysical. This transformation is thus presented, by the pro-choice ideology, as a sort of magical event. Or else, an act of State arbitrariness. Both are irrational, dangerous, and obscurantist.

So much for those who think that anti-abortion stances are exclusively religious stances and for the others – shallow and misguided disciples of Rorty and even Kant – who think that one is enlightened if one is pro-choice. Actually, being pro-choice is obscurantist, as it invokes either magical thinking or State arbitrariness.One reaction I got, however, was not 'immaturely cynical', but historically ignorant. It was about Roman history: 'The Roman civilisation was quite successful and persisted for centuries while people strove to become and treasured to be Roman citizens.' What is the Roman civilisation that persisted for centuries the reader referred to? There was no Roman civilisation which persisted for centuries! Roman civilisation was a constantly-evolving phenomenon. Roman civilisation was not a monolith. Roman law – the basis of Roman civilisation – underwent tremendous transformations by absorbing elements of Jewish law through Christianity and Hellenic elements prior to the ascendency of Christianity. Later on, Western "Roman" Law evolved separately from Byzantine Roman Law, absorbing many notions from Germanic laws. And, on the eve of the Barbarian Invasions, Roman citizenship had become worthless, because everybody had become a Roman. Where does this pro-abortion notion of Roman civilisation end? With the Fall of the Western Roman Empire? With Charlemagne's death? With the Renaissance of the 12th century? With the Fall of Constantinople?

Lastly, the *nec plus ultra* of inane arguments is that abortion is fine because it is accepted in many parts of the world. But so was slavery in the past! My hero is and will remain till my last breath, William Wilberforce. I read a few books on slavery which convinced me of its inherent evil; but my convictions were galvanised when two years ago I visited Gorée Island in Senegal, the Old World's western-most land, the port of departure of thousands upon thousands of slaves toward New World plantations. What I saw, and more importantly, felt there, further strengthened my admiration for Wilberforce, a man who had the moral fortitude to fight against a practice (enslaving people and trading them) that was considered acceptable (and even beneficial) in his times. So no amount of browbeating can make me back one inch from my position, and I urge all pro-life supporters not to be disheartened by the arrogance of those who, by espousing the dominant ideology of the day, think they know better. They know nothing. Which is why the debate is difficult. How can you debate those who turn up wearing the T-shirt of a Premier Ideology League team?

Cynically Socialist

OFFICIAL STATISTICS SHOW THAT EIGHTY THOUSAND PEOPLE IN MALTA ARE RISKING POVERTY AT A TIME WHEN THE PARTY IN GOVERNMENT CYNICALLY CLAIMS TO BE SOCIALIST. Socialism (some elements of which are shared by the Christian Democrats) means that you do politics to take care of the weak and the vulnerable. How is Muscat's government doing that when the number of people risking poverty has grown by 10% in 10 years? That's no joke.

A few are making a killing; as

many as 80,000 are at the risk of poverty! This is not socialism! This is shameless neo-liberalism, disgusting laissez-faire that allows one and all to do their thing undisturbed as then some magical, hidden hand will take care of everybody. Not only are there 80,000 people in Malta in dire straits, but more than 25% of the over-65s face the same predicament. Traditionally, the older generations were the darlings of Socialism. This self-deluded Best Administration in Europe keeps looking the other way when some fifteen thousand people are experiencing 'severe material deprivation'! These are the real challenges facing the country.

The introduction of abortion, or the legalisation of cannabis for recreational purposes, or the legalisation of prostitution – presented to us as if they were the real challenges – are only expedients to allow a few people to laugh all the way to the bank (at least to those branches that will survive the cull) by offering services to those who don't know what to do with their extra cash. The Italian poet Pier Paolo Pasolini (1922-1975) said in the early 1970s that these are objectives that spoilt brats (*figli di papà*) aspire to achieve. In one of his poems, he criticises the predecessors of today's neo-liberals. Ask yourselves if The Invincible does not fit the identikit.

You have daddy's boy faces
You were born with silver spoons
in your mouths.
Good pedigrees, do not lie.
You all have the same naughty look.
You are fearful, uncertain,
desperate
(great) but you also know how to be
bullies, blackmailers, and brazen:
petty bourgeois characteristics,
friends.

Pasolini's critique is as valid today as it was in the 1970s. He understood that these false challenges divert political energy from the important battles, such as the war on poverty, toward selfish objectives which put individual "self-expression" before social solidarity.

As usual, *cui bono*? Who stands to gain from all this? Certain types of businesses, that grow fat on selling "self-expression" products and services: abortion clinics, Amsterdam-type coffee shops, brothels... the list is endless. When the economy comes before the human being, every aspect of the human experience is scrutinised under the money-making microscope, to be analysed and mapped so that new ways of extracting cash out of people are devised. The economy grows, and grows, and grows, while the individual is deprived of tangible wealth (savings, mostly) and intangible wealth (family ties, self-respect, psychological well-being).

* * *

ONE NIGHT, I DREAMT THAT I DE-
SCENDED INTO AN UNDERGROUND
CAR PARK WHERE THE SECURITY
GUARD GAVE ME AN ENVELOPE
WHICH I OPENED AND FOUND FULL
OF PHOTOS OF MY LATE FATHER.
When I woke up, an idea freely as-
sociated itself with the memory of
the dream.

My unconscious had referred to
The Odyssey: the car park was the
Underworld and the security guard,
Hades God of the Dead.

Let me quote what Achilles tells
Odysseus when they meet in the
Underworld:

> Let me hear no smooth talk
> of death from you, Odysseus, light
>   of councils.
> Better, I say, to break sod as a farm
>   hand
> for some poor country man, or
>   iron rations,
> than lord it over all the exhausted
>   dead.

In death, Achilles learns a wisdom
to which he had been blind in life:
nothing matters but life.

My Personal Library

Peter Stein's *Roman Law in
European History* (1999) is an
excellent primer.

It discusses the evolution of
Roman Law (the basis of Roman
civilisation) and its influence on
Europe.

It is a very short book
– 137 pages – but contains a
lot of pointers if one wants
to understand the impact of
Roman Law in the ancient world
and its continued unifying
influence throughout medieval
and modern Europe.

Like a Fly in the Jungle

IN INTERNATIONAL LAW THERE IS A FICTION: ALL STATES ARE EQUAL IN THE INTERNATIONAL SYSTEM. The reality is that it is just that: fiction. Some States are stronger, others are weaker and power is reflected in how they treat, and are treated by, other States. In the world of *realpolitik*, power (be it military or economic, or both) sets the rules of the game.

When we look at our own little State, we immediately realise that we are as powerful as a fly in the jungle, while other States are lions, elephants, gorillas... We exist as an independent state only because we are tolerated by the system, not because we can really stand on our own two feet. It also means that our Prime Minister understands international politics as much as that fly in the jungle. He seems to think that gambling in international politics is for everybody, and that an understanding of the link between cause and effect is a bonus. So now he is gambling with the country's reputation. But his gambling is very much like the fly's. The fly is not attracted to pollen, or to fruits, or to blood, or to decaying food, like most other insects. No, the fly is attracted to other stuff. And it's in that such other stuff that the Invincible's gambling will ultimately get us. In deep "such other stuff". And when that such other stuff will start hitting the fan, I don't know how we're going to get out of it untainted and not smelling foul.

A source from the banking sector told a newspaper last week that 'some banks do not want to touch high-risk sectors such as gaming, medical marijuana and cryptocurrencies. We are ringing all the alarm bells on this front.' This is the equivalent of "such other stuff". And just like the fly is attracted to it, so is The Invincible.

So we are as powerful as a fly in the jungle, and like flies we fly around...

Pro-Life Budget?

LET US NOT BE FOOLED BY THE APPARENTLY PRO-LIFE INITIATIVE FOUND IN THE 2020 BUDGET. If taken by itself, it's a very good initiative. But in the wider context of the ongoing debate, in which a vociferous minority is clamouring for the legalisation of abortion, it is highly suspicious. That this minority can clamour with such intensity is indicative of official support from behind the scenes.

So to grasp the meaning of the new benefit of €300 to parents for every newborn or adoption to help out with the costs, one has to keep in mind the context. It's a bit like that famous kiss used to betray somebody who was supposedly a friend... a kiss, a universally-recognised symbol of friendship and love, was used for the vilest gesture of all: betrayal.

The context depends very much on what is being increasingly perceived as the real ideology driving this government: neo-liberalism.

Government believes in *laissez-faire*, allowing (almost) everyone to do whatever they think best, and then, somewhere along the line, a hidden hand will fix any problems that may have arisen.

Like the equality of States in the international system, this too is fiction. Because chaos cannot breed order. The natural way with things is the exact opposite: order descends into chaos. For order to come out of chaos, you need a lot of hard work and discipline, and to keep away from the path of least resistance.

With this ideology of *laissez-faire* as backdrop, we can properly understand what this seemingly pro-life measure really means.

In the wider context of symbolic discourse, this government is implying that whatever you choose, the State will let you do (*laisser faire*) and will support you.

If you want to have a child, the State will give you €300. If you start the process to have a child but then change your mind... the implication

seems to be that a day will come, perhaps in the not-too-distant future, when the State will help you with that too.

So the €300 benefit is not a pro-life measure. It is a deviously pro-choice preparatory measure, paving the way for things yet to come. Our struggle against the devaluation of life does not stem solely from religious or abstract thinking. It is deeply rooted in practical considerations, as the devaluation of life brings widespread cynicism in its wake. Considering an unborn child as a mere "bunch of cells" or an old person as a "useless human wreck well past its use-by-date" is not just an aberration against morality and religion.

It can impact you and your life, and leave you without cover under the bombardment of other people's selfishness.

That bunch of cells could be your son/daughter whom your wife/partner goes to eliminate behind your back.

That useless old wreck could be you, in your old age.

Sena Missjoni fl-Albanija (1997) and its sequel *Lura fl-Albanija 1998-2001: Nissoktaw il-mixja 'l quddiem* (2002) are two touching memoirs by the late Ġwann Frendo, O.P. (1938–2003), who devoted his life to showering brotherly love on people he didn't know. It is such a strange ideal to pursue, probably has always been, but I would say particularly in these times of "self-realisation" and consumerism.

These books describe the Maltese Catholic mission in post-Communist Albania, and are characterised by paradox – a "naïve" man seeks to attain utopian objectives but is also wise to the ways of the world (he speaks of Albanian politicians who *'thammġu bil-korruzzjoni u l-flus'*). For the tepid believer or the non-believer, they are precious snapshots of the society of this obscure country. For the believer, they are testament to the fact that we can all live an ideal.

I know another Dominican who has accumulated a wealth of knowledge on Albania. I hope he will one day produce a book to convey it, like his predecessor Ġwann Frendo O.P. did.

Mercenary Today

IF POLITICS – POLITICS IN A DE-MOCRACY – WERE SIMPLE, HUMANS WOULD BE RE-ADMITTED AS TEN-ANTS IN THE GARDEN OF EDEN. Instead, ever since that mythical eviction, things have always been extraordinarily complex.

If democracy had still been a primitive political process, we would gather in assemblies and vote on important matters by show of hands. But democracy has become a complex affair, with all adult members of society voting, not on all matters, but to choose those who will then vote on all matters on their behalf. But even this setup, though complex, would be simple. Democracy is more complex still. Remember that human nature is what it is. Remember that one man and one woman constantly under God's watchful eye could not find the strength to resist eating the "forbidden fruit"... just imagine how a group of men and women can resist eating many "forbidden fruits". And since human nature is what it is, there is the need for a watchful eye to keep constant watch on the men and women elected to vote on all matters on behalf of their electors. The need is to make sure that they don't eat the forbidden fruit. This God-like watchful eye belongs to the Press. Without the Press, our representatives would eat as many forbidden fruits as they please. Obviously, if the representatives want to eat the forbidden fruit and not pay for it, all they have to do is to enlist the support of the Press. By commandeering journalists, the representatives reduce the Free Press to a Mercenary Press.

I believe it is still fresh in everybody's mind that certain members of the Press receive or used to receive phone calls at 1 a.m. from the Prime Minister's Chief of Staff (the same Chief of Staff who opened the secret Panama company purportedly to carry on recycling business in the Gulf States while carrying the Prime Minister's attaché case in and out of Castille). It is clear to me that the cozy relationship between the Prime Minister's Chief of Staff and Salvu Balzan – so cozy that one of the them called the other at 1 o'clock in the morning – can only mean that the Press is not Free, that instead it is a Mercenary.

That by itself should have been enough. But we were given more evidence of this: the attack last September on former Labour Minister and Deputy Leader, lawyer Joe Brincat. I will not repeat the rubbish published by Mr Balzan's yellow-press paper on Dr Brincat. I will only say that it is disgusting that Dr Brincat, as you will recall, took a public authority to task for what he believed to be an abuse and a few days later he had to take Salvu Balzan to court because Mr Balzan published rubbish on him. This case shows two things. One, that, as is publicly known, Mr Balzan is a mercenary, and we all know of whom. Two, that we are living in a culture in which doing the right thing – as Dr Brincat seems to have done – attracts punishment from the Press (or parts of it) rather than encouragement. The Press – that should serve as the watchful eye to prevent the people's representatives and political appointees from helping themselves – actually punishes somebody who blew the whistle on somebody else who seems to have helped themselves. This is the ultimate perversion.

If I may be forgiven for using a metaphor borrowed from law, Joseph Muscat's biggest shortcoming is to equate a power-of-attorney with a title of ownership. He thinks that a *prokura* means you have acquired the thing. A *prokura*, a power-of-attorney, means that you administer something on behalf of its lawful owner – as a politician he is administering the country on behalf of the people and has to give account to them, but the country is not his to do with it as he pleases.

The pattern seems clear. You criticise or expose Muscat and his entourage, you get attacked by Salvu Balzan. I do not think Mr Balzan does it for fun.

The Common Good

AMONG THE MANY THINGS I LEARNT FROM A GREAT, BUT UNDERRATED MIND, GIUSEPPE MIFSUD BONNI-CI, WAS THE IMPORTANCE OF "THE COMMON GOOD". He used to make an intelligent distinction between **il-ġid komuni** and **it-tajjeb komuni**. The Common Good is an idea(l) that informs practical reasoning within a political community, in its bid to find ways how to serve common interests. Its role in the political thinking about the public and private dimensions of social life is central.

What do I mean by the "public dimension of social life"? "Public life" refers to that situation in which the members of a political community share an effort to achieve certain objectives because they have common interests. On the other hand, "private dimension" refers to the personal projects that each of us seeks to achieve. As members of the political community, each one of us participates in the community's public life while living our private lives. This necessarily raises a number of questions. For example, about when we are supposed to base our decisions on the common good. Are only legislators and civil servants bound by the common good?

What about journalists, CEOs, even consumers? Aren't these bound by the common good? And then, why should we care about the common good? Would there be something wrong if we all withdrew from "the common interest" to focus only on our own private lives? Joseph Muscat – "The Invincible" of his imagination – has built his entire political edifice on the foundations of egotism. He addresses each member of the political community not as a member of a community but as an individual voter, as an atom floating in the void. For Muscat, individual interest is more important than the common good. This is what he understands by "liberalism" – the liberty of the individual to do as s/he pleases.

The truth is that the price will one day be paid by all of us collectively. It will be private profit at public expense. But The Invincible will not be around when the day of reckoning dawns. We will, however. And we – all of us, whether we made hay while this particular sun shone or not – will all have to pick up the pieces of a shattered environment and of the shelled family unit, and we will all have to pay the price. As a community. As a community we will have to pay the price for the profit made by individuals. The need for the common good is increasingly daily. But it is surrounded by a fog that disappears slowly. At first, only a few will see it through the fog. At that early stage, the price to be paid by the community will still be low. As time passes, more people will see it. And the more the need for the common good becomes visible, the higher the price will have become.

But political change can take long to materialise. Time is always on the side of those who use politics for private profit.

My Personal Library

Nigel Warburton's *A Little History of Philosophy* (2011) is just that, 'a little history of philosophy'. The 'little' in the title is not an adjective; instead, "a little" is a determiner, a pronoun ("A Small Amount of History of Philosophy"). Because indeed, it gives the reader not a short history of philosophy but only a small amount of history of philosophy.

This doesn't mean that the book isn't important. It's actually very important, but not for the reasons its publishers think it is. It outlines, quickly and succinctly, the selection of philosophical thinking that justifies the current dominant ideology: neo-liberalism, the ideology that informs Joseph Muscat's and other governments in the contemporary world.

It includes philosophers from the classic canon, like St Augustine, Boethius, Machiavelli, Hobbes, Locke, Spinoza... and others from the contemporary Crazy Canon, like Peter Singer (the Australian philosopher who believes that there are circumstances when saving a pig's life is more ethical than keeping a human foetus alive – which, if I'm seeing things right, is the philosophy espoused by Salvu Balzan and a couple of weird characters engaged in his Freak Show).

The book seems biased; it leaves out certain names that should appear in any History of Philosophy, be it Full or Concise. This is why I say that the title means "a small amount of" and not a "short/concise/small" history of philosophy. I might complain about the book's Eurocentric approach: it mentions only philosophers who are either European or of European descent. Is it possible that Asia and the Islamic world produced nothing of worth in philosophy? Confucius and Avicenna, say, mean nothing to the author? I might complain about the author's decision to leave out European philosophers like J.G. Fichte or Mary Midgley or Giorgio Agamben. But I will only complain about the author's choice to leave out Aquinas and the Star of Contemporary Philosophy, Slavoj Žižek. This is unforgivable. How can you write a history of philosophy and ignore Aquinas, whether you agree or disagree with his views? How can you write such a book at the beginning of the 21st century and ignore Žižek, the contemporary philosopher whose lectures sell out like rock concerts? It's like writing a book on rock music and ignoring Elvis.

Orbot il-Ħmara, Ġuż!

... *FEJN JGĦIDLEK SIDHA* – A SLIGHT VARIANT ON A MALTESE PROVERB THAT COULD BE TRANSLATED AS "TIE THE JENNY WHERE HER OWNER TELLS YOU". (In reality, the proverb refers to the "donkey" not the "jenny".) The jenny in our case is the Republic of Malta, that belongs to the People, not to the Administration.

The sovereignty of this country belongs to the People. The People does need a leader, but the leader of a country is not the equivalent of the owner of a company. Joseph Muscat took over the Labour Party and transformed it from a workers' movement into a Liberal Movement, without really explaining what his plans were. Now, having taken over the country, Muscat wants to conform it to his ideas, by reforming the Constitution. He would be justified in imposing his Revolution had he explained his ideas in a book published in advance, so as to allow to People to acquaint itself with, and digest them. Instead, like a Fairy Godmother of the French literary genre *préciosité*, Muscat promised certain Cinderella lobbies that he would grant their wishes; in return these Cinderella lobbies have guaranteed his success at the polls, enabling him to bypass the normal process followed in mature democracies, whereby a Revolution is preceded by a detailed manifesto that enables the (thinking part of the) People to understand and actively (and knowingly) support the project being proposed.

But while promising an earthquake, Muscat never quite considered it necessary to inform the electorate in advance what it would consist of. Indeed one of his ministers even flaunted her satisfaction at how cunning they all were at hoodwinking the electorate. She stopped short of calling voters ħmir. (For those interested in learning Maltese, ħmar is donkey, ħmara jenny, ħmir the plural.)

Muscat's bypassing the political ritual that is customary in developed democracies has no precedent in Maltese politics. Dom Mintoff wrote short political treatises, e.g. *How Britain Rules Malta* and *Malta Betrayed: Truncheons and Tyrants*; the Nationalists published *Perspektiv*; Alfred Sant penned *Malta's European Challenge* and *Is-Soċjaliżmu fi Żminijietna*. They all aimed to allow voters to weigh their respective visions. This is normal practice in developed democracies. In Italy: Muscat's (former?) best buddy Matteo Renzi published *Un'altra strada. Idee per l'Italia di domani* and *Avanti. Perché l'Italia non si ferma*; his nemeses, Matteo Salvini: *Io sono Matteo Salvini. In-*tervista allo specchio and *Secondo Matteo. Follia e coraggio per cambiare il paese*, and Giorgia Meloni: *Noi crediamo. Viaggio nella meglio gioventù d'Italia*. In Britain, Muscat's one-time hero: *Cameron on Cameron: Conversations with Dylan Jones* (self-evidently) by David Cameron and Dylan Jones. In France: *Révolution: Réconcilier la France* by Emmanuel Macron, the man with whom Muscat has shared an advisor... and so on and so forth. In the Real Europe – not the Europe of Muscatian Propaganda – politicians (even if sometimes only formally) respect the electorate, and allow the electorate to make informed decisions. It is only Malta's Joseph Muscat who is planning a Revolution without having told the People in advance what his vision is about, in writing. He only caused to be published a photo album full of propaganda, a few weeks before a snap election, without any real attempt to explain his vision in words. He has treated the People as if we were a pace of ħmir.

He wants to reform the Constitution, but we don't really know what his ideas for reform consist of. It's all shrouded in Muscatian mystery. On top of that, the reform will be in the hands of a President of Malta who is an excellent doctor but, I am reliably informed in writing by people who are very close to His Excellency, is quite unsure about his knowledge on human rights, an integral part of any modern Constitution. This is worrying. The *ħmara* belongs to the People; Muscat should tie her were the jenny's owner – the People – tells him. But there's a slight possibility that Muscat got mixed up by Biblical symbolism, according to which riding a donkey represents an act of kingship. Let's not be fooled, however, as the world is wonderful: when the king rides the donkey, it is also the best time of the donkey's life because it is ridden by the king – as Chesterton reminds us in his famous poem:

> Fools! For I also had my hour;
> One far fierce hour and sweet:
> There was a shout about my ears,
> And palms before my feet.

So perhaps Muscat thinks that the jenny is the People, and he is riding her and then tying her where he thinks best. *Jorbot il-ħmara fejn jgħidlu moħħu, waqt li lilna joħroġna ta' ħmir.*

Stop Dummitt, dammit!

THE ITALIAN NEWSPAPER *IL GIORNALE* HAS REPORTED THIS WEEK THAT THE CANADIAN ACADEMIC CHRISTOPHER DUMMITT, ASSOCIATE PROFESSOR AT TRENT UNIVERSITY, PETERBOROUGH, WHO BASED HIS ENTIRE CAREER ON GENDER STUDIES, HAS ADMITTED THAT HE HAD MADE IT ALL UP! He not only admitted that much of gender stuff is pure ideology, but he also owned up to having falsified the conclusions of his research.

Dummitt is an authority on the subject. His book, *The Manly Modern: Masculinity in the Postwar Years* (2007) has been defined as the 'first major book on the history of masculinity in Canada'. It argued that "gender" was a social and cultural construct, forming part of a vision in which sex is not determined, and biology is subject to human action, consonant with post-modern, social constructionist ideas.

And now, Dummitt, the renowned gender ideologue and teacher, offers his *mea culpa*, in an essay entitled 'Confessions of a Social Constructionist' published in Quillette last September. He candidly writes that,

> now my big idea is
> everywhere. It shows up
> especially in the talking points
> about trans rights, and policy
> regarding trans athletes in
> sports. It is being written into
> laws that essentially threaten
> repercussions for anyone
> who suggests that sex might
> be a biological reality. Such a
> statement, for many activists,
> is tantamount to hate speech.

If you take the position ... that gender is at least partly based on sex, and that there really are two sexes (male and female), as biologists have known since the dawn of their science, uber-progressives will claim you are denying a trans person's identity, which is to say, wishing ontological harm upon another human being.

He further argues that the radical progressives are 'wrong'. He admits, hand on heart, that 'I was wrong. Or, to be a bit more accurate, I got things partly right. But then, for the rest, I basically just made it up. In my defence, I wasn't alone. Everyone was (and is) making it up. That's how the gender-studies field works.'[38]

So much for Fairy Godmother Muscat and his Cinderella lobbies.

38   You   can   find   the confession   here: https://quillette. com/2019/09/17/i-basically-just-made-it-up-confessions-of-a-social-constructionist/.

My Personal Library

I think it was thirty years ago that I read this for the very first time. I translated it (and other works by the same author) to Maltese and wanted to publish it, but those were different times, and publishers were afraid of "Oscar Wilde".

I appreciated and still appreciate Wilde not as the icon of whatever, but for his wit. My father had read to me a couple of Wilde's farces in my pre-teens, and we had laughed a lot together.

Today, I see (once again) that laughter and tears are interchangeable.

Anyway, Chesterton's take on the donkey and the king reminded me of this poem in prose, from *Wilde's Essays and Lectures*:

> When Narcissus died the pool of his pleasure changed from a cup of sweet waters into a cup of salt tears, and the Oreads came weeping through the woodland that they might sing to the pool and give it comfort.
> And when they saw that the pool had changed from a cup of sweet waters

into a cup of salt tears, they loosened the green tresses of their hair and cried to the pool and said, "We do not wonder that you should mourn in this manner for Narcissus, so beautiful was he."

"But was Narcissus beautiful?" said the pool.

"Who should know that better than you?" answered the Oreads. "Us did he ever pass by, but you he sought for, and would lie on your banks and look down at you, and in the mirror of your waters he would mirror his own beauty."

And the pool answered, "But I loved Narcissus because, as he lay on my banks and looked down at me, in the mirror of his eyes I saw ever my own beauty mirrored."

The precise psychological dynamic expressed in the closing lines is echoed in that scene in one of García Márquez's novels when Oscar Wilde meets the pornographer Frank Miller under a lamp-post one foggy London night.

Keith Schembri,[39] Dead Man Walking

NEEDLESS TO SAY, THIS IS A META-PHOR. But indeed, Keith Schembri is politically finished. And if his boss has any sense, he should realise this and fire him immediately. Ironically but not naïvely, the Leader of the Opposition Adrian Delia is giving the Prime Minister the best advice possible.

The timeline
ON MARCH 6, 2016, DURING A NATIONAL PROTEST AGAINST COR-RUPTION, THEN-PN LEADER SIMON BUSUTTIL PUBLICLY STATED THAT MR SCHEMBRI WAS INVOLVED IN CORRUPTION. Mr Schembri reacted by taking Dr Busuttil to court for libel. The stunt had an effect on the electorate.

On October 16, 2017, Mr Schembri declared under oath that he had never received kickbacks.

On March 22, 2018, Mr Schembri challenged Dr Busuttil to face the 'truth' in Court when he (Mr Schembri) would testify again. But on that day, Mr Schembri did not turn up in Court. And again on November 23, 2018, he did not turn up in Court. One year later, on

---

39   Keith Schembri, Joseph Muscat's Chief of Staff, resigned on the 26 November 2019, 13 days after this essay appeared on *The Malta Independent*.

November 11, 2019, Mr Schembri did turn up in Court but instead of testifying, he withdrew the case he himself had lodged. *The Malta Independent* reported the crux of the matter thus:

> Schembri's lawyer Pawlu Lia told the court that his client had been advised not to answer questions about facts under a magisterial inquiry on 17 Black. The court said that irrespective of what is said in inquiries, the questions would be admissible. If the questions are incriminating, the witness has a right not to answer them, said the magistrate. Schembri twice refused to answer the questions, with the court warning him it would take sanctions if he refuses to answer. He then proceeded to withdraw the defamation suit.

Mr Schembri is involved in a magisterial inquiry on 17 Black. He tried using this involvement – about which further down – to avoid answering questions in a case he himself lodged.

Schembri's untenable position
CLEARLY, HOWEVER, MR SCHEMBRI'S INVOLVEMENT IN THE MAGISTERIAL INQUIRY MAKES HIS POSITION UNTENABLE. This is not only the opinion of the Opposition and of a number of NGOs and individuals, but it is the normal practice in mature (and not-so-mature) democracies. In a functioning democracy, somebody in Mr Schembri's predicament would simply leave or be chucked out.

Let's have a look at precedents from the past 20 years, and the reasons for the resignations:

2001:   **Henry McLeish**, First Minister of Scotland, over allegations of improper financial dealings.

2004:   **James McGreevey**, Governor of New Jersey, after being mired in extortion scandals.

2005:   **Greg Sorbara**, Finance Minister of Ontario, resigned while under investigation.
David Blunkett, British Secretary of State for Work and Pensions, resigned after breaking the Ministerial Code regarding private business appointments.

2006:   **Laila Freivalds**, Swedish foreign minister, in response to a number of scandals.

2008:   **Peter Hain**, British Work and Pensions and Wales Secretary, after the Electoral Commission referred investigations over political funding to the Police.

Eliot Spitzer, Governor of New York, over claims of involvement in a prostitution ring.

2010: **David Laws,** UK Chief Secretary to the Treasury, forced to resign over expenses abuse allegations, after it emerged he had channelled tens of thousands of pounds in public money to his long-time partner.

2012: **Pál Schmitt,** President of Hungary, in a plagiarism scandal.

David Petraeus, Director of the US Central Intelligence Agency, for an extramarital affair.

Michael Palmer, resigned as Singapore's Speaker of Parliament for an extramarital affair.

2013: **Annette Schavan,** Education Minister of Germany, after her doctorate was revoked for plagiarism.

2016: **Sigmundur Davíð Gunnlaugsson,** resigned as Prime Minister of Iceland due to the Panama Papers scandal.

2017: **Robert J. Bentley,** resigned as Governor of Alabama due to his involvement in a sex scandal with his political aide Rebekah Mason.

Raúl Fernando Sendic Rodríguez, resigned as Vice-President of Uruguay at the conclusion of an investigation regarding his use of public funds while President of a State-owned company.

Michael Fallon resigned as UK Secretary of State for Defence after allegations of harassment.

Priti Patel, forced to resign as UK Secretary of State for International Development after undisclosed meetings with Israeli officials on holiday in the country.

2018: **Robert Fico,** resigned as Prime Minister of Slovakia in the wake of mass demonstrations against his governing coalition following the murder of Ján Kuciak, a journalist who was investigating possible ties between government officials and an Italian organised crime syndicate at the time he and his *fiancée* were gunned down in their home.

Amber Rudd, resigned as UK Secretary of State for the Home Department following misleading Parliament in the aftermath of the Windrush scandal.

2019: **Ricardo Antonio Rosselló Nevares** resigned as Governor of Puerto Rico as important members of his cabinet are currently accused on corruption charges for more than $15 million.

Ramush Haradinaj resigned as Prime Minister of Kosovo after being summoned by the Kosovo Specialist Chambers and Specialist Prosecutor's Office to be interviewed as a suspect.

Evo Morales resigned as President of Bolivia on 10 November after an OAS audit revealed irregularities in the 2019 Bolivian general election.

From the above, it is clear that the accepted practice in functioning democracies is that people in situations that are similar to Keith Schembri's either resign out of their own accord or are forced to resign.

That the Prime Minister keeps sheltering Mr Schembri says a lot about two things. One, the undeniable meltdown of the country's political institutions – as the PN has been rightly pointing out for quite some time now. (The problem is that political education is somewhat lacking in this country, so the PN is speaking a language only the few can understand. For the many, it is a foreign language.) Two, that Mr Schembri has a lot to hide and that, by implication, so does the Prime Minister. Even if it were merely the shadow of a doubt, in a functioning democracy this would be enough to make politicians and their aides, resign. We really have a constitutional crisis on our hands.

The President of the Republic should find residual powers and act.

Now.

Revolutions and Constitutions

THE MUSCAT YEARS WILL BE RE-MEMBERED AS MARKED BY AN URGE TO REVOLUTIONISE THE CONSTITU-TION WHICH CAME TO NAUGHT, AND COMPLETE IGNORANCE OR IG-NORING OF THE CURRENT CONSTI-TUTION. Needless to say, all revolutions have a long history of eating up their progenitors.

Muscat the Revolutionary has been eaten up by his own revolution.

Muscat's revolution was not really and truly a Progressive one, but a revolution in laxity, in corruption. He tried to legalise moral corruption as a distraction from his revolution in institutional corruption – the two faces of the same Janus-Corruption.

More importantly, his insistence on a New Republic, a New Constitution, was meant to hit two birds with one stone: keep the people distracted by dangling this possibly much-expected carrot while, at the same time, imply that since the current Constitution is on its way out, it need not really be observed.

Equally important is Joseph Muscat's constitutional insensibility. Again, another proof – if any were indeed needed – of his not being really a statesman. Unlike his predecessors (all of them),

Muscat seems completely oblivious to the true meaning and significance of a constitutional setup. For him, the State is a private company of which he is the majority shareholder.

His greatest flaw, I think, is his misunderstanding of the Modern State and of the power that majorities engender.

The Movies this Week

THE KEITH SCHEMBRI MOVIE
SHOULD END WITH HIS STEPPING
DOWN. Why? Because the implications of his shameful retreat in
Court are clear. If Mr Schembri
cannot answer questions posed
to him in a libel case he himself
opened otherwise he incriminates
himself, then he is, by his own admission, guilty of something. This
makes his current position untenable. Now that I've said what I had to
say about politics, I will write about
a subject which is close to my heart.
I ask you to forgive me; I'll write as
if I'm writing to my Future Self.

Dreams
IF I HAD MORE THAN ONE LIFE,
I'D CHOOSE TO BE A FILM HISTO-
RIAN. I'd spend time studying how
Italian (so-called spaghetti or Za-
pata) Westerns recycle silent-film
material. For instance, I recently
watched the 1926 silent movie
The General, starring Buster Kea-
ton, realising that *The Five-Man
Army* (1969, starring Bud Spencer,
sound track scored by Ennio Mor-
ricone whose birthday was just
a few days ago, directed by Don
Taylor) copies scenes, almost shot-
by-shot, from it. Whereas Sergio
Leone found himself in copyright
hot water with Akira Kurosawa for
copying scenes shot-by-shot, Don

Taylor probably got away with it
because *The General* had become
public domain in 1954.

Today, we would call that copying, intertextuality, that is to say the
post-modern practice of inserting
previous literary or artistic material
(or even references) into the work
at hand without a formal citation.
Then again, this is not a 20th century thing. Lucian, the 1st century
poet and writer, could be "accused"
of intertextuality – he constantly
refers to Greek cultural history and
literature in his poetry and prose.

Film is the medium *par excellence* of our times. It articulates
our dreams, grants us our wishes,
teaches us how to live. As I said, if
I had another life, I wouldn't have
enrolled in the law course (and the
other courses I followed afterward,
like history and history of law, and
even historical sociology and management...) and would have enrolled
for film studies. Why, if I could go
back in time, say 28 years, I would
tell my Younger Self to choose that
particular path in life.

Who knows how many others
my age share this same wish! Of
going back 20, 25 even 30 years to
tell their Younger Self that, despite
all the pompous self-assuredness,
experience now teaches them that
they should choose otherwise. Well,
isn't this the theme of a movie, starring Will Smith, that was released

a few weeks ago: *Gemini Man*, the story of a man who encounters his 23-year-old clone and tells him not to become a hired assassin like himself but to go to university to study something else?

In a way, it reminds you of the theme of one of Sergio Leone's immortal movies, one of the best movies ever made: *The Good, The Bad and the Ugly* (1966), in which two middle-aged men trying to scrape though during the American Civil War, happen to discover a treasure. How many of us don't dream of finding a hidden treasure that would enable us to escape from the humdrum civil war of everyday life?

Movies are – as an Indian film distribution company says in its name – a Dream Factory. They fulfil our dreams for us. They induce us to suspend disbelief, and to believe – in child-like fashion – that life is essentially easy. They follow the plotlines devised centuries ago by Aristotle, of where to place the crisis in the plot and how to work the solution to it. As if each crisis has a solution. That's probably the most recurrent dream: that all crises have a solution. Giovanni Bonello recently told me, during an email exchange that had nothing to do with movies, that we have been taught to think mathematically, in the sense that we've been brainwashed to believe that every problem has a solution, like in mathematics. Real life isn't like that at all: some problems don't have solutions.

I think this is best captured in that scene in Scorsese's *The Last Temptation of Christ* (1988), when the Devil appears to the Christ on the Golgotha in the guise of a small, blonde, female angel and tells Him that God's message is that there's no need for Him to die on the cross, He can climb down and go and have a family, like every other regular guy. Had this been in Italian, I would have written, *come ogni altro povero cristo, o povero diavolo.*

Movies peddle the fantasy that for every problem there's a solution, solutions aren't difficult to find, and we should follow our desires. In a sense, all movies are "pornographic". I'm borrowing this idea from Eli Roth, for whom Quentin Tarantino's *Inglourious Basterds* (2009) is 'kosher porn', in the sense that the Jewish viewer gets gratification in the form of vengeance for Nazi atrocities. Mr Roth clearly extended the meaning of "porn", as none of Mr Tarantino's movies depict obscene scenes (even if you factor in his somewhat disturbing fixation with toes). They're "pornographic" because they offer fantasy-ish gratification. *Django Unchained* (2012), for instance, is "nigger-violence-porn". Somebody on the *Economist* online comments-board wrote, 'So let's be clear: it's OK to make violence-porn so long as there's some recondite dialog and pretty mountains in the background? Tarantino represents the worst of Hollywood – an obsession with guns, the glorification of violence, and a "there's-never-any-consequence" motif.' In this sense, the second part of *Grindhouse* (*Death Proof*, 2007) is "feminist-violence-porn".

Mr Tarantino does it in an artful but in-your-face way. Others are either more subtle or even more callous. Let's ignore the callous and focus on the subtle, who may be doing it consciously or unconsciously. In the documentary *The Pervert's Guide to Ideology* (2012), Slavoj Žižek revels in psycho-analysing movies like Cameron's *Titanic* (1997) and proposes that movies are dream factories emitting ideology-CO_2. In the case of *Titanic*, the theme is class struggle: the sinking of the ship is necessary to rescue the fantasy of a romance between two lovers hailing from different classes (not just passenger but social) as love can't live long between the classes.

Family dynamics could be the hidden theme of movies that use extravagant settings, such as interstellar or historical wars. The real issue would be deep-seated parent-child relationship traumas. Star Wars is an obvious example: 'I'm your

father' is probably the real theme of the entire saga. *Joker* blames a decadent urban (cosmopolitan?) environment and a mother's psychosis for the protagonist's criminal behaviour. The lunatic Joker is a criminal because a rotten society and a rotten mother made him so; it ain't his fault.

Then there are productions in which a family is tightly-knit but its relationship, as a unit, with society is weird: *The Addams Family*, say. Two interesting things happened to the mid-1960s original TV show.

One, it was unexpectedly cancelled, after only two seasons, when ratings were still high.

Two, psychiatrists at the time observed that, though the family is bizarre and completely out-of-synch with society, the dynamics between the family's members are actually close to the ideal everybody should aspire to. Husband and wife are sincerely attracted to one another; the parents watch over the children; a grandmother and a celibate uncle live with the nuclear family, supporting, and being supported by, it. It is indeed all presented in an almost-demented black-humour way, but the family dynamics are enviable. One wonders whether Tolstoy's opening line for *Anna Karenina* applies to the Addamses as well, 'All happy families resemble one another, but each unhappy family is unhappy in its own way.' If the Addamses are a happy family, are all happy families like them?

There's another tightly-knit, bizarre silver-screen family: the Corleones. Their relationship with society is "unusual", but we love them. After all, they're only into prostitution and gambling (somehow reminds you of this country's Muscat Administration, somehow), and the Godfather clearly says *No!* when Virgil Sollozzo offers him to joint venture on a drug deal (I'm not sure what to say here about the present Muscat Administration, with its pro-joint-smoking razz-matazz). We share the Godfather's distress when the machine-guns of the other Mob families riddle his son with bullets, and we cry when he passes away in his tomato garden, as if a great patriarch-hero has just died before our eyes. We all admire him because he loves his Family and he deals with problems like a Man, with a capital "M". The Corleones are a tightly-knit family, sure, but are they happy? And, are all pro-family people actually... Mafiosi?

That and many other questions I'll never answer as I'll neither have a second life nor the chance to have that chat with that starry-eyed 18-year-old boy, my Younger Self. My film-historian or film-critic dream is destined to stay in the drawer, with a few other dreams. Dreary life goes on, taking us all to the inevitable grave. 'In the long run,' as my economist friend loves reminding me (quoting his own hero), 'we're all dead'.

The University of Hollywood
AND YET, AS PEOPLE WHO THINK, WE HAVE TO LOOK WITH CRITICAL EYES AT WHAT HOLLYWOOD TEACHES (OR TRIES TO TEACH) US. Hollywood wants us all to graduate in Neo-liberal Studies, to master the ideology of our times, that a woman (and she alone) has the right to "terminate a pregnancy", that marriage is not only between man and woman, that your gender is for you to choose, and other such concepts.

The ideology is hammered into our heads and those who reject it are labelled *Addamses* or *Corleones* or *retrogrades* or *bigots*. Those who, puppy-like, absorb the training and, dog-like, respond to the master's voice, feel superior, invigorated by the self-importance that being a good dog instils in you. I feel an irresistible urge to quote a Pink Floyd song,

> I've got a little black book with
> my poems in
> Got a bag with a toothbrush
> and a comb in
> When I'm a good dog, they

sometimes throw me a
bone in
I got elastic bands keepin' my
shoes on
Got those swollen-hand blues
I got thirteen channels of shit
on the T.V. to choose
from ...
I've got the obligatory Hendrix
perm
And the inevitable pinhole
burns
All down the front of my
favourite satin shirt
I've got nicotine stains on my
fingers
I've got a silver spoon on a
chain
Got a grand piano to prop up
my mortal remains
I've got wild staring eyes
And I've got a strong urge to fly
But I got nowhere to fly to

It's called *Nobody Home*. After you conform to the dictates of the dominant (neo-liberal, anti-family) ideology, you discover that you do have 'a pair of Gohills boots' but you also have 'fading roots'. That's the current ideology: no-roots, no-family ('nobody home') self-centred existence behind the wall of isolation, surrounded by material possessions and conforming to current fads, and being available to the needs of the Market and of the Powerful Masters who/which pull its strings.

My Personal Library

In quick succession, a few books for film aficionados. *Mafia Movies: A Reader*, edited by Dana Renga, discusses some of the genre's best, not just Coppola, Scorsese, and Chase, but also Italians like Michele Placido, Damiano Damiani, and Francesco Rosi.

For diehard Godfather fans: Jenny Jones' *The Annotated Godfather: The Complete Screenplay* and *Francis Ford Coppola's The Godfather Trilogy*, edited by Nick Browne.

Jon Lewis' *The Godfather* gives some background to the film but also some cinematographic history, including the notion that gangster money might have financed the movie and saved Paramount Studios and the rest of Hollywood in the process.

The same theme is further developed in a book which, for some reason I forget, I own in French: Tim Adler's *La Mafia à Hollywood* – Hollywood survived in the 1970s and '80s with Mafia money, and in the '90s Giancarlo Parretti bought MGM with money coming from the Mafia and Crédit Lyonnais.

Constitutional Abuse, Again

THE SITUATION IS UNPRECEDENT-ED, AS EVEN THE PRESIDENT OF THE REPUBLIC HAS POINTED OUT. Not only is the situation unprecedented, but it seems to be totally out of control. Joseph Muscat, now Prime-inister-in-Limbo, surviving by the skin of his teeth amid a chorus of calls for his resignation, is inventing rules as he goes along, in a constitutional scenario that has no precedent. Finally accepting the inevitable, Muscat has announced his resignation. But he won't resign immediately. He single-handedly decided he will resign in January 2020.

He justified the delay on the basis that this is the minimum timeframe for the Labour Party's internal organs to elect a new Leader. He has clarified that he will be limiting himself to day-to-day administration, without elaborating on what. Will he behave like a caretaker Prime Minister?

Many issues are raised, even of an institutional nature, and constitutional experts should air their views. Particularly since it seems that the statute of the Labour Party is taking precedence over the country's constitutional setup. The Constitution states that 'wherever there shall be occasion for the appointment of a Prime Minis-ter, the President shall appoint as Prime Minister the member of the House of Representatives who, in his judgment, is best able to command the support of a majority of the members of that House'. There is no mention of internal Party elections. And yet, Muscat is unilaterally subjugating the country's constitutional setup to the statute of his political party. The line of demarcation between State and Party is being blurred right before our eyes, seemingly with impunity. Bloomberg published an opinion piece a couple of days ago: 'Malta Proves Oligarchs Aren't All Eastern European'. 'A government crisis is a reminder that official corruption — and violence — can shake even seemingly stable countries.'

The present scenario is unprecedented. We have never had a Prime Minister who found himself in such a legal and political morass. It is unprecedented, the constitutional document does not seem to contemplate such a scenario, and, moreover, Muscat is doing as he pleases in his last days. We have to refer to the hallowed British constitutional theorist A.V. Dicey, who wrote that there are other, non-legal rules that also make up the constitutional setup: 'conventions, understandings, habits, or practices which, though they may regulate the conduct of the several members of the sovereign power are not in reality laws at all since they are not enforced by the Courts. This portion of constitutional law may, for the sake of distinction, be termed the "conventions of the constitution," or constitutional morality'. In this case, "understandings" is the operative word.

We have to resort to "constitutional morality"; in other words, we have to understand what is right and what is wrong. We have to ask ourselves the following. Given that:

(a) Muscat's closest aide is probably involved in an assassination and in money laundering;

(b) Muscat's trusted Finance Minister, Economy Minister and former Tourism Minister are to face a criminal inquiry on the health privatisation deal;

(c) Yorgen Fenech has claimed that he knows of a number of instances of government corruption (which should obviously lead to investigations by all competent bodies, not just the police – namely the FIAU, the MFSA, tax department, and so on);

(d) other facts may come to the fore as the police and other bodies continue investigating and interrogating people; and

(e) Muscat himself might have criminal responsibility (by commission or omission) and might face charges and even imprisonment;

is it right that Muscat should remain Prime Minister, with full powers, until he decides that it is a convenient time to go? Or is it right that he should go immediately?

I am surprised that the President hasn't publicly reacted to the unilateral decision taken by Muscat. Under Article 85 of the constitutional document, the President can and 'shall act in accordance with his own deliberate judgment' in certain circumstances involving the removal and appointment of the Prime Minister. I'm sure that with a little lateral thinking and intelligent interpretation, the President can find a way to allow constitutional morality to reign supreme.

I'll say it frankly. I do not exclude that Muscat has not resigned and is abusing of the silence of the constitutional document – but not of the constitutional set up – not only to be in a position to help friends and allies and to clean up as many traces of malfeasance as he can, but also to prepare his escape from the country if it comes to the worst. Knowing him, when he said he will stay away from politics, he might have meant just that.

The Rise and the Fall

THE END IS NEAR. He faces the final curtain but he'll still state his case, of which he's certain. He has lived a life that's full, but he still has a few regrets. Then again, they're too few to mention. He did what he had to do, and saw it through without exemption. He planned each charted course and each careful step. Yes, there were times when he bit off more than he could chew, but through it all, when there was doubt, he ate it up and spit it out; he faced it all and he stood tall. He has loved, laughed and cried, had his fill, his share of losing... That's his worldview, his self-delusion and his perception of the world.

How does the world see him?
HIS "OFFICIAL" STEEL-SOLDIER BIOGRAPHER[40] HAS QUICKLY DISTANCED HIMSELF FROM HIM, TELLING HIM THAT 'HE SHOULD HAVE RESIGNED IMMEDIATELY'. So it is up to us to draft a first biographical sketch of this man who promised zero tolerance for corruption and delivered the most corrupt government in the country's history, a vain and conceited man who turned out to be a petty political picaroon.

The Rise
THE RISE WAS IGNOBLE, MUCH LIKE

---

40   Cyrus Engerer.

THE FALL WOULD BE ELEVEN YEARS LATER. In 2008, Labour had been tipped off about an obscene project that would have ruined Mistra Bay, involving a Government backbencher who had been posing as Malta's number-one paladin of the cause of the environment. He had deceived his own party, as they were completely unaware what he was up to. It seems that Joseph Muscat alerted the backbencher's party which took immediate remedial action, managing to control the damage and eventually turn the tables. Muscat's party lost the election – in my opinion mostly because of the information he smuggled to the other party – but Labour's loss opened the mouth of the cave where Ali Baba found the treasure.

A seat in the House was sought and pressure was piled on MP Joseph Cuschieri. At the time, *In-Nazzjon* published an article claiming that Mr Cuschieri was promised a salaried job at the Labour National HQ in return for the sacrifice. Some time later, Mr Cuschieri probably realised that he had got a raw deal and decided he wanted a *quid pro quo*: Muscat had taken his seat in this parliament, Mr Cuschieri wanted Muscat's seat in the other parliament. But it seems that Labour's media were instructed not to be too enthusiastic about the idea. Mr Cuschieri did eventually make it, thanks to the coming into effect of the Treaty provisions which changed the composition of Parliament, but he suffered a lot, even physically, during the wait. In 2008, I had emailed Muscat asking him whether he didn't think he was too young for such an ambitious move. He replied that he knew what he was doing.

The Style

IT TURNS OUT THAT HE ONLY THOUGHT HE KNEW WHAT HE WAS DOING, NOT ONLY WAS HE TOO YOUNG, BUT HE ALSO HAD NOT BEEN THROUGH ANY REAL DEFINING EXPERIENCE, WHICH COULD BRING OUT THE MAN INSIDE HIM. His only experiences were flitting around Alfred Sant and then betraying his leader-mentor; first resisting Malta's EU membership and then rushing to become one of Malta's first MEPs. Neither define a Man. Compare him with another former MEP – Simon Busuttil, who also had no experience in Malta's Parliament. Dr Busuttil has demonstrated tenacity, grit, and, most of all, guts. Dr Busuttil's steely determination has allowed him to continue his struggle against the rot in the country, and, on a personal level, to forge a political style by striking the hammer of his resolve on the anvil of adversity. These three years of blood, toil, tears and sweat not only earned him a fortune in terms of moral authority but also served to make his potential take shape before our eyes. Simon Busuttil has gone through his own Odyssey and is now on Ithaca.

What was Muscat's Odyssey? There's no Odyssey to talk of. There's no defining moment. He was a charmer, a sweet talker, an eloquent orator, a seducer... but even a sleazy second-hand car-dealer has these attributes. He was a puppet, a pauper, a pirate, a poet, a pawn and... a king. But there was not a single historical moment in which Muscat fought on the side of Good in the great battle against Evil. The politically illiterate mistook his pig-headed defence of Konrad Mizzi and the other one as his Odyssey. He did everything not to disabuse them of their delusion: he adopted a narrative that depicted him as a Ulysses of sorts. But only the politically illiterate fell for it. Ultimately, as he himself admitted during an interview held in Japan in July 2018, he was all for 'leadership which goes beyond being seen to do something. For me,' he said, 'that's the greatest type of leadership. Leadership where people don't realise what you're doing until it's done'. His words can be understood in so many, many senses. But I think that he managed in that moment of pure, unadulterated narcissism, when he was so deeply in love with his own image in the pool, to put his political style in a nutshell. There you have it. He thought he would be Ulysses; instead, he was only Narcissus.

The Content

MUSCAT'S POLITICAL PREPARED-NESS WAS CONSISTENTLY SHALLOW. Just like when he said that at first he was against same-sex couples adopting children, but then after reading one book, he changed his mind. How can you be a serious politician when you change a (supposedly) deeply-held opinion after reading one book! You can find Muscat's PhD thesis online. Read it, and you will catch yourself unconsciously posing the question, 'Is it possible that he wrote this?' There are entire excerpts where I could distinctly hear another voice dictating while a wild-eyed Muscat furiously jots down.

The Secretaries

CHAPTER 22 OF *THE PRINCE* IS WHERE MACHIAVELLI GIVES US A MOST IMPORTANT LESSON.

> The choice of servants is of no little importance to a prince... the first opinion which one forms of a prince, and of his understanding, is by observing the men he has around him; and when they are capable and faithful he may al-

ways be considered wise, because he has known how to recognise the capable and keep them faithful. But when they are otherwise, one cannot form a good opinion of him, for the prime error which he made was in choosing them.

Take all of Muscat's predecessors and compare their secretaries with his secretaries.[41] Muscat surrounded himself with wheeler-dealers and fixers rather than intellectually-endowed people. He seemed attracted to people with faulty characters; honest people repelled him. He has had to admit that he felt betrayed by Keith Schembri. I cannot agree with his assessment. If his top secretary was a venomous snake, he has only himself to blame when the snake finally bit him. It's in the snake's nature to bite.

---

41   In 2016, Evarist Saliba wrote this online about my father, who had been a secretary to a Prime Minister. Mr Saliba was referring to many years before that: 'I knew [Frans Sammut] also when I was the acting secretary at the Ministry of Foreign Affairs. One day, I was instructed to call him to persuade him to come back to work at the Ministry. ... His response was that I had disturbed him from his work in his garden. He made it clear that his standards did not permit him to work any longer at the Ministry.' Such standards I'm sure were shared by others who were secretaries to the Prime Minister before the Muscat Administration.

The Allies

MUSCAT THOUGHT HE COULD COUNT ON HIS MERCENARY ALLIES. He thought he could depend on Salvu Balzan, say. But when the end was nigh, Mr Balzan reiterated with supersonic speed that the Prime Minister must resign on the spot. Muscat was unable to see through Mr Balzan's mercenary nature. Had he been wise, he would have understood Mr Balzan. He could have read what Mr Balzan wrote in his rag when I published my book on the Panama Papers scandal: 'I have not read the book, but will do everything humanly possible not to touch a copy'. He even called me "polemicist", that is somebody who writes about controversial subjects. For Mr Balzan, the Panama Papers were controversial. He couldn't work out what the Panama companies were in reality... Either Mr Balzan has the IQ of an orang-utan and couldn't extrapolate where the Panama companies would eventually land Muscat, or else he's an opportunist who milks people in power up till the moment they start their descent into the hell of political oblivion.

Muscat was quickly abandoned by other allies too. I already mentioned his "official" steel-soldier biographer. Then there's the Book Council Chairman, who enjoyed Muscat's complete backing when he jousted with Education Minister Evarist Bartolo. Now that Muscat's destiny seems to be the rubbish heap of history, Mark Camilleri, in Flash-like fashion, put a huge distance between himself and his former, but now-disgraced patron. For Minister Owen Bonnici, certainly not the sharpest knife in the drawer, Muscat is like a messiah: such leaders are born once every 25 years. As I said, not the sharpest knife in the drawer.

But to my mind, the most important ally of all was Michelle Muscat. Her role throughout the great pageant that the Muscat Years have been, was to follow the Eva Perón script. You might remember Tomás Eloy Martínez's *The Perón Novel* and *Santa Evita*, in which Evita had to symbolise the people, so that as she loved President Juan Perón, so would the people love him.

Do you remember, in the happy days of the 2008 Messianic revolution, when Muscat told his followers, '*Ħobbuwha għax hi tħobbkom!*' (diphthong included on purpose to reflect faithfully his strong village accent)?

The message there was inverted. 'Love her because she loves you' was in reality an inverted imperative: 'You love me because she loves me, and she's one of you': the Evita-Perón-People triangle. Yes, this had been brilliant.

The Fall

MUSCAT HAS FALLEN; INVICTUS HAS BEEN DEFEATED, BY HIS OWN HAND. He has lost all credibility. The MEPs who were on Malta this week said it clearly: Muscat has been discredited in European circles. They also added – another voice in an ever-growing univocal chorus – that he should leave immediately. For how can he function properly in the European bodies and guarantee he won't tamper with all there is to tamper with? Of his many mistakes, the greatest was to choose a shady figure to be his right-hand man and (if we want to be generous here) to be unable to see through him.

Epilogue

MY MOTHER HAS DRAWN MY ATTENTION TO SOMETHING I'D LIKE TO SHARE. While staring at the chaotic scenes of Muscat's prolonged fall on television like stout Cortez when with eagle eyes he stared at the Pacific, she told me, 'You know, I'm sorry for those two innocent girls.'

At first, my mother's words had no effect on me. But then, upon further reflection, I realised that she was right, and I shared her pity and sympathy for those two innocent girls who, out of no fault of their own, are probably going through a lot. It is never fair – never ever – that children have to pay for the misdeeds of their parents.

My Personal Library

'There's the scarlet thread of murder running through the colourless skein of life, and our duty is to unravel it, and isolate it, and expose every inch of it.' Thus says Sherlock Holmes to his friend and chronicler Dr Watson in a speech on the nature of his work as consultant-detective, delivered in *A Study in Scarlet*, the 1887 detective novel by Scottish author Arthur Conan Doyle that marks the first appearance of the most famous detective duo in popular fiction.

The story is about kidnapping, murder, and enslavement, and deals with an organisation which pretends to be made up of saints but is in reality made up of despicable criminals.

The Legacy

HAVING PRECIPITATED HIS OWN POLITICAL DEMISE, WHAT WILL JOSEPH MUSCAT BEQUEATH TO THE NATION? We have the Father of the Maltese Language, the Father of Independent Malta, the Father of European Malta. What will Muscat be remembered as being the father of? The Father of Corrupt Malta?

Fortification against tragedy
SOME LABOURITES ARE GOING THROUGH WHAT LOOKS LIKE A PERSONAL TRAGEDY. They reposed their trust in the blue-eyed wonder-boy and they've been betrayed. Now they're discovering they lack inner "fortification" against tragedy. They're aghast at the evidence they had so clamoured for believing that it didn't exist, and awash with feelings of helplessness now that it has emerged. Muscat's Farewell Tour, organised to lubricate his transition from Top Man to the political Great Beyond, is meant to fortify them, to offer them solace for the tragedy he himself inflicted upon them.

Such paradoxes are the norm with Muscat. They're so well-crafted and intricate that the vast majority might never even deconstruct and work them out. He's a master trickster. Just consider how he delivered identity politics to the upper classes while treating the lower classes with the most unabashedly patriarchal paternalism. And this when one of the fundamentals of identity politics is the anti-patriarchal stance! He capitalised on both the ignorance of the lower classes and the roseate spectacles worn by the upper classes. The latter were both beneficiaries of Muscat's identity politics and his unwitting alibi – thanks to them Muscat was routinely treated as a hero in certain European circles, and this permitted his cronies to busy themselves with their lurid affairs away from the public eye.

These paradoxes make up a great part of his legacy.

A split party:
neo-liberals v. socialists
THE BOTTOM-LINE MESSAGE IN MUSCAT'S FAREWELL TOUR SPEECHES IS THAT THE ELECTION OF A NEW LEADER WILL FURTHER UNITE THE LABOUR PARTY. We should not for a moment assume that this is a slogan meant to describe the current situation. It is a slogan that serves as an imperative. When Muscat says 'The election will further unite the Party' he is in reality imparting an order: 'The result is not important; party unity is. Therefore, I'm ordering you to forget all differences and be united.' Frankly, he's right. I mean, he's right to impart this order to his followers.

But at the same time, Muscat's order means that his legacy includes a split party. It couldn't be otherwise.

I have already written that Muscat had misappropriated Labour, replacing – without any mandate – its social-democratic ethos with neo-liberalism. This usurpation has recently induced a number of self-styled "socialists" to write a post-resignation letter to the Labour Party asking that the Party be restored to its socialist roots.

One can question their sincerity given the timing, but that's hardly the point.

The point is that Labour is split in two: the Muscatians (neo-liberals, cultural Marxists, anarchists, pro-abortionists, pro-EU, couldn't-care-less-about-the-workers "realists", etc) and the old-school (Mintoffian) Socialists (socially conservative, traditional Western-European-Marxists (as opposed to Soviet Marxists), pro-family, EU-suspicious, pro-worker-rights "idealists", etc).

Muscat managed to hold these two currents together and separate at the same time, and it was no mean feat. He succeeded because he embraced political amorality with a smile in his heart – the same amorality which led him to be blind to the rats running about the ship.

His successor will not find it easy to follow in Muscat's footsteps, because now there will be heightened supervision within Labour (once bitten, twice shy and all that).

Muscat's successor will have to learn schizophrenic skills and hone them: moral in one field, amoral in others.

Life experience teaches that such schizophrenia is so stressful, it never lasts long. Few minds can entertain two opposite ideas at the same time. Ask any wife who starts suspecting her husband's cheating on her – she realises from the small, almost-imperceptible signs of her husband's stress at leading a double life, at trying to make two opposite ideas (fall in love with another woman but keep being nice, though not too nice, to the wife) co-exist in one head.

The big problem, however, is that some people want politicians that are administrators (minister is semantically close to administer) whereas others want a leader who assumes the role of parent. Muscat succeeded in being a bit of both.

He was an administrator to those who wanted neo-liberalism and a parent to those who do not even begin to understand that politics should be a contest between ideas not tribal warfare or clan war.

This will be the big challenge for his successor, and possibly his downfall too.

A demoralised party

DESPITE THE HYPE, RELATIVELY FEW PEOPLE ATTENDED THE MAWK-ISH FAREWELL TOUR EVENTS. And rightly so. As I'm a Żebbuġi, I'll limit my analysis to the Żebbuġin. I think it was obvious that the vast majority of Żebbuġi Labourites would keep away from the theatre and the lovey-dovey couple, as they figured out the trick. Years ago, Guido de Marco told me something he learned from the time he had an office in Ħaż-Żebbuġ: the Żebbuġin always seek a second opinion. Says something about the character of this people who alone in Malta use the word *ġarnus* (from the Sicilian *giarnusu*), meaning a particularly obstinate person. They understand when they see somebody obstinately wanting to milk the cow till the last drop. Muscat *il-Ġarnus*, Muscat the Obstinate, is bequeathing a demoralised party. Though they won't readily admit it, party members from all over Malta are grasping what Muscat did to them and to the country, and feel sorry for both.

They will obviously overburden the new leader with hope and expectation. Chance is, they will be disappointed again, because the new leader is only human (or possibly because, to quote the deep wisdom that Owen Bonnici shared with us, messiahs like Joseph 'are born once every 25 years').

The major conundrum Labour will have to solve is to discover why Aristotle was right when he wrote that virtue lies in the middle.

The intermittent Constitution fuss

THE MUSCAT LEGACY (*EREDITÀ* NOT *LEGAT!*) INCLUDES THE CASTRATED URGE TO REVOLUTIONISE THE CONSTITUTION, AND THE CONCURRENT IGNORANCE OR IGNORING OF THE CURRENT CONSTITUTION. For six years, Muscat promised a new constitutional document, but never elaborated on the details. Every now and then, he would allow a lot of fuss to dominate the public arena, heightening expectations about his promised constitutional changes. He started a real and gaudy revolution, in so-called "civil rights" which, coupled with the fuss on constitutional change, served to distract from his third, concurrent but concealed, "revolution": institutionalised corruption.

His purposefully vague insistence on a New Constitution was also meant to hit another bird with the same stone: since the current constitution is on its way out, it need not really be observed. This enabled him to usher in a sort of "authoritarian populism" – the enormous majority at the polls emboldened him to amass as much power as possible in the Executive, and, pointedly, in his hands. No wonder the Venice Commission was shocked.

This urge to revolutionise the Constitution was castrated for two reasons. One, the fuss helped to divert attention from the rot. Two, unlike all his predecessors, Muscat seems to have been oblivious to the true significance of a constitutional setup. Future historians will doubtlessly find among his greatest flaws, his inexplicable misunderstanding of the Modern State and his cynical nonchalance toward the temptations that landslide victories engender.

Economic chimera

MUSCAT REPEATEDLY PROMISED HIS FOLLOWERS THAT THE ECONOMIC BOOM HE TAKES CREDIT FOR WOULD CONTINUE FOR A LONG TIME. He never reminded his followers that his predecessor had agreed a financial package with the EU of over one billion euros. Equally important, he never explained to his followers that, in addition to that injection of cash, Malta's economy enjoyed healthy growth thanks to the ballooning of the population. A few weeks ago, Minister José Herrera told us that the population has now grown to more than 700,000! This population growth has brought about the economic boom – but the bases of this boom are volatile.

Muscat's legacy (*eredità* not *legat!*) will include a shock when the artificial fattening of the economy stops and leaner times knock on the Nation's door. Already certain industries have begun complaining that the political environment no longer affords them the stability they need to operate. Don't be surprised if the country goes to the dogs.

International reputation

THE INTERNATIONAL FALLOUT FROM MUSCAT'S MESS IS WITHOUT PRECEDENT. As there are no natural resources on the islands or beneath the surrounding seabed, Malta depends on foreign direct investment. FDI requires political stability, a trustworthy workforce, a functioning legal system, an efficient banking system and, most importantly, a good reputation. EU membership certified that we had all of that. Now, thanks to Muscat's administration, the certificate of quality has been torn up. Now, after Muscat's devastation, we'll have to start afresh.

Epilogue

IN *LIFE IS BEAUTIFUL*, ROBERTO BENIGNI'S CHARACTER PRETENDS THAT IMPRISONMENT IN A NAZI CONCENTRATION CAMP IS A GAME, TO SHIELD HIS YOUNG SON FROM THE TRAUMA. Muscat might be doing the same. Perhaps he wanted to overstay his welcome at Castille to do a Benigni thing. Consider the private audience with Pope Francis.

I looked at the faces of the two innocent Muscat sisters in the photos with His Holiness. Perhaps the Holy Father was playing a role in a Benigni-like masquerade, shielding the children from their unholy father's narcissistic recklessness.

Consider the surreal farewell events around Malta. Again, if they have the effect of not traumatising those two girls, I sort of close one eye.

But truth be told, I rather suspect Muscat cares very little about doing a Benigni thing, and is instead diabolically protecting himself as he slowly comes to terms with his self-delusion.

Ultimately, it seems that he genuinely believed that because he had the power and the glory, then the kingdom would be his forever and ever.

My Personal Library

Aquilina's Maltese-English, English-Maltese dictionaries seem to be loved and loathed at the same time. I've heard complaints that Aquilina simply compiled terms from previous dictionaries.

To me that's more of a plus than a minus. Defects abound in Aquilina – I once wrote a 6,000-word study on one word which Aquilina took from Vassalli's *Lexicon* while discarding Vassalli's precise definition and proposing an alternative definition based on assertion.

Yet, Aquilina's remains one of a handful of authoritative Maltese lexicons. It's a pity that a new mentality has taken root in the country that believes the people have the last word in matters linguistic.

There's a tendency to forget that it's the experts who sieve through the mass of popular linguistic initiatives because the people is not always right. At the end, the experts have to measure themselves against the Father of the Maltese Language.

And So This is Christmas

IT IS CHRISTMAS, SHOULD WE TALK ABOUT JOSEPH MUSCAT? A reader left an interesting comment beneath the online version of 'The Rise and the Fall'. Referring to a sentence in my article – 'It is never fair – never ever – for children to have to pay for the misdeeds of their parents' – he wrote, 'It may not be fair but it is reality and has been ever since the parents were kicked out of Paradise. It seems "fair" was not a high priority for God.' I reacted with a sarcastic comment, which was not nice of me. So, since this is Christmas, I tell that reader I'm sorry and all that.

But the comment served to inspire this piece. This reader's comment probably came from a free association of ideas... the rise and fall of Joseph Muscat... the fall of Man... Paradise lost... the Garden of Eden. Christmas – though this might come as a surprise to some people – is not an excuse to binge-buy, overeat, and revel; it is the celebration of the birth of Jesus, who, according to the story, was born to make good for the silliness of Adam in the Garden of Eden, when the first man listened to his wife and both ate the fruit that God forbade them to eat. Why was it an "apple"? Whereas there's no mention of "apple" in the Genesis story, there is an ancient tradition according to which the "forbidden fruit" was a red apple. The renowned psychologist Jordan Peterson suggests in one of his lectures that the forbidden fruit is a red apple because red signifies "ripeness". It was therefore a ripe fruit which the first man accepted from his wife.[42]

When God got angry at Adam's silliness, God cursed the serpent and the ground; God did not curse Adam. It was after these two curses and God's decision to greatly increase the woman's pangs in child-bearing that the first man called his wife Eve, 'because she was the mother of all living'. According to tradition, the name "Eve" is related to the Hebrew word for *life*. ("Adam" is related to the Hebrew word for *red*.) According to another tradition, the name of God is the third person singular of the verb in Hebrew related to *life*.

Despite the insistence on Life, the punishment for eating the fruit was Death. The story can be read

---

42   (The early Church also believed the fig was the "forbidden fruit" because Adam covered himself with a fig leaf when he realized he was naked (they assumed he had just eaten from it and covered himself with the nearest leaf). There are echoes of the fig tree in the Gospel and Augustine hears the voice which invites him to "take up and read" when weeping beneath a fig tree. – *Ed.*)

on many levels, but one level should strike us most. When the serpent convinced the woman to eat, the serpent told her, 'You will not die; for God knows that when you eat of it your eyes will be opened, and you will be like God, knowing good and evil.' You'll notice that the claims made by the serpent were twofold. One, that the punishment promised by God was not true; two, that by disobeying God, the two humans would 'be like God'. This theme is found elsewhere in Genesis, for instance in the Tower of Babel story, as it seems that man can't learn the lesson, keeps falling prey to hubris and wanting to be like God, and keeps incurring God's wrath and punishment. Even if you read this through the eyes of the non-believer, you will still perceive the archetype, and how to interpret what happened to silly Joseph Muscat who fell prey to hubris and to his delusions of grandeur.

In Muscat's case, he might have thought he became a god (many men of power have suffered from this self-delusion – the Roman emperors even made it state policy to be considered as a divinity). But the way I see it, Muscat was more like the serpent. He tempted the "innocent" Maltese electorate ('Those who craved to be duped and now expect commiseration because they were betrayed', as Giovanni Bonello privately told me a few days ago – I'm quoting him with his permission by the way); he tempted them using deception. The Genesis serpent is also known as *The Deceiver*.

Genesis is such a powerful text because it is archetypal. Some serious and other, less serious scholars try to divine its numerological secrets. Others consider it of divine inspiration. I think it's divine.

Deception
MUSCAT DECEIVED THE MALTESE PEOPLE IN MANY WAYS. Not just by pretending not to understand the Panama Papers scandal in 2016 and doggedly defending the 'gang who brought shame on our country'[43] when instead he should have instantly fired them. He deceived the Maltese people by promising long-lasting economic prosperity while pushing forward short-termism. We might experience the implications in the not-too-distant future, even though I hope I'm wrong.

He also deceived the Maltese people by promising a twisted idea of equality. By equality one usually means equality of opportunity. One does not mean that people are personally equal. Equality of opportunity means that, irrespective of

---

43   'Malta bigger than "gang who brought shame", President on Republic Day', *The Times of Malta*, 13 December 2019.

one's condition and family origins, if one is intelligent one gets the opportunity to move up in life. This revolutionary idea comes from the first article of the French Revolution's *Declaration of the Rights of Man and of the Citizen*: 'Men are born and remain free and equal in rights'. Everybody should have the same opportunity to advance in life. Ultimately, equality is a Christian idea: in his letter to the Galatians, St Paul explains that there is equal opportunity for salvation in Christ(ianity).

The other type of equality – the one that pretends that all are personally equal – is what one finds in totalitarian systems. But in such systems, as George Orwell pointed out in *Animal Farm*, some animals end up more equal than others. Because in totalitarian systems there is a law for the animals and a law for the gods, as Evarist Bartolo reminded us in 2016. Muscat deceived the people by promising a warped vision of equality. Earlier this year, during the TV talk-show *Xtra*, Muscat said that he 'want[ed] the Maltese youths to get the skilled jobs' and 'Maltese workers to be managers or doctors'. These words only served further to confuse the people, as he deceivingly fomented the subversive, racist idea that all should be managers and doctors, all should get skilled jobs, whereas the other jobs would be taken up by foreigners. This was vile deception. How can you ignore the intelligence quotient of people? Muscat's deceptive equality is deceptive because it promises to those with a lower IQ that they can be like those with a higher IQ. It's like telling short peo-

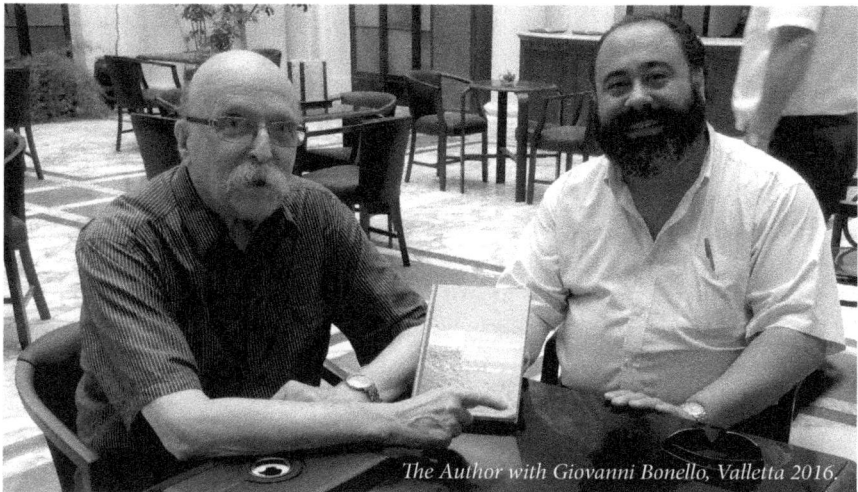

The Author with Giovanni Bonello, Valletta 2016.

ple they can have a career in basketball if they want to, or heavy-set people that they can be jockeys or ballerinas, or the tone-deaf they can become professional singers. This is pure and irresponsible deception. And the less intelligent believed it, swallowing the lie that they are really equal to the more intelligent!

Equality of opportunity means that anybody who has what it takes can become anything they want. Muscatian equality means that everybody is like everybody else if they want to. This is chaos! Diabolical chaos!

Chaos
THE JUDEO-CHRISTIAN TRADITION PROPOSES THE IDEA THAT ORDER BRINGS A FUNCTIONING STATE AND A PROSPEROUS SOCIETY BUT AT ITS HEIGHT, ORDER IS BETRAYED BY CORRUPTION AND THE STATE AND SOCIETY FALL INTO CHAOS. Corruption happens when public administration is no longer carried out according to the principles of morality.

Malta's constitutional setup is basely on Britain's. According to the British constitutional theorist A.V. Dicey, there are two types of constitutional rules: those that are enforceable in Court and those that make up "constitutional morality" – what is right and what is wrong. But salvation is not achieved through

the State *per se*. Salvation is achieved through the truthful individual, through the individual who speaks the truth and leads everybody else toward the "utopian" State. When the leader of a nation does not follow (constitutional) morality, when he deceives, he leads to chaos. The crisis that has hit our country with the force of a gale wind is constitutional chaos. This chaos feeds primarily on ignorance. Even in his last days, Muscat has embarked on yet another attempt at spreading ignorance. I have recently discovered that there is a new branch of knowledge which actually studies the systematic spread of ignorance. It is known as *agnotology* and it is the study of culturally induced ignorance or doubt. Look carefully at what Joseph and Michelle Muscat are doing at the moment, aided and abetted by the Labour-owned and Labour-leaning media. You will see that they are spreading unknowledge and doubt. In other words, they are spreading chaos.

This has been the overall effect of Muscat's politics. He injected into the country a culture of ignorance, of "everything goes", of impunity. His politics have opened the gates for chaos. When the PN was campaigning for rule of law it was implicitly campaigning against chaos. But now Chaos is here. Muscat leaves a chaotic country behind

My Personal Library

The Bible is the most important book ever. Saydon's Maltese translation is particularly dear to me. It should be to Maltese what the King James version is to English. But few people read it, saying it is "difficult".

I claim that that difficulty makes it so precious. Scripture should be difficult because it needs to be read over and over before the meaning is grasped. I disagree with those who want the Bible to be translated into everyday language.

It is said that music heals the soul. But surely, it's not shallow music that heals the soul. It's music structured on many levels that you unravel over time, music that initially attracts you not because it's cantabile but because of a partially-veiled beauty you can't put your finger on, not immediately at least. Then you listen to it attentively and, in time, you crack the cipher. When you achieve that level of intimacy with a piece of music (a fugue by Bach, say, or a romanza by Beethoven, or even, in certain circumstances, *Any Colour You Like* by Pink Floyd), then your soul starts to heal. And when you read about the structure of these musical pieces, your brain starts glimpsing why they heal your soul.

The same with Scripture. Scripture should not be approached like a pop song; it should be approached like those pieces of music that attract you with a promise but deliver only after careful listening – not with the ears; with the soul. Scripture is like the woman of your life... you uncover her true self the deeper you know her.

If you are interested in Pink Floyd music, a number of university professors and lecturers contributed to a book called *'Speak to Me': The Legacy of Pink Floyd's The Dark Side of the Moon* (2005).

Part II deals with the music: structure, tonal coherence, modulation...

him. One has to wonder whether we have the resources – human, financial, and cultural – to restore order out of chaos.

Living the Frank Sinatra repertoire
MUSCAT'S STYLE – SPREADING WHAT HE CALLED "POSITIVITY" AIMED TO CREATE THE FEEL-GOOD FACTOR – REMINDS ME A LOT OF FRANK SINATRA'S REPERTOIRE. There seems to be a common theme in many Sinatra songs: the post-war feel-good factor. According to one author, Sinatra was the personification of 1950s America: 'cocky, eye on the main chance, optimistic, and full of the sense of possibility'.[44]

Listen to songs like *That's Life* and *New York, New York* and it's as if Muscat were singing them. Muscat even explicitly used the title of one Sinatra song – *The Best Is Yet To Come* – during the 2017 election campaign.

But then, listen also to the Sinatra version of *Bad Bad Leroy Brown* and *Mack The Knife* – these two songs somehow also feature in Muscat's political biography.

Then there's the song *I Get A Kick Out Of You* of which there are two versions: one mentions cocaine, the other doesn't.

---

44   Tom Santopietro (2008): *Sinatra in Hollywood: The Film Career of a Screen Icon* (New York: T.Dunne/ St Martin's Press).

The Last Days

MUSCAT'S LAST DAYS COINCIDED WITH THE LAST DAYS OF 2019, A YEAR THAT WILL REMAIN ETCHED IN MALTESE HISTORY LIKE 1919, THOUGH FOR DIFFERENT REASONS.

What could have been but was not
IN JULY 2018, FORMER LABOUR MINISTER JOE DEBONO GRECH, A GOOD-HEARTED MAN WITH THE VOICE OF A DOBERMAN, WAS INTERVIEWED ON THAT WASTE-OF-AIRTIME TV SHOW CALLED *XTRA*. The interview was then transcribed on the mercenary newspaper which belongs, in part, to *Xtra*'s presenter, Salvu Balzan. In the newspaper's shoddy English translation, Mr Debono Grech says, 'Muscat managed to become a statist – which none of us expected.'

Clearly, Mr Debono Grech had said *statista* in Maltese, but for *Mercenary Today*, since *ġurnalista* is *journalist*, *statista* has to be *statist*. What do they care that *statista* is *statesman* whereas *statist* is "an advocate of a political system in which the state has substantial centralised control over social and economic affairs"?

One could say of Salvu Balzan what Mr Debono Grech said of Disgraced Muscat: "Balzan managed to become a journalist – which none of us expected." Only that, as the more intelligent expected, neither became either.

Expectations... One would expect that when Muscat was a one-year-old toddler, during the *quċċija* he chose the statesman gizmo. When he was slightly older but his princely face still smeared with royal snot, people would ask him, 'What do you want to become when you grow up?' and he would answer, 'A statesman, a statesman!' ('*Statista! Statista!*').

Instead, and tragically, Muscat grew up to become an amoral man. Morality was for him something to be derided. The main connotation of his unnerving, slightly malevolent Cheshire-cat grin was that he had knowledge that you, the beholder, were not aware of. I think that knowledge was that morality is unnecessary ballast that keeps the hot-air balloon from rising to reach the heights it's meant to reach. But now that the hot air has gone, something Alice-in-Wonderland-like has happened. Whereas in that children's novel, the Cheshire cat disappears leaving the unnerving grin behind, in Malta, the unnerving grin has disappeared leaving an enervated Cheshire-cat politico behind.

A statesman does not live politics as a get-rich-quick scheme (was the Bulgari watch just a tip... of a huge iceberg?). Muscat wanted to become a statesman; he became the central figure of a medieval tragedy instead.

Muscat's birthday
On January 22, 2020, 10 days after his planned resignation, it will be the former Invictus' birthday, his forth-sixth. At forty-six years of age, he's at his peak, full of energy and vim, endowed with enough life experience to understand what he really wants and how to get it and to know the ways of the world and how to achieve his full potential. He has now reached the point when he's too old to be young but too young to be old, when the investments he made in himself during the first half of his life can be brought to bear fruit. This is the time in the life of an alpha male when he can lead others not on the basis of institutional authority or a cornucopia of promises, but because the horizontal forehead lines, the faux-tame force of the voice, the dignified salt and pepper in the hair, and the wild violence he could potentially unleash but chooses not to, all conspire to make charismatic authority ooze naturally from every single pore in his body.

And yet, having reached this juncture, the former Invictus has castrated himself. His name has become worthless. Even on his Ph.D. rumours have been making the rounds for ages, which he never bothered to dispel because it would have looked petty and infra dig. So now with his top academic qualification sullied by doubts raised and never quelled; with the edifice of his political track record having been pulled down by the wrecking ball of his reckless blind faith in a man who has no scruples, no culture, no values, nothing but cynical materialist utilitarianism; with his reputation swept away by a destructive whirlwind that had started off as a breeze of chutzpah and self-confidence and then grew into full-blown arrogance and overconfidence as time went by... his downfall now is a tragedy. Not just for himself, but for the entire nation: his private failure is like an oil stain that spread all over the fabric of the nation's reputation. The "genius" – as that lady screeched at him after his Farewell Tour stop in Naxxar – turned out to be another benighted victim of the Dunning-Kruger effect. For if the ten Labour victories were secured by the sweat of Keith Schembri's brow, how does the genius of the *ġenju* feature in the story?

Born Again?

Are we to believe that the raging fires of scandal kindled Muscat's spiritual rebirth? The Prime-Minister-King under whose reign the Maltese State took a hard-line anti-Church stance, passed legislation that defies Catholic teaching on marriage, and tolerated pro-abortion manifestations (when abortion is a crime in Malta – would the State have tolerated, say, pro-fraud, pro-homophobia, or pro-rape manifestations?)... this decidedly anti-Catholic Prime-Minister-King first visited the Bishop of Rome, then attended the Christmas midnight mass in the Church of the Nativity in Bethlehem!

(The bills for the trips triggered by this recent spiritual awakening were, alas, footed by the taxpayer.)

The man's effrontery knows no limits. The spoilt brat who was elected Prime Minister but crowned himself King, never managed to grasp the notion that the respect for limits is what makes us mature men and women. His self-perception is seriously constrained by his inability to see where the limits are and that lack of limitation annihilates being. We are witnessing the self-annihilation of a man who presented himself as a statesman in the making but proved himself to be just the embodiment of a brand craftily packaged by the shrewd Schembri.

Limits there are. A little water gives life, but if it keeps on raining, the levee eventually breaks and the flood carries everything away, leaving chaos where there would have been order. The hypocritical use of religion to impress the gullible is highly damaging. Like the chaos he's creating in his last days.The doctor who in August 2012 said about Dom Mintoff's 1998 actions: 'I'm not saying his mind wasn't there but this high fever could have affected him', now can't diagnose Muscat and save the nation further embarrassment and chaos?

The President of Malta

THE LAST DAYS OF THE FORMER INVICTUS ARE MARKED BY THE SIGNATURE DISRESPECTFUL APPROACH ENCAPSULATING HIS PHILOSOPHY ON PUBLIC LIFE AND THE NATION'S INSTITUTIONS. That the President of Malta is drawn into this public display of disregard at the constitutional setup of the country, is also an ignominy.

It is not clear who is advising President Vella, but it seems to me that it's unimaginative advice he's receiving, that the constitutional setup is made up only of the constitutional document. This is wrong. There is the constitutional document but there's also constitutional morality. (As Dicey teaches.) However, I am not surprised. I have it in writing from people very close to the President that His Excellency feels quite unsure about his knowledge of human rights (an integral

part of our constitutional setup). It would therefore follow that he could also feel unsure about constitutional morality. But His Excellency should follow his doctor instinct and transcend whatever legal advice he's receiving. This country has had a political infarct and needs a device to arrest fibrillation of the ventricular muscles of the nation's heart – a presidential defibrillator. When a doctor is faced with an infarct situation, he does not consult a lawyer on the legal niceties. A doctor has to save the patient, without wasting precious time, acting quickly with vision, courage, and moral integrity. These are the very qualities that Karmenu Mifsud Bonnici and many Labourites had seen in George Vella in 1992, when Dr Vella was offered the leadership of the Labour Party. These are again the qualities that the Maltese nation now needs to see in Dr Vella. He has to act, and the constitutional setup affords him that. On December 10, in a move that the editorial of this newspaper called 'a double blow to democracy', Parliament went into Christmas recess – three full weeks before Christmas – to reconvene three weeks into the new year. This decision was taken without consulting the Opposition. During this record-breaking seven-week recess, there is no way for a majority of MPs to express themselves in the only legally valid way possible, through the House itself. The President is claiming that he can remove the Prime Minister only if such a majority expresses itself yet he knows that they cannot do it because Parliament rose for this seven-week-long recess.

The wool has been pulled over everybody's eyes, to benefit Muscat. But the President has to resist it. The entire nation can see that the ball of leadership is now in the President's court, just like the ball of constitutional morality. The very restrictive interpretation of a constitutional setup that excludes everything except the constitutional document is noxious to the health of the nation.

B-Movie Days

WHAT WE ARE ALL WITNESSING IN MUSCAT'S LAST DAYS IS SOMETHING CLOSE TO A CRIME THRILLER. Day after day, we get carried away by new revelations, almost all scandalous in nature, many of which could verge on the criminal.

Muscat's prolonged stay in office may serve to satisfy psychological needs, but it may also be a ruse to attain last-minute crime-related objectives. There are so many things we don't know and that we might never get to know. So many that we probably don't even know that we don't know them. Even if Muscat is not up to something (difficult to believe knowing him, but let's give him the benefit of the doubt), the indelible impression Muscat is leaving is that he's covering up evidence. This impression will haunt him all his life, but he seems oblivious to it. He has been told by the Opposition to leave, for the good of the nation. A true friend would also tell him to leave, but for his own good.

A wise man knows that it often happens that your own good and the nation's converge... and that your enemy could be giving you the friendliest advice.

My Personal Library

Procopius (c. 500 – c. after 565) was legal adviser to Belisarius, the Emperor Justinian's chief military commander in the campaign to regain the Empire's lost Western half. In *The Secret History*, which he probably wrote in 550 AD, Procopius criticised harshly both Emperor Justinian and his wife Theodora and his chief commander Belisarius and his wife Antonia. The former Procopius called, "demons in human form"; the latter, incompetent and treacherous.

The Secret History exposes the secret motivations behind the public actions as well as the private lives of the Emperor and those close to him. Justinian is portrayed as venal, prodigal, cruel, and incompetent, while his wife Theodora as vulgar and insatiably lustful, envious and fearfully mean-spirited, full of shrewdness and cold-blooded self-interest. By uncovering the secrets of the powerful, *The Secret History* reminds me of the attempts to uncover the truth on the ownership of the third secret Panama company.

Some Lessons Learnt

As we watch Muscat's sun setting behind the hills of shame, let's have a look at some lessons we can learn from the bad experience the country's been through.

We don't need another hero

Is ours a messianic system? Are we perennially waiting for a messiah who will establish some heavenly kingdom?

Are we a theocracy neurotically expecting a miracle-worker or are we a democratic republic founded on our own work?

Muscat, a politician with more than half his Twitter followers made up of fake accounts, mixed up concepts for an already-mixed up people.

He portrayed himself as a messiah – that is to say, a religious figure – while he delivered the ultra-secular, ultra-liberal Kingdom of the God of Money.

Do we need a messiah for this country, or do we need a talented political class with a vision that is shared and discussed by a team rather than imposed by a know-it-all spoilt brat whose judgment was compromised when he meaningfully shook hands on the fourth floor and struck pre-election back-street deals?

Friends will be friends

THE PRIME MINISTER'S FRIENDS CAN PLAY A ROLE IN THE COUNTRY'S HISTORY THAT'S UNEXPECTED AND POLITICALLY UNHEALTHY. Prime Minister Muscat's friends ended up being like the courtesans of the absolute kings of yore. Muscat surrounded himself with friends who became the noose snaring the country's neck. Keith Schembri was linked to corruption and murder, but also to an energy rip-off that promises to strangle the nation over time. Neville Gafà got immersed in still-to-be-fully-explained "missions" to Libya. Nexia BT big-shots were lodged in Castille apparently to devise secret corporate structures for persons so important that their names couldn't be mentioned in emails. This circle of friends destroyed Muscat while damaging the country more than the Stukas of WWII.

All this indicates our country's institutional weakness, that there are no mechanisms at law which could stop such abuses. The Prime Minister's advisors cannot be businessmen, and worse still businessmen with a finger in every pie. They cannot be ideologues who push minority aspirations to the exclusion of others. Even though minorities have to be listened to, the Government cannot become a dictatorship of the "*minoritariat*".

The advisors cannot just be quick-witted; they have to be intellectuals and academics, who don't flatter the man but give him advice based on intelligence and knowledge not ideology or self-interest.

The fixer

IN THEORY, ANYBODY COULD BECOME PRIME MINISTER. In practice, we need politicians who are not fixers (and certainly don't portray themselves as such) and are not awarded the accolade of Man of the Year for Corruption. Isn't it ironic that while Muscat was enacting legislation against corruption, his crew of picaroons were busy concocting devious schemes and peculation?

We don't need fixers or power-mongers who with immature cynicism meddle with the State's institutions and with society. We need people who have gone through real experiences in life, listened to the troubles of real people (from the employee to the professional to the business magnate), and then know how to mediate between social forces and seek the common good... a leader for whom Us is more important than I, and for whom Us incorporates Them as well.

We don't need fixers who use public resources to fix and further their own careers, to attain high office in international institutions. We need politicians who seek the common good, who seek to distribute wealth fairly and efficiently, who seek to create an advanced society for all of its members. In practice, we don't need fixers but politicians who are well-versed in constitutionalism. If the State is like an orchestra, the constitutional score cannot be played by ear; it has to be studied and the person occupying the most constitutionally important position, i.e. the conductor, has to know the music more than the musicians who follow his baton. All of Muscat's post-Independence predecessors had undertaken formal education in matters constitutional. Giorgio Borg Olivier, Karmenu Mifsud Bonnici, Eddie Fenech Adami, and Lawrence Gonzi were lawyers while Alfred Sant had studied at the École Nationale d'Administration. As for Dom Mintoff, he had been so long in politics that he knew the ins and outs through long exposure. Only Muscat was constitutionally illiterate... and we need to avoid having another Prime Minister equally ignorant in these matters.

The Rime Of The Ancient Mariner
DURING THE GOZO STOP IN HIS SURREAL FAREWELL TOUR, MUSCAT LET US KNOW THAT HE INTENDS TO BE A MARINER ON THE NEW CAPTAIN'S SHIP. How will this new subplot in the national soap opera unfold? (Politics, that should about plans for future action and solutions for present problems, has under Muscat degenerated into a pathetic third-rate *telenovela*.)

Coleridge's poem *The Rime of the Ancient Mariner* tells us how calamities befall a ship after one of her sailors kills an albatross. Steve Harris' song rendition captures the essence of what happened soon after the killing:

> The mariner kills the bird of good
> omen
> His shipmates cry against what
> he's done
> But when the fog clears, they
> justify him
> And make themselves a part of
> the crime.

Let this lesson be learnt by those who need to learn it.

Us and them
MALTA IS, OR SHOULD BE, A NEUTRAL STATE ACTIVELY PURSUING PEACE, SECURITY AND SOCIAL PROGRESS AMONG ALL NATIONS. Previous Prime Ministers worked hard in this direction – just consider the Fenech Adami administration's hosting of the Bush-Gorbachev Summit way back in 1989 and Alfred Sant's role in the meeting between Palestine's Yasser Arafat and right-wing Israeli politician David Levy in 1996.

What has Muscat done in this regard? Not only did he not pursue peace, security and social progress policies, but he actually somehow got in trouble with Russia (we still don't really know the details). So much so that in July 2019, Russia vetoed Malta's attempt to place two oil smuggling suspects on a United Nations sanctions list. (These individuals were at the centre of a €30 million fuel smuggling ring involving Libya and Italian Mafia associates.) What had Muscat been up to in this case? We don't need Prime Ministers who think they're so smart they can outwit global or regional powers. We're a micro-State and we have to behave as such. So, no delusions of grandeur or other bouts of megalomania from future Prime Ministers.

We don't need Prime Ministers who accept expensive gifts from big businessmen. Decent Prime Ministers would tell such people not to buy gifts but to donate the money to charity and to the needy instead. Why, is Muscat so needy that he needs a bottle of wine and a wristwatch?

(The questions raised on gifts made to the State and office-holders prior to 2013 seem to insinuate a certain neediness, which could be more psychological than financial.)

When you examine these people's behaviour under the morality microscope, you understand their underclass worldview and *modus operandi*... Why does the electorate give the benefit of the doubt to a politician? In general. And, in particular, why give it to a politician who, when he could choose, didn't give others the same benefit? Why give this benefit to Muscat when he pushed Godfrey Farrugia to resign over the erection of a tent outside Mater Dei Hospital? Why, when he fired Manwel Mallia because Dr Mallia's chauffeur opened fire not on the Minister's orders?

In both cases, the benefit of the doubt could have been a reasonable option for Muscat. Instead he chose to give both of them the sack. So why afford Muscat the benefit of the doubt for unreasonably protecting his Chief of Staff and Madame-de-Pompadour Minister when they were caught red-handed owning secret offshore corporate structures clearly opened to receive funds from suspect sources?

I'm not arguing about Muscat's intentions here. I'm questioning the reasoning of the majority of the electorate. Why the leniency? Why the readiness to forgive, or, at least, to afford the benefit of the doubt? One could argue that Muscat is a narcissistic psychopath who can fool thousands of people. Could be, even though I don't subscribe to this school of thought. Something tells me that there's a different angle to the story. Sometimes people want to be hoodwinked. The victim sometimes wants to be the victim. It's a bit like that controversial scene from *Gone With The Wind* when, at the bottom of that imposing staircase, Scarlett wants to be "ravished" by Rhett. The electorate seemed to enjoy being Wily Muscat's accomplice-victim in his shenanigans. As if people knew what was going on and still wanted to participate. In a sense, it was like an archetypal Biblical story, when a people decides collectively to break the covenant with the Sacred, the "Sacred" being a byword for morality.

Individuals were willing to give up their responsibility of their own relationship to the Truth to Muscat and constantly lie to themselves.

And now because of this collective behaviour, read what has been written about us in the international press in the last days of 2019. On November 27, *Bloomberg* argued that 'Malta proves oligarches aren't all Eastern Europeans. ... Oligarchs who purchase political influence aren't just a post-Communist phenomenon.'

On December 3, *The Guardian* claimed that 'only now, two years after Daphne Caruana Galizia's murder, is it becoming clear just how rotten the [Maltese] State really is.'

My Personal Library

In the dystopian novel trilogy *The Hunger Games*, the *Bildungsroman* written by Suzanne Collins, the dictatorial government seated in Capitol City continuously issues slogans to convince the people that Panem (of which Capitol is the capital) is indeed the best country to be in and that the rulers of Panem are protecting the population and showed mercy in the "dark days", for which the population needs to be grateful. Slogans (or propaganda) are the deliberate and systematic attempt to shape perceptions, manipulate cognitions, and direct behaviour to achieve a response that furthers the desired intent of the propagandist. This is what the rulers of Capitol are continuously engaged in throughout the novels.

If you watched Joseph Muscat's end-of-year (but also end-of-career) speech, you would be excused if you thought you were reading *The Hunger Games* and its portrayal of the propaganda of the rulers of Capitol.

On December 4, *The Telegraph* described how 'Malta went from perfect holidays destination to scandal-ridden State.'

On December 5, *The Atlantic* wrote that 'Malta is not just a Mediterranean backwater; it's a back door – into Europe's banking system, into the visa-free travel accorded by its European passports, into the protection of European rule of law and the values of human rights and the free press that the EU has been created to uphold. It is hard to imagine the government of any other EU country staying intact under similar circumstances.'

On December 11, *The Economist* observed that 'amid all the uncertainties on Malta today, one thing seems clear ... A country that was once Europe's bridge to Africa and the Middle East has now become a pariah.'

Thank you, Muscat. Thank you so very much.

It Finally Happened

IT FINALLY HAPPENED: WE'RE SLIGHTLY MAD. Actually, we're not just *slightly* mad, we're *really* mad. At Muscat who has hijacked our politics. Maltese society has abandoned all semblance of mature political discussion on matters of national import and got lost in Muscat's labyrinth.

Consider the recent events in Libya. They are indicating that Russia and Turkey have assumed a larger role as regional powers in the Mediterranean. Malta's foreign policy seems to be working through proxies, when we are one of Libya's neighbours.

Public discussion and scrutiny of politics means we should be analysing this new development; instead, the nation is wasting its limited resources on the mess created by Muscat and his evil shadow, and on pushing for a malfunctioning State to investigate malfeasance...

Just look at France to see how a functioning State works. The French are tackling the Libya crisis head-on and at the same time they will try their former President Nicolas Sarkozy this coming October for corruption, and all this while the people have been demonstrating for weeks on end. The French try their former President (who toppled Libya's Qaddafi in 2011) for corruption; One TV fetes the outgoing Prime Minister as a national hero.

The aftermath

Today was Muscat's last day as Prime Minister. At least, *de jure*. Let's see what happens *de facto*. (He promised – or was it a threat? – he'll remain active but on the sidelines.)

Is Muscat a psychopath who climbs the ladder and cuts the rungs, not caring at all if the ladder maintains itself, and perfectly willing to have it destroyed after he's exhausted it? I know that there are many who subscribe to this school of thought. I'm not one of them. Also because it seems that he wants that ladder to stay, possibly because he (and his wife) think they haven't exhausted it yet.

Muscat's self-perception is important for us to understand what he's still capable of. Objectively speaking, he was born under a lucky star.

From a subjective point of view, however, he probably marinates himself in self-pity, spiced with his sensation of having endured terrible suffering, particularly when he was Alfred Sant's acolyte. (He keeps forgetting that this role was not imposed on him; he sought it and was only too happy to keep it.)

He probably resents the office boy who ran around during fateful Executive Committee meetings convened to vote on by-election choices, handing out scraps of paper with numbers written on them. That boy – the arm that executed the orders that made or broke political careers – probably resented the humiliation but also revelled in the importance it bestowed on him. I suspect that he carries this psychological scar, and it somehow engenders within him a sense of entitlement that, in turn, has been contagious and infected both his inner circle (I cannot otherwise decipher Neville Gafà's delusional public statements) and his followers. This could explain the psychological dynamics of the surreal farewell tour and concurrent campaign for the new leader. Needless to say, there could be more pragmatic reasons behind what we witnessed, but it's still too early to say.

Muscat should have resigned a long while ago. And I don't mean in November or December of 2019. I mean even before. In particular, I mean when Daphne Caruana Galizia was assassinated. I have repeatedly quoted precedents – particularly, Francesco Cossiga's, when the Italian Minister of the Interior resigned to carry the political responsibility for Aldo Moro's assassination. When I first mentioned this, I wrote that Mr Cossiga was obviously not criminally responsible for the assassination, implying that the same could be said of Muscat.

As things have now developed, I'm seriously reconsidering my statement. If one were to be stricter, Muscat should have resigned when his right-hand man, his evil shadow, was caught red-handed owning secret offshore corporate structures meant to receive God knows what money. I obviously don't know what former Police Commissioner Cassar declared behind closed doors during the ongoing Inquiry, but the fact that investigations on Schembri began on 8 April 2016 (a few weeks after the Panama Papers scandal erupted) and Mr Cassar resigned a mere twenty days later is, to say the least, bizarre.

Muscat as myrmidon

CERTAIN PEOPLE RECOGNISE WHO'S GOOD AND WHO'S EVIL QUICKLY, NOT TO SAY IMMEDIATELY. Others take more time, if they ever manage, particularly when the evil wear the clothes of the good. The Italian proverb *l'abito non fa il monaco* (literal translation: "the monk is not by the habit made") means little if anything to them. They are easily beguiled by smart suits, child-like golden smiles, and hollow rhetoric.

Then again, we live in morally ambiguous times. Consider the silly actress who recently bragged that she owed her success to her abortion. She portrayed killing her own child in the womb as a strategically intelligent move for her career. Her life was not threatened, there had been no rape, the child wasn't deformed (the usual three excuses for abortion) – it was essentially an act of selfishness; she destroyed a life for her career; and the media portray her as a heroine. How can people understand right from wrong, when they're constantly fed this rubbish?

Why do I mention abortion? Because much of the pro-abortion rhetoric is like Muscat's: based on subtle misrepresentations, illogical arguments, non sequiturs, and all the other techniques used by manipulators. The rhetoric's success is predicated on the inability of people to see through invalid arguments than on the arguments having any inherent validity. Muscat mastered such rhetorical trickery, with such gay abandon and consistency that it's good material for a PhD. Consider the latest example: Jacob Borg's legitimate question to Muscat about Muscat's Dubai trip (while he was still Prime Minister) and Muscat's obscene answer: 'It's none of your business'. The obscenity was missed by the majority – Muscat again used his rhetorical abilities to obfuscate the issue. The public was again fed rubbish.

The latest instalment in this never-ending charade is the almost-imperceptible shift in the narrative the public's being fed. Analyse how Muscat, who for a short moment was coming out as the evil man he really is, has begun to morph into a goodie again, while the blame shifts unto his evil shadow, Keith Schembri.

There's a clear effort to deflect guilt from Muscat unto Schembri. It's a subtle shift in the narrative, meant to present Schembri as Prime Minister in all but name and Muscat as Schembri's myrmidon. It's the umpteenth attempt to pull the wool over the people's eyes. If we want to resist the indecent proposal to absolve Muscat of Schembri's sins, we have to ask: if indeed Muscat was simply Evil Schembri's myrmidon, how to explain Konrad Mizzi? Mizzi is the man who, when last December Muscat declared he would be soon resigning (but then took his time), told him, 'I love you – our project is still alive.'

If my memory serves me right, it was Muscat who brought Mizzi in as the third leg of the energy-deal tripod, not Schembri. If indeed the unholy trinity was created by Muscat, not Schembri, then the narrative of an evil Schembri who manipulated a ginger boy Muscat amounts to rubbish, and Muscat is as evil as Schembri.

Schembri's business too is none of our business?

In November 2018, the newspapers reported Muscat saying that he did not 'interfere with his chief of staff's business affairs'. Actually, since Schembri told us he had divested himself of all his business interests, there should have been nothing for Muscat to interfere with in the first place. Be that as it may, there are a few questions to ask about Schembri's business affairs.

Starting from 2013, did Schembri's companies use his powerful role as chief of staff to a Prime Minister who "does not interfere with [his] business affairs", to push their products and drive competitors out of the market? What kind of direct orders did the Police, Army, and other State entities place with Schembri's companies from 2013 onward? Do we know anything about these dealings?

How many tenders were Schembri's companies awarded post-2013? Was everything above board? Schembri's companies import paper, machinery, power tools, foodstuffs, wines, beers, and so on. Did these companies increase their sales to State entities from 2013 onward? How and why were their products chosen?

In September 2019, the papers ran stories claiming that Schembri's fortune had sky-rocketed in the previous five years.

In May 2016, Schembri had written an article claiming that 'a political conspiracy' was afoot 'over [his] business group' and that serving as 'chief of staff to the Prime Minister [...] ha[d] come at great cost to [his] business interests.'

'I serve this country and its prime minister,' he wrote, 'with no expectation of gratitude or reward'. Was he ever grilled on all this unadulterated rubbish? Now that Muscat's era is over, there should be nothing to hinder a thorough investigation of Schembri's companies' dealings. And while they're at it, they should also thoroughly investigate all the companies Yorgen Fenech was involved in, in view of his declaration that there were many instances of corruption. If this country wants to get back on track, it has to go through this painful experience.

The French have charged their former President Nicolas Sarkozy with attempting to persuade a high-ranking magistrate to leak confidential information about another investigation targeting him. He will face a three-week-long criminal trial in October 2020.

If we want our ability to manage our own State to be taken seriously and if we want to find our way out of the labyrinth Muscat threw us in, we have to (*not* should *but* have to) investigate our own office-holders, for malfeasance that's far more serious than anything Mr Sarkozy is being charged with.

My Personal Library

The Cambridge University Press publication *The Psychology of Politicians*, edited by Ashley Weinberg (2012) has a silly Nicolas Sarkozy laughing like a monkey on its cover. But that's not the point. The point is that Dr Weinberg herself writes (p. 16):

> Perhaps the time is well overdue to ask that the process by which leaders are selected, and their functioning monitored, is one which includes assessments of their suitability against more objective criteria than if they can win power. [...] This is not to say that there is such a thing as an ideal set of psychological attributes for politicians [...] Nevertheless there are advantages to regular and reliable health screening of serving politicians, which could help to flag up serious misgivings about the behaviour of a leader. As history shows, only in major crises does the question begin to be asked audibly, 'Should this person be in charge?' As with selection, health screening of politicians is likely to be challenging to introduce, but constitutes a necessary precaution against political abuse.

IN HIS INAUGURAL SPEECH, NEWLY-INSTALLED PRIME MINISTER ROBERT ABELA SAID HE WANTED TO 'KEEP JOSEPH MUSCAT'S "MOVEMENT" ALIVE AND KICKING'. What this will mean beyond the rhetoric is not clear yet, particularly since Muscat's "movement" lacked balance and depended entirely on its imbalance to succeed. Time will tell what Dr Abela really means by his early statements, mostly because Muscat's "movement" was based on a huge misunderstanding: Muscat deluded himself he was a liberal. Real liberalism is, in one of its manifestations, the pursuit of happiness, as the Americans have declaimed in their (liberal and stunningly beautiful) Constitution. I won't go into the feasibility of the project of pursuing happiness, as that pursuit might be endless given that happiness might just be a mirage in a desert of misery and desolation.

Be that as it may. The pursuit of happiness isn't the pursuit of pleasure. Pleasure doesn't engender happiness and happiness isn't necessarily pleasure. In actual fact, pleasure might just augment the desire for more pleasure – consider the mechanism behind the overdose: a relentless search for more pleasure which doesn't bring more happiness but death. Happiness – as even the Greek philosophers who taught about seeking happiness in this life, pointed out – is learning how to avoid pain and how to satisfy one's needs adequately. Muscat's liberalism is *hedonist*, it seeks pleasure; it doesn't seek happiness in the sense I've just described.

This was one of Muscat's biggest "philosophical" mistakes – I'm using "philosophical" because I feel like being generous with the man who has been kicked out of the number-one job in the country because of his lax attitude and insatiability. He always wanted more, and more, and more. In reality, his wasn't "philosophy"; it was a mentality.

The Mejjet bil-Ġuħ Mentality

MEJJET BIL-ĠUĦ LITERALLY MEANS "FAMISHED" IN THE SENSE OF "PECKISH". But it is also calqued on the Italian *morto di fame* (literally, *starved to death*) which is synonymous with words like *bramosia, cupidigia, avidità, smania* – all of which mean, more or less, the excessive greed of the excessively famished, who devour (not eat) with a wild look in their eyes. If you remember the movies of Bud Spencer and Terence Hill: the former is usually hungry, the latter *un morto di fame*.

Muscat governed with the *morto di fame* mentality, as if he never had

had anything in his life, exuding an excessive urgency to make hay while the sun shines, even tolerating and protecting his two closest aides when they were caught red-handed owning very fishy secret offshore corporate structures.

This *mejjet bil-ġuħ* mentality must have been the what's-it-called that attracted the flies to the what's-it-called-hole on the Fourth Floor; the same flies Anġlu Farrugia is now hinting he didn't have a big enough flyswatter to strike them with.

If we are to believe Sandro Chetcuti, the Nationalists had told him about the need to diversify since "development" as Mr Chetcuti understands it was no longer sustainable. The "developers" recognised Muscat's *mejjet bil-ġuħ* mentality and seduced him.

Yes, I claim that it wasn't Muscat who seduced the "developers" but the other way round – the "developers" seduced (an admittedly easy) Muscat.

Had Muscat not been slave to his *mejjet bil-ġuħ* mentality, he would have put the national interest first. And the country would not have been thus ruined. But give Ċirillu a pair of trousers, and being the *bravu* he is, you know what he'll do, and you also know where he'll wipe after he's done it. And the flies keep going back to him, as they like it.

Lord of the Flies

IT MUST BE AN OBSCENE BEING WHO, IN A MATTER OF DAYS, FIRST VISITS POPE FRANCIS ACCOMPANIED BY HIS TWO INNOCENT CHILDREN, THEN ATTENDS MIDNIGHT MASS AT THE NATIVITY CHURCH IN BETHLEHEM, AND THEN FIRST THING HE DOES UPON RESIGNING IS TO HINT HE WILL CAMPAIGN FOR THE INTRODUCTION OF ABORTION. This could finally become the textbook example of "obscenity".

This obscene creature said he owed it to future generations. What does he owe to future generations? That they be killed in their mothers' wombs?

This obscene Beelzebub, this Lord of the Flies, knows that the illiterate segment of the electorate adores him and is easily carried away by his demonic rhetoric. But more importantly, this Deceiver also knows that there's a small but powerful percentage of the thinking electorate that's warmly receptive to his obscene ideas. On this game Muscat the Obscene has now set his mind. He will keep rousing the rabble while using the ultra-liberal part of the electorate to shield himself from possible official procedures relating to corruption and other illegalities. He is crudely and rudely hinting at immunity in exchange for his role in introducing (or not) abortion in this country.

The new Prime Minister has declared that he'll fight Muscat the Obscene's pro-abortion efforts. This is, I believe, wishful thinking. Muscat the Obscene's understanding of the economy is probably considerably better than Dr Abela's; he also understands that in time, Dr Abela might need the support of that percentage of the electorate that respects Muscat the Obscene.

Let's keep in mind that it often happens that politicians miscalculate how much power they really have, and as a first-term lawmaker, Dr Abela is still fresh to real politics. One reason why many politicians don't keep their word isn't because they're not honourable people, but because circumstances are much stronger than the politician could ever have dreamt, and s/he must bow before to them to survive. Muscat the Obscene said he wants to be a sailor on a boat captained by another – let's see whether and how he'll rock the boat.

Politics as entertainment

A CERTAIN, UNSOPHISTICATED SEGMENT OF THE ELECTORATE, VIEW POLITICS AS ENTERTAINMENT, ON A PAR WITH FOOTBALL. They possibly view it as even better than football because it's a sort of interactive game. Whereas in football you just watch (and bet, if you're the betting type), in politics you watch, you bet, but also you participate by voting, bribing, etc. However, this is not Politics.

This column is probably read by the converted, so there's no need for any preaching. Then again, it's always good to share convictions with like-minded people. Particularly with regard to politics, which are nothing but the art of surviving in a hostile world where nobody owes you a living but where you should not behave like a *mejjet bilġuħ* either: politics is surviving in a community with limited resources. Politics is not point scoring but problem solving.

Let us pray that God listens to our national anthem and does grant judiciousness to he who governs Malta and strength to those who make the economy grow.

Post-Muscat Stress Disorder

'Muscat's sarcasm and cynicism had of late become nauseating. At least now, the sarcasm and forced smiles have evaporated. The country has breathed a sigh of relief. There's still a lot to be done, but the country has already breathed a sigh of relief.' I'm quoting from a Franco Debono Facebook post. I think he's right. The sarcasm, the forced smiles... everything had really become nauseating. But, apart from breathing the sigh of relief, has the country also got rid of Muscat?

I don't think so.

Prime Minister Abela seems to be doing his best to distance himself as much as possible from Muscat's legacy. Even newly-installed Education Minister Owen Bonnici has taken two important steps: terminating Anthony Degiovanni's consultancy contract, after the well-known online commentator was caught tampering with the Council of Europe rapporteur's Wikipedia page; and initiating an investigation into a tender won by a company belonging to Keith Schembri. (We are also interested, and probably more, in the *direct orders*, Minister.)

Will this be enough to cut the ties with Muscat's legacy (*wirt* not *legat*)?

No.

If Robert Abela wants to cleanse

his Government, and Malta's reputation, he has to ensure that top political actors assume their political *and criminal* responsibility for their acts. Otherwise, it will just be Act II of *Omnivores: The Farce of the Few, The Tragedy of the Nation*. In the sense that the protagonist of Act I would have been Muscat; of Act II, Dr Abela. (I say the "Omnivores", because these people eat everything they see, as a friend has suggested to me recently.)

It is true that the country needs to return to normality. But it's equally true that the institutional and psychological trauma the nation has been through needs to be addressed. Treating the trauma and the ensuing stress will make the return to normality not only speedier but also permanent. I'd like not to be misunderstood: I certainly don't mean that what Muscat did was in any way politically comparable to what the Nazis did; not only the scale but also the substance were infinitely different. That said, there's a striking psychological similarity.

For the Germans, the Nazi period is still traumatic. After the war, they needed to come to terms with the fact that they had momentarily exited civilisation and started inhabiting another space, governed by an alien morality.

When, after the war, they expected to be re-admitted to civilisation, they had to come to terms with what they, as a nation, had done. The Germans have a word for this process of coming to terms: *Vergangenheitsbewältigung* and it means 'public debate within a country on a problematic period of its recent history'.

"Problematic" refers to traumatic events that raise sensitive questions of collective culpability; in Germany, it refers to embarrassment about and often remorse for Germans' complicity in the war crimes, the Holocaust, and the other atrocities of the Second World War.

As I said – and I'm repeating particularly for the sake of the (now-unemployed?) nitwits who post silly comments to try to deviate attention from the main point – I'm *not* implying that what Muscat did is politically comparable to what the Nazis did. But what happened under Muscat has been traumatic to the country. Malta needs its own *Vergangenheitsbewältgung* but this has to be done in an environment in which it is *tangibly felt* that the country is being run like a normal country.

Indeed, the Labourites have to shoulder most of the responsibility. But they're not alone. Those who embraced the *Moviment* have to shoulder their responsibilities too. And even those of us who refuted the crazy *Moviment* and the Labour Party that passively allowed itself to be manipulated, even we are involved in this "coming to terms" process. Because we share in the national embarrassment caused by the acts of the others. They did things, but their actions embarrass both them *and us*.

In practical terms, however, criminal investigations have to be put in place to investigate the role of Joseph Muscat, Keith Schembri and possibly others not only in Daphne Caruana Galizia's assassination but also in rampant corruption, collusion, and prevarication. All dealings with government entities involving Schembri's companies have to be investigated, and criminal action initiated where foul play is suspected. Most if not all of the big government contracts have to be investigated, as the stench feels strong and the deals feel dirty.

January 22

ON WEDNESDAY JANUARY 22, 2020, I DELIVERED A PUBLIC LECTURE IN VALLETTA ON A NEW DISCOVERY I'VE MADE REGARDING MIKIEL ANTON VASSALLI, ON A POINT THAT'S BEEN BAFFLING RESEARCHERS FOR THE PAST 70/80 YEARS. The following day I was talking on the phone to a friend who attended the lecture and who also researches on Vas-

salli. I remarked that Vassalli had been baptised on May 4th and that my father, who had written Vassalli's fictitious autobiography, died on May 4th. My friend quickly retorted that *his* birthday was... May 4th. Simple coincidences? The power of destiny?

On January 22, the day I delivered the Vassalli lecture, Muscat was celebrating his birthday. That this was a coincidence, I can vouch for. But also on that day, January 22, pro-choice maniacs in the US were celebrating the *Roe v. Wade* anniversary. *Roe v. Wade* is the US Supreme Court judgment that legalised abortion in the United States. Muscat is the former Prime Minister of Malta who seems keen on legalising abortion in Malta. That *Roe v. Wade* was decided on January 22 and Muscat was also born on January 22 (but a year later), is a coincidence about which we're all free to speculate. Is it a simple coincidence? Is it destiny?

Twenty-two. According to the *smorfia* – the Neapolitan tradition of interpreting dreams by associating them with numbers and then betting on those numbers in the state lottery – the number 22 is associated with the madman, the maniac.

However, the *tarocchi*, the tarots, have a slightly different meaning. Some tarot systems refer to the madman by the number 0, meaning limitless energy that has no particular shape. Other tarot systems assign a meaning to the number 22 that's similar to that assigned by the *smorfia*. In this latter tarot interpretation, the madman can be seen as a beginning, as will and action.

The madman in Muscat's case could be the will to a new start, in football, a game in which 11 men play 11 other men, adding up to 22 players on the pitch. In Italian, *dare i numeri* (literally, "to give numbers") means *to talk nonsense*.

Mafia

I believe it is universally accepted that the greatest Mafia movie of them all is Francis Ford Coppola's *The Godfather* trilogy based on Mario Puzo's bestseller. I consider it a long movie divided into three parts.

The main theme, to my mind, is intergenerational transmission of power, first from Mafia kingpin Vito Corleone to his son Michael, and then from Michael Corleone to his nephew Vincent Mancini. There are other themes, such as the corrupt Senator who demands a bribe to grant the Corleones a casino licence, and is then set up by them when he goes to a brothel they run. There's a corrupt Chief of Police, who ends up shot in the face by Michael Corleone. There's the mutual betrayal between brothers, when Fredo sides with Casino owner Moe Green against his brother Michael, and then Michael has Fredo shot when he's out fishing on the lake. There's the theme of abortion, when Michael's wife tells him she has aborted their third child because she didn't want the child to come into their world of mafia, killings, and crime. There's prostitution, which, like gambling, isn't considered serious enough to burden the otherwise easily-troubled conscience of Vito Corleone, who doesn't accept to take part in a drug deal because they don't deal in drugs. There's the Commission meeting when Vito Corleone threatens his colleagues from the other four of the Five Families after his son had been riddled with machine-gun bullets. There's the theme of big real estate business and corrupt bankers. There's Michael's visit to the future Pope. There's the repeated theme that the transmission of power to a new Godfather means the retirement of the old Godfather, a veritable hero.

And so on and so forth... there are so many themes in those 539 minutes of cinematographic genius.

But then you stop reminiscing as you realise that the themes masterfully elaborated in the trilogy are the very same themes that keep recurring when one thinks of Muscat's six years in office: casino tenders (see the letter the doctor delivered to Yorgen Fenech while he was "in the can"), politicians and brothels, Police Chiefs, betrayals among fraternal friends, abortion, prostitution, hypocrisy toward drugs, real estate business, corrupt bankers, tense threat-characterised meetings of the powerful sitting round a table, visits to the Holy Father... and the ritualised transmission of power to the new boss while the former boss' retirement is portrayed like that of a hero.

It's as if these people watched *The Godfather* over and over again, and then scripted their political lives according to Mario Puzo's and Francis Ford Coppola's script for the movie. True, the Corleones are Sicilians. But I have to refer to the Neapolitan *smorfia*: madmen! Mad to think they could get away with murder. Literally.

On second thoughts, they still can. Unless Robert Abela proves his mettle and makes sure that tainted politicians and their henchmen end up "in the can".

My Personal Library

Catch-22 (1961), a satirical war novel by Joseph Heller, is considered among the best novels of the twentieth century. Although the narrator seems to know everything about everything and everyone, the narration does not follow a straight time-line; it describes events from the angle of different characters and the reader has to work out the story-line by him- or herself.

It is set during World War II, even though critics have found that that is an excuse to allow the author obliquely to refer to the Korean War. He ultimately wants to show the absurdity of war and military life through the experiences of the characters, as they strive to keep their sanity while carrying out their military duties with their ultimate aim being homecoming.

Resignation and Ideology

DO I MEAN THAT WE SHOULD RE-
SIGN OURSELVES TO THE IDEOLO-
GIES OF IMPUNITY AND WHITE-
WASHING? Not at all!

Joseph Muscat was an expert at whitewashing, at attempting to stop people finding out the true facts about a situation. Now that events have proved to be bigger than any one individual's will, we are begin-ning to look into the abyss that was Muscat's evil premiership.

The whitewashing ideology has to stop. Likewise, the impunity ideology. This can only be feasi-bly achieved if politicians decide to police themselves. After all, the unwritten constitution inspiring Westminster-model constitutions was based on this principle: poli-ticians should honourably apply checks and balances on each other, as members of clubs would. This might have been the case in the 19th century; it is now clear that this tradition has withered away. Civil society has to keep piling on the pressure, even upping the ante. What do we stand to gain, at least as individuals? Little. We won't be taking home any bigger paycheque. What do we lose if we're passive? A lot. Once politicians think they can get away with murder, democracy fades away like an old photograph, to be replaced by the portrait of the

Leader who dictates what's to be done. We all stand to lose – tan-gibly and intangibly – if democ-racy's gone. It is indeed worrying that Prime Minister Abela should brag that his ability to foresee the outcome of the constitutional case concerning the people's Caruana Galizia memorial induced him to dictate that government employees shouldn't touch the memorial. If the PM's respect for human rights stems from his being so clever as to pre-empt a court decision, then we're really in a sorry state. If the PM had democracy at heart, he'd educate his followers as to the meaning of allowing even those you disagree with to relay a public message at the institutions. At the same time, he would fire his Educa-tion Minister. By extending a warm welcome to Owen Bonnici, the PM's sending the wrong message: you can flout the constitution with impunity. The ideology of impunity has to be eradicated – only the PM can do this. He has to make it cat-egorically clear that Justyne Caruan-a's political hara-kiri won't absolve her husband of any wrongdoing if he really passed on sensitive infor-mation to Yorgen Fenech. To es-tablish the facts, serious investiga-tions must be launched. Similarly, if Joseph Muscat was in any way an accessory, investigations must be carried out and, if need be, Muscat should be prosecuted, just like Nicolas Sarkozy in France. Only these "drastic" actions will save democracy in Malta... drastic for the Maltese but run-of-the-mill for the (other) Europeans.

Distorted narrative

THE EXTRAORDINARILY SAD MURDER OF CHANTELLE CHETCUTI HAS GIVEN RISE TO A NARRATIVE WHICH, TO MY MIND, IS BEST DESCRIBED AS DISTORTED. My intention is **not** to discuss the murder. Instead I want to focus on the pro-abortion women organisation the name of which escapes me, that quickly organised a demonstration in Valletta to protest against "patriarchy". *Patriarchy* means a society controlled by men in which men use their power to their own advantage. But, because "patriarchy" is a figment of certain radical feminists' imagination, we shouldn't allow the thorny issue of domestic violence to be manipulated into a feminist issue because it's two-way traffic, as scientific research demonstrates.

It's absolutely not true that we live in a society controlled by men in which men use their supposed power to their own advantage. In reality, we live in a society in which there are equal opportunities, and women can *choose* to have a career as much as men do. That women don't in actual fact make such a choice is a conscious decision made by individual women, who, upon weighing the pros and cons, find that it is more psychologically and emotionally rewarding to have a family and children than to be married to a career. It's all nice and exciting when you're in your 20s; but as they approach 35, many intelligent women realise that at age 50 they won't be wishing to spend their evenings with their feline friend. So it's not a question of "patriarchy" – it's a question of rational choices made by rational women.

Science demonstrates that women tend to mate with equal or better men. Intelligent and successful women tend to find equally or more intelligent and successful men who can therefore assume the role of making enough money for the women to pursue their more important goal – having their own children. That's how women's brains are hardwired; no amount of ideology can wipe out psychological traits evolved over some 350 million years.

This ideology is actually recent. While reading Engels' 1845 *Condition of the Working Class in England*, I found this little gem: 'the reign of the wife over the husband, as inevitably brought about by the factory system, is inhuman...'.

If Engels is correct, then not only do we not have patriarchy, but we have matriarchy and its origins lie in the Industrial Revolution!Be that as it may. It's clear that the patriarchy narrative is only an excuse to ride the abortion hobby-horse. It's almost an obsession: this radical feminist ideology has psychological not philosophical roots.

Then, psychological studies paint a picture that could shock politically-correct sensibilities. A 2000 study (by J. Archer) suggests that 'women engage in slightly more physical aggression than men in intimate relationships but sustain more injuries'. During the British Psychological Society's 2014 symposium 'Developments in Intimate Partner Violence Research and Practice', Dr Elizabeth Bates from the University of Cumbria presented a study suggesting that '[w]omen are more likely to be verbally and physically aggressive towards their partners'. 'Analysis showed that women were more likely to be physically aggressive to their partners than men and that men were more likely to be physically aggressive to their same-sex others. Furthermore, women engaged in significantly higher levels of controlling behaviour than men, which significantly predicted physical aggression in both sexes.' Dr Bates expounded:

> Previous studies have sought to explain male violence towards women as rising from patriarchal values, which motivate men to seek to control women's behaviour, using violence if necessary. This study found that women demonstrated a desire to control their partners and were more likely to use physical aggression than men. This suggests that IPV may not be motivated by patriarchal values and needs to be studied within the context of other forms of aggression, which has potential implications for interventions.

A 2018 study called 'Aggression in Women: Behaviour, Brain and Hormones' argues that

> [r]esearch consistently reports that women use *indirect aggression* to an equivalent or greater extent than men. Indirect aggression occurs when someone harms another while masking the aggressive intent[:] spreading false rumors, gossiping, excluding others from a social group, making insinuations without direct accusation, and criticizing others' appearance or personality. Some studies using data from the criminal justice system (e.g., police reports, pre-trial information and victim statements) of IPV offenders highlight commonalities regarding the use of IPV in women and men. These studies reported that defendants of both genders are equally likely to engage in harassing behavior (e.g., trespassing and stalking), and

to have been physically abusive by punching, hitting, slapping, or stabbing. Findings from these forensic studies suggest women are equally likely to use severe forms of violence as men and to severely injure their partners.

Bottom line: **less** ideology and **more** science.

The response to this horrific murder should be neither an increase in incarceration periods nor indoctrination at schools. Instead, we need a campaign to favour a shift in attitudes: from rights-based to duties-based. No longer 'He's my man/She's my woman', but 'I'm her man/I'm his woman'. But this runs counter to neoliberal thought, the dominant ideology of late capitalism, that is highly individualistic but for the benefit of Big Capital.

Brave new world

WHAT THE HECK! There are five doctors who are probably out to make money by opening an abortion clinic in Malta. Why not? It's the free market! Let's allow (and therefore encourage) women to terminate their own unborn children. What's wrong with that? Then, let's allow them to terminate their born children. A foetus, an infant... what's the difference? Aren't they both hindrances to achieving one's goals in life?

Let's assist people who want to terminate their own lives. It's dignity!

Let's allow people to marry more than one person at a time, of different sexes or of the same sex, or both. It's love!

Let's sterilise the defective, the criminal, the insane, the bigots, the Jews (why not?), the Catholics, and all non-conformists. It's long-term planning!

Let's allow complete strangers to co-habit in big dormitories as if they were family. Let's tolerate siblings to copulate, even reproduce (there's always abortion). It's freedom!

Let's stop giving names to people. Let's use barcodes instead. It's liberation!

Let's stop dating and mating. Let's engineer new humans in the laboratory by matching and manipulating their DNA. Let's rid ourselves of the rejects, using their aborted body parts for industrial research. It's efficiency!

Let's introduce DNA material from other species to create mutant humans able to do things that today's humans can't. It's evolution!

Let's place integrated circuits in babies, and bionic parts too, to enhance their abilities – cognitive intellectual physical – for the armed forces to deploy them in combat and aeronautics to colonise Mars, and for industry to employ them on toxic production lines. It's progress! And let's call it Neoliberalia!

Let's celebrate the complete equality of everybody and their free will!

Every individual's wish to be elevated to command and religiously executed!

It will be Paradise!

And lastly, let's burn subversive literature, especially Dostoyevsky and Chesterton.

My Personal Library

In *The Explanation of Ideology: Family Structures and Social Systems* (1985), Emmanuel Todd proposes the idea that the success of 20th-century ideologies (communism, liberalism, Catholicism, etc) depended more on family structures than anything else.

For instance, in France,

> [p]rovinces where the family structure is authoritarian and the marriage age high [...] send conservative, Catholic deputies to the National Assembly. Authoritarian family regions where the marriage age is low [...] form socialist bastions. Exogamous community family zones develop a special affection for the Communist Party. The centre-west, an absolute nuclear family region [...] was driven by the republican and predominantly egalitarian dynamic of the overall system towards the Catholic Right...

If Todd is correct, then we Maltese might reconsider our pointless Anglo-mania. England and Malta probably have different family structures; English ideology therefore cannot be transplanted to Maltese society with ease. In our fanatical urge to copy all things English, we might find that we caused our society to collapse.

"Thank you for existing"

WHEN WE STILL LIVED IN THE BEST OF TIMES UNDER HER SPOUSE'S REIGN OF PROGRESS, WHEN THE SYSTEM RAN ON POSITIVE THOUGHT AND MONEY GREW INSTEAD OF TREES, WHEN PHENOMENAL DEALS WERE STRUCK IN STYLE AND CAPITAL-P PROJECTS CASH-COWED THE LAND, WHEN CHIEFS-OF-STAFF WERE CHIEFLY CATALYTIC AND THE ONLY LIMIT WAS BUT THE SKY, THEN, MY FRIENDS, WE WERE ALL CAREFREE AND SERENE AND TRANSFIXED BY MRS MUSCAT'S TASTES IN FASHION.

Michelle Muscat, Joseph Muscat's wife, carved out a para-constitutional role for herself as "Prime Minister's Spouse". She seemed to have entertained a hazy notion of political accountancy, and carried her role in the electoral campaign forward to the Profit-and-Loss account of governing the nation, obviously engrossed in her notion of herself as more profit than loss. It seems to have never crossed her mind to work out this foggy pseudo-constitutional idea of hers. She created a para-constitutional role but never asked herself on what basis. Did she create her public role on the basis of her private (marriage) contract with her husband? Had they divorced, would she have lost her "constitutional" role? The ab-surdity of her constitutional thinking was rivalled only by the absurdity of her fashion choices.

We owe a lot to Daphne Caruana Galizia's sartorial analysis in this department. She had first brought to our attention the hilarious outfits worn by Mrs Muscat, and then, from one particular photograph we all remember, the comparison that begged itself, the comparison to Eva Perón.

Evita and Perón

EVA NÉE DUARTE WAS THE WIFE OF THE CAUDILLO OF ARGENTINA, JUAN PERÓN. Together they founded the Justicialist Party in 1947, to supersede the Labour Party. The following year, Argentina's women acquired the right to vote, and the First Lady founded the Peronist Women's Party.

We know neither the exact circumstances in which Eva met Perón nor the exact words that ignited their love story, that was to engulf all of Argentina in a burning triangle of passion, power and populism. Tomás Eloy Martínez, the Argentine novelist, interviewed Perón in 1969, and later used the material gathered to write two of his more brilliant novels, *The Perón Novel* (1985) and *Santa Evita* (1995). In the latter, Martínez fictionalises the fateful encounter between Evita and Perón.

Perón has just delivered a speech, describing himself as a humble soldier who had been granted the honour of protecting the working masses of Argentina. Evita turns her great dark eyes on him as he returns to his seat.

"Colonel."
"What is it, my girl?"
"Thank you for existing."

Evita and Michelle
LIKE MICHELLE, EVITA WAS FIRST LADY FOR SIX YEARS (1946-52). In a 1951 speech, Evita told the *descamisados*, the "shirtless", the poorest of the poor, of Argentina: "I have only one thing that matters, and I have it in my heart. It sets my soul aflame, it wounds my flesh and burns in my sinews: it's love for the people and for Perón."

In his book *Postmodernity in Latin America: The Argentine Paradigm*, Santiago Colás writes, "If their romance was the symbolic and real cement holding together the Peronist movement, then the movement, in turn, sustained their marriage: 'Now I love Perón differently, as I did not love him before: before I loved him for himself... now I love him because my people also love him!'"

In her autobiography, Evita wrote, "To divorce himself from the people, the head of the government would have to begin by divorcing his own wife!" "Perón and his wife," writes Mónica Esti Rein in *Politics and Education in Argentina 1946-1962*, "thus became the most prominent figures in the country, around whom everything in the 'new Argentina' revolved.

The adulation they enjoyed and the personality cult of which they were the center recall similar examples from other undemocratic regimes. This personality cult, orchestrated from the presidential palace, was designed to help mobilize the masses and unify them around the regime.

By this means, Perón and Evita became the glue holding the Argentine nation together – or such was their ambition, at least."

Why did Martínez...
... THUS FICTIONALISE THE ENCOUNTER? Because in that scene, Evita speaks on the People's behalf and the successful politician is s/he who receives such declarations from the People, whether explicitly or implicitly. The successful politician is thanked for existing, for satisfying a general need. If nobody thanks you for existing, then you're not a good politician and your future in politics is bleak and sterile. You'd better start seeking greener pastures.

No ghetto in Malta

WHILE I'M WRITING THIS, I'M LIS-
TENING TO A 1973 SONG CALLED
"ACROSS 110TH STREET", BY BOBBY
WOMACK. I'm not actually listening
to it on speakers or headphones; it's
simply playing over and over again
in my ears, I can't get it out of my
head. It's a song about the black
ghetto in Harlem, New York City,
and was the soundtrack of a blax-
ploitation movie of the same name,
starring Anthony Quinn and Ya-
phet Kotto. However, I first heard
it on Quentin Tarantino's *Jackie
Brown* (1997). But it was Anthony
Quinn's film which set me thinking.
And the lyrics to "Across the 110th
Street", which explain the struggles
of the blacks, for whom

> Trying to break out of the
>   ghetto was a day to day
>   fight
> Been down so long, getting up
>   didn't cross my mind
> But I knew there was a better
>   way of life that I was just
>   trying to find
> You don't know what you'll do
>   until you're put under
>   pressure.

Back in 1973, a few critics understood that Quinn's movie had
a number of messages to convey
about the dreadful, miserable lives
of the blacks in Harlem. There's
one particularly poignant scene
in which a protagonist justifies his
participation in a robbery that ended in a bloodbath by arguing that
he's 42 and black, has no education
and a medical condition, and thus
has no prospects in life. He simply
wishes a better life.

Earlier this year, the State of
New York passed the Reproductive
Health Act to resist any attempt by
the Supreme Court or the Trump
Administration to reverse *Roe v.
Wade*, the 1973 court decision that
affirmed American women's constitutional right to access abortion.
Unable to offer proper social welfare, New York can only offer abortion as a solution. Where there's
social welfare, there's no need for
abortion. And those who make it
their mission to poison the minds
of the young – such as those who
are conspiring to convince University students to bear the abortion
standard – should keep in mind
that, despite the ravings of backbencher Muscat, Malta isn't New
York. Malta has social welfare and
doesn't need abortion.

Unless, that is, their aim is to facilitate cynical immaturity, not just
of a few youngsters but of others
who learnt nothing from the university of life.

In the meantime, it's expected
that the US Supreme Court could
soon overturn *Roe v. Wade*. At
least this is how Mary Ziegler's recent publication *Abortion and the*

Law in America: Roe v. Wade to the Present (Cambridge) is being marketed.

Anniversary
LAST MONDAY WAS THE NINTH ANNIVERSARY OF THE PASSING AWAY OF MY DIRECT ANCESTOR. When I decided to stop supporting Muscat's Labour, *Sensiela Kotba Soċjalisti* – which my father had helped to found – gave away his books for free, as if to distance themselves from whom they perceived as his demented offspring. It must have been another egomaniac order from the Corrupt Man of the Year himself, who thinks he's God's gift to Malta. What a preposterous mindset.

History has already shown us that I and those like me who denounced him, were right: Muscat was an embarrassment to the entire country. Time will tell if his direct successor will ensure that justice is served. Frankly, I doubt it. Instead of giving backbencher Muscat a wide berth, Prime Minister Bobby Abela has Muscat advising the Government on the post-COVID-19 economic recovery. That Bobby Abela was weak was evident from even before the beginning; that he was *so* weak, I must admit, comes as a bit of a surprise.

On Monday the space-time continuum of my thoughts was bent by the black hole of my father's death.

What had he felt, nine years before to the day, when he breathed his final breath?

How did it feel when he fell into the final void?

Was it weightlessness, was it dread?

Was it nothingness, was it cold?

Were all the lights suddenly switched off?

Did it hurt?

He probably crossed the frontier into the unknown beyond too soon.

Then again, who knows why we die when we die, why we're born when we're born.

But also, who knows whether we ever manage to become our own father and mother, or – according to backbencher Muscat's demented policies – our own Parent 1 and Parent 2?

My Personal Library

When I write these short references to books, I usually look at the books on my shelves and let them inspire me. This time, I want to write about a book that, as far as I know, has still not been published. Quentin Tarantino spoke about it during a conversation with Martin Scorsese, published on the *Directors Guild of America Quarterly* in 2019.

Scorsese says, "The more pictures you make, the more there is to learn."

Tarantino answers, "Right now, I'm working on a book. And I've got this character who had been in World War II and he saw a lot of bloodshed there. And now he's back home, and it's like the '50s, and he doesn't respond to movies anymore. He finds them juvenile after everything that he's been through. As far as he's concerned, Hollywood movies are movies. And so then, all of a sudden, he starts hearing about these foreign movies by Kurosawa and Fellini… And so he's like, 'Well, maybe they might have something more than this phony Hollywood stuff.' So he finds himself drawn to these things and some of them he likes and some of them he doesn't like and some of them he doesn't understand, but he knows he's seeing something."

Many people must have watched many movies during the Covid lockdown. So it's good to keep in mind that most – though not all – Hollywood movies are juvenile.

Which reminds me of something P.G. Wodehouse wrote in one of his autobiographies. Wodehouse's publisher would give Wodehouse's manuscripts to his 14-year-old nephew to read. If the boy laughed, Wodehouse's new book was printed. If not, the manuscript would be returned as rejected.

The entertainment industry has always been meant for the adolescent mentality. The showbiz approach is analysed in Clint Eastwood's *White Hunter, Black Heart*, a 1990 movie that's exquisitely shot and fared badly at the Box Office.

EPILOGUE
Was Joseph Muscat great? Was he a hero?

PERHAPS IT IS STILL TOO EARLY, AND PERHAPS EACH AGE WILL DELIVER ITS OWN VERDICT ON THE MAN. But I will still try to answer these two questions.

I met him for the first time in the early 1990s and was impressed by his cunning. I remember Feliċ Agius, then editor of Labour's Sunday weekly *KullĦadd*, in the hallway of the Super One complex in Marsa, encouraging him to contest the 1996 elections, and Muscat saying, with a smirk of self-satisfaction on his face caused by Agius' sincere invitation, that it was not the right time yet. Years later, we met in a professional setting, and again I was impressed by his acumen: he would interrupt me half-way through my explanations of the provisions of the Civil Code and finish my sentences, correctly. My father had observed the same quality in him, namely his extraordinarily quick wits.

But while it might be true that his IQ was clearly high, Muscat scored low on the value scale. Even if he was keeping bad comapny (think of Keith Schembri) and was led down the path of evil as a result, Muscat still bears responsibility for choosing the path of evil. He was unable to sit at the same table with the rich and be content with the power and the glory. He could have become a legend among mortal men, the Maltese Alexander the Great (if you like history) or Captain James Kirk (if you prefer fiction). Instead, he allowed the song of the sirens to lure him away from the man he could have been. He neither had wax in his ears to avoid hearing their song, nor was he tied to the mast to avoid being drawn by their invitation. Instead, he was carried away by the pressure exerted by the wicked and the greedy, and demolished all he had been painstakingly building since the early 1990s.

It's not a tragedy, though, and he's not a hero. He is a fool who threw away the great potential Destiny had bestowed upon him, to chase mirages that brought only ignominy. His political death did not see him cremated on a long ship set on fire to carry his soul to Valhalla, the enormous hall where dead warriors rest. On the contrary, his political death saw him burning in Gehenna, the abode of the dead wicked.

Will his legacy survive? That question is predicated on another: what is his legacy?

He left behind a *laissez-faire* Malta, plagued by arrogance on different levels of society. He left behind an ugly Malta, with more buildings and "development" than these small islands can sustain. He left behind a jumble sale of "civil liberties" which I, as a social conservative, think will only harm Malta in the long run (even though they will earn some people a lot of money in the process). In his moment of despair, when he was in the throes of his political demise, only days after he paid a visit to the Pope and to the Nativity Chapel in Bethlehem, he promised he would campaign for the legalisation of abortion in Malta. This was his nadir, his complete moral meltdown, his *cri de coeur* to his radical liberal allies as the ghost was leaving his political body. Muscat's swansong will be remembered as his invitation to make it legal to kill unborn babies in their mother's womb.

It is true that a time might come when killing unborn babies will be normalised, when such a practice will become an everyday occurrence free of remorse. "Philosophers" like Rorty and Singer already contemplate such a heartless world, in which women will be taught that their unborn babies are a burden and may be killed because they become persons only after birth. They will be taught that crossing the neck of the uterus magically bestows personhood on the hitherto non-person. This future society will be post-religious (post-Christian for sure) but will embrace *Magick* and superstition. For only a superstitious outlook can accept the idea that an unborn human being is not a member of humanity that deserves legal protection and that such legal protection becomes effective only upon passage through the cervix. There is nothing rational or scientific in the belief that parturition bestows a legal status, given that the baby is alive before and after the birth. This passage from unworthy to worthy of protection is but a legal fiction.

Be that as it may. For such a future society, Muscat will be a man ahead of his time, a flawed genius who embraced the right vision but was burnt by the fire of human frailty. But for a future society which will resemble my Ideal City, Muscat will remain the great marketing expert who preached a *carpe diem* gospel, miscalculating the true extent of his abilities. Like many intelligent people, he thought that nobody was as intelligent as he and that he was so bright he could overcome all the adversities that would come his way. But despite his obvious Machiavellian approach, he failed to keep in mind two of *The Prince*'s most important lessons: a Prince survives who is not only endowed with Prowess but is also blessed with good Fortune, and employs good secretaries.

Muscat erred by believing that his quick wits and above-average IQ would deliver him from all troubles. This is the arrogance of the intellect which he might have acquainted himself with had he read literature (Milton, say) and philosophy (Machiavelli, say), instead of wasting his time travelling to Italian stadiums to watch football games. "Learn! Learn! Learn!" as the Soviets used to say!

Index of Names

Index of Movies

Index of Publications

Adler, Tim: *La Mafia à Hollywood* Nouveau Monde 2009 *262*

Ali, Tariq: *The Obama Syndrome: Surrender at Home, War Abroad* Verso Books 2010 *58*

Aquilina, Kevin: *Constitutional Law in Malta* Wolters Kluwer 2018 *52*

Bonello, Giovanni: *Misunderstanding the Constitution* BDL 2018 *144, 212*

Boonin, David: *A Defense of Abortion* Cambridge University Press 2002 *49, 164*

Brown, Dan: *The Da Vinci Code* Doubleday 2003 *33*

Browne, Nick (ed.): *Francis Ford Coppola's The Godfather Trilogy* Cambridge University Press 1999 *262, 301*

Browning, Robert: *Childe Roland to the Dark Tower Came* 1855 *123*

Butterfield, Herbert: *The Whig Interpretation of History* W. W. Norton 1931 (1965) *xi*

Cameron, David & Jones, Dylan: *Cameron on Cameron: Conversations with Dylan Jones* HarperCollins 2010 *250*

Camilleri, Andrea: *Il re di Girgenti* Sellerio 2001 *197*
La mossa del cavallo Rizzoli 1999 *197*

Carbasse, Jean-Marie: *Histoire du droit pénal et de la justice criminelle* Presses Universitaires de France 2014 *52*

Carlyle, Thomas: *On Heroes, Hero-Worship, and the Heroic in History* 1841 *xviii*

Carroll, Lewis: *Alice's Adventures in Wonderland* 1865 *228*
Through the Looking-Glass, and What Alice Found There 1871 *228*

Cervantes, Miguel de: *Don Quixote* 1605, 1615 *67*

Cesarini, Antonella: *Una rivoluzione in forma di legge. Malta 1974: storia di una anomala revisione costituzionale* CEDAM 1997 *46*

Chaucer, Geoffrey: *Canterbury Tales* c. 1400 *177*

Chilton, Bruce, Evans, Craig A. & Neusner, Jacob: *The Missing Jesus: Rabbinic Judaism and the New Testament* Brill 2002 *30*

Cipolla, Carlo M.: *Allegro ma non troppo* il Mulino 1988 *77*

Colás, Santiago: *Postmodernity in Latin America: The Argentine Paradigm* Duke University Press 1994 *309*

Coleridge, Samuel Taylor: *The Rime of the Ancient Mariner* 1798 *287*

Collins, Suzanne: *The Hunger Games* Scholastic Press 2008 *289*

Collodi, Carlo: *Pinocchio* 1883 *11*

Conrad, Joseph: *The Nigger of the Narcissus* 1897 *7*

Glajar, Valentina & Radulescu, Domnica: *Vampirettes, Wretches and Amazons: Western Representations of East European Women* East European Monographs 2004 *129*

Goldberg, Jonah: *Liberal Fascism: The Secret History of the American Left, From Mussolini to the Politics of Change* Random House 2009 *xi, 100, 120, 121*

Graham, Carol: *Happiness around the World: The Paradox of Happy Peasants and Miserable Millionaires* Oxford University Press 2009 *xvi*

Gray, John: *Liberalism* University of Minnesota Press 1986 *73*
False Dawn: The Delusions of Global Capitalism The New Press 1998 *73*

Greene, Richard (ed.): *The Sopranos and philosophy: I Kill Therefore I Am* Open Court 2004 *225*

Hall, Radclyffe: *The Well of Loneliness* 1928 *35*

Heller, Joseph: *Catch-22* Simon & Schuster 1961 *302*

Hitler, Adolf: *Mein Kampf* Pimlico 1994 *154, 160*

Hodgson Burnett, Frances: *Little Lord Fauntleroy* 1885 *125*

Holz, Rose: *The Birth Control Clinic in a Marketplace World* University of Rochester Press 2012 *142*

Homer: *The Odyssey* Collector's Library 2004 *242*

Huxley, Aldous: *Brave New World* 1932 *166, 207*

Hymowitz, Kay S.: *Manning Up: How the Rise of Women Has Turned Men into Boys* Basic Books 2012 *129*

Inglehart, Ronald & Welzel, Christian: *Modernization, Cultural Change, and Democracy:The Human Development Sequence* Cambridge University Press 2005 *238*

Jacoby, Henry & Irwin, William (eds.): *Doctor House and Philosophy: Everybody Lies* Wiley 2008 *225*

Jones, Jenny: *The Annotated Godfather: The Complete Screenplay* Hachette 2009 *262*

Jung, C.G.: *Psychology and Religion* Yale University Press 1960 *123*

Kirk, Russell: *Enemies of the Permanent Things: Observations of Abnormality in Literature and Politics* Cluny Media 2016 *xvi*

Koskenniemi, Martti: *The Gentle Civilizer of Nations: The Rise and Fall of International Law 1870-1960* Cambridge University Press 2001 *7, 56, 162*

Ledda, Gavino: *Padre Padrone: l'educazione di un pastore* Feltrinelli 1975 *127*

Leopardi, Giacomo: *Canti* 1831 *26-27*

Lewis, Jon: *The Godfather* Bloomsbury 2019 *262*

Lewis, Richard: *When Cultures Collide: Managing Successfully Across Cultures* Nicholas Brealey 1999 *111*

Livio, Mario: *Brilliant Blunders* Simon & Schuster 2014 *37*

Luttrell, Anthony: *The Making of Christian Malta* Routledge 2017 (2002) *62*

Machiavelli, Niccolò: *The Prince* 1513 *167, 177, 267, 314*

Macron, Emmanuel: *Révolution: Réconcilier la France* Scribe 2017 *250*

Meloni, Giorgia: *Noi crediamo. Viaggio nella meglio gioventù d'Italia* Sperling & Kupfer 2011 *250*

Mercieca, Sir Arturo: *The Making and Unmaking of a Maltese Chief Justice* Giov. Muscat 1969 *160*

Midgley, Mary: *The Myths We Live By* Taylor & Francis 2011 *xvii, xxvii*

Mifsud Bonnici, Guiseppe & Sammut, Mark A.: *Il-Liġi, il-Morali u r-Raġuni* Kotba-Argo 2008 *xxiv, 38, 134, 221*

Mifsud Bonnici, Ugo: *Kif Sirna Repubblika* PIN 1999 *46*

Mintoff, Dom: *How Britain Rules Malta* 130, 250
Malta Betrayed: Truncheons and Tyrants 250

Mizzi, Achille: *Ġenesi* Horizons 2017 *62-63*

Nicoll, Allardyce: *The World of Harlequin* Cambridge University Press 1963 *233*

Nietzsche, Friedrich: *Thus Spoke Zarathustra* 1883-1885 *193*

Orwell, George: *Animal Farm* Secker and Warburg 1945 *277*

Pearce, Philippa: *Tom's Midnight Garden* Oxford University Press 1958 *40*

Pennetta, Enzo: *L'Ultimo Uomo: Malthus, Darwin, Huxley e l'invenzione dell'antropologia capitalista* GOG 2017 *164, 166, 167*

Pratkanis, A. & Aronson, E.: *Age of Propaganda: The Everyday Use and Abuse of Persuasion* WH Freeman 1992 *117*

Procopius: *The Secret History* Penguin 1981 *285*

Reisch, George A.: *Pink Floyd and Philosophy: Careful with that Axiom, Eugene* Open Court 2007 *225*

Reising, Russell (ed.): *'Speak to Me': The Legacy of Pink Floyd's The Dark Side of the Moon* Ashgate 2005 *279*

Renga, Dana: *Mafia Movies: A Reader* University of Toronto Press 2019 *262*

Renzi, Matteo: *Avanti. Perché l'Italia non si ferma* Feltrinelli 2017 *250*
Un'altra strada. Idee per l'Italia di domani Marsilio 2019 *250*

Rossiaud, Jacques: *La prostituzione nel Medioevo* Laterza 1984 *20*

Sacks, Rabbi Lord Jonathan: *The Great Partnership: God, Science and the Search for Meaning* Hodder & Stoughton 2011 *93*

Salvini, Matteo: *Secondo Matteo. Follia*

Xuereb, Charles: *France in the Maltese Collective Memory* Malta University Press 2014   *59*

Zemmour, Éric: *Petit Frère* Denoel 2008   *95*

Ziegler, Mary: *Abortion and the Law in America: Roe v. Wade to the Present* Cambridge University Press 2020   *310, 311*

Žižek, Slavoj: *Living in the End Times* Verso 2018   *29, 88*

www.ingramcontent.com/pod-product-compliance
Lightning Source LLC
Chambersburg PA
CBHW030148310326
41914CB00086B/14